The Face of Glory

The Face of Glory

Creativity, Consciousness and Civilization

William Anderson

BLOOMSBURY

BY THE SAME AUTHOR

POETRY

Haddow Sonata
Humans, Beasts and Birds
The Waking Dream
What I am is Stillness

OTHER WORKS

Castles of Europe
Cathedrals in Britain and Europe
Dante the Maker
Holy Places of the British Isles
Cecil Collins: The Quest for the Great Happiness
Green Man: The Archetype of Our Oneness with the Earth

First published 1996

This paperback edition published 1996

The moral right of the author has been asserted

Bloomsbury Publishing Plc, 38 Soho Square, London W1V 5DF

A CIP catalogue record for this book is available from the British Library

ISBN 0 7475 2938 8

10 9 8 7 6 5 4 3 2 1

Typeset in Great Britain by Hewer Text Composition Services, Edinburgh

Printed in Great Britain by Clays Ltd, St Ives plc

For Jennifer

Contents

Illustrations

Frontispiece: *Resurrection*, 1952, a detail showing the face of Christ from the drawing by Cecil Collins' in the Britten–Pears Foundation, Aldeburgh. Clive Hicks.

Figure 1. The Face of Glory appears at the top of this statue of Shiva and Parvati. Surrounded by celestial beings, with his mouth touched by Shiva's sceptre, the Face of Glory pours out the stylized vegetation that forms the aureole of the god and goddess. Orissa; twelfth century AD. Copyright British Museum.

Figure 2. The Green Man: a vaulting boss from St Bénigne, Dijon, later thirteenth century, retaining its original paintwork. The carving, now in the Musée archéologique, Dijon, is remarkable for the individuality of the face and the precision of the leaves. Clive Hicks.

Figure 3. Three Green Men from the south portal of Chartres Cathedral, c. 1220. The plants portrayed are vine, acanthus and oak (left to right). Clive Hicks.

Figure 4. The theatre at Epidauros. Clive Hicks.

Figure 5. From the ball court at Chichen Itzá: a carving showing a decapitated player with his blood spurting as serpents turning into vegetation. Clive Hicks.

Figure 6. The façade of the Casa de Montéjo, 1542, in Mérida, with the giant Spanish soldiers with their axes. Clive Hicks.

Figure 7. The heads of Green Men on which the Spanish soldiers in figure 6 stand. Clive Hicks.

Figure 8. Christ the Pantocrator: the mosaic in the apse of the cathedral of Monreale, Sicily, 1172–76. The Ancient Art & Architecture Collection.

Figure 9. The ambulatory of Chartres Cathedral, first half of thirteenth century. Clive Hicks.

The Face of Glory

Introduction: The Face of Glory

The Face of Glory signifies divine creative energy. The face is that of a man or of a man with the mouth of a lion, with fierce bulbous eyes and with vegetation pouring out of the sides of his mouth and with a mane of leaves and flowers. How I first became conscious of this image offers an instance of the altered state of awareness which attends or precipitates discovery, invention and inspiration.

I was waiting with my travelling companions and others to enter a fifteenth-century Jain temple in Jaisalmer. The custodian, a small elderly gentleman wearing a big turban and armed with a thick stick, had decided to shut the temple twenty minutes early. I stood behind the custodian while a crowd of young men argued with him, demanding to be let in. I was happy to let others conduct the argument: I was already full of impressions and did not mind whether I saw the temple or not. The argument got hotter in tone: someone must have been very rude to the custodian. He swept his stick over his shoulder to threaten them and in doing so he hit me on the jaw. It was very painful and I yelped. He was much too busy shouting to hear me but one of the young men had seen. He stopped the argument and turned the custodian around to look at me clasping my jaw. The old man's resistance collapsed at his shame in having struck a visitor to his country and we were let into the temple after all.

We entered the cool white temple and heard the brass bell being rung to attract the attention of the Jain saviour whose statue faced us on our entrance. I began to look at the richly carved decoration on the columns and walls, on which the clear warm winter light fell through the interstices of stone screens. There in the carvings I began to see face after face disgorging vegetation, and the experience was like being hit on the jaw all over again – though in a much less painful way – because I realized that these images were a new aspect of the Green Man, the image of the relationship between nature and humanity I had already studied and written about.

It was a shock in several ways. The image seemed to be telling me it was not finished with me yet. I was brought up sharp by the realization that I had been passing similar images many times in India and not seeing them for what they were. I needed a blow on the jaw to wake up to them. Once I had seen these images – which I was soon to learn bore the name of the Kirtimukha or Face of Glory – wherever I went in India from that time onwards I saw them by the hundred (figure 1). Once the new pattern entered my awareness I saw what I had been wholly blind to. It was also an exciting experience because I was being given a further gift from the reservoir of images from the past, comparable to the one I was given when I climbed to the parapet of the spire of the minster in Freiburg im Breisgau and discovered that the eight ribs of the spire all issued from the heads of Green Men. It was after that discovery that I found wherever I went in Europe the Green Man seemed to be making himself appear to me – and it was after he presented himself as a poem to me that I realized I had to write a book about him.[1]

The image of the Green Man, first developed in Europe from the cults of Dionysos in the south and from the Celtic god Cernunnos in the north and west, recurs in most of the important movements in western culture up to the early twentieth century – when, to a large extent, it vanishes. The Green Man possesses the most lively ability to slip from one movement to another so that he always presents a new aspect of his nature in symbolizing whatever is most dynamic and important in a particular period. He is there in the mystery religions of the Roman Empire, he is taken up into Christian art from the fourth century onwards, he appears in Christian Celtic art such as the Book of Kells, he is there for the revival of architecture and sculpture in the art of the Romanesque, and he undergoes a great transformation in Gothic art (figure 2) when his portrayals are given individual human faces and the vegetation out of which he springs or which he disgorges is also identifiable as an individual nameable species such as the oak, the vine or the acanthus (figure 3). He appears as a symbol of learning and of fecundity in the Renaissance, in the works of Donatello, Michelangelo and Mantegna, for example. He also appears in the first printed books and was placed on the title pages of some of Luther's most important works. He survives the breaking of images in Protestant countries and is taken up in Baroque and later architecture so that, for example, he is to be found throughout the Palace of Versailles. He is connected with the works of the early scientific age and he enjoys a riotous parade in friezes and sculptures on the official and commercial buildings of the later nineteenth century throughout North America and western Europe, presumably as a symbol of prosperity. He disappears with the banishment of decoration from buildings in the twentieth century but he has now returned in a new context: that of the environmental movement. As a creature with the dual nature of man and leaf he is a symbol of the relationship between humanity and nature and he has come back to warn and to help us in meeting the creative challenge presented to us by our new understanding of the planet and our need for a harmonious relationship with the cycles and interconnections of the natural world.

In his greatest representations the Green Man is a symbol of divine and human creativity. As he is shown at Chartres Cathedral, for example, he is associated with the beginning and end of time in the sculptures of the three great portals. He was to the Gothic masters their chief image of the creative power on which they had to draw to create their masterpieces, the power of making that was as beyond themselves as the power that made the universe is above and includes all physical things. To return to the Face of Glory, there is a similar theme behind his origins.

This is the legend of how the Face of Glory came into being.

Jalandhara, the Titan king, has conquered most of the world. He hears that the god Shiva is leaving the Himalayas after a long period living as an ascetic in order to marry the goddess Parvati. Jalandhara wishes to marry Parvati himself, thereby humiliating Shiva and asserting his dominance. He sends as a messenger to Shiva the demon Rahu, whose usual function is to cause the eclipse of the moon. (Rahu consists only of a head and a mask so that when he swallows the moon he has no stomach to digest her and she always escapes.) Rahu appears before Shiva and demands Parvati. He points out that Jalandhara now owns everything the gods once owned and as Shiva has been an ascetic living in a cemetery he would be unable to maintain Parvati in a proper style. At this all the outrage of the god is concentrated in the chakra between his eyebrows and he expels from that point a terrifying man with the mouth of a lion, with his hair standing on end and with flames pouring from his eyes. The man chases after Rahu in order to devour him.

Though he flees, Rahu knows he cannot escape. He has only one hope: he implores the protection of the god. Addressed in this way the god may not refuse: Rahu comes under his protection and cannot be harmed even by Shiva's emanation. Nevertheless the man with the lion mouth who has been created by Shiva's anger is ravenous with hunger and demands something else to eat.

Shiva says: 'Why don't you eat your feet and hands?'

The man with the lion mouth begins obediently to eat his feet and hands but he is so hungry he cannot stop and devours the whole of his body up to the neck, leaving only his face and head. Shiva smiles at what remains of him and tells him that, henceforth, he will be known as the Face of Glory and ordains that he should always remain at his door.

As the Kirtimukha or Face of Glory he therefore appears on the lintels of temples dedicated to Shiva and at the top of the aureoles in carvings of the god. He also appears disgorging vegetation in the aureoles above other gods and goddesses as the expression of their power. He is known as Vanaspati, 'Lord-Spirit of the Woods, Patron of the Wilderness, King of Vegetation', and he is our protector in the jungle and the forests of life.[2]

The story is about the control and transformation of fierce and violent emotions. Shiva is portrayed with his neck painted blue to represent the poison he swallowed that would have destroyed humanity. Here he does something similar: he transforms the energy of his fury into the Face of Glory. So the Green Man in his Indian form is an image of violent emotion transfigured into protective benevolence, an act of the highest civilizing and artistic importance. The aggressive force which provides the energy creators and makers of civilizations need for their work must be tempered and guided by the principles of mercy and compassion.

Images comparable to the Green Man and the Face of Glory are to be found in the art and legends of many cultures, from Islam, China and pre-Columbian Mexico, for example. They are all aspects of a universal image or archetype and his return into our awareness now is an instance of a gift from the Great Memory, a hypothesis I develop in Part I of this book.

In most of the cultures in which the archetype of the Green Man appears, he is closely connected with the archetype of the Goddess. He plays several roles: he is the son, the lover and the guardian of the Goddess. The Face of Glory plays the role of the guardian when Shiva creates him to defend Parvati. In the Danube civilization of the sixth millennium BC he appears as a proto-Dionysos figure in relation to the Goddess. In historical times he is shown frequently in association with the Virgin Mary in the sculpture of the Gothic period. Whenever there is a strong new statement of the feminine ideal, there is also likely to be a new aspect of the Green Man made current: this is what has happened in recent years in relation to our understanding of the environment. As the name of the ancient Greek Earth goddess Gaia has been brought back to symbolize the unified complexities of the biosphere, so too there has been a major recurrence of interest in the Green Man.

In this context the Green Man can be seen on three levels of meaning. The first is as an image of the vital processes of life: he symbolizes the fact that we are all made of leaves. He is the process of photosynthesis: he is the child of the marriage of Sun and Earth; he is the living face of the biosphere.

In this sense he returns to humanity at a time when we have an awareness of the globe on which we live that none of our ancestors could ever have had. The second level of meaning concerns our inner life as individuals and our collective life as members of humanity. On this level he is the manifestation of the creative force within us: he is the terror of challenge and fear that must be faced but also he is, when faced, the source of freedom and inventive directions for turning the chaotic energy of fear into the ordered energy of art and science. Our creativity is aroused by challenge and he is the challenger who stirs our creative responses into action. The third level of meaning to be found in him is universal in the true sense of the word: he is the mouthpiece of creation. The leaves that pour through his mouth are the works of space and time. We come out of his mouth. As the Face of Glory he is the terrifying and yet protective emanation of the creating deity and, as the Green Man on the tympana of our great cathedrals, his is the mouth through which the Logos is uttered.

The comparable figure in Islamic lore is that of Khidr, the guide of Moses in the Koran.[3] His name means the Verdant One and his mysterious visitations are known only by the sight of his green footprints. To the Sufis he is the inner guide and source of inspiration to the seeker, the thinker and the artist. He is, it may be said, the creative state when the maker is so full of the wealth of understanding and imagery that is offered him, he does not recognize himself.

Like Khidr, his other self, the Green Man knows far more than we know. In the doctrines of the Dionysiac mysteries, the young Dionysos was created from the mind of Zeus and therefore possessed all the wisdom of the father of the gods. When the Titans in their jealousy tore him apart and burned him, humanity was created from his ashes so that all human beings contain his divine knowledge. Dionysos was called the mundane intellect, the universal mind in which we all share. Both Dionysos and Shiva were late arrivals in their respective pantheons: their legends show them as able to perform marvels and tasks that their fellow deities find impossible or balk at. They are both destroyers and renamers, fountains of spontaneity and givers of life. As they are images of creation on the great scale of the universe, so they are also images of the creativity of our own souls.

As the soul includes the mind, so the Green Man includes the wood or forest which is the ancient symbol of the human mind. Medieval writers called the mind *mens silva*, the mind as the wildwood. Dante is lost in the *selva selvaggia* at the outset of his journey in *The Divine Comedy*. Sometimes the forest of the mind is full of kindly messages and intimations, as in Baudelaire's sonnet '*Correspondances*':

L'homme y passe à travers des forêts de symboles
Qui l'observent avec des regards familiers

and sometimes it is full of muttering menace. We flee there as outlaws from the grim sheriffs of conventional thought only to find the wild animals of thwarted energies and the carrion birds nourished on old grudges. Yet it is there that we will find the help of the child princess, the wise woman or the Green Man himself.

Like the wildwood, the Green Man can often seem grim and menacing in his portrayals and that is not surprising because life is often grim and menacing. The Green Man has come back now in the context of environmental threats to say to us: 'I am Life. Life is a challenge. How are you going to meet my challenge?' That challenge is to equal and surpass the creativity of our forebears in finding solutions and harmonious resolutions to problems on a scale humanity has never had to meet before.

The challenge also is to discover more about the nature of creativity itself. It may be an obvious point – but it is also one not generally considered – that if we learn more of the ways in which creativity works, we may be able to put our creativity to more efficient uses.

Creativity is the linking point between all fields of human endeavour and thought, especially between art, religion and science; it also provides special ways of studying consciousness. Furthermore, as all civilizations depend on the creativity of individuals or small groups of individuals for their origins and their maintenance, the study of creativity should enhance our knowledge and understanding of civilization. Our present civilizations are being forced into change through the new awareness in mankind that we share the single home of our planet. Much of the damage that humanity has inflicted on the environment has been made possible by the effects of man's own creativity; the discovery that he could manipulate matter in its atomic and molecular nature to make new chemicals in order to increase yields, to kill off unwanted pests and weeds, and to preserve and distribute the vast surpluses of food that are only made possible by the use of agrochemicals; the discovery that he could refine fossil remains in oil, coal and gas to create new means of transport on land and sea and in the air and to generate electricity; and the discovery that he could tap the energies of nuclear power. It is as though the Green Man glares at us from his ruined forests and his blighted mosses and grasslands to say: 'This is what you have done to me and mine and to yourselves. The revenge is not mine; it is yours upon yourselves and your children.'

Yet the only way to evade our self-inflicted fates is through our own creativity, to evolve a science that takes into account the effects of any new invention or chemical or source of power. That will depend on our creative ability on other levels, the deep levels of the psyche, the inner environment of all humanity which is where pollution and degradation truly begin. The challenge of tackling environmental problems has already produced many remarkable new insights and understandings and here perhaps it is also the Green Man smiling at us in his benign aspects.

There is an archetypal relationship between the colours green and gold, found in many cultures and often associated with the Green Man, and this signifies the link between creativity and civilization. From ancient Mexico there are carvings showing the maize plant from which humanity first grew: the golden corn cobs are replaced by human heads. The Aztec corn god Xipe Totec is the god of spring who has to shed his skin for new growth to arise, and in a Nahua poem it is said of him: 'Emerald is my heart. I shall see the gold water.'[4] Osiris, who has a green face as judge in the underworld, undergoes a further mystical transformation into the golden sun god Ra. In the folk song 'Greensleeves' the refrain goes: 'Greensleeves is my delight, Greensleeves is my heart of gold.' In alchemy the stage of the Green Lion is a preliminary to the transmutation of gold. It was when he was already embarked on his studies of alchemy that C. G. Jung was led to his reinterpretation of Christian symbolism by a vision of the crucified Christ with his body made of greenish gold which appeared at the foot of his bed. Jung saw in the green and the gold the quality of life that the alchemists saw in both man and nature. It was an expression of the life spirit, the soul of the world, the Anthropos who animates the whole cosmos.[5]

The basis of the imagery is agricultural; the green shoots that sprout from the mummy of Osiris will yield golden stalks and ears of wheat at harvest. All civilizations depend on a similar transformation in their staple foods and, as the Green Man becomes the Gold Man, the process symbolizes the necessary change when the green of life becomes the gold of civilization. It also symbolizes the psychological alchemy in ourselves when the energy of life we are given to create with is transmuted by the touch of the gold of consciousness.

In the three parts of the book which follow I want to consider how the green of creative energy arises in the first place and how it is changed into the gold of civilization. I see creativity as a cycle, a cycle of dramatist, actor and audience in the case of the theatre or of research scientist, chemical engineer or manufacturer, and user in the case of scientific technology. On this cycle the relationship between creativity and civilization depends. Civilizations die without the renewal of the creative flame within them. The flame of creativity is spent without the fuel of experience and inspiration and without the oxygen of appreciation, understanding and patronage.

What links creativity and civilization is the performer, the impresario, the executant, the patron, the publisher, the engineer or builder. Through such people the cycle of enjoyment is carried through to the cultivated spectators and audiences on which civilized societies depend. This cycle of enjoyment was described by the tenth-century Sanskrit writer Abhinavagupta thus:

> artistic creation is the direct or unconventionalized expression of a feeling of passion generalized, that is, freed from distinctions in time or space and therefore from individual relationships and practical interest, by an inner force in the poet himself. This state of consciousness expressed in the poem is transferred to the actor or the reciter and to the spectator. All three – poet, actor and spectator – in the serene contemplation of the work of art, form in reality a single knowing subject, merged together by the same sensations and the same purified joy.[6]

Thus the poem is sown in the creative imagination of the poet by the experience of *rasa*, the delight of tasting one's own consciousness. The poem is the tree; the activity of the artist, that is, the representation, is the flower; and the fruit is the experience of tasting by the spectators. The special link between the poet and the spectator is recognized here: as the creative imagination is latent in the poet until woken by *rasa*, so the cultivated spectator is one in whom all the states of being are dormant until he sees them brought to life on the stage, when through the magic of the theatre he is lifted to the state of bliss which is *ananda*.

The cycle of creativity Abhinavagupta describes in this passage is also the cycle of civilization. People of cultivated emotion, once they have experienced that state of bliss, will need to come to it again and again throughout their lives. They and their fellow spectators will make sure that the artist and the performers are provided with what they need to continue to produce and perform their works.

Civilized societies are those in which the experience of bliss, the delight in *rasa*, is recognized as one of the highest goods and where, among the reasons for work, productivity and administration, is the provision of that experience for all members of that society who desire it.

Recent studies of early man have tended to emphasize two particular elements in the development of humanity. One of these concerns the capacity for symbolic thought and the part it has played from earliest times in creative achievements, in social organization and in communication. The other concerns the way in which man's capacity for creativity has helped to decide his evolutionary development.[7] In other words the possession of an imagination capable of metaphorical association and the ability to solve the problems encountered in a variety of environments make human creativity a natural endowment.

When we consider the cycle of creativity as the cycle of civilization, a true civilization, one that provides happiness for its members and a balanced relationship with its environment, then we can say that, if it is natural for man to be creative, then it is natural for civilizations, the fruit of many conjoined and repeated creative acts, to come into being. Civilization, therefore, is not at its best an excrescence or parasitic outgrowth from nature, but the true flowering and development of humanity in nature. We can see this on a long time scale when we think of many of the great landscapes of the world: they are beautiful not because they have been left to themselves. They are beautiful because over thousands of years man has worked on them and maintained a just relationship with their soil and their hills, waters and plains. That just relationship is always the product of a civilized influence, stabilizing, accepted throughout the community, and seemingly at times so right in its effects when judged by modern scientific and ecological standards that they suggest the existence of lost or dormant sciences. Another way of looking at the problems of the environment is this: Nature is already a civilization; she has the division of labour, the interdependence of lives, the checks and balances to maintain harmony, her artists, poets and creators in her moods and adaptations. She has been granted all this by the universal consciousness from which she issues. She has already achieved a civilization for all her myriads of species living together on Earth as a whole. We have to realize the potentiality in the sphere of human spirit of what she has already achieved.

In speaking here of universal consciousness I am anticipating a theme to be developed later in this book. My interpretation of the creative cycle is based on the premiss that everything that exists bears the sign of its creation and is an image capable of leading our thoughts to universal consciousness. The world is matter in mind: as Baudelaire puts it: 'The whole universe is a store of images and signs to which imagination will give a place and a relative value; it is a kind of pasture that imagination must digest and transform.'[8] I find in the symbolist method a way of describing creativity that lies between the poles of science and religion. Perhaps the science of the future will possess the means of describing the creative cycle far more fully than anything I have been able to state here, but present-day science has not reached that stage yet: it cannot account for consciousness, inspiration, memory or enjoyment. The great religions, with their philosophical and theological traditions, can give accounts of them but their accounts are not neutral: they are expressed in terms of their belief structures. The widening of our horizons of knowledge beyond the separate cultures and religions of the past owes most to the application of the scientific attitude and the related comparative method: it has been accompanied and supported by symbolism, a movement in the human spirit which has too often been seen wholly as a literary movement but which has been essential to the development of science, and of psychology in particular. We may not be scientists or theologians but we are all symbolists in that we all possess the capacity for metaphorical thinking; it is natural for us to express the ineffable and to explore the unknown through similes, analogies, metaphors and symbols.

We are facing change on a global scale: we will need to draw on all the inventiveness and creativity potentially existing in ourselves to make those changes fruitful. The symbolist method would help us to understand that we are infinitely cleverer, infinitely wiser, infinitely more creative than we allow ourselves to be: we are collectively the Fool walking towards the unseen abyss while he carries on his back the bag containing the magic instruments which would enable him to become the Juggler. We all possess that bag and its contents, which are our creative response to the challenges of life.

Among those magic instruments are the myths and archetypal images such as the Green Man or the Face of Glory. They also include our capacities for intuition and for those states of creativity and appreciation I will characterize in the course of this book as the Eternal Feminine. Such states make us more open to the special kind of knowledge that is conveyed to us through atmosphere.

The atmospheres of places, buildings and great artefacts frequently offer us the experience of the living myth, the state in which the inner and the outer significances of our own experience come together in image and symbol. As illustrations of the bent of my thought I give three examples to give point to my meanings: one from the ancient world, one from the modern world, and one that combines both the ancient and the modern worlds.

The first illustration is that of the site of Epidauros on the eastern side of the Argolid in Greece. It is chiefly and rightly famous for its theatre, scooped from the hillside, with its perfect acoustics (figure 4). The theatre is still in use but it is only part of a wider complex of buildings devoted to the healing and the wholeness of man that comprised the shrine of Asklepios, the god of medicine.

The site of Epidauros is a wide natural mound rising from a broad valley whose flanks rise up to mountains. Wherever you walk there you feel the presence of the mountain summits protecting and blessing both you and the place. Among the ruins you come across the Temple of Asklepios and beside it the remains of the *abaton*, or portico where those seeking healing slept after making the appropriate sacrifices. During the night the god would visit them in their dreams and he would either cure them or give instructions for what they had to do to be healed. The next morning the priest doctors of Asklepios would listen to the patients' accounts of their dreams and would prescribe one or more of the cures available at Epidauros. These could range from medical treatment with herbs to surgery, courses of exercise in the palaestra, listening to poetry and music or attending the plays in the theatre, or making offerings in the temples of other gods that were on the site. Every aspect of man's nature that could receive a hurt or be subject to illness, it appears, could find a cure there.

One comes away from Epidauros with the fragrance of a lost wholeness, with a desire for a medicine that starts, as with the dream of the god, from being connected with one's deeper self and for a medicine that acknowledged once more the healing power of art, architecture and music – instead of the exhausted members of the modern medical profession and the hideous buildings in which too frequently they and their patients are confined.

Like the cure at Epidauros, my next illustration starts with a dream. A German chemist, Friedrich August Kekulé von Stradonitz, was working in London in the 1850s. Chemists were then struggling to make sense of the nature of chemicals derived from living things and from materials such as coal and oil derived from organic remains. Because of their origins these chemicals were called organic chemicals; all of them were found to be compounds of the element carbon. The chemistry of carbon is still known as organic chemistry although thousands of the compounds with which organic chemists deal do not occur naturally in plants or animals but are designed and made in laboratories. These include plastics, synthetic fibres, anaesthetics and the drugs available to modern medicine. One important organic chemical from which a multitude of others can be made is benzene. Kekulé was studying the structure of benzene and getting nowhere with his research. He fell into a doze in front of the fire in his lodgings in Clapham and a hypnagogic experience came to him. It was of a whirling serpent biting its tail, the ancient symbol of eternity.[9] He saw a new significance in it: he was being offered the structure of benzene, not as a chain or in any other form, but as a ring. He discovered in that moment a major key to understanding organic chemistry. Kekulé's dream had momentous consequences: without it there would have been no automotive industry, no oil-powered air flight, and no synthetic materials such as plastics. What he had learned from his dream enabled chemists first to work out the different structures of the various chemicals they extracted from coal or crude oil – and then, because they understood the structures, to devise new materials which they could make out of the naturally occurring chemicals. Thus they learned to make substitutes for wood, stone, metals, leather, wool and cotton. One such material which has found more and more uses over the past fifty years is polyurethane.

We are surrounded by polyurethanes in one or more of their uses in most aspects of our lives. We sleep on polyurethane foam, we sit on polyurethane at home and when we travel in a motorcar or fly through the air; the very ink on this page was printed on it by a polyurethane roller. Polyurethanes are one of the most efficient forms of insulation in use today. Their introduction is probably the chief reason why the domestic refrigerator, formerly owned only by the richer classes, is now a common possession throughout the developed world. They have also contributed greatly to the social and economic changes brought about by the introduction of supermarkets and the transport of frozen and cooled foods on which the supermarkets depend as well as providing the insulated storage for the butter mountain, the wine lakes and the other food surpluses of the European Union.

On a visit to a huge site of the chemical industry beside a Lancashire estuary, I was shown the plant where one of the chief constituents of polyurethane, a chemical known for short as MDI, is made. A visit to a chemical plant tests the imagination because you cannot see any of the processes happening. Death would come quickly if you tried to look. My guide was the plant manager, a chemist who held in his knowledge and imagination all the processes and changes that were happening in the vessels and pipes. A sequence of transformations based on the molecular structures worked out by Kekulé and his successors was taking place: a derivative of benzene was being combined with a derivative of natural gas. This in turn was being joined in a temporary marriage with a combination of chlorine and carbon monoxide; the chlorine would then be driven off, leaving the mixture from which MDI is formed. Climbing up and down metal staircases, gazing at juddering vats, with my guide describing the sequence of chemical changes, I had the illusion that I was close to something like a living being in the plant – an impression reinforced in the control room where I saw the screens relaying information about what was happening in each vessel, which valves were closed until particular processes were finished, which parts were flowing and what the pressures were, all as though I were watching a screen monitoring the progress of a patient in a hospital or an animal in a zoo.

At the end of the process I saw the drums being filled with MDI that would be sent to factories all round the world. I could not see there the final stage of the MDI being combined with another chemical, called a polyol, which actually forms the polyurethane, though I had watched it elsewhere. The two liquids are poured together and they react instantaneously to form a solid. It is an extraordinary sight. It could be taken as an image of the creative process itself, when in the artist's mind a powerful and emotion-arousing impression reacts instantaneously with his prepared skills and desire to create, or when the scientist echoes the cry of Archimedes: 'Eureka!' The reaction is indeed used to make things: parts of motorcars, refrigerators, buildings, shoes, packaging, all that is useful or adds to comfort or convenience – and little that adds to beauty.

To put the matter more kindly, the results of this process create nothing that is as beautiful and as awe-inspiring as the grim half-beauty of the plant itself. There as I stood among the vibrating life of the plant I thought of the work of modern artists such as Fernand Léger who have tried to convey the fascination of machinery. This, I thought, was a greater art in its way and more inspiring, simply because in the work of those artists, their pipes and constructions are merely impressions of machinery, whereas here, every artefact and valve had meaning and purpose because they were put there with intention and knowledge. That feeling was reinforced by the atmosphere of the place created by all the thoughts and all the careers that had been devoted to the making and the running of the plant and its predecessors ever since, over a hundred years ago, Barrow ironmasters had first discovered rock salt beneath the estuarine meadows and had used it to found an alkali industry.

What troubled me also were certain thoughts that took a long time to become clear. They come back to the issue of beauty. Something is missing from the product. It can be used to make a myriad artefacts but it cannot be impregnated with the sense of humanity in the way that stone or wood leave the craftsman's hands changed not only by his handiwork but also by the quality of attention he has given to them. Nor, in general, can it be made more beautiful by repeated use – unlike the handle of a garden spade, for example. All the effort has been given that investigative genius, commercial power and high finance can provide to finding out about the nature of substances and how to manipulate them into new materials for useful and saleable objects. It is as though when man learned how to manipulate the molecular levels of matter, he was given a toy to distract him from the fact that he was himself being manipulated on a higher level by forces that wanted to replace his natural taste with imitations of the natural substances with which he had hitherto worked and to cut him off from direct experience both of the outer world and of what lies beyond and includes the molecular and atomic worlds within himself. It is also as though he has been deluded by studying minor causes into thinking that his knowledge is deep enough to anticipate the effects of any discovery he makes and any new substance he introduces into the world. Or, to put it another way, as man's power over nature increased through his use of science, he should have made an equivalent progress in moral and aesthetic depth: he should have increased his ability to control that power by thought and emotion developed to a new degree of unity. Instead, he has raped the world like a necrophiliac, believing the world to be dead – but the world is turning out to be alive and demanding justice.

An ancient rape and a modern rape are the themes of my last illustration. This is the site of the Mysteries of Eleusis, the most flattened of all the ruins of Greece, and now bordered by a motorway and surrounded by oil refineries, petrochemical plants and dockyards.[10] The legend of Eleusis is this: Demeter, the goddess of fertility, had a beautiful daughter, Persephone, in whom she delighted. Hades, the brother of Zeus, had no wife and he desired Persephone. A conspiracy of the gods ensured that Persephone was enticed by beautiful flowers to a place in Sicily where the earth opened and Hades appeared to seize Persephone and bury her in his underground kingdom. In her grief Demeter wandered the Earth looking for Persephone and no one could or would tell her news of her. She came to Eleusis, where the King and Queen greeted her kindly and gave her hospitality. Demeter resolved she would cease her wandering and she sat on the stone, still to be seen at Eleusis, called the 'mirthless rock'. There she came to a decision: since no one would help her, she would withdraw her own help to others. She took away the power to bear fruit from every plant. Nothing would deter her: she was bringing about death for every living creature. Gods and men besought Zeus to intervene. He nodded his ambrosial locks on Mount Olympus and the message went to Hades that he must return Persephone to her mother instantly. Persephone, in the underworld, had refused all food, knowing that if she ate there, she could not return. Nevertheless she had eaten three pips of a pomegranate and this meant that every year she had to return to Hades for three months, thus instituting the season of winter.

In her joy at the return of Persephone, Demeter taught Triptolemos, a son of the royal house of Eleusis, how to sow and reap corn and she gave him a winged chariot in which he travelled the world, teaching the knowledge to all men. She also founded the Mysteries of Eleusis, annual rites of initiation open to free men and women and to slaves. The candidates for initiation performed preliminary rites in Athens in February of each year and in the autumn they walked the fifteen miles from Athens to Eleusis known as the Sacred Way. There they were greeted with ritual dances and songs and admitted through the gates that led to the great covered hall, or *telesterion*, where they experienced the Mysteries.[11]

It was death for the uninitiated to pass into the shrine and, though Alcibiades was thought to have mocked the Mysteries and Aeschylus to have revealed too much of them in one of his plays, no one told in full what they learned. The wheat ear and the grape were important in the rites, precursors of the bread and the wine that later became the elements of the Christian Eucharist. At the height of the ceremonies it is recorded that the hierophant chanted: 'The Great Goddess has borne a sacred child. Brimo has borne Brimos.' This child may have been one of the avatars of Dionysos and therefore one of the precursors of the Green Man. This connects with another rumour about the Mysteries of Eleusis: that Demeter, as a recompense for her sufferings, was the mother of Dionysos in his third incarnation. After this announcement the hierophant held up the wheat ear for all to see, and celebrations and banqueting followed.

These rites were performed for some 1,500 years until they came to an end in about AD 395. What gave them their power and authority over so many centuries remains a matter of fruitful wonder. It may be that the experience was literally ineffable. I have heard it suggested that the essence of the initiation was a near-death experience in which the initiate was given personal and convincing evidence of immortality and the rebirth of the soul. The initiates would then go back to their various lives to fulfil their particular destinies with a trust and a vigour that would have enabled them to face whatever challenges life presented to them. In a culture that had only a weak and undeveloped conception of the afterlife, the renewal in every generation of a trust in immortality in people of every kind and rank must have influenced society in a subtle and important way. They could not say what they had seen but their ensuing lives and the influence they exercised would have been a leaven in the world, extending far beyond what we know of that influence through, for example, the Attic dramatists and the dialogues of Plato.

The influence is still there in the remains of the shrine of Eleusis Its atmosphere of solitude and holiness is all the more palpable for the evidence of the modern rape of the Earth that surrounds it. The closeness of the motorway that straddles the Sacred Way, the tall crackers in which crude oil is refined, the clouds of yellow smoke that float across the bay obscuring the cliffs of Salamis, and the dingy streets through which one approaches the rusty iron gates of the shrine are enough to make one expect to find Demeter once more upon the mirthless rock, rigid with outrage at the polluted air that keeps the beauty of her daughter locked underground. But for our visit in April, Persephone had returned: the ruins brimmed with vetches foaming with mauves and purples: the dark crimson Greek poppies thrust out of cracks in the marble. The meadows round the sacred well were studded with yellow camomile, standing upright as though they were the *korai* of the rite poised for their dances to begin.

A holy place such as Eleusis is charged with an atmosphere that survives the overturning of temples and the scorn of later religions. Such an atmosphere is the emotional reality of these places. How the trace of human greatness, of the transformation of grief into the triumph of civilization, and of the revelation of the divine, enters into the stones, natural forms and plants of such places is a mystery denied to our generation, to us who know about matter, or who pay willingly for others to know about matter and its transformations in the refineries and the chemical plants such as those that surround Eleusis. It is the mystery of the all-containing consciousness.

There was another association in my mind, the association that had particularly roused our desire to go to Eleusis. This was the poem by the poet Angelos Sikelianos (1884–1951), 'The Sacred Way'.[12] Driven by an unnamed grief, Sikelianos set out to walk the length of the Sacred Way from Athens to Eleusis. Passing by ox-drawn carts and motorcars, he came to a solitary part where he saw a rock. As he sat on the rock, he saw three shadows come round a corner. A gypsy pulling two shuffling bears on chains came towards him. The moment the gypsy saw him he began beating a tambourine and he tugged at the chains to make the bears stand on their hind legs. The bigger of the bears was the mother: her forehead was decorated with blue beads and a white talisman was placed on her head. To Sikelianos she seemed to be an image of the Great Goddess. The gypsy pulled at the chain that led to the ring in the young bear's nostril, still red with blood from having been recently pierced. The mother bear growled with pain, stood upright and began to dance vigorously while she gazed all the time at her child. Sikelianos says that he was withdrawn from time by the sight of her. He saw nothing but the gigantic bear with the blue beads dancing and out of her pitiful love, witnessing to the whole world a primeval and universal suffering.

The soul still is, as it was, in Hades. The poet dropped a drachma in the tambourine. The gypsy went on his way, dragging the two bears with him. As Sikelianos walked, his heart groaned. 'Will the time ever come when the soul of the bear and the gypsy and my own soul which I call initiated will rejoice together?' As the twilight fell, the darkness poured into his heart like the waves into a sinking ship. When his heart seemed utterly drowned in that blackness, he heard a murmur above him, a murmur that seemed to say: 'It will come.'

As for myself, being as complicit in my means of travelling to Eleusis in the pollution of the environment and the destruction of the beauty I revere as Sikelianos was in the suffering of the bears, I also felt in the atmosphere of the shrine a presence of hope and of joy as though the wisdom that awaits our understanding was radiantly existent, as though the crushing of the spiritual by the devotion to material things and material explanations was an illusion easily and soon to be dispelled, and as though the joy of the creative act will feed again the shoots of a new civilization as it springs out of the inexhaustible wealth of the one consciousness.

Part I

The Great Memory
and the source of creativity

1

The creative imagination

The view to the downs is arched by two trees, a deciduous ash and an evergreen ilex. Behind me is an oak and I sit beneath its shady canopy. The lower branches of the oak hang to my eye level, their leaves making bright-green roundels where the midday sun catches them. The meadow beyond is pale brown with seedheads. Across the meadow I look at a copse of beeches whose black shadows tumble down a hillside. Above the crowns of the beeches I see the line of the downs – a rich blue line of hills with their horizon sharply defined against the heat-filled August sky.

The horizon of the downs is a source of continuous fascination; it marks the boundary of seen and not seen; it signifies the point of departure for imagination and invention to create worlds beyond the limit of sight. Death, new life, fears, hopes and the unexpected are all tingling in the line where sky meets earth. It is a further stage in the divisions of experience that, in sense terms, begin from the warm summer air on my skin reminding me of what is within my body and what is outside that body.

For imagination there is no such division. It can create black night even at such a noon as this. It can fly over that horizon and conceive a million possible worlds and universes. It can shrink itself into the ambitions of a looper caterpillar hanging by its thread from an oak leaf. At the moment it wants to do nothing but to sink into the mood of the summer.

I feel myself in Nature. The heat commands stillness from every plant and creature except for the silent flutterings of the butterflies and the last spasm of an exhausted breeze in the leaves above me; and their slight motion only tends to emphasize the stillness of all other things. It is a time of contentment, of the gathered harvest and the ripening of fruit still to be picked. The Green Man has become the Gold Man. Once again life has been successful.

But is it just unthinking life and witless nature that have been successful? Imagination, having soaked itself with the mood of the day, stirs me to think of the success of past generations as evidenced by this ancient landscape.

What I see and enjoy here is the result of human creativity and inventiveness interacting with geological structures such as chalk, clay and greensand and with grasses, scrub, trees, worms, bacteria, wildlife and the animals domesticated and introduced by man.

Everywhere before me there is the obvious or inferred evidence of human inventiveness and toil. Everywhere there is evidence of choice, of what man has chosen to do with nature; there are, probably, few trees of all the hundreds in this view that were not deliberately planted. Each different plough that worked these fields had to be invented or devised by human hands and brains. The very grass seeds in the lawn were selected and chosen originally from all the variety available in nature. Someone had to invent the first table for me to be able to sit and write at a table today. Some geniuses among our remotest ancestors discovered the relationship between sounds and meaning, between names and forms, so that we can communicate with one another today. Each succeeding culture, race or civilization that has affected this landscape had its own technology and its own imaginative concept of the world, its social structures and religious beliefs that nourished some arts and could accept some novelties but defended itself as against invaders from other novelties or introductions. This landscape, with its evidence of the interplay between different kinds of human energies, between the extension of the chemical energy in human muscles into machines and tools and the exercise of mental and emotional energies helps us consider the natures of the creative imagination and of civilization and of the relationship between them.

In their present state the downs look as though they have always seemed as they are now. Their bareness, the rounded moulding of their slopes, their almost total lack of human habitation, all speak of a primordial antiquity. Yet once they were covered in thick forest which was cut down by the first farmers in these islands. The men who cut down the forest, using axes chipped from the flint nodules they mined from the chalk with deer horns, revealed the line of the downs whose whiteness they perhaps held in veneration as a sign of the Great Goddess. Their successors would have built the wooden temple, or Woodhenge, just beyond the horizon, traces of which have just been revealed by the cutting of a new road. They or their followers in time would have brought here the metal-working skills of the Bronze Age in the period when the barrows were raised for their princes and princesses on the edge of the downs.

Later invaders have come, each bringing new myths, faiths and technologies: the Celts with their mastery of iron, their pantheistic faith and belief in immortality, and their hero myths, who constructed as their tribal and religious centres the hillforts such as Chanctonbury

Ring visible in the far west; the Romans, who brought the gods, the plants, the architecture and the technology of their sophisticated Mediterranean society and built villas and roads in the valley beneath the downs: the South Saxons, who would have brought in and adapted some of the most crucial inventions of the Dark Ages such as the heavy plough and the stirrup; and the Normans, supreme masters of the technology of their time, who conquered England through their victory at Hastings thirty miles eastwards and made their power absolute through building castles such as those at Lewes and Bramber to guard the passes through the downs cut by rivers flowing to the sea.

The later Romano-Britons, the South Saxons and the Normans were all in turn the witnesses, the subjects and sometimes the agents of another kind of conquest. This was the conquest by Christian missionaries of the old religions, the animist and participatory cults of ancient Europe. In destroying the old cults, by cutting down the sacred groves and denouncing the spirits of earth, air and water as demons powerless before the name of Christ, the missionaries of the Dark Ages gave to their flocks, without it being at all their prime intention, a new licence to change and modify their environment. This change of attitude to Nature, that she was there to be exploited and used, not to be propitiated and feared, has been called one of the greatest psychic revolutions in the history of mankind.[1] To this revolution, which first becomes plain in the eighth century, is attributed the later supremacy of western science and technology. It was in fact a revolution in man's imaginative conception of the world.

This landscape must have been one of the last places in England to retain the old attitudes to nature simply because the South Saxons were the latest as a people to submit to Christianity. By the time the Norman rule was thoroughly established here in the twelfth century, the countryside would have exhibited many of the machines and mechanical aids that a thrusting, expanding Europe had welcomed from the East or had invented for itself. One of these introductions was the windmill. Up to a hundred and fifty years ago the horizon of the downs would have looked quite different: an army of windmills had been set up on the high ground to capture the energy of the sea winds from the Channel.

The exploitation of the land continued. By the fifteenth century brick-making skills had been introduced from Holland and north Germany and the rich local deposits of clay were being worked. This brought about the later evolution of our characteristic Sussex brick and tile-hung houses. North of us stretched the great Forest of the Weald where the charcoal burners supplied the iron founders who made the cannon for the fleets that defended Protestant Britain from the Spaniards, the French and the Dutch and that were to win the Dutch and French colonies in North America for England.

By the later eighteenth century the industry had declined and the countryside settled back into rurality, only to be invaded once more by a succession of inventions; the railway from London, the motorcar and the new highways it requires, the pylons carrying electricity, the gas pipes, the water mains, aircraft in the skies and the nearby airports, and the ceaseless flow of information poured into every house by television and radio. Every now and then in deepening dusk we can see the slow passage of a satellite above the downs at its task of spying or transmitting messages or watching the weather or relaying programmes.

Again, although the landscape seems so eternally rural, until recently there was not a sheep visible that had not been dipped in chemicals, and there is probably not a field that has not been fed with artificial fertilizers or dosed with selective herbicides, just as, from sowing to harvesting, every craft and technique that once raised our crops has been superseded by mechanized farming. It seems so beautiful, so protected by legislation and popular feeling that no one would ever want it to change more than it does with the alternating beauties of the seasons – but there are deposits of oil under the downs and it could only need a severe break in our supplies of fossil fuel for yet another round of exploitation to begin, and it would require a conversion in our attitudes to nature, a revolution in our imaginative concepts comparable to the changes when the first farmers cut down the primeval forest or our ancestors in the Dark Ages abjured the old gods, for such a temptation to be resisted. But that may be what the return of the archetype of the Green Man is indicating to us now as necessary to our survival – and also necessary before new aspects of our own creativity and new forms of knowledge can be revealed.

Every change to this landscape caused by a newly introduced technology, every inspired use of those technologies in the cause of art and religion such as the churches nestling under the downs, has arisen because of a revelation, a fresh understanding or simply a bright idea in an individual's head, in some cases thousands of miles away – as in the case of the nameless soul beyond the high Pamir who, looking at wind-turned Buddhist prayer wheels, thought of adapting the device to grinding corn or the mason in the thirteenth century who, weary of humping earth or stones, either invented or introduced the wheelbarrow. All these changes have arisen first in the imaginations of individuals and have been greeted or delayed in their acceptance according to whether the imaginations of their contemporaries could see the need for them and could accommodate them to their beliefs and social forms.

From the energies generated by chemical, physical or nuclear means we turn to the energies in the human soul and the creative imagination that may direct their energies or set them in new paths of work. What I mean by the creative imagination is the faculty of coordination in ourselves that makes images of what we are to do or make or be. It draws on our intuitive and physical natures, on our emotions and our intellectual powers, on our dream life and our waking life. It is what makes our experience and the impressions we receive truly our own. It is imagination that limits or expands possibilities and explanations. The greatness of our science is in part owed to the fact that its progenitors and their successors *imagined* the world to be capable of rational explanation and to be founded upon laws, rather than on the powers of deities and spirits. That greatness is also owed to the world-transforming energy that is channelled through the imagination when it is coordinated with the observation and total attention that we find, for example, vivifying the writings of Charles Darwin, whether he is describing the action of earthworms in creating topsoil or the communication of emotion in the Animal Kingdom.

Darwin described the imagination as 'one of the noblest prerogatives of man'.[2] The dominant metaphor in his writings on evolution is that of the tree of life, first manifesting itself as a rough sketch of branches marking the separate development of phyla and species set down in his notebooks during the voyage of the *Beagle* and later recurring many times with its leader branch from the main trunk of life culminating in man as though he was finding the strength for his thoughts in the archetype of the Green Man, quite unconsciously turning back to this ancient symbol in order to create new paths for the scientific imagination to travel on.

Darwin's use of the word 'imagination' in such a context reflects the exalted stage the word had been raised to in the English language by poets of the Romantic era such as Coleridge and Wordsworth. Imagination was a term of medieval faculty psychology: it was used in general to describe the faculty of absorbing and distributing the impressions of sense images. The functions we now give to the creative imagination were in the Middle Ages described as those of *fantasia*. It was through his *alta fantasia* that Dante was taken up into the vision of the Trinity at the end of his *Paradiso*. In the market of words *fantasia* lost its value and declined, in English, into fancy, while imagination in its creative sense has grown in value though it still keeps in other uses the meanings of delusion, groundless hopes or hallucination.

What it can mean to us in understanding our own natures is strikingly revealed in the phrase we may use of someone we cannot persuade to agree with us: 'He has no imagination.' We mean, of course, by it that his imagination is not the same as ours, but the full implications of the expression are terrifying and dehumanizing. They would mean that the individual of whom we disapprove has no ability to understand a story, that he cannot make metaphors or similes, that he cannot dream or daydream, that he cannot conceive of any friend in their absence, that he cannot think of other worlds or lands, or sympathize with others, and that just as he may have no fears or hopes about the future, he is permanently ignorant of the past. Even this short list shows how much we depend upon our imaginations and how much we owe our sense of ourselves to imagination.

The variety of different kinds of imagination – the auditory, the visual, the imagination of empathy and the different combinations brought out by the exercise of varied talents – provokes the question of whether there is indeed one creative imagination with common characteristics that are revealed in any field of human action or whether there are a host of different kinds of imagination brought into play by genetic and environmental factors and whose differences are far more obvious than any casual resemblances. Do the scientist, the artist, the engineer, the inventive cook and the inspired preacher have anything in common besides a passionate desire to innovate in their particular fields and an equally passionate desire to be rewarded either on Earth or in Heaven for their efforts? Is there a link between, say, the imagination of the unknown wheelwright who invented the whippletree which enabled horses and cart drivers to manoeuvre round corners in narrow streets in medieval cities (it is the ancestor of our articulated lorries), the imagination of a member of the Bach family composing an intricate piece of music and the imagination of an entomologist whose particular gift is for the taxonomy of earwigs? The first example is a solution to what must have been an urgent practical problem; the second is an example of someone born to a particular profession and producing music, for which there was great contemporary need at religious and social occasions; the third is a trained scientist, working either in a university or in the research institute of a company interested in pest control, using a combination of intellectual powers and powers based on memory for his work. Apart from all three supplying social and economic needs in their time, what links them together is that they are all applying or discovering patterns. We know nothing about the inventor of the whippletree except that he or she must have existed at some time between the late thirteenth and the early fourteenth century. Almost certainly he or she must have seen how the principle of a device already invented, such as a threshing flail, could be applied to the shaft of a cart, or got the idea from contemplating the articulation of his or her own limbs or even by noticing the articulation of insect bodies such as ants or earwigs which enable the insects to dive into the narrowest holes and negotiate the tightest of corners. He or she would have seen a pattern or principle that could be applied in a new way. The member of the Bach family is making patterns of sound and the entomologist is discovering patterns in nature.[3]

Though I say that the composer is *making* patterns while the entomologist discovers them, it could equally well be said that it is the composer who is the discoverer because he listens to a pre-existent harmony and therefore lays bare what is already there and that the entomologist is the creator of a fiction because he is imposing on nature a pattern that may be coherent and intelligible to himself and his peers but is nevertheless a construct of their shared imaginative view of living things.

We recognize patterns through the repetition of motifs, through the periodicity of the motions of the stars, through the rhythms of verse and of music. The seventeenth-century Japanese poet Bashō had an insight on his travels into the relationship between poetry and the rhythms of living. He had passed through the gate of Shirakawa, which marked the entrance to the regions of the north and which also was a traditional theme of poetry. Asked by another poet what he had written at the gate, he had to confess he was so taken by the countryside and the works of older poets, he had written nothing of worth. In his shame, he wrote the following:

First impulse to art:
Songs of peasants planting rice
In the distant north.[4]

Out of the stillness of the valleys pour the songs of the peasants that give them the rhythm for rising and bending as they plant the rice seedlings in the flat, sky-reflecting paddy fields. Out of the stillness of the primal mind is uttered the word, or Logos, whose reverberations set up the repeated patterns of matter and living form. From the mouth of the Green Man, whose mysterious mind we can only guess at from the varied expression in his eyes, pour out the leaves, flowers and fruits whose seeds will give birth to and support the repeated generations of all plants and all the chains of living creatures that will feed on them. From the one quintessential element come the dances and transmutations of the four elements of matter: earth, water, fire and air.

Rhythm and pattern are necessary both to the execution of works of art and their communication – as with poetry, music and the dance. A painter may feel the beginnings of a painting as a certain contrast of rhythms; in his execution of the painting his brush will move in a series of changing rhythms, soft and fierce, strong and gentle, the effects of which on us will be a resonant and vibrant response. The detail of the drawing *Resurrection* (frontispiece) shows the rhythm built up by repeated pencil strokes. The architect, having heard or seen the inner harmony that will bring his building together as a whole, creates façades that move and impress us through massed repetitions of stone or brick, broken by the patterns of recession formed by windows, alcoves and doors, themselves held within and divided by the greater beats of columns or pilasters.

Many of the most fundamental discoveries in science have arisen from the search for patterns or rhythms. The Periodic Table – its very name means a pattern of recurrence – was discovered in such a way. By the end of the eighteenth century so many elements had been discovered that scientists were looking for relationships between the elements. Döbereiner discovered triads or patterns of three in certain relationships. When Dimitri Mendeleev was given the overall scheme of the Periodic Table in a dream, he was able to predict from three gaps in his table that certain elements must exist even though they had not at that time been isolated and identified. He was to be proved right with the later discovery of all three elements.

In the arts rhythm has a particular purpose: it is to transmit and to re-create in the reader, spectator or listener the mood of the poet, the artist or composer. It arises in the mood of the creative artist, often as the original inspiration or resonating as part of the nature of the given image or theme. It is when we absorb the mood of a work of art and are engrossed in it that we experience something of the same coordination of our faculties and of our emotions and powers of attention that I ascribe to the creative imagination. In essence our creative imaginations and our appreciative imaginations are one.

As the creative imagination enables us to share knowledge and experience, as it gives unity and expansion of understanding to our minds, as it creates in us the mood in which we become most welcoming to the universal, so imagination enhances our humanity. The potentiality of the imagination for expressing and communicating universal truths is one recognized by many thinkers and poets. Thus Mary Warnock says: 'The imagination, especially as it is exercised in the creative arts, is that which can draw out general implications from individual instances, can see and cause others to see, the universal in the particular.'[5] Coleridge in one of his most famous passages in prose spoke of the 'Primary Imagination' as being 'the repetition in the finite mind of the eternal act of creation in the infinite I AM'[6] and elsewhere he wrote of the purpose of imagination as being to find unity in multiplicity.[7] William Blake had an equally grand conception of imagination: 'The Imagination is not a State: it is the Human Existence itself.'[8] He meant by this that imagination is not a faculty or condition subject to change, but the continuum of meaningful life.

To Blake we are all within the divine imagination of Jesus, united with that imagination when we acknowledge the unity of our selfhood with Him, and subject to degrees of false perceptions and understandings of the world in so far as we assert our separate selfhoods. Hell is an illusion because it is our own illusion: no God created Hell or sent us there: we will have done it ourselves through the impurity of our imaginations.

The creative imagination is the faculty in our natures that individuates the experience and knowledge of the past and turns it into something new that creates or affects the future. For traditional religious and philosophical views of the human psyche it provides one of the ways in which the greater understanding, emotion and wisdom of the worlds beyond time can enter our awareness and descend into human affairs. One symbol for this process is the cross, with its upright being the shaft of eternity passing through the horizontal bar of linear time. The upright shaft represents the light of consciousness illuminating the processes of history and time which are thought of as passing along the line of the horizontal bar of the cross. One of the great differences between traditional views and the accepted western scientific view is that for the latter, there is no cross because there is no vertical shaft to the cross. Everything is explained in terms of cause and effect working along the course of linear time and this requirement has imposed limitations on the scientific imagination which extends in its influence far beyond the discourse of those formally trained as scientists.

Older systems of thought, such as the Neo-Platonic tradition and the Advaita system, consider imagination as an attribute of God. According to these philosophies it is the task of man to raise his imagination to the divine imagination and be guided and instructed by that. The scientific imagination in contrast allows no superior to itself and it denies the fruitfulness or use of other modes of investigation. It brooks no other god than its own view of truth.

As the scientific imagination has extended the span of the universe, so it has narrowed its gaze to investigate matter in smaller and smaller particles: the two processes are part of a necessary polarity because many advances in modern cosmology have been related to the discovery of the behaviour of matter at the atomic and subatomic levels. The invisibly vast universe is interpreted in terms of invisibly minuscule particles. In whichever direction investigation goes, no mind beyond that of the observer is discovered and no imagination ever worked to make the universe which is revealed to the mind of the observer. The mind and the imagination of the observer, like the universe, are the outcome of mechanisms that are logically explicable as arising from ultimately random causes.

T. H. Huxley and Charles Darwin accused the opponents of evolutionary theory of a want of imagination in failing to grasp its scope. Curiously enough, many of their followers have limited the concept of imagination by providing an explanation of the origins of the imagination in evolutionary terms. To them the human imagination has arisen in response to the challenges of competition, out of man's need to find food, make shelters, procreate and defend himself; from learning when to stand and fight or when to flee, man progressed to social and tribal groupings and to devising walls and defences that would make flight unnecessary and inventing weapons that would make victory certain. Even what may seem the most gratuitous and individual part of our imaginative capacities, our ability to dream, has been given an evolutionary interpretation: dreams are rehearsals for all the dangers and eventualities we may have to encounter in our waking life. The human being, according to the various theories dominant in the ambience of the scientific imagination, is a largely closed system. It is both autonomous, in that it possesses no contact with a source of intelligence greater than what is possible within its own species, and without autonomy, in that what it does know and live by is the product of its genetic and social inheritance, its present environment and the traumas and sufferings of the womb and early childhood. Because of a particular conjunction of genetic and environmental factors it may be especially gifted in one or more fields. Through a fortunate combination of mental and physical coordination with the right education and appreciative milieu, it may give pleasure through the arts, heal and increase the sum of human knowledge through medicine and the sciences or refine thought through philosophy. In terms of the various descriptions of the origins and employment of these creative powers it is simply a successful animal that has adapted to the complex organization of a particular ant heap. It bears the right smells for acceptance and is rewarded according to the hierarchy of prizes given for those smells. Within the terms of the various descriptions there is no room for what would be considered the human qualities of such a human being, his or her imaginative sympathy, moral depth, and profound intelligence, as being of value in their own right. Their status as virtues is a delusion: as delusions, they may be valuable because they contribute to the powerful delusions which maintain the equilibrium of a social organization by soothing and reassuring its collective members, but when they are compared with the standards of biological success, of adaptation to an environment or organization, of achieving a relative longevity, of reproducing oneself or contributing to the continuity of reproduction in the hive or ant heap, they are no more than epiphenomena.

The starkness of these theories have been too much for many of those who have introduced and held them. They have masked their grimness from themselves and others by adopting a general humanitarian philosophy which can owe nothing to theories expressed in biological or social terms. The values of the humanitarian philosophy come from a quite different source, the secularized Christianity and the classical upbringing of the philosophers of the Enlightenment with their hopes of so ameliorating the lot of humanity that at some time in the future the kingdom of Heaven will be established on Earth. Such was the philosophy that sustained the liberal and humane Charles Darwin after he had lost the faith of his upbringing and such has been the philosophy made use of by politicians who sought to put into practice the logic of their scientifically derived theories about human society.

Most older traditions speak of a Golden Age in the past, an age that may recur as part of a great cycle of time in the future but certainly does not exist now. To the philosophers of the Enlightenment and the scientists and politicians whom they influenced, man has emerged out of a past of barbarism and superstition and they found it necessary to place their Golden Age in the future. Doctrines of the evolution of man became inextricably bound to the vision of an imagined future, guided by scientific and technological advances. The idea of progress took over from triumphalist Christianity the imagery of conquest; pain, suffering, hunger, repression and social injustice would be eliminated or alleviated and the secrets of nature and the universe would be discovered and used to destroy superstition and create a perfect society. The vision was probably necessary to the many notable achievements of the scientific age but it has also led to the present environmental crisis which has led in turn to a crisis of the scientific imagination.

One of the latest promises leading to a future Golden Age is offered by genetic engineering. The theory is that, as we are the product of our genetic inheritance and have virtually no choice over our appearance, character and talents, so we are unconsciously the slaves of our genes. Genetic engineering will liberate us from our state of slavery: we will be able to modify and improve everything in our bodies and mental dispositions that we dislike, fear or wish to change and we will be the makers of the future through the mastery of our heredity. The techniques are already being applied to plants and to domesticated animals.

The promise is one in a long series of imagined futures offered by various discoveries and inventions, from the steam engine to radium and to cheap and safe sources of nuclear energy. None of the promises have the predictive value science can boast of having achieved in so many fields. They are part of the collective myth of science and it is to collective myths and the image of man implicit in them that this first part of the book returns again and again.

Myths may also be extremely fruitful, as we can see from the other aspect of what created the myth of the Golden Future: the humanitarian and freedom-loving urge for future perfection. As an example of a work of art with universal appeal inspired by that urge, I take Beethoven's Ninth Symphony, the 'Choral', with its setting in the last movement of Schiller's 'Ode to Joy'. It provides an example of the complex interdependence of skills that our western civilization has evolved. Though I will discuss the work again in Chapter 7 in relation to Schiller's and Beethoven's creative processes and in Chapter 13 in relation to its effects on an audience, here I am most interested in what was necessary for Schiller to write the 'Ode to Joy' and for Beethoven to compose his Ninth Symphony. First of all, we have the poet and composer themselves: two gifted individuals both fired by the same ideals of liberating the human spirit and a belief in the perfectibility of man. The processes each went through to compose the works combined in the symphony, let them remain in black boxes for the time being. For what went into the black box of Schiller's creative processes, there was necessary the coming-of-age of German literary language under the guidance of Goethe and his contemporaries and the philosophers of the Enlightenment; there was necessary the rediscovery in Germany of ancient Greece, and her art, literature and history; there was necessary the creation of a reading public and therefore a network of publishers, printers and booksellers through the cities of the German-speaking world; there was necessary the reports of the American Revolution and the realization, even in the least significant of German princely states, that new ideas were abroad and that the relationships of ruler to ruled and between man and man would be altered for ever. As Schiller put it in an earlier version of the 'Ode to Joy': *'Bettler werden Fürstenbrüder'* (Beggars become the brothers of princes). What the transmission of all this information and these new ideas depended on was the technology of printing, which in turn arose from the dreams of master printers each determined to create ever more elegant and appropriate typefaces, format and layouts in order to communicate more efficiently and pleasurably.

Turning to what went into the black box of Beethoven's creative processes, we see all the same influences that affected Schiller, including those from ancient Greece: the reading public was also in general the musical public, whether it was centred on the princely courts or was composed of the middle classes of cities such as Vienna or Prague. To the reports of the American Revolution can be added the more immediate effects and influences of the French Revolution and the Napoleonic Wars. What was also necessary in Beethoven's case was the tradition of musical composition and performance into which he was born; not only were Haydn and Mozart and a host of other composers necessary to him but every development of instrumental and choral polyphony going back to the twelfth century. What had become necessary for that tradition was the extraordinary range of crafts and inventions that were required to make the instruments of an orchestra: the work in many metals, the valves of the woodwind and the brass, the choice of different woods, the varnishes of the stringed instruments, the vellum of the drums and the catgut, sheepgut and wires of the strings. Behind every instrument was the dream of a craftsman or succession of craftsmen to create a new voice for the expression of human emotions or to add a new sonority or tone to combinations of instruments. Behind every instrument that has been adopted to make the consort of sounds familiar to us in the orchestra today were probably thousands of experiments that failed – the ophicleide, the arpeggione and the bass-serpent are at least remembered if not played – and yet all that effort that we interpret as failure was almost certainly necessary to Beethoven's inheritance and creativity because it is evidence of a passionate desire and will in society to make and to hear new music. When Beethoven, Umlauf the conductor, the orchestra, the soloists and choir came together in the Kärntnertor Theatre in Vienna on 7 May 1824 for the first performance of the Ninth Symphony, what were they giving to the world, especially in the cantata of the last movement? In the capital of an empire ruled by one of the most reactionary governments of the period, they were offering a work inspired not only by Schiller's words but also by the examples of music composed for mass celebrations in the early days of the French Revolution: they were also offering, with their combined skills and talents, a vision of the future when all the millions of the Earth would be enfolded in a single embrace. They were offering hope, the chief virtue by which civilization survives and makes its way into the future, and they were offering the living presence of the myth of the Golden Future – a myth of a time when all men and women would live in unity as conscious individuals.

Schiller calls Joy the spark of the gods and the daughter of Elysium. She lives in a holy place within our own souls which we approach when we are drunk with divine fire. Into that holy place she entices us that we may become more deeply aware, whether as makers or appreciators, of the power of the creative imagination and of what that imagination draws on, the interdependence of myth and memory.

2

Myth and the Great Memory

Mount Parnassus raises its snow-covered summit and flanks above the sacred chasm of Delphi where the ruins of the chief shrine of Apollo in the ancient world stand uncovered for the tourist to visit. Once the pythoness, the priestess of Apollo, sat on a bronze tripod in a cave and, inspired by the god, uttered prophecies in verse to the representatives of the cities of the Hellenic world. Now there remains only a small fraction of the buildings, the memorials, the temples and the treasuries, and the museum can show an even smaller proportion of the hundreds of statues and works of art that generations of patrons and artists lavished upon this site. So forgotten and unesteemed was the site after the oracle fell silent in the reign of Julian the Apostate that an entire village was built over the ruins and this had to be removed before what was left of classical Delphi could be seen again. What has also been revealed is the power of the site to move and inspire: every orchid, every tree, every sight of a rock nuthatch darting over a stone takes on a visionary quality or seems to be signalling a message. It is as though the god still smiles and stands beside your right elbow, tantalizing you with unremitting but barely interpretable prophecies.

Heraclitus in the sixth century said of Apollo: 'The Lord whose oracle is at Delphi neither speaks nor conceals but gives signs.'[1] The sign he indicated to me was to look on Mount Parnassus and Delphi as being like emblems of the relationship of myth to civilization. Civilizations rise and fall, are forgotten and remembered, but what was there at the beginning of each civilization and what remains to comfort and encourage survivors in intervening dark ages is myth – universal in all societies. Delphi gives us the ever-living presence of the past and the evidence of past creativity but it is to Parnassus and to the myths associated with the mountain that we have to look for the secrets of the source of creativity. The higher you climb, the more you become aware of the overpowering presence of Mount Parnassus.

The myth of Parnassus begins with the union of sky and earth. The sky god Zeus fell in love with the Titaness Mnemosyne or Memory. From their embraces were born the nine Muses of the arts and sciences. When the Muses began to offer their inspirations to men, no one could understand them. They wandered on the slopes of Parnassus uttering incoherent cries. It was only when Apollo arrived to claim the site of Delphi for his own (it takes its name from his swimming from Delos in the form of a dolphin) that he came across the Muses and taught them, giving order, meaning and measure to their songs and dances. Then they were able to communicate their inspirations to men and women. There came, later, an association with Dionysos, who, as the child of Zeus, the god of spontaneous energy and the inspirer of the theatre, was especially linked with the Muses of comedy and tragedy. It could also be said that the Muses collectively are Dionysos. The twin peaks of Parnassus were sacred to the guiding gods of the Muses, the lower peak, Nyssa, being dedicated to Dionysos and the higher peak, Cirrha, to Apollo. Thus the green of Dionysos is raised to the gold of the sun god Apollo. When Dante begins his *Paradiso* he calls on Cirrha, the peak of Apollo, to aid him in describing the transcendental realms; a big flame follows a little spark and perhaps, following his example, other, greater poets will arouse an echo with their better words from Cirrha.[2]

The myth can be understood on an individual level – how divine inspiration comes to the poet as the lightning flash of Zeus striking the earth of buried memory giving birth to the voice of the Muse or as the shout of Dionysos whose utterances are interpreted by the sun consciousness of Apollo. It can also be understood on the scale of a civilization: Zeus woos and makes love to the dark nymph Memory. The divine imagination impregnates the humus of the collective memory of a society and fathers the arts.

This legend is an example of how myth conveys wisdom and truth that would be cold and unmemorable if expressed in other forms. The function of all great myths is to lead us back to the oneness of God.[3] Thus the story of the Muses leads us back to the lightning flash of Zeus. Myths such as those told in the *Mahābhārata* are instinct with a mind-expanding power that transfigures the imaginations of readers and audiences so that they see the drama of creation as a spectacle of fascination and redemption. Everything that can be imagined as an aspect of the primal nature of God, whether benign or fierce, is revealed in the drama as leading ultimately to justice and to the recognition of love. The charm, the authority, the attractive force of myths are owed on the one hand to the sense of trust they inspire in what otherwise is inexplicable and on the other hand to the depth of human experience they convey: this last is so even when they are stories of gods and demigods because these deities are depicted as human incarnations of the deity, as in the cases of Krishna and Rama, or as immortals with all the temperaments, faculties and features of human beings, as in the case of the gods of Olympus.

The making of a body of myth at the beginning of a culture or society must be one of the most creative acts of which the human spirit is capable. I say this from inference of the effect of myth rather than direct evidence because, in fact, for most sets of myths, such as the Indian, the Chinese, the Japanese, the Mayan and Aztec, the Greek and the Nordic myths, though we may be able to set dates to the likely period of their origins, we know practically nothing about the men and women who possessed the universality of experience and the knowledge of what was required for the future of their peoples in order to create them. Such originators create what will be the foundations of the memory of the races and the civilizations in the future that they will influence, as in the following example.

The culture of the Australian Aborigines is thought to have remained unchanged for tens of thousands of years up to the colonization of Australia. In their societies they remained close to their founding myths. Imagination and tribal memory are one. Imagination and individual memory are also closely united and enable members of some tribes to perform extraordinary feats: the memory of the ancestral routes across the continent is preserved in song and members of a tribe can travel vast distances guided by the unfolding instructions of legend and topography combined, revealed to them as they chant the songlines.[4] It beggars our understanding just to think of the knowledge and imaginative power required to create a tradition such as the songlines – to hold a continent in one's mind, without maps, without writings, and to devise routes across it that could be transmitted through generations over thousands of years.

Their technology is also intimately related to their heritage of myth. Simple as their technology may seem when set against western machines, what tools they have are themselves treated as sacred objects and are used to an astonishing degree of dexterity and efficiency for the purposes of survival in a hard and hostile environment. The environment is, of course, hostile in a western sense: to a people that knows no other land, their environment is what it is and to them all its features are mythic, recognizable in terms of what shelter they provide or what dangers they forebode in relation to ancestral stories and the ever-present sense of the numinous. Each individual lives again the life of his ancestors as a drama or story: they are attuned to the Great Memory of their race.

Like those few Lapps who have kept to their Stone Age culture and like the remaining Bushmen, the Aborigines have the richest of interior lives with their systems of myths and stories that are integrated with their songs, poems and dances and with their food gathering and the rest of their communal lives. They have no gratuitous art and too much inventiveness would disturb their culture and the ecological balance of their environment. Their chief creative act is to survive and to enjoy what is given or earned in the spirit of the guiding myth and the ancestors.

One of the effects of myth on such societies is to keep them the same from generation to generation. It is a conserving force. In other societies such as ours, subject to frequent change, myth still plays an important but opposite part. It is an agent of that change: it becomes a radical and revolutionary force.[5] This is what happened when in twelfth-century Europe the Arthurian legends were released upon the imaginations of listeners and readers while at the same time a much wider currency was given to the 250 stories from classical myth told by Ovid in his *Metamorphoses* and to the legendary history of Alexander the Great. The Church no longer feared either the Celtic or the classical religions and could allow these stories to circulate: very often it was clerics who played a major part in transmitting them. The effect of them was to change emotional attitudes on a wide scale: the love element in the Arthurian stories aroused passionate interest and discussions, the stories from ancient Greece and Rome provided examples and images of the variety of the human soul which Christianity had never in its own terms managed to define or express, and the Alexander stories fed the desire for exploration and conquest so keen in the years of the first Crusades. The recurrence of myth in European and western society has since that time nearly always signalled and brought about change – as, for example, the rediscovery of Teutonic myth in the Romantic period has had enormous historical consequences.

The contrasting effects of myth I portray above are two aspects of the process I call the Great Memory. In comparatively static societies myth and the Great Memory are one and they are one also with the ideal or image of what their tribal members aspire to in their lives. In dynamic societies there is a continual process of forgetting aspects of the past as changes in fashion, ideas, technology and political and spiritual aspirations overwhelm them. The same process, however, in the course of time brings them back so that we live in a state of anamnesis, the act of unforgetting the past that frequently determines the future.

I approach the exposition of the Great Memory by describing a recurrent theme in the poetry that has helped to make European civilization. The theme is that of civil war – the very opposite of the theme of joy and universal brotherhood that resounds in Schiller's words and Beethoven's setting in the Ninth Symphony. It is a theme that goes back to our earliest literature because it appears first in Homer's *Iliad* in the wars between the Greeks and the Trojans who share a common culture and religion, in the quarrels between the Greeks themselves, and in the divisions among the gods of Olympus.

In the *Iliad* Homer – or the Homeric poets – went back to a remote and legendary past to create what became, in effect, the scriptures or holy writ of the Greek world and the prime authority on the gods of Olympus. Similarly the Athenian dramatists rarely took a contemporary or recent theme for their tragedies: they too went to the legendary past for subjects through which they could express their present conflicts, doubts and terrors.

In Virgil, we find even more clearly an example of how the poet can draw on the Great Memory. His early career was overshadowed by the last struggles of the civil wars that brought the Roman republic to an end. Augustus, having triumphed in those wars, now had the responsibility of giving law and order not just to Rome but to her possessions that covered the entire Mediterranean basin and far into central and northwest Europe. To find a common bond to unite the myriad peoples under his rule he went back to the past. With the help of antiquarians and scholars, he invented a new state religion, based on the Capitoline deities of Rome and on Etruscan ritual and practice, which was particularly important in drawing the imperial army, with its units drawn from all races and tribes, into cohesion, with its systems of oaths and devotion to the emperor. Into this endeavour he brought Virgil with his request that he should write an epic that would be the Latin equivalent of Homer. So Virgil turned to the very story Homer had told to create a new myth of the origins of Rome. It was a new myth, not in the sense that he invented the traditions of the Trojan origins of the founders of Rome, but that he took the family traditions of the Julian clan with its legendary descent from the goddess Venus and turned them into a universal myth in which all participators in Roman culture could share. He turned an inheritance through a bloodline into an inheritance through the spirit. More than that, he drew on what was probably the experience of his own initiation into one or more of the mystery religions to bestow on a far wider audience than could have come into direct contact with those privileged sects a view of the afterlife that is infinitely more hopeful than anything else in Latin literature of his period, apart from Cicero's *Dream of Scipio*. By going back to the past and by making Aeneas descend to the underworld, he was able, through the mouth of Anchises prophesying the future, to give a new definition to all that was best in the civilizing mission of Rome. To go to the dead is to go into the Great Memory.

Dante too went to the past and to the dead of all ages in *The Divine Comedy*. The guide who led him down through the circles of Hell and up to the summit of Mount Purgatory in the southern hemisphere was Virgil, the poet of a just empire. Writing in a period when much of Europe was riven by strife between popes and emperors, Dante appealed to the time of Augustus when Christ was born in an era of peace. If Virgil drew together many traditions, Roman, Greek, Etruscan, Celtic, Phoenician and probably Hebrew, to make his epic, Dante synthesized a much wider range of references: not only those inherited from the Latin poets, but the science and learning of Islam, probably including the story of the ascent of the prophet Mohammed to heaven on his steed Buraq, the corpus of the Judaeo-Christian writings, including the Church Fathers and the scholastic philosophers, the tradition of the troubadours and the Arthurian romances, Celtic legends of the afterworld and all the history and experience of an Italy and a Europe altered for ever by the Crusades. His mind was open to every influence and it was as though the Great Memory poured its gifts into him because of his openness. Out of all these influences he made a synthesis in his poem, among the effects of which have been these. He set a model the rest of Europe could follow in creating from the vernacular what Erich Auerbach called a language of the intellect;[6] that is, a language capable of expressing the range of emotions and thoughts necessary for a complete civilization. He invented a new way of presenting characters by making them create themselves out of their own words in the dramatic monologues or dialogues of *The Divine Comedy*; this invention has influenced nearly every form of literature and drama since his day. He began the process of the redemption of the learning and beliefs of the classical world, by, for example, placing certain of the heathen heroes in Paradise and by stating that the gods of the ancients were angels mistakenly adored by men. In this he announces and prepares for the Florentine Renaissance. By absorbing all the available information on the geography of Earth and on astronomy, he created the most complete visual image of Earth and the heavens according to the Ptolemaic system achieved by that date. By the centrality of the imagery of the Sun and of light in his poem, he prepared the imaginations of men for the Copernican world system as he did for the voyages of discovery in his description of the journey of Ulysses beyond the Pillars of Hercules. Above all, through his love of Beatrice, he gave new strength to the idea that the love between man and woman is a way to God. I say more of Beatrice and of other aspects of Dante's writings later. Here I am concerned to show the beneficent and creative effect of a mind capable of receiving the gifts of the Great Memory and synthesizing them into something new through poetry. Dante takes a primal myth, the myth of the hero who goes to find himself, one that goes back in time at least as far as the *Epic of Gilgamesh* and that he has inherited from Virgil and, through Virgil, from Homer, and in making his own version of it, he inalterably changes the imaginative possibilities of literature in the future.

One of the ways in which he does this is through the transformation of images. From his earliest work to his late elegies in Latin he gave descriptions of his creative processes. In cantos 15 and 17 of the *Purgatorio* he describes a series of intense mental pictures or waking dreams that come to him in the course of his journey and these are probably drawn from his own experience of how his inspirations often came to him. They resemble descriptions by Blake and Coleridge of similar experiences (see page 165). Those mental pictures come to him on either side of a meeting with Marco Lombardo who relates to him the journey of the simple soul after it issues from the hand of God. What that soul needs for its progression through life is two guides working together, the emperor and the pope. The balance is wanting and mankind, individually and collectively, goes astray. The traditional image for the relationship between pope and emperor was the Sun and the Moon, and as the Sun is more powerful than the Moon, so, in the eyes of the Church, the pope was more worthy of reverence than the emperor ($7,644\frac{1}{2}$ times more worthy according to one cardinal who calculated the relative luminosities of the Sun and the Moon[7]). Dante substituted the image of two Suns for the emperor and pope instead of the imagery of the Sun and the Moon, possibly influenced by a Byzantine source, but almost certainly he found the images arising in his creative imagination as an answer to his reflections on the condition of humanity torn apart by civil war.

Civil war – war between those naturally bound by blood, affection and common loyalties to live in amity – is the most terrible kind of conflict because it is strife within a family on an enlarged scale. As a subject or theme it runs through Virgil, Dante and Shakespeare. The arrival of Aeneas in Italy provokes the civil war that occupies the later books of the *Aeneid*. The conflict between the Guelph and Ghibelline factions which in the thirteenth century divided the city-states of Italy internally and against one another is the running bass to *The Divine Comedy*. Dante himself was exiled from Florence on account of the struggle between the White and Black factions of the city. Virgil left the *Aeneid* unfinished at the point at which Aeneas kills Turnus, his chief opponent among the leaders of Italy: we do not know what final resolution he might have given to his poem. In Dante the solution is clear: the coming of an emperor, guided by philosophers, who will work in harmony with the papacy freed of the temptation and troubles of earthly possessions and rule.

In Shakespeare the resolution is expressed through the image of marriage. As Dante exalted human love as a legitimate pathway to God, so Shakespeare gave a new idealization to marriage both in human terms and as a symbol of accord between the divine and the temporal.

Where the marriage is thwarted, as between Hamlet and Ophelia, or is corrupted, as in *Macbeth*, the forces of internal division or civil war triumph. Civil war and the consequences of the usurpation of legitimate authority run as themes throughout Shakespeare's work from *Henry VI* to *The Tempest*. The Wars of the Roses had ended only eighty years before his birth and the Tudor settlement of England and Wales was achieved against strong opposition and a series of unsuccessful rebellions, often aided during the reign of Elizabeth by the arch-enemy Spain. The political and religious apologists for the Tudor monarchy turned to myth in order to establish the ancient independence and sovereignty of the British Isles; they wrote of the Trojan origins of the first founders of Britain as described by Geoffrey of Monmouth and of Arthur and they appealed to the myth of the Golden Age when the nymph Astraea, or Justice, would return to Earth. Astraea is the virgin of Virgil's prophetic fourth eclogue and Dante had earlier made use of the same image, seeing her as the divine law from which descends the natural law which should inform and guide the laws of mankind.

This too, as mediated through the Tudor chroniclers and political theorists, was part of Shakespeare's inheritance of legend, myth and philosophy. What he inherited included much or all of what had been available to Dante but extended into wider fields. Either directly or through translation he had the culture of ancient Greece which had been denied to Dante: he had Plato in the interpretations of Marsilio Ficino and Baldassare Castiglione who had created a new philosophy for living from the Neo-Platonic tradition; he had Plutarch for fresh insights into the characters and history of antiquity; he had a fuller range of classical mythology for his images and references; he had the model of Seneca's five-act tragedies for his plays; he had the tradition of the *Romaunt of the Rose* grounded in a strong background of achievement in native English verse which had also absorbed all that could be learned from Dante, Petrarch and their followers; he had the new fusion of symbolism and cosmology introduced by the Renaissance magical philosophers; though born into a Protestant country he was the heir of the western Catholic tradition and of the Gothic north, of ancient rural traditions, of the hunt and the farm and of the long experience of the trades and professions of the towns and cities; and what to Dante had been a matter of fruitful and creative speculation but not of direct knowledge or confirmed experience – that is, the knowledge of what lay beyond the Pillars of Hercules – was to Shakespeare a matter of common and daily report since the route to the Indies eastwards had been discovered and his own countrymen were now founding settlements in the New World.

What did he do with these treasures from the Great Memory? I only touch on one aspect of his rich and magnanimous spirit when I say he created new syntheses of ancient myths. Hardly a single plot or legend or story of his plays are of his original creation: he took what the past offered and projected back on to the past both the spirit of his time and an understanding of the need for reconciliation that did not exist in those periods, thereby permanently altering our picture of the past, whether of ancient Rome or of late-medieval England. The theme of civil war which had already arisen in his earlier works written during the later years of Elizabeth I – such as the three parts of *Henry VI*, the two parts of *Henry IV*, the tragedy of *Richard II* and, as a memory of the strife of the Italian city-states, *Romeo and Juliet* – continued with a renewed sense of mission when James VI of Scotland on his accession to the throne of England in 1603 brought the kingdoms of England and Scotland under the rule of a single monarch. If we look at the range of historical periods from which Shakespeare drew his stories, it could seem as though he was with deliberate intent drawing on all the traditions and legends that had gone to make the geographical expression of Great Britain into the beginnings of a political unity. To take these periods in rough historical order – not in order of writing – they start with the pre-Roman Celtic *King Lear* and with the Homeric story of *Troilus and Cressida*; they continue with the first impact of Rome on Britain in *Cymbeline*, with the early Roman republic in *Coriolanus* and with the plays based on Plutarch's accounts of the end of that republic. From the Dark Ages he brings in the Viking-Celtic traditions of the time of *Macbeth* and the Norse-Scandinavian setting of *Hamlet*. From the Anglo-Norman period of the early Plantagenets he gives us *King John* and from the later Plantagenets he brings in the long-lasting connections with France through the Hundred Years' War, which forms part of the background to the civil strife of the Wars of the Roses which begin from the time of the wrongful disthronement and murder of *Richard II*. Even several of the comedies that are set in no particular period, such as *As You Like It*, have unjust usurpation as a necessary part of the plot or, as in the case of *Love's Labour's Lost*, the neglect by a ruler of his responsibilities that could lead to civil war. In the later plays Shakespeare provides various forms of resolution to each of the traditions on which he draws: for the Roman plays, Antony and Cleopatra die on the physical level but they are united eternally in the afterworld; for the Wars of the Roses a symbolic ending to the strife comes with the birth of the infant Elizabeth in *Henry VIII*; for the Celtic plays, *Cymbeline* ends with the saving of a marriage and the resolution of the conflict with Rome; for the plays with mythical or imaginary settings, *The Winter's Tale* and *The Tempest* end with sublime acts of forgiveness. Even in those works, such as *Hamlet*, *King Lear* and *Macbeth*, where the tragedy is absolute, each play ends with the re-establishment of government based on true right and law, by Fortinbras, Albany and Malcolm respectively.

In his ranging over the racial memories, histories and legends that the Great Memory was offering to him and his contemporaries, Shakespeare was fulfilling one of the functions of a great poet. That is to sum up and recapitulate within the concentrated language of poetry all the experience of the past that will be needed in the future, the lessons of how to endure suffering, how to battle against wrong, how to triumph wisely in victory and how to bring about harmony. Another function of the great poet which goes back to the mythic origins of his craft is to be a prophet. The strength of his prophecy lies more in the emotional and spiritual preparation which he gives to later generations than in the prediction of events – though one cannot help asking whether it is entirely fortuitous that twenty-six years after Shakespeare's death, following a creative lifetime spent in warning of the dangers and consequences of civil war, the English Civil War broke out. With his profound political sense he would have seen the causes of later discontent in the execution of the Earl of Essex and the imprisonment of Sir Walter Raleigh, but those events came after the first statement of the theme in his work. If his plays could not avert the Civil War, they certainly inspired some of the main and assistant actors to carry out their parts in the real drama. Charles I constantly read his Shakespeare on campaign: one can only hope he drew more comfort from it than he did from Virgil when, one day in the Bodleian Library in Oxford, in the company of Lord Falkland, he consulted the *sortes virgilianae*, the method of telling the future by opening the *Aeneid* at random and placing a finger on the page for the message that could be interpreted from it. His finger touched the passage on the death of Priam, ending with the line which Sir John Denham was later to translate: 'A headless Carcass, and a nameless thing.'[8]

As a result of the Civil War the theatre died in England for nearly two decades. After the Restoration of the monarchy in 1660 Shakespeare was revived for performance but it was only after the final resolution of the conflicts of the Civil War in the Glorious Revolution of 1688 that he came to be recognized as the greatest of English poets and dramatists – the necessary prelude to the later recognition throughout the world, both in translation and with the spread of English influence through conquest and colonization, of his universal genius.

I have taken three poets who, though of different periods, belong to a brotherhood of intent and spirit, with the purpose of showing how, through the alchemy of inspiration, the various traditions offered them by the Great Memory are transformed into fresh contributions to art and civilization. There are many other, later examples of poets who have achieved similar syntheses, such as J. W. von Goethe, A. S. Pushkin and W. B. Yeats. Goethe in *Faust Part II* married the Gothic north in Faust to the ancient classical south in Helen, who is brought back from the dead by an appeal to the Mothers, the beings who rule primal matter according to the *Kabbalah*. In the same play he shows the meaninglessness and horror of civil war in the battles of the Emperor. Pushkin brought together the culture of eighteenth-century France with the history and legends of ancient Russia, assuming the mantle of Shakespeare in writing the verse play *Boris Godunov*, a story of usurpation and civil war, modelling himself on Walter Scott in writing the novel *The Captain's Daughter* set around the Pugachev rebellion, about which he also wrote a history, and in his other works, such as *The Bronze Horseman*, struggling with the problem of authority. As for Yeats, in him the ancient themes continue: inspired first of all by the mythology of Ireland which had been published in his early youth by scholars and collectors of folklore, open to the discoveries of French Symbolism and to the new influences of eastern thought and religion first through the theosophical movement and later through his friendships with Rabindranath Tagore and Purohit Swami, he too had to undergo the experience of civil war, a war which, he feared, his own words had helped to bring about. In his old age he turned to the theme of Byzantium, creating a new myth of the empire of art and feeling, and to prophesying a Second Coming.

The profundity of Yeats's verse is owed to the fact that more than any other poet of the English-speaking world in the twentieth century he responded to a process that began before his birth and that has been accelerating since his death. It is the accumulation of knowledge about the past which is being recovered on a scale unknown in recorded history. Our minds today are like our museums: full of unassimilable impressions and pieces of knowledge that have to be kept in basements because we are incapable of assessing their worth or cataloguing them. What is on show in the accessible galleries of our minds is the choice of fashion rather than the pick of judgment. We take refuge in becoming specialists, in cultivating our little fields of study, trying to ignore what the Great Memory is pressing on us. What Virgil, Dante and Shakespeare all possessed was a conception of what man should and could be in his wholeness. Those conceptions of an ideal human being gave them the discrimination with which they could choose among the gifts of the Great Memory. If we now are offered the gifts of the Great Memory on an unprecedented scale, we need an ideal of what we should be, an ideal through which we gain an understanding of the creative process, and the discrimination to choose and assimilate from the past.

Among the gifts of the Great Memory since the mid-nineteenth century has been a recovery of the myths of peoples from all over the world. The collecting, collation and interpretation of these myths, often by scholars with a rationalist bent such as Sir James Frazer, have provided us potentially with the encapsulated history and experience of countless peoples, many of whom have now vanished from the Earth. The effect of the recovery and recording of myth on an international scale has been the opposite of what earlier rationalist scholars may have intended. As the resemblances and the shared archetypes came to be studied and recognized, so new significances were found in them and also the meaning attached to the word myth changed. (Its very pronunciation in English also changed: from mythe with the y pronounced as in why to myth with the y pronounced as in pith.) The meanings for 'myth' given in the Oxford Dictionary a century ago nearly all have a pejorative association of fiction. Myth was used as a term for a fabulous invention, often involving the supernatural as an explanation for natural occurrences, in contradistinction to legend which could be allowed some basis of truth in historical occurrences. With the weakening of the hold of traditional religions on thought, with the influence of Symbolist art and literature, and with the interest shown by various schools of analysis in myth, the meaning of the word has changed to a story of symbolic narrative that expresses truth on many levels. Myth is now closer in our understanding to parable as the expression of deep psychological truth and to heraldry as the symbolic representation of the destiny of a people or clan concentrated in an image.

One of the greatest opportunities given us by the explosion of information technology in our time and by the effect of that technology in awakening more and more images and ideas from the Great Memory has been the awareness of Earth as a whole which we now enjoy. Virgil's Mediterranean basin and his underworld, Dante's Earth hollowed with the rings of Hell and with its southern hemisphere of water, landless except for Mount Purgatory, and Shakespeare's

> all things rare
> That heaven's air in this huge rondure hems[9]

await an even grander expression in verse that will express for mankind the beauty of an Earth known for the first time from outside herself Already the science of ecology has turned to classical myth to name the self-regulating interdependence of living creatures and their environments in Earth's biosphere. She is once again called Gaia, the Earth mother, by the scientist James Lovelock at the suggestion of William Golding. Perhaps a further stage in our understanding of our own natures will come about when we develop an ecology of the spirit, a knowledge of the interdependence of human minds. In the study of that ecology of the spirit it will be found that myths and great ideas are like living beings that may seem to die but pass into the Great Memory which gives them new birth in the dreams of multitudes and the inspirations of individuals. We need a new art and a new poetry universal in its appeal that will transform the myths of the past into a new understanding of consciousness and the world we inhabit.

To return to a theme that was expressed above, our conception of the unity of the globe is now so different from even a few decades ago that we are beginning to see that all wars are civil wars within the family of humanity. If mankind needed poets in the past to lay bare the causes of war and to pronounce the words of healing, how much more do we need them now! Those who come to perform this service for us will win the necessary energy to change the future, paradoxically, by what they draw out of the past from the depths of the Great Memory. They must pray for the guidance of symbols just as Aeneas, knowing he had to descend to Hades, prayed to be led to the Golden Bough, the possession of which would give him safety in the underworld. Even as he prayed, two doves sent by his mother Venus appeared before him and led him towards an ilex tree. Shining out of the ilex was the Golden Bough which Aeneas plucked and carried back to the Sibyl who was to be his guide on the journey.[10] The poets of the coming age must also discover what is the Golden Bough for them, the green that has turned into gold to guard them in the strata of the past.

3

The Great Memory in art, religion and politics

There is something both strange and stirring to the imagination about a site once devoted to heroic achievements in sport and now abandoned, such as the stadia at Delphi and Olympia. Imagination fills them with spectators and the more than ghostly runners, wrestlers and discus throwers seem to be vibrantly present in the memory of the place. Such an atmosphere fills the ball court of the Mayan and Toltec rulers of Chichen Itzá, one of the greatest cities to have been uncovered from the jungle of Yucatán. The ball court, with its massive clean-cut walls, with the stone rings protruding as the goals of the game, and with temples placed on the walkway of one of the walls, has acoustics as fine as a Greek theatre, as though the spectators listened to the sounds made by the players as attentively as they watched them. Along the base of the walls runs a sequence of sculptures depicting the cosmic significance of the game, where the players, it is thought, were re-enacting the sports of the gods and the ball itself was the sun. One of the players is decapitated: his blood streaks out from his neck across the sky as serpents turning into vegetation (figure 5). All this was buried and forgotten for hundreds of years and has now been recovered: a time when sport was practised as part of religion has been remembered at a time when sport, for the majority, *is* religion.

The vegetation growing from the beheaded player has links with an image associated with the Spanish conquest of Yucatán. In the main square of the city of Mérida there stands the house of the family of conquistadors who first seized the surrounding region from the native Mayan princes and peoples. It is the Casa de Montéjo built in 1542. The main portal of the Casa de Montéjo is a superb Renaissance façade, covered with rich carvings which were probably the work of Mayan sculptors working under the direction of a Spanish friar from engravings of contemporary Spanish buildings. The most forceful carvings depict two huge Spanish soldiers: each carries an axe and wears a helmet that echoes in its curves the blades of the axes (figure 6). You have to look very carefully to see what they are standing on: their feet press upon the heads of Green Men whose mouths are open for the utterance of a continuous scream of pain (figure 7).

In these faces of the Green Man – here representing the natural man, the Indians who were to be chastised into Christianity – the Mayan craftsmen carved their reaction to the horrors enacted by the conquerors: the abandonment of their great and beautiful cities to the jungle, the silencing of their priests and poets, the burning of their sacred books and the extinction of their science and medicine. In absorbing the message these faces convey, we can see also that the brutality of the colonizers towards the Mayan Indians is related closely to the brutality of western attitudes to the natural world.

Soldiers, landowners and priests did all they could to repress the ancient culture of the Mayans and to cast it into oblivion – and yet what the rest of the world travels to Yucatán today to see is not the grim fortified churches of the Conquistadors nor the crumbling mansions of their descendants but the great Mayan cities such as Chichen Itzá and Uxmal with their stupendous architecture, their pyramids, temples and ball courts. It is as though there is a slow justice in the workings of history. The life and inspiration that went to make a civilization in the past are impressed upon the collective memory of humanity so that when the right moment comes they will be recalled, remembered and will play new parts in the history of the future – in other words, they will fulfil the process of the Great Memory. Just as in a literal sense the rockface falls away to reveal the cave of the Dead Sea scrolls or the plough turns up the shinbones of oxen inscribed with the earliest Chinese ideograms, so there are shifts in the landscape of the mind or unexpected discoveries that bring new and forgotten knowledge into the light of day.

There is another simple analogy to illustrate the Great Memory. Just as many individuals find themselves drawn back to the experiences of their childhood that determine the course of their creative lives and find in the memories of those experiences the renewal of their inspiration, so, on the wider scale of dynamic societies such as ours, the impulse to create something new is charged by a return to some forgotten aspect of the past.

The hypothesis of the Great Memory is this:

1) All great civilizations are founded upon ideal images of man and woman which provide the standards by which each civilization judges its achievements. Through such concepts of an ideal human being the civilization projects its imaginative grasp of the future.

2) In dynamic societies, most important social, political and cultural events are preceded or accompanied by the recovery of some forgotten, dormant idea, emotion or image from the past or by a wholly new interpretation of an idea, emotion or image.

3) The assimilation of the past with the imaginative grasp of the future is brought about by the creators, patrons and audience of a civilization and the completeness of the assimilation depends on the presence in that society of enough men and women who fulfil the ideals of that civilization – in other words, on the level of consciousness in that society. If that level is high – as in the case of Gothic civilization – there will take place a notable advance for humanity. If it is low, then great ideas and discoveries will rapidly be distorted and adapted for criminal and tyrannical ends – as in Nazi Germany.

The chief matter for the Great Memory in each civilization will lie in its founding myth or revelation which will also bring about a new interpretation or explanation of the purpose and nature of creation. What triggers the recovery of the past from the Great Memory includes war, conquest, political adjustments, natural disasters and the effect of the introduction of applications of science and new technologies and techniques. The techniques may include methods of thinking, of analysis and of study as well as craft or artistic or laboratory techniques. As an instance of how a scholarly technique can have an effect on wider attitudes to the past, we can point to the techniques of textual analysis first devised for the study of classical texts in the Renaissance. One of the first casualties of these techniques was the Donation, a document purporting to be the gift of the Western Empire by the Emperor Constantine to the papacy and on which the claims of the popes to temporal supremacy were based: Lorenzo Valla proved this to be a forgery. Those techniques applied later to Christian texts and the scripture of other religions have had, as we shall see in relation to India and the discovery of the common roots of the Indo-Aryan languages, profound political and spiritual consequences.

To illustrate the effect of the past on new cultural and religious movements I give seven short examples from the history of Judaeo-Christian civilization from the sixth to the seventeenth centuries. In each case I relate the movement to technical and scientific introductions.

Byzantium

In the reign of the Emperor Justinian (527–65) there was a rebirth of Neo-Platonism in the context of eastern Christianity with a special emphasis on aesthetics. Justinian desired to recreate the Temple of Solomon in Byzantium and he commissioned the architects Anthemius of Tralles and Isidorus of Miletus to build the great church of Hagia

Sofia, which they completed in 537. The style of Hagia Sofia influences all future Byzantine sacred buildings and much of the mosque architecture of Islam. The new style, arising from the twin influences from the past, Neo-Platonic aesthetics and the dream of Jerusalem, is made possible by technical advances such as the raising of the dome from pendentives.

The Matter of Britain and the Matter of France

The Matter of Britain is the cycle of Arthurian legends recovered from largely Celtic and older Latin sources in the twelfth century and retold in French, German, Old English and other languages. They are stories dating back not only to the historical Arthur of the fifth century but to Celtic and perhaps pre-Celtic myths over the preceding two thousand years. From being the private heritage of beleaguered Welsh, Cornish and Breton clans they become the rage of Europe, especially when, combined with the legends of Glastonbury and the Grail, they provide ideals of Christian knighthood. One of the reasons for their popularity is that they include marvellous and intriguing love stories that people relate to their own experience; another is that in their retelling the heroes of the past acquire all the military technology of the present. As with the earlier Matter of France, which includes the legends of Charlemagne and his paladins, the Arthurian legends become the myth of chivalry, the social and military caste whose power depends on the horse and the combination of stirrup, new kinds of harness, efficient body armour, and the couched lance that made the mounted knight a redoubtable foe and a dominant master.

Gothic civilization

Gothic civilization is created at three places close to Paris between 1120 and 1150: St-Denis, Sens and Chartres. It arises from a synthesis of many influences from the past – the rediscovered writings of Dionysius the Areopagite with its symbolism of light, the recurrence of images from the pagan past such as the Green Man, the rebirth of the Eternal Feminine whereby the Virgin Mary assumes the roles of the Neolithic Great Mother Goddess and of the goddesses of antiquity, the desire to recreate Solomon's Temple, a turning back to classical influences in architecture, and a revived interest, especially at Chartres, in Neo-Platonism and the cosmologies and mystical mathematics associated with that school. All these were brought together to make the greatest aesthetic revolution since Roman times. The synthesis was made possible by new applications in building of the principle of the opposition of forces, as seen in the pointed arch, ribbed vaulting and the flying buttress, as well as other technical innovations. These techniques were employed in constructing the great cathedrals which are themselves expressions of an ideal of the universal human being (see Chapter 4).

The scholastic movement and the development of vernacular literatures

The rediscovery of Aristotle and of Dionysius the Areopagite helped to fire the new confidence in the powers of the human mind which characterizes scholasticism. Scholasticism had its own ideal man – a man who had transformed his powers of thought so that his thought concorded with the thought of Christ and the angels. The terms evolved in the discussions of the scholastics were in a Latin which they tried to make free of associations (in other words, an objective and scientific language). These terms were, when translated, to have a profound influence on turning the great vernacular languages of Europe into languages of the intellect. I can write these quite difficult ideas down in the English language and you, the reader, can grasp them because writers such as Chaucer in his translation of Boethius and the unknown author of the *Cloud of Unknowing* (who also translated Dionysius the Areopagite) had to go to the immense effort of finding English equivalents for abstract ideas first expressed in Greek and Latin. Meister Eckhart performed the same function for German through his sermons and his influence on the Rhineland mystics. Dante and his contemporaries such as Guido Cavalcanti and the astronomer Ristoro d'Arezzo did the same for Italian. The requirements of expressing and commenting on the freshly recovered texts and ideas led to new techniques for laying out and designing the pages of books on grid patterns that could accommodate texts and their commentaries on the same page. The craft of graphic design which has been used on this book is an invention of this period. These techniques reflect the new techniques in logical thinking and philosophical discussion and the need for philosophers to define precisely the stages of their thinking.

The Renaissance

The Renaissance depended on the recovery of neglected or lost Hebrew, Greek and Latin texts and traditions, notably the *Kabbalah*, the works of Plato and those attributed to Hermes Trismegistus, as well as on the new study of Vitruvius and classical buildings and sculpture. The technical advances of the time are innumerable, from improvements in shipping design to the invention of printing and the widespread development of engraving techniques. The ideals of humanity which brought Renaissance civilization to so high a peak are discussed in the following chapter.

The Reformation

The Reformation was an appeal to the pristine values of early Christianity against the corruption of the late-medieval Church. Its leaders drew on the scholarship of the Renaissance and the access to original texts made possible by the revived study of Greek and Hebrew in addition to Latin. Its influence depended on the invention of printing and its survival against ferocious reaction depended on gunpowder.

The seventeenth-century origins of science

The founding of the Royal Society was preceded by a vision of the recovery of the Golden Age such as that expressed by Francis Bacon (see pages 89–90) and shared by many of its first members and their contemporaries. Milton's reinterpretation of the Judaeo-Christian creation myth in *Paradise Lost* is mirrored in the urge among members of the Royal Society to find out the origins and the causes of things. Their inspiration was as much religious – and often heterodox – as what we would call scientific. Sir Isaac Newton spent far more time and effort on exploring alchemy, astrology, and number symbolism in the Bible and on the proportions of Solomon's Temple than he did on the *Principia* and the *Opticks*. And what was he looking for? An explanation of the principle of life to counteract and balance the principle of gravity enunciated in the *Principia*. The ideals of humanity current in this period are discussed in Chapters 5 and 6.

What I have been describing in these examples is both a process and a pattern of recurrent rememberings. They are not only recurrences of ideas and themes but of passionate emotions and energies. The pattern and the emotional charge can both be seen in the history of religion. As most religions depend for their authority on a past revelation, so anyone wishing to introduce changes makes his or her appeal to that revelation and to the original purity of practice and doctrine at the time of the founding of the religion or of one of its later cults or sects. Thus the Cistercian movement at the turn of the eleventh century began as a return to the original simplicity of the Rule of St Benedict and as a reaction against the luxury and artistic splendour of the Cluniac order. The many sects that preceded St Francis a century later made their appeal to primitive Christianity and the poverty of the apostles. I have already mentioned the Reformation as a rediscovery of the past and since that time there have been many examples showing the same pattern. Queen Elizabeth's first archbishop of Canterbury, Matthew Parker, justified the independence of the Church of England from Rome by reference to what he saw as the independence of the Church in Anglo-Saxon times. The effects of scholarly investigation may be much wider than the intentions of the original investigators. Who would have thought that the Liturgical Movement which began as an investigation into early liturgies would lead to the end of the Tridentine Mass and the introduction of vernacular services in the Roman Catholic Church? Or that the discovery of the gnostic texts of Nag-Hammadi with their evidence of the centrality of the feminine principle among some early Christian sects would help to fuel the arguments of the movement for the ordination of women?

The power of the influence of the past is also to be seen in political and social movements. I give in what follows examples of the Great Memory at work on significant events in European and world history from the sixteenth century onwards.

In writing about Shakespeare and the theme of civil war in the last chapter, I mentioned the influence of Tudor historians, chroniclers and political apologists on his work. Contemporaries of Shakespeare were also recreating the history of the British Isles in their works, such as the *Polyolbion* of Michael Drayton and the passages in *The Faerie Queene* where Spenser, through the mouth of Merlin speaking to Britomart, retells some of the mythical history of Britain as preserved by Geoffrey of Monmouth and others.[1] The impulse to write on these themes arose from the need to assert the ancient freedoms of first England and then the British Isles from foreign domination. Once the threat of Spanish invasion receded, tensions that had been held in check in a time of national emergency came into the open. It was then that the past became a source of argument to fuel current debates and dissensions. Thus there arose a debate on the Normans and the Saxons. The period Archbishop Parker had turned to in order to justify religious freedom, now fed the desire for political freedom. The Norman Conquest of 1066 could be seen as a crushing of the ancient liberties of the native Anglo-Saxon population. The barons who had followed William the Conqueror had stolen the land and usurped the privileges of a free people and those rights should be restored to their descendants. The extent to which this theme penetrated popular awareness can be seen from the reports of the

Leveller debates held in Putney in 1647 when Cromwell and Fairfax were faced with what was an insurrection in their own army. As John Wildman said in the second debate: 'we have been under slavery, that's acknowledged by all. Our very laws were made by our conquerors . . .'[2]

Equally important in this period was the return of Magna Carta. Written probably by Archbishop Stephen Langton, Magna Carta was the agreement the Barons of England forced King John to sign in 1215. It established among its clauses the rights of freemen to justice against the arbitrary rule of King John – meaning in effect the rights of the barons, their families, dependants and higher vassals. Its importance was regarded as substantial for some time after its signing because it was reissued several times throughout the thirteenth century and into the fourteenth. Then it was largely forgotten. Shakespeare made no use of it in his play *King John*; it was mentioned in none of his sources. In the year of Shakespeare's death, 1616, a learned judge, Sir Edward Coke, who had crossed swords with James I over the royal prerogative, was dismissed from his seat on the bench. He and other antiquarian lawyers brought Magna Carta back into public discussion as evidence that royal rule in the past had depended on a contract between monarch and people and not on the doctrine of divine right that James had promulgated in his own writings.[3] In the new life that was given to Magna Carta by its reinterpretation, the clauses concerning the rights of free men were interpreted as applying to all Englishmen, not just to the ruling class.

With this interpretation, from being no more than one of thousands of other legal transactions on dried-up parchment with no current significance, Magna Carta was to become a symbol of essential freedoms. What now applied to all Englishmen could be called on by those overseas of English descent, as did the leaders of the American Revolution, and then was extended to all those nations that were to adopt English constitutional practices. The revival of Magna Carta and its subsequent history can be thought to be a distortion of its original intention: but the principles underlying what it meant when first forced upon King John and what it meant in the period leading to the Civil War and later are the same. It was written by a wise and great man, a scholar, poet and statesman, who would have studied and understood the principles of natural justice, and it is his wisdom that resonates across time in its provisions.

The desire for natural justice underlies my next example of the past being brought to the aid of the present. This is the Celtic revival with its subsequent effect on the development of Irish nationalism.

Here it was the work of scholars and editors of the ancient Irish texts, the collectors of folklore, the writers and poets rediscovering one of the richest yet most neglected sources of myth in Europe, who restored a noble past to their fellow countrymen and gave them the images and the ideals to find again their sense of national identity, crushed for long years by the influence and power of England. The fruits of such a gift from the Great Memory may be beneficent – as I remarked in writing of Yeats in the last chapter – but they may also be cruel and sinister in their effect. One of the repeated themes in Irish legends is of the self-sacrifice and death of the hero. In the Dublin Post Office, the centre of the 1916 uprising, the memorial to those who took part in the attempt is not a Celtic cross: it is a grisly and realistic bronze statue of the death of Cuchulainn. It is a startling revelation of the archetypal power of the spirit of self-sacrifice underlying Irish nationalism – the same spirit that has driven the hunger strikers and the bombers of the IRA. ·

The history of nationalism in recent centuries is, in fact, a story of the remembering or recovery of heroic pasts and legendary freedoms – whether it is the recentring of their national culture on the *Kalevala* by the Finns, or the naming of their state after a mysterious archaeological site by the Zimbabweans.

The recovery of national identity does not come about only by publishing forgotten chronicles or epics: in all the European countries that achieved independence either just before or after the First World War there were movements to record folk music and to link music to the sense of national identity. In certain cases composers were as much the creators of these new nations as their statesmen and politicians; the examples of Edvard Grieg for Norway, Anton Dvořák for the future Czechoslovakia and Jean Sibelius for Finland demonstrate this point because the wider world, though not knowing their languages or literature, could understand and feel the individual essence of ancient peoples and their history from the music and therefore came to acknowledge their right to independence. Some of these composers, Sibelius especially, passed far beyond the influence of folk music, to make their works a new sound world that, even more powerfully voicing the knowledge of the Great Memory, resurrects vanished springs, lost forests and heroic deeds and journeys.

Sometimes what is remembered points to contemporary unresolved problems: in Mexico the dilemma is how to reconcile the repressed pre-Columbian past with the imported Hispano-Christian language and culture. The scars that this struggle has left on the national awareness are summed up in an image taken from a fresco by Diego Rivera which appears on one of the current Mexican banknotes. The image shows one of Cortez's men-at-arms on horseback, locked in struggle with one of Montezuma's Eagle Knights. They are joined in a chiasmus of death: the Christian steel-tipped lance transfixes the Aztec warrior: the Aztec obsidian spear slices through the Christian soldier. Rivera's painting dates from the period following the Mexican Revolution when the reaction against the Hispanic heritage and against the Christian priesthood was at its most violent and cruel.

Since then, as with the uncovering of the Mayan cities, the balance of cultural appreciation has shifted so that the remarkable Anthropological Museum in Mexico City with its collections of the art and sculpture of all epochs of pre-Columbian society is now as much a national shrine as the pilgrimage church of the Virgin of Guadalupe. Equally the conventional image of the Aztecs as a blood-drenched and blood-hungry society has been altered by the translation and circulation of the marvellous literature in the Nahua language. What we find in that Nahua literature and mythology is a surpassing tenderness and feeling for the beauty of the world and its transience – and in the legends of Quetzalcoatl and his life of sacrifice we find something of the ideals that guided the societies of pre-Columbian Central America.

The relaxation of the tyrannies behind the Iron Curtain has revealed many more examples of races and peoples who have guarded in secret the traditions of their ancestors and depend upon them for the strengthening of their sense of national identity. The present struggles in what was Yugoslavia are a return to the religious enmities between Catholics and Orthodox Christians and between the Christians and Muslims, living again ancestral warfare and each turning to their history and their traditional religion for justification.

Political necessity sometimes dictates strange revivals. The late Shah of Iran needed a past for his parvenu dynasty and he also needed a past that would help rather than interfere with his plans for the modernization of his country. The Islamic traditions were too conservative for his plans and therefore he centred his appeal to the past on the pre-Islamic Great Kings of Persia, chiefly Cyrus the Great – a period unrecorded in the Islamic traditions of his own country and known only from Greek historians and the discoveries of archaeologists at Persepolis and other sites.[4] His regime was overturned by one that makes its appeal to another past – the Shiite tradition of Ali, the cousin and son-in-law of the Prophet whose murder in AD 661 led to the division of Islam into its two main sects of Shiites and Sunnites.

An example similar to the Shah's attempt to use a forgotten period in his country's history is provided by Israel in what has been called the Masada complex. The story of the defence of Masada in AD 73, the last outpost of the Jews to resist the Romans after the destruction of Jerusalem until the besieged committed suicide rather than surrender, played no part in

Jewish history and traditions. It was recorded only in Greek by the historian Josephus, who was regarded as a renegade. It was brought into the general awareness of Jews through a poem by Yitzhak Lamdan published in 1927. This poem included the line: 'Masada shall not fall again.' With Yigael Yadin's excavations at Masada after the founding of the state of Israel, the Masada story grew into a legend of immense power, focusing the needs of Israelis to feel that they must never again be dispersed. It has produced a national complex comparable to the part played by the Great Trek in the mythology of the Boers.[5]

These examples I have given are of *unpredictable* gifts of the Great Memory and they are often like the rediscovery of a lost childhood in the origins of a people or culture. But what happens when a people reject the childhood they have been given or rise up and throw out their parents – as happened in the American and French Revolutions? In these great events too we can see the processes of the Great Memory at work: what is remembered is reinterpreted and used in a different way. Take, for example, the idea of republicanism: there were several examples of republics in Europe in the mid-eighteenth century, such as Venice and Geneva, but they were as conservative in their outlook and political structures as the monarchies they bordered. No one to any extent would have thought of them as providing the models for alternative constitutions or forms of government for, say, the government of France. Yet in a few years, a citizen of Geneva, Jean-Jacques Rousseau, fired by his reading of Plutarch and Livy on the republic of Rome and of Machiavelli on the Florentine city-state, had introduced through his writings, especially *Du contrat social*, a conception of republicanism that was radical and revolutionary and that involved the mass of the citizenry in the processes of decision-making.

Both the American and French Revolutions were preceded by a revolution in the arts and architecture – the Neo-Classical style. This style is most obviously a reaction against the exuberance of the Baroque and Rococo periods. It is also a reflection of the contemporary movements in philosophy and political thought – the appeal to reason and the belief that human society can be organized on the basis of reason that was common to the *philosophes* in France, the thinkers of the *Aufklärung* in Germany and the rationalists of Edinburgh and Glasgow in Scotland. Like most such movements it was also a return to the greater purity of antique models: travellers, writers and architects, often quite unconnected with one another, such as the German Johann Joachim Winckelmann and the Scot James Stewart – known as Athenian Stewart because of his enthusiasm for Greece – helped to set the guidelines for the style which provided the stage settings and the imagery for the autocracy of Catherine the Great in St Petersburg, the vicissitudes of the Prussian Hohenzollerns in Berlin, the expansion of the commercial and professional classes in London, Edinburgh and Dublin and the two events with which I am concerned here, the American and French revolutions and their sequel, the empire of Napoleon I.

The leaders of both these revolutions were all largely trained in the classical studies which had formed the ground of education since the Renaissance. When the signers of the Declaration of Independence broke the bonds of loyalty to their king and and their mother country, they not only appealed to the libertarian tradition in England, notably Magna Carta and the Bill of Rights, but they turned to the past that Rousseau had indicated to them, for a different form of government, republican Rome and the city-states of classical Greece. It was even proposed in one of the debates in Philadelphia that they should abandon English because it was the language of the oppressor and adopt ancient Greek. They adopted as far as they could the names of Roman institutions and buildings such as the Senate and the Capitol and in the heraldry and coinage of their new state they combined the images of Roman power, such as the eagle, with imagery from classical and Egyptian sources familiar to them from Masonry, also a powerful movement in reviving forgotten symbolism, imagery that is still to be seen in the pyramid with the blazing eye that separates its summit from its base on the US one-dollar bill.

The American Revolution was one of the chief inspirations of the events that led to the French Revolution. One difference was that the French were not throwing off the yoke of rulers three thousand miles away. Paris was rebelling against Versailles a mere twelve miles distant. What Paris rejected in the Bourbons was a complex of religious and social assumptions, the tradition of St Louis, the identification of Christianity with the monarch, the ranks of an aristocracy that had sacrificed power in order to retain its privileges, and the titles and regulations of feudalism. The artists and architects had already prepared the imaginations of the revolutionaries with the past to which they would turn for inspirations. Among the most impressive works shown in the salons of the 1780s were paintings by Jacques-Louis David depicting examples of Roman courage and savagery from the early history of Rome. There, too, the works of Jean-Baptiste Greuze, in a milder form, extolled the Roman simplicity of family life. Hubert Robert brought a new grandeur and menace to the painting of Roman architecture and ruins, while popular writings on Roman and Greek history provided the models and inspiration for the cultivation of republican virtue.

There is one influence in particular that seems to run throughout the education and reading of many of those who were to play leading roles in the French Revolution. It was the *Lives* of Plutarch, which I have already mentioned in connection with Rousseau. A priest of Delphi in the first century AD, Plutarch wrote a series of lives of heroes, statesmen, generals and other prominent figures, setting Greek notables in parallel with Roman notables. Since the sixteenth century, when his works had been translated into the main vernacular languages, Plutarch had been a fruitful source of themes for plays, such as Shakespeare's *Julius Caesar* and *Antony and Cleopatra*. With the decay of the influence of the Church by the end of the eighteenth century, Plutarch's *Lives* became for many an alternative Old Testament. More than a source of instruction or of literary and artistic themes, his works were an incitement to action and the inspiration of political virtue. The interpretations depended on the natures and motives of the revolutionary leaders. Robespierre, Saint-Just and David, for example, found in stories such as that of the Elder Brutus executing his sons for conspiracy against the republic a justification for their belief that the revolution would only be made complete by a rejection of all personal feelings and that the soil should be drenched in the blood of the impure. To Madame Roland and Camille Desmoulins it was the example of people who remained true to their ideals in the vicissitudes of life that drew them to Plutarch. To the young artillery officer Napoleon Bonaparte the *Lives* were his instruction in the leadership which he knew was to be his destiny.

Plutarch provides an example of an influence on the leaders of a great historical movement. What is more astonishing is the extent to which imagery and nomenclature from the classical past permeated so rapidly the awareness of ordinary people. When the revolutionaries decided to change all weights and measurements, they turned to Greek and Latin for their metres, their grammes, their Fructidors and Thermidors, and these fast became everyday usage. One of the strangest influences comes from the beginnings of archaeology: when the first excavations were made at Pompeii and Herculaneum, great interest was aroused in the evidence of the Roman mystery religions, including that of the Great Goddess Cybele, whose priests would castrate themselves in her honour, suffering the same fate as her lover Attis. Attis was shown wearing the Phrygian cap. This cap of liberty became part of the insignia of the revolution: it was worn by the sans-culottes, it appeared on all printed documents of the revolution and in Strasbourg a huge bronze model of the Phrygian cap was placed on top of the cathedral spire, then the highest building in Europe, to signify the defeat of the *ancien régime*.

When Napoleon created his empire, he was not only dependent on the imagery of the emperors of Rome, but he had to turn to another past to counteract the ancient authority of the Bourbons. The Bourbon right to rule went back to Hugh Capet, who was the first of the line to become king of France in 987. Napoleon went back to the older dynasty of Charlemagne, the first Holy Roman Emperor. His brothers and marshals were made subordinate kings and princes as Charlemagne had chosen his paladins to secure his rule. Napoleon dispossessed the pope of his territories on the grounds that the pope was in league with heretics and he, as the heir of Charlemagne, had the right to keep the Church in check. Though, unlike his brothers, he did not have fake genealogies drawn up showing the descent of the Bonapartes from Charlemagne, he was particularly alive to the importance of emotive symbols. 'It is with baubles that mankind is governed,' he once said. To replace the lilies of the Bourbons he turned to another discovery of archaeology. The tomb of a Merovingian prince had been discovered just before the revolution; it was thought to be that of Clovis, the first Christian king of France. In the tomb was the remains of a cloak that was studded with golden bees. Napoleon took the golden bees as part of the insignia of his dynasty: it signified at once the industry he hoped to foster once his wars were over, the swarming millions of Europe over which he and his family would reign, and the gold of the civilization that would issue from his rule. His coronation robes in which he stood in Notre Dame as the aged pope shuffled towards him bearing the crown which he seized and placed on his head, were studded with these golden bees – as are still the hangings round his throne in the palace of Fontainebleau. To the revival of Carolingian and Merovingian sources we can add a third influence from the same period: when the young Ingres was commissioned to paint Napoleon in his coronation robes, he portrayed him in the attitude of Byzantine emperors as shown in ivory carvings.

There are fascinating currents and countercurrents in these influences from the past. The French Revolution seems to abolish or reject the Middle Ages: all traces of feudalism in rank, privilege or the survivals of serfdom are erased; the Church with its medieval institutions of monasticism is made nonexistent; great numbers of the finest buildings of the Middle Ages, the cathedrals and great churches are destroyed or severely damaged; the goddess of Reason is enthroned in Notre Dame. A few years later we find Napoleon turning to the very period in which feudalism had its remote beginnings for the legitimation and the symbols of his rule.

There was another strong influence from the past on Napoleon's early reading in addition to Plutarch and that was *Ossian*, the much disputed account of Celtic heroes, said by its author James Macpherson to be a translation of a lost Gaelic epic. Turgid, repetitive and gloomy though *Ossian* may seem to us now, to the generation of Napoleon it was the authentic voice of a heroic age, all the more refreshing in that it came from a source different from the accustomed writers of Greece and Rome. Napoleon thought of it as the greatest work he had ever read and it probably provided him with the closest he ever came to a personal religion. At Malmaison there is a painting commissioned as a gift to him during the Consulate from the artist Ann-Louis Girodet in 1800 depicting the apotheosis of French heroes who had died for their country in the recent wars being welcomed into an afterlife peopled by Ossian, Fingal and other heroes of Celtic legend. The dead French generals, realistically though ideally portrayed in the uniforms of the Revolutionary Army, walk into a mist of white souls greeting them with songs to the accompaniment of a blind harper. An eerie, not to say sinister work, it has a curious characteristic in that, so strong is the Neo-Classical influence on the artist, the Celts are portrayed as though they were ancient Greeks, rather than woad-painted, bearded barbarians.

The popularity of Ossian is matched in this period by the revival of the Nordic myths in Denmark, again portrayed in Neo-Classical guise. This search for pasts other than the classical is characteristic of the period and of the rediscovery of the Middle Ages which is contemporaneous with the rise of Neo-Classicism.

The rediscovery of the Middle Ages is as important in political, social and cultural terms as the influence of classical history on the French Revolution. It was to feed the right-wing reaction against the French Revolution and Napoleon. There is a painting by Heinrich Olivier (1815) at Dessau of the three monarchs who formed the Holy Alliance; Alexander I of Russia, Francis of Austria and Frederick-William III of Prussia, all portrayed as medieval knights swearing to support Christianity and to crush radical and revolutionary movements wherever they might be found. The return to the Middle Ages was also curiously enough to be an inspiration to the beginnings of socialism. English socialism grew in part – through John Ruskin, William Morris and others – from a desire to return to the craftsmanship and respect for the labourer of the Middle Ages The writings of Victor Hugo, Jules Michelet and, later, Charles Péguy were to have a similar effect on French socialism. In certain ways it offers more striking evidence of the Great Memory because of the way it rose up in different parts of Europe, seemingly in a spontaneous manner.

What are the impulses that drive an Italian priest to publish the forgotten medieval chronicles of his country, an English bishop to edit ballads and poems from the Middle Ages, a Swiss critic to translate the *Nibelungenlied* into modern German, a Russian scholar to discover the *Slovo o Polku Igoreve* (the epic on which Borodin's opera *Prince Igor* was later based), a Danish poet to write poems and plays based on forgotten Nordic legends – all quite independently of one another?[6] And what drives such writers as Goethe, Walter Scott, William Blake and Chateaubriand to discover medieval art, history and literature for themselves in their boyhood and young manhood? They are examples of synchronicity – the phenomenon well known in science when investigators make the same discoveries within weeks of one another. And how do we account for the movement for the collection of folk tales and folk song, the compilation of dictionaries of popular and ancient speech, and the publication of ancient folk ballads and epics, and contemporary imitations such as Scott's *Minstrelsy of the Scottish Border* (1803), Achim von Arnim and Clemens Brentano's *Des Knaben Wunderhorn* (1806), the Brothers Grimm and their *Fairy Tales* (1812), Thomas Moore's *Irish Melodies* (1807–34), Joseph Dubrovsky's *History of the Bohemian Language* (1818), and Vuk Karajic's *Serb Dictionary* (1818) and *Serbian Folksong* (1823–33)?[7]

One common cause, whether entertained consciously or not, was an incipient ideal of humanity, the ideal peasant, uncorrupted by industrial society, who was the European counterpart of the noble savage. To Johann Gottfried von Herder, the friend of Goethe and one of his most important influences, folk poetry (in which he included Homer and Shakespeare) was the only true poetry and behind his thought was a conception of poets capable of ecstatic inspiration far beyond mere rational speculation. Out of these incipient ideals came the lyrics of Goethe with a directness of speech and emotional truth that made them the voice not only of Goethe but of anyone who spoke them. The lyric impulse inspiring hundreds of other poets was taken up by the series of composers from Mozart to Richard Strauss who created the style of lieder singing, a special sound world that is a transformation of the folk and peasant life of the past uttered through the personae of men and women who are themselves ideals because of the honesty and sense of truth with which they confess or relate the sufferings and the joys of existence.

Another common cause was to rediscover the ideals of humanity underlying medieval art, literature and thought. The influence of the rediscovery of the Middle Ages is to be seen in nearly every field of art, literature, philosophy, religion and politics. It supported a great revival in the fortunes of the Catholic Church just as it encouraged the revival of Catholic traditions in other churches such as the effect of the Oxford Movement on the Church of England. Churches, cathedrals and universities across North America bear witness to the effect of the revival of Gothic and Romanesque architecture, as do most of the cities of western Europe. The completion of Cologne Cathedral, left unfinished in the Middle Ages, was one of the most significant acts of German nationalism leading to the unification of Germany under the Hohenzollern emperors in 1871. The compilation of the hundreds of volumes of the *Monumenta Germanica Historica*, the grandest scholarly series ever printed, was also inspired by nationalist motives in order to enable Germans to rediscover their ancient past.

At the same time that German students dreamed of the revival of medieval institutions and of a German empire and that English undergraduates were exploring the medieval origins of the western Catholic traditions, something similar was happening in the still largely enclosed world of Japan. There young men, disgusted by the weakness of the shogunate in its decline and by the indignities of the treaties forced on their country by foreign nations, were inspired by their rediscovery of indigenous Japanese traditions such as the myths of the sun goddess and by their hopes for a Japan that would be ruled in truth by the emperor of divine origins and not by regents, to turn for their ideals to a semi-mythical past, an ancient time before Buddhism or any other foreign creed had corrupted the purity of the 'Shinto' heritage. It is a curious fact that the movement that led to the modernization of Japan and the subsequent dominant position of that country in the world began as a wholly reactionary movement to restore the direct role of the emperor and to expel the foreigners. The oligarchs who brought about the Meiji Restoration in 1868 were quick to realize that if they were to expel the foreigners, they had to learn from them first, about their political institutions, their science and their technology – and so they turned to the recently re-created German Empire for models of its government and parliamentary bodies and its universities. To maintain their own vision of their antique imperial institutions they had to go to an empire that not only had modernization forced upon it by the nostalgia for its medieval past, but actually owed its restoration to that nostalgia.[8]

The revival of Shinto studies began in the late eighteenth century, long before the Meiji Restoration and contemporaneously with another movement to which we come again in Chapter 6. This was the mutual discovery by English judges and administrators and Bengali pundits of the wealth of Vedic and later Sanskrit thought and literature. Educated as classicists and aware of the significance of the Renaissance in the making and preservation of their own cultural traditions, the English, in studying Indian tradition and thought, expected to bring about a comparable renaissance in India. It is an interesting example of how an awareness of a historical pattern can influence and, indeed, make history.

The rediscovery of the Middle Ages still proceeds, and perhaps the most significant discoveries still to be made are those that relate to the questions of how it was that Europe and its later settlements in North

America came to develop scientific knowledge and its applications and to use these to master and control the environment to an extent unknown in any other culture, and to what purposes that knowledge should be most fruitfully put. I have touched on the importance of the change in attitude to nature brought about by the Christian missionaries of the Dark Ages. The purposes to which we direct our knowledge depends, however, on how we see our ultimate purpose as human beings – in other words, on our images of ourselves as human beings and the ideals by which we live and to which we aspire. It is the strength of these ideals that permits us either to control the immense energies of the past or to be swept along by them.

The exploration of the Middle Ages requires our modern imaginations, fed with awareness of many cultures, to try to enter into the imaginations of peoples a thousand years or so ago. We have to understand what confined or limited imagination in societies of the past as well as what expanded it or made it grow. We can see this in relation to the great cultures of Meso-America. These differed from those of early medieval Europe not so much in their technology – they possessed the wheel even if they only used it in toys, they knew how to work metals even if they restricted its use to wonderful jewellery – but in the fact that they did not have to take into account the existence of peoples wholly different in cultures and aspirations from their own.[9] Despite their many languages and despite the ferocious wars they conducted with one another, there was a remarkable cultural homogeneity throughout their societies. The Old World of Europe, Asia and North Africa was characterized by a constant clash and synthesis of civilizations. Even if they imagined their neighbour as a damned infidel, crusaders and Muslims *had* to imagine each other. The New World experienced no interchange comparable to the invasions of the Celts, the expansion of Greek thought, the campaigns of Alexander the Great or the spread of religions such as Buddhism, Christianity and Islam. Octavio Paz has characterized its isolation as the fatal limitation of America: to be able to imagine the *other* is to have built up defences and to be prepared for the unexpected and the new.[10] He compares the lack of defences of Amerindians against European and Asian viruses to the vulnerability of their civilizations when confronted with European influences. The last defence of the Aztecs in the final battle for Tenochtitlán was to construct a great paper serpent into which they put all the spiritual and magical powers of the universe. So desperate were they in making this serpent, they did it certain that not only would the Spaniards die but they themselves would also perish and with them the whole universe would disappear. It was the equivalent of a bomb that would blow everything to pieces. The Spaniards, faced with this monster, hacked it to pieces with their steel swords.[11] The resistance of the Aztecs collapsed.

To set against the homogeneous cultures that built the great pyramids of Yucatán, Monte Alban and Teotihuacán, I choose the cathedral of Monreale in Sicily. Built by the Norman King William II 1172–76, it demonstrates in its construction and its superb mosaics the interchange of cultures which characterize the Old World: Muslim craftsmen made the lower register of abstract mosaics and the wooden ceilings and Byzantine Greek and Sicilian artists made the mosaics which tell the Jewish story of the creation and history of the world in the upper reaches of the nave on walls carried on Roman pillars. The aisle and choir tell the story of Christ's life while the apse is dominated by the great mosaic of the ascended Christ as the Pantocrator, the ruler of creation (figure 8), an image that has been traced in its origins back to the famous statue of Zeus by Phidias at Olympia (see page 314). The patron of the church, King William, had himself portrayed as receiving his authority to rule direct from heaven and therefore independently of the pope. His grandson, the Emperor Frederick II, was to engage in furious battles with the papacy over this same question. But still, whether popes or monarchs claimed the supreme authority under heaven, they all as European Christians believed in their right to rule the rest of the world as given them from the Pantocrator Christ. That right to rule has descended not only in the colonial tradition but in the attitudes underlying western science and technology and it colours our images of our own humanity. In our materialism, our reductionism and our acceptance of ugliness and pollution in our surroundings, we are in danger of being as blind and deaf to the Other as the Aztecs were limited by their isolation in their imaginations. The Other, here, encompasses the symbols and images of the Great Memory: we need to cultivate our imaginations in order to understand the power of the imagination. It was through the cultivation of the imagination that past civilizations achieved their heights. To explore one particular instance of this cultivation we go to another cathedral, one in the ambience of which western science first developed – the cathedral of Chartres.

4

Image of woman: images of man

When we stand at midday at the crossing of Chartres Cathedral we are symbolically at the midpoint of time and at the still heart of the universe. We stand between the memory of the past and the memory of the future, between the northern rose window, showing the Virgin presiding over what is gone, and the risen Christ promising what is to come in the southern rose window. Everywhere around us are the faces of people looking up with their lips parted and their eyes full of wonder and we see in them a mirror of how our own expressions must appear to them. The wonder in our faces is not only at the beauty of the symbols, patterns and colours of the stained glass and the interplay and chequering of their reflections cast on the stone columns and capitals but at the hugeness of our own humanity. By entering the cathedral we have stepped inside the symbolic realization of universal humanity: the ground plan represents a human being with the arms stretched out into the transepts, the legs and body down the nave with the sexual organs where the labyrinth is set into the pavement and with the head forming the sanctuary and the rounded chevet and ambulatory of the eastern end (figure 9). At the crossing we are close to the heart of Adam Kadmon lying supine as when he was first formed from the dust while around us are the tree trunks of another Eden in the columns of stone – and it is through the stilling of the heart in ourselves that we are most touched and awakened by what we see and experience here.

As we walk about the cathedral, we move as much through an ambience of mind as of space. The mind symbolically represented and almost palpably present is that of the second Adam, Jesus Christ, and the wisdom that suffuses that mind is that of the Virgin Mary, identified with the Sapientia, or divine knowledge of the Solomonic books of the Old Testament. This wisdom is the theme of the sculptures of the Royal Portal, the three doors that open into the cathedral in the west front surrounded and surmounted by carvings showing all the paths of knowledge, science and art under the guidance of the Virgin seated on the throne of wisdom, all the labours of

66

man and the works of time associated with the Ascension, and, over the centre door, Christ in majesty blessing the world as the symbol of what unites contemplation and action in the oneness of truth.

Chartres was the greatest shrine of the Virgin in western Europe, possessing the relic of the silk shift believed to have been worn by the Virgin at the birth of Christ. It is especially the cathedral of the Incarnation and therefore of birth and life: no one was ever buried there. As a centre of learning, science and art it was the hearth of the most important civilizing force in Europe. Western science and cosmology were born there; the most advanced techniques of the time in building and in crafts were brought to a new pitch of excellence in the demands made by the rebuilding after the great fire of 1194 destroyed the old Romanesque cathedral; and the western conception of the worth of the individual soul received its first statement in the column statues of the Royal Portal and in the later statues of the north and south portals (figure 10). The building itself is regarded as pre-eminent among the surviving great churches of the Gothic period, partly because its sculptures and stained glass largely escaped the iconoclasts of the Reformation and the French Revolution, and partly because of the emotions it arouses, and its atmosphere of a profound and satisfying joy.

As the cathedral celebrates the Incarnation of God as man, so it is evidence of the incarnation of divine inspiration in art – of how an inward thought or image charged with emotion can be realized in the physical terms of stone, metal and glass so that they transmit the same emotion of the inward experience. Longinus, writing in the first century AD, ascribed the fundamental source of creative power in literature to the quality of magnanimity or greatness of soul[1] – and magnanimity at the heart of civilization is what we are most impressed by at Chartres. We see it in the representations of the highest ideals of humanity in Christ and his mother and we know it by inference from the works of those who designed and created the Royal Portal, the western towers and the conception of the major part of the cathedral built in the twenty-six years following the fire of 1194. Much is known about every aspect of Chartres, about the scholars and thinkers who would have worked together with the architects and sculptors on the iconographical schemes, about the preceding development of the Gothic style at St-Denis, about the enthusiasm that drove nobles and peasants to drag the carts carrying the stones and provisions for the building of the southwest tower, and about the symbolism, mathematical and mystical, that dictated the proportions and the disposition of the building, but we do not know the names of those chiefly responsible for the remodelling and rebuilding of the cathedral between 1150 and 1220. In terms of comparable influence it is as though the plays of Shakespeare, the works of Plato, the *Principia* of Isaac Newton and the theology of Thomas Aquinas were all available to us but their authors were anonymous. This is not an unfamiliar position for us to be in when we look for the founders of civilizations: we do not know who actually wrote the Gospels just as we do not know the authors of the myths that feed our literature and art. In the case of the great sculptors and architects of Chartres, what we do know about them is that they were inspired by new ideals of man and woman. We know that the perfection of humanity was a great theme in the thinking of the school of Chartres: Bernard Sylvester and Alan of Lille both wrote about the creation of perfect man and John of Salisbury, Bishop of Chartres, was influenced in his political writings such as *Policraticus* and in his other works by comparable ideals. When we turn back to the cathedral as an image of man·and to the works of art there which also celebrate ideals of humanity, we can trace how profound inner experience married to superlative talents may transform gifts and traditions from the past into a new impulse of civilization.

We trace the inner experience of these men particularly in the greatest ideals of humanity they represented, namely Christ and his mother. The Christ in Majesty over the Royal Portal is one of a series of representations of the Son of God in the tympana of other, earlier great churches such as those at Moissac, Autun and Vézelay. There Christ is always represented as much larger in size than any other figure. Here at Chartres he can be shown in more moderate proportion because his authority comes from the expressive power of the carving. What is particularly new here is the humanity and approachability of this Christ shown as 'he who makes all things new'. He is the ultimate standard of truth for all the forms of knowledge pursued in his service. What is new beyond everything else is that he is a happy Christ: unlike the stern or sorrowing Christs of the Romanesque, he is smiling. It is one of the first smiles achieved in sculpture since classical antiquity and the boldness of emphasizing his humanity may reflect the conscious influence of statues from classical times.

An ideal of humanity may be expressed in other ways than figural representation. As was said earlier, the eastward parts of a church symbolize the neck and head of a man so that, for example, the choir sings in the position of the throat of the imagined universal man and the faithful approaching the high altar receive the host on their tongues at the point at which his mouth would be. Even in the greatest Romanesque churches, though their builders were familiar with the symbolism of the ground plan representing a man, the apse occupied little space in proportion to the rest of the church.[2] It was the achievement of the first Gothic masters at St-Denis to expand the space and increase the lighting of the sanctuary and apse. I think it is no coincidence that this expansion of the area symbolizing the human head comes at the very time when the first scholastic philosophers were rediscovering the powers of the human mind. Aided by another gift of the Great Memory, the recovery of the works of Aristotle from Islam, these philosophers had a simple ambition: it was to be able to think like a universal or perfect man; in other words, to think on the scale, and with the profundity, of Christ.

Many were the experiments to devise the most perfect form of the chevet, or eastern end symbolizing the human head, in the course of the twelfth century, most notably at the two other great centres of scholastic philosophy, Laon and Paris. At Chartres perfection was found by making the eastern part of the cathedral the same length from the crossing as the nave and with the grandeur of a double ambulatory to ease the circulation of pilgrims. When we walk in that ambulatory we can think of ourselves as walking through the mind of Christ in spaces filled with divine wisdom of which we, the shafted colours and the polished stones, are the consequences.

The same emphasis on the humanity of Christ is also to be seen in the representations of the Virgin at Chartres. With the emphasis on her humanity she is also raised to new positions of glory: never before had she been represented on the tympanum of a great church in the position of honour she is given in the Royal Portal. What was in effect the new art of stained glass offered fresh opportunities for representing her, as in the earliest windows at Chartres, the Tree of Jesse and the window known as *Notre Dame de la Belle Verrière*: it was a topos of the Incarnation that Jesus was in his mother 'as the sun that shines through glass'. She is shown, most gloriously, surrounded by her genealogy in the rose window of the north transept where she appears as the wisdom of the cosmos (figure 11). In that window she is shown with a black face.

The question of why her face is black leads us into other examples of gifts from the Great Memory. As well as the shift of the Virgin, the cathedral also possessed a miracle-working statue of the Black Virgin. The original statue was destroyed in the French Revolution: it was believed to be of great antiquity but, going by the many other surviving examples of Black Virgins, it was probably late tenth or eleventh century in origin. These Black Virgins are nearly always to be found in places that archaeology has shown to be associated with the goddesses of antiquity. Churches raised on the sites of temples or shrines to Venus, Diana, Cybele and Isis acquired cult statues of the Black Virgin, often with miraculous stories attached to them such as that they were discovered in a tree or, as at Boulogne, arrived from the sea in an unattended boat. The form of these hieratic sculptures can be traced back to several ancient sources: the original cult statue of Cybele had a black meteorite in the place of its face and the earliest sources of the representations of a mother with a child on her lap were the Egyptian statues of Isis with her infant son Horus.

The appearance of these Black Virgins in the eleventh and twelfth centuries is part of a gradual and general movement throughout western Europe that in various ways improved the lot of women, redressing the balance of their position in society, and restored ideals of femininity. Women as great heiresses or rulers such as Matilda of Tuscany, the Empress Maud, and Eleanor of Aquitaine were playing parts in international politics unheard of since the Roman Empire. In literature and art restored from the past the role of women in the Celtic legends that formed the Arthurian cycle helped to change imaginative attitudes. Perhaps under Sufi influences, the poets of southern France began to idealize their mistresses and beloveds in ways that permanently affected the chivalry of Europe. Among the most extraordinary ways in which forgotten themes from the past were revived in this period is the way in which the patterns associated with the Neolithic Great Goddess – the chevron, the spiral and the lozenge – appear as some of the chief ornamentations of later Romanesque churches such as Durham, and the associated image of the Sheila-na-gig, the goddess revealing her genitals as the source of life, was carved on so many churches.[3]

The chief pattern in the rose window of the north transept at Chartres is formed by lozenges swirling about the central panel of the Black Virgin. Black and comely, she has a look of loving kindness in her face, light years away from the reserved, staring faces of the earlier Black Virgins of which she is the transformation. Something happened at Chartres to bring about this transformation and among its effects in its influence on other sacred art throughout Europe was that the Virgin grew younger, so that at Rheims, Regensburg, Ely and Florence she became less and less the goddess reborn and more and more the smiling happy girl who accepted the gift of godhead in her. As she changed, so all the other representations of women in art and literature also changed.

One of the most influential of all the new representations of women is the portrayal of Beatrice Portinari by Dante. In the record of his love for Beatrice set down in *La Vita Nuova*, Dante created the first autobiographical work devoted to the psychological understanding of love. In this he was greatly helped by his friend Guido Cavalcanti, who had brought to the tradition of the troubadour lyric the scientific and medical theories of the time that explained the relationship between body, mind and spirit, otherwise known as faculty psychology. This faculty psychology was the common property of Christian and Islamic cultures and just as the great

poet Ibn Arabi had earlier claimed that God is revealed in the beloved
to the gaze of each lover, so Dante, Cavalcanti and their friends in the
association known as the *fedeli d'amore* (or faithful followers of love) saw in
the women who were the objects of their love the paths to higher knowledge
and experience. The *fedeli d'amore* had a hierarchy based on the experience
of love. Only someone who possessed the *cor gentile*, the noble heart, could
understand what they expressed in their poems; here the social concept of
nobility was transformed into an aristocracy of the soul. Their aim was
to awaken within themselves a higher organ of consciousness, *l'intelletto
d'amore*, 'the intellect of love', which was not just a fine phrase but a
potential awaiting manifestation within the human soul. Through this
awakening of the intellect of love, they would be able to understand the
divine wisdom, Sapientia, which was incarnate for them in the ladies who
inspired their love. They aspired through their loves to a communion of
the spirit, a level of awareness in which their consciousness and their
creativity would be identical – and, because they saw so many levels of
meaning in their beloveds, it is difficult sometimes to distinguish when
they are speaking of young Florentine ladies or of the states of union and
ecstasy to which they are transported by their love.

La *Vita Nuova* tells the story of how Dante fell in love with the
eight-year-old Beatrice at a party in Florence when he himself was almost
nine. Under the guidance of a figure he calls Love who is both his conscience
and muse and who appears to him in dreams and visions, at the age of
eighteen he wrote a poem about Beatrice that won him the friendship of
Guido Cavalcanti. Throughout the work Dante draws quite open parallels
between Beatrice and Christ and he celebrated her as a miracle: 'Crowned
and clothed in humility, she walked, showing no pride in what she saw or
heard Many would say as she went by: she is no woman but one of the
loveliest angels of heaven. And others said: she is a miracle: Blessed be the
Lord who works such marvels.'[4] When she died at the age of twenty-four it
is as though her city was widowed and Dante describes with heartbreaking
sorrow his state of bereavement until he is given two visions of Beatrice
in glory. He is, he says, inspired to write of her what has never been said
of any woman.

This passage is a promise of *The Divine Comedy* in which Beatrice
plays a very different part. In *La Vita Nuova* Beatrice is seen, described and
glorified but she never speaks directly. In the chief work of Dante's middle
period, the *Convivio*, she is, briefly, a silent presence. In *The Divine Comedy*
she is the instigator of his journey through the three worlds of the afterlife
and in her meeting with him on the top of Mount Purgatory she is again
a type of Christ. She appears out of the rising sun at dawn to berate Dante

for forgetting her and for ignoring the inspirations she has sent him. She is the woman priest who presides at the procession of the Holy Sacrament and who hears his confession. She is witty, intelligent, formidably learned in all the works of the Fathers, and the accumulated science and knowledge of the earthly and heavenly worlds: she is, Virgil says of her, 'the light between the truth and intellect';[5] her beauty grows with the beauty of Dante's verse as they ascend together through the heavens. Dante ascends from sphere to sphere only by looking at her eyes. Beatrice is she 'who imparadises my mind': it is as a reflection in her eyes that he first sees the point of light around which all creation revolves; and it is through her that he comes to experience in himself 'the love that moves the sun and other stars'.

Beatrice is the joy of the creative imagination on the hugest scale; only through her can Dante expand his conceptions and love to the understanding of the universe. Can she be at the same time the girl who lives in the next street, the young lady who marries a banker of the Bardi family? So Dante says. One of Dante's earliest commentators, who was probably a friend, writes that she was 'a noble Florentine lady who in this life gave out a miraculous radiance by her beauty and the purity of her morals'.[6] This commentator, Guido da Pisa, gives symbolic meanings to her as well: she is the sacred science of theology, she is the spiritual life and, mystically, she is divine grace infused in man in this world and the life in glory – *vita beata* – that man may expect and hope for.

Virtue can be real to us only as it is manifested in a human being; ideals can have force and influence only as they are realized consistently in human behaviour. The impact that Beatrice has had on succeeding generations is owed to Dante's experience of her human greatness; hers is the realized ideal that redeems the monsters and horrors of the past thrown up by the Great Memory into Dante's imagination.

The process of transformation brought about at Chartres through a new statement of the redemptive power of the feminine and through Dante's praise of Beatrice is part of a pattern that we can see in European civilizations long before the Middle Ages and it has recurred again in many forms since that time. The ideal may be realized in a living woman, as with the teacher of Socrates, Diotima, or it may be the allegorical or visionary expression of a great tradition, as when Boethius in his prison cell was comforted by the vision of Philosophy as a great and beautiful woman with her head in the stars. It recurs, in fact, whenever the Neo-Platonic tradition is remembered and understood anew, though it is not tied to that tradition. What Diotima told Socrates about the ascent of the lover to truth, from the love of an individual through the love of the many to the love of the One, was later developed into a ladder of ascent to God so that we find it in St Augustine, in St Bonaventure and in Dante's *Divine Comedy*.[7]

When the philosophers of the Florentine Academy, chiefly Marsilio Ficino, rediscovered the original statement of the theme of the ladder in Plato's *Symposium* which had been lost to the West for centuries, they used it to set out a new statement of the feminine ideal which they related to the mystical ladder of ascent. They devised a new philosophy of love which they expressed as the ascent from the terrestrial Venus of physical attraction and earthly passions to the celestial Venus of divine love and imagination; it was an ascent into greater and greater creativity and the doctrine of the two Venuses inspired many Florentine artists such as Botticelli and Michelangelo. The doctrine was spread further afield through the popularity of Castiglione's *Il Cortegiano*; in that work he gave to the mouth of Pietro Bembo a speech on the nature of love which is a radiant and ecstatic expression of the doctrine. This was, through Sir Thomas Hoby's translation into English, to inspire, as we shall see, Shakespeare and many of his contemporaries. Thus, once again, we see how the revival of a forgotten idea from the past, given new meaning by being related to ideals of human achievement, in this case the Renaissance ideals of the *uomo universale* and the lady who mirrors the celestial Venus, can have the widest of civilizing influences.

The ideas also influenced in their youth two of the greatest artists of the Venetian school, Titian and Giorgione. Titian is thought to have drawn on the doctrine of the terrestrial Venus and celestial Venus in his *Sacred and Profane Love* (in the Villa Borghese in Rome) of about 1515. He is also thought to have expressed it in another early work, *Le Concert champêtre* in the Louvre, long attributed to Giorgione but now universally given to Titian (figure 12). *Le Concert champêtre* is a large pastoral work which shows, in a north Italian landscape, two beautiful naked women with two young men.[8] One of the women stands beside a marble well, drawing water from it; the other woman sits with her back to us; she holds a flute and she listens to the intense conversation between the two young men. Of these two, one is a lute player, a courtier dressed in splendid crimson and black silk and particoloured hose, and the other is a young shepherd with a mop of dark hair: the shepherd boy is fascinated by the music and the conversation of the lute player. The mood of this mysterious painting excites our wonder as it arouses our pleasure; we puzzle over the meaning and the occasion of the association of the four people as thousands of others have puzzled in the past. Do the young men ignore the two naked women because they do not see them, except in so far as the women are their own natures at the time the painting depicts? What is being said in the interchange between the lute player and the shepherd? What is the nature of the extraordinary tension between their two heads so that a discharge of electricity seems to divide and yet connect the halves of the canvas? The Renaissance humanists had recovered much of the art and the literature of the ancient world but, apart from writings about the theory of music, they had no music of the classical period. Yet they were convinced that music was both a means to the ascent of the mystical ladder and an expression of what may be learned on the ascent. Ficino would recite poetry that he composed extempore accompanying himself on the lyre (or *lira da braccio*) to the admiration of his friends; stringed instruments such as the *lira da braccio* and the lute were considered according to ancient views much more capable of reproducing the higher and heavenly harmonies than wind instruments such as the flute. Thus it has been suggested that the shepherd boy is being taught to abandon the flute held here by the terrestrial Venus in favour of the music of the lute which signifies the wisdom and the inspiration of the celestial Venus, she who is already drawing the water of genius from the well, beneath the evergreen tree which contrasts with the deciduous beech and oak of the shepherd's old life depicted on his side of the picture.

So influential was the doctrine of the two Venuses that it had effects upon the way in which the Virgin Mary was portrayed. It is obvious to any eye that the naked Venus of Botticelli is the same ideal girl whom he painted when she was clothed as the Virgin. The influence of the doctrine is to be felt in the mood of paintings as much as in visual resemblances and in none more so than in a work by Giorgione.

In the cathedral of Giorgione's city, Castelfranco Veneto, is hung his work *The Virgin and Child with St George and St Francis* (figure 13). Because of its extreme value and of attempts to steal it, we can see it only through the interstices of a stout metal grille. As we look, we may get the feeling that it is we who are imprisoned, not the painting, such are the immensity of freedom and expansion of understanding it conveys. Like Titian, Giorgione was deeply affected by the magical philosophy of the Renaissance and many of his other works such as the *Tempesta* are inspired by the symbolism and the mystical inner feeling of that philosophy. Here the mystery is conveyed through a fusion of classical and Gothic themes. The Virgin is seated on a chair of state as the earlier Virgin of Chartres is seated on the throne of wisdom, but here the chair and its architectural surround are of classical simplicity. Below her is a pavement of black and white marble squares on which the saints stand. St George is in the full armour of a medieval knight and he holds his lance rested against his left shoulder with its pennon with the cross hanging down; behind him stands the walled Gothic city of Castelfranco. Behind St Francis is a wilderness of trees and mountains with a temple in the distance. The horizon of the sea links both landscapes. Virgin and Child make the apex of a triangle bringing together the active life of St George and the contemplative life of St Francis, signified further by the scenes behind them.

St George looks out at us, his eyes shadowed by his helmet, while St Francis gazes to the ground as his gesture shows the nail wound in his left hand. The Christ child is relaxed, half asleep in his mother's right arm. Her left hand is resting gently on the arm of her throne: all the peace in the world seems to be expressed in her motionless fingers. She sits in stillness and the mood of her conscious reverie flows out from her beautiful face as though the quality of light with which the painting is filled is transfigured by her inner nature. There is almost certainly a cosmic significance in the design of the plinth on which her throne is set with rich brocades hanging on the plain stone to signify the source of creativity in higher worlds and in the pavement of black and white squares which signify the world of time and the alternation of night and day. The mood of profound reverie expressed by the Virgin holds the figures of the saints: they are as motionless in their minds as in their bodies. They reflect on their experience, on the experience of humanity and on what has brought them together, which is the incarnated Word of the Christ child. What brings in particular St George and St Francis together is that they both in different ways know the life and sufferings of Christ. Through the gift of the stigmata received at La Verna, St Francis experienced the wounds of the crucifixion. In his martyrdom St George died three times; twice St Michael brought his scattered limbs together at the command of Christ, who brought about his resurrection. At his third execution he was allowed to die. It is not strange that two such men who have known such mysteries should be brought together before the throne of the Virgin. They rise above the world of time to live within the eternal dream of Virgin and Child – ideals of the two paths to the truth that is in Christ. This work could never have been painted and could not have its abiding sense of calm unless Giorgione had had the influence of the preceding artists of the Renaissance who had absorbed the doctrine of the heavenly Venus as the climax of the mystical ladder, signified in the throne.

If the doctrine of the two Venuses affected the representations of the Virgin in those regions that remained Catholic, it also provided an ideal independent of formal religion in many Protestant states. The effect of the Great Memory can be destructive as well as innovative: when the leaders of the Reformation looked back in history with grim rationality to study the doctrines and practices of the primitive Church, they found no justification in scripture or the Fathers for the cults of the Virgin that had provided joy and solace for so many centuries. So, for much of northern Europe, the shrines were despoiled and the statues were broken or burned like heretics.

In England from 1558 onwards the cult of the Virgin was replaced by the cult of the Virgin Queen Elizabeth and increasingly throughout her reign the doctrine of the heavenly Venus made its influence felt, in many new expressions of the feminine ideal. These range from Sir Walter Raleigh's passionate 'Complaint of the Ocean to Cynthia', his poem addressed to Queen Elizabeth when she had him imprisoned in the Tower of London, to Spenser's four Hymns on Platonic themes of love and beauty and many passages in *The Faerie Queene*, such as the description of the Temple of Venus in Book IV, Canto X, and from the sonnets of Samuel Daniel to the poems of Fulke Greville. The influence runs throughout Shakespeare, from the portrayal of Silvia in the early *Two Gentlemen of Verona* to the heroines of his last plays. The four marriages with which *As You Like It* concludes – between Orlando and Rosalind, Oliver and Celia, Silvius and Phoebe, and Touchstone and Audrey – are twice graded according to the degree of love each pair has attained on the ladder of ascent. Equally the themes recur throughout the tangled story of the Sonnets, in the course of which, whatever the vicissitudes of the passionate friendship, and the betrayal by mistress and friend, Shakespeare speaks of the love that is enduring, unchanging, universal:

For nothing this wide universe I call
Save thou, my rose: in it thou art my all.[9]

As Shakespeare spread the new ideal of the Eternal Feminine beyond his circle to the many thousands who saw and read his plays, so Philip Sidney, through the effect of his entrancing tale *The Countess of Pembroke's Arcadia*, published after his death, had an equally wide effect on manners and civilized society through the portrayal of his beautiful, wise and brave heroines, the sisters Pamela and Philoclea. The *Arcadia* went into fourteen editions up to 1725, following its first publication in 1593, and it was translated into the main European languages. It is to my mind just about the most enjoyable book in the world for its ever-memorable emblem-like images, its alternations of poetry and prose, of adventure and contemplation, of failure and success, and the way it encompasses all degrees of love and all varieties of human virtue and vice. It reaches its grandest and most terrifying flights in the story of the imprisonment of Pamela and Philoclea by their wicked aunt Cecropia and in the debates between Pamela and her aunt and the mental tortures and physical deprivations inflicted by the aunt on Pamela. Pamela became a type of someone who rises above suffering and the presence of death to gain a state of perfect acceptance: according to tradition Charles I on the scaffold quoted from her prayer.

> O all-seeing light and eternal life of all things, to whom nothing is either so great that it may resist, or so small that it is contemned; look upon my misery with Thine eye of mercy, and let Thine infinite power vouchsafe to limit out some proportion of deliverance unto me, as to Thee shall seem most convenient. Let not injury, O Lord, triumph over me, and let my faults by Thy hand be corrected, and make not mine unjust enemy the minister of Thy justice . . .[10]

So the prayer begins and Sidney makes also one of his vivid paintings in words as he describes Pamela kneeling on the ground

> as if devotion had borrowed her body to make of itself a most beautiful representation; with her eyes so lifted to the skyward that one would have thought they had begun to fly thitherward to take their place among their fellow stars; her naked hands raising up their whole length and, as it were, kissing one another, as if the right had been the picture of Zeal and the left of Humbleness . . .[11]

Michael Drayton (1563–1631), similarly inspired by the same doctrine, wrote this the night before he died:

> So well I love thee, as without thee I
> Love nothing; if I might choose, I'd rather dye
> Than be one day debarred thy company.

Men who share with beasts and plants merely their animal and vegetable lives are themselves beasts, but to Drayton, 'He only lives, that deadly is in love.' As the corn must die in order to multiply, so Love, which is the seed of the world, must die in order to increase. Then he speaks of how the many pieces of a broken looking-glass may each show forth the same face:

Proportions, features, graces just the same
And in the smallest piece as well the name
Of fairest one deserves, as in the richest frame.

So all my Thoughts are pieces but of you
Which put together makes a glass so true
As I therein no other's face but yours can view.[12]

What characterizes all the works inspired by the ideal of the Eternal Feminine mentioned so far in this chapter, whether they are on the huge and public scale of a cathedral or the intimate and private scale of a sonnet, is that they convey calm and certainty. They reflect a stillness of the mind and this stillness may help us to understand what the Eternal Feminine may mean in an inward sense. Meister Eckhart asks us to understand the Incarnation in an inner moral sense; he says that the Virgin is the soul in such a state of purity that the Son may be born within it.[13] What is the soul when it is pure? It is tranquil and accepting; its emptiness is filled with love and its efforts are made effortless because its choices are made for it. It is in a state when it realizes the potentiality of the consciousness ready to reveal itself, which is another way of saying the incarnation of the divine mind and imagination.

In that state, illuminated by pure consciousness, the soul possesses the wisdom which is characteristic of the Eternal Feminine in all its manifestations. So on the scale of society, when enough individuals have that experience of the Eternal Feminine, the gifts of the Great Memory can be changed and used fruitfully under the guidance of a great ideal of humanity.

We can take the idea further: that when the soul is pure enough for an idea, an inspiration, an archetype to be born in it, then the Incarnation extends into the physical and lived existence of the recipient. In the case of architects like those who created Chartres or artists such as Giorgione and Titian, they are literally the means of transforming matter, whether it is the stone from the quarries of La Berchère or the pigments formed of clays, minerals and vegetables with which they work. The subject or meaning, to represent which they transform the materials of their arts, is the transformation of life and consciousness.

To illustrate this I give the examples of St Francis and his follower St Anthony of Padua. There were many sects in the late twelfth century that turned to the ideal of poverty set by Christ and the Apostles: these movements can be seen as examples of the Great Memory at work as I described earlier in relation to the ways in which new religious movements arise. St Francis, inspired by the ideal of poverty, in his great innocence set in motion a powerful revolution, by being, in becoming empty to God, the ideal of the poor in spirit to which he aspired. A spiritual troubadour, he was devoted to a feminine ideal whom he called the Lady Poverty.

From St Francis's life pour many civilizing streams, the preaching of his friars which brought about a new democratization of Christianity, the learning of Franciscan theologians, new styles in Gothic architecture, a new sensibility to nature, animals and plants which is reflected in art and literature, and a blazing awareness of the love of God. For a man whose surviving genuine literary remains cover a few pages, this is an astounding influence.

We see similar effects in the pilgrim church of Il Santo at Padua where St Anthony of Padua (1195–1231) is buried. Of all St Francis's followers he seems to have mirrored him most, in the directness and purity of his soul, in his sensibility to nature and created things and in his miracles. Padua was the chief scene of his work where in 1222 the university which was to become famous for its medical school was founded. So universally regarded were St Anthony's virtues that he was canonized almost immediately after his death in 1231 and in 1232 work began on building his church. The architect, Fra Girolami degli Eremitani, married Gothic influences then new to Italy with the Byzantine model of St Venice to create a church extraordinary in its exterior with its six domes surmounted by a conical dome and mind-expanding in its interior spatial arrangements. The works of art it contains are rich even by the standards of great Italian churches. Donatello and his assistants made the statues and altar furnishings of the high altar. Cardinal Bembo, who uttered the inspired oration on the ascent to the heavenly Venus recorded in Castiglione's *Il Cortegiano*, is buried in the nave under a tomb designed by Palladio. As for the shrine of the saint, the finest sculptors of the north Italian Renaissance, Jacopo Sansovino and Tullio Lombardo among them, carved the nine reliefs portraying scenes from the life of the saint that encase the interior round the tomb. As you follow the pilgrims round the tomb and like them place your hand on the green mottled marble slab of St Anthony's sarcophagus, you may feel, as I did there, that the true evidence of creativity and civilization is in the life and continued presence of the man in whose honour all these supreme works of art were made. The popular cult of St Anthony of Padua pays little attention to the ferocious denouncer of clerical corruption he was in life but it reflects the strong femininity of his nature. He is the saint of instant intuition, the presence we call on when we need immediate help: he represents the part of the mind that can remember where we last put our keys or the winning lottery ticket. This femininity also appears in his cult statues which show him as a beardless youth with a lily in his hand and carrying the Christ child, as though he, virgin, could give birth to Christ, in Eckhart's sense, through the purity of his soul.

What we experience in Il Santo as the effect of one man's life or what we learn from the *Divine Comedy* as a result of the short existence of Beatrice Portinari, we see on the much wider scale of the founders of religions and civilizations. Of those teachers such as Christ, the Buddha, and Krishna it can be said that their words and actions were so memorable that what they said and did so imprinted the minds of their companions that there was no need for them to write their own scriptures or develop the implications of their insights. That was for others, over hundreds of years, to do.

The influence on the future of such men is extraordinary. As an artist may receive an inspiration that lasts a few seconds but takes years to implement, so they in a matter of moments transmit their own experience in a way that changes the lives of future generations. They give an instruction or make an observation and codes of behaviour, manners, morals, dietary instructions affecting millions yet to be born, will be devised from a few words. They pass through a town or a village and a shrine inspiring patrons and artists to surpass one another in emulation and devotion will be built, attracting pilgrims for centuries. The civilizations that issue from the short periods of their existence on Earth are like the time-bodies of their souls, and each succeeding renewal of civilization within their influence, as with the Christian civilizations of the West, or each development within a converted country, as with the spread of Buddhism, will explore a further aspect of their souls.

Theirs is the greatest and noblest form of creativity. They are the truth they teach and there is no division in their natures. They are directly inspired in the sense Christ spoke of when he said, 'the words I speak to you, I speak not of myself: but the Father that dwelleth in me, he doeth the work',[14] or they may be said to be inspiration itself because they are permanently in a state of cosmic consciousness, the state to which their followers aspire. They are, most supremely, what the Great Memory remembers.

Giving the Sermon on the Mount, Christ utters the nine Beatitudes which he fulfils himself by his attitude and behaviour throughout the Passion and which are a model for human perfection through the path of nonresistance to evil. In the *Dhammapada* the Buddha says: 'What we are today comes from our thoughts of yesterday, and our present thoughts build our life of tomorrow: our life is the creation of our mind. If a man speaks or acts with a pure mind, joy follows him as his own shadow.'[15] Through such statements he created an ideal of humanity all the more powerful for the detachment he himself showed in the events and temptations leading to his enlightenment. In the *Bhagavad-Gita* Krishna reveals to Arjuna the universality of human nature when man discovers his true self: 'He who sees Me in everything and everything in Me, him shall I never forsake, nor shall he lose me.'[16] Such a man in all the vicissitudes of life remains steady and still in his being. Revealing himself in his true nature as the Self of the universe and as the author of the drama of life, Krishna celebrates his nature which is the essence of human nature:

> I am the Gambling of the cheat and the Splendour of the splendid;
> I am Victory; I am Effort; and I am the Purity of the pure . . .
> O Arjuna! I sustain this universe with only a small part of Myself.[17]

'He who cultivates his Real Self achieves the Absolute. When he achieves the Absolute the human elements will drop away, but the heavenly qualities will come to his assistance.'[18] Thus Chuang Tzu described the heavenly qualities of his master Lao Tzu. Lao Tzu sat still like a corpse and yet revealed himself as a dragon. From his profound stillness a sound came forth as thunder as if issuing from all Heaven and Earth.

We in the West are accustomed to think of creativity as action, as the drive to make and do spurred on by inner conflicts in the solipsistic enclosed individual. Taoist thought gives us a different and more relaxed conception – of creativity as surrender, reflection, absorption in the images of a tradition or of nature – in the way that Dante speaks of the spheres of Heaven moving as an effect of the silent contemplation of the angels[19] or, as an eighth-century Chinese poet wrote:

> The wild geese fly across the long sky above.
> Their image is reflected upon the chilly water below.
> The geese do not mean to cast their image on the water;
> Nor does the water mean to hold the image of the geese.[20]

Of such a moment of observation Chang Chung-yuan says: 'Our minds are simply God's mirror, reflecting the "here-now" of creation.'[21]

Human beings cannot live without an ideal of what they could be – whether it is the founding hero or god or totem of a tribe or the Buddha under the bo tree before whom all the temptations and attacks of Mara are powerless. Our need for an ideal is not so much for a symbolic leader or hero: it is a recognition of the lack of completeness in ourselves which is solaced by the awareness from the example of others that the lack may be made good and that the talent for seeking certainty and inner stillness, which is one of the talents given to all human beings, whatever they may be deprived of in other ways by heredity or environment, may be cultivated with hope of success.

It is through such ideals that men and women control and turn to fruitful purposes the giant potentially creative energies in the Great Memory.

Even where the response to the offerings of the Great Memory is not equal to the challenge, there is a psychic necessity to devise a human ideal that sums up the philosophy of a movement or party. When that ideal is false or twisted or incomplete, then great dangers await humanity, as we can see from the distortions of civilization and the ideals of humanity presented to us in the twentieth century by Fascism, Nazism and communism.

Each of these movements was in its individual way powered by recent discoveries about the past and by the return of ancient ideas and shibboleths. Each of them was prepared for by literary and artistic movements and each of them drew on evolutionary theory and the reinterpretation of the past that Charles Darwin and Alfred Russel Wallace had brought about. Fascism had its heralds in the Futurist movement and in poets and writers such as Gabriele D'Annunzio, desperate to revive a lost spirit of manhood in the newly created Italian nation. Mussolini made his appeal to the more cruel and bombastic sides of Roman imperialism: the fasces, the rods for beatings wrapped round the axes for execution once borne in front of Roman magistrates, were made the insignia of his movement. Thus what was once a symbol of law was appropriated by a political movement that enforced its supremacy by organized and licensed terrorism. The ideal of the movement was a physical type based on Roman statues of young men but where, in the case of the originals, the statues represented gods or heroes with godlike powers, the Fascist ideal reveals little trace of mental or spiritual powers (figure 14). Mussolini in his speech in Naples before the March on Rome on 24 October 1922 appealed to the memory of the Roman Empire.[22] He frequently returned to the theme of *Romanità*. 'Rome is our point of departure and our point of reference; it is our symbol and, if you like, our myth,' he said in 1935. Two years later he was patron of a vast display of Roman antiquities, the Mostra Augustea della Romanità, the point of which, to him, was to emphasize his historical role as the new Augustus who was going to reconquer the Mediterranean world for Italy and repossess it as ancient Rome had once done.

Popular Darwinism also played a preponderant part in the rapid

FIGURE 1. The Face of Glory appears at the top of this statue of Shiva and Parvati. Surrounded by celestial beings, with his mouth touched by Shiva's sceptre, the Face of Glory pours out the stylized vegetation that forms the aureole of the god and goddess. Orissa; twelfth century AD.

FIGURE 2. The Green Man: a vaulting boss from St Bénigne, Dijon, later thirteenth century, retaining its original paintwork. The carving, now in the Musée archéologique, Dijon, is remarkable for the individuality of the face and precision of the leaves.

FIGURE 3. Three Green Men from the south portal of Chartres
Cathedral, c. 1220. The plants portrayed are vine, acanthus and oak
(left to right).

FIGURE 4. The theatre at Epidauros.

left
FIGURE 5. From the ball court at Chichen Itzá: a carving showing a decapitated player with his blood spurting as serpents turning into vegetation.

bottom left
FIGURE 6. The façade of the Casa de Montéjo, 1542, in Mérida, with the giant Spanish soldiers with their axes.

bottom right
FIGURE 7. The heads of Green Men on which the Spanish soldiers in figure 6 stand.

FIGURE 8. Christ the Pantocrator:
the mosaic in the apse of the
cathedral of Monreale, Sicily,
1172-76.

FIGURE 9. The ambulatory of Chartres
Cathedral, first half of thirteenth
century.

FIGURE 10. Column statues on the
Royal Portal, Chartres, c. 1150: the
first statements of the western ideal of
the individual.

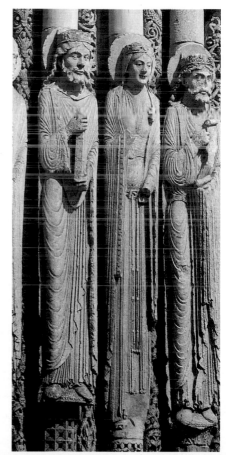

FIGURE 11. The rose window of the Virgin in the north transept of Chartres Cathedral.

FIGURE 12. *Le Concert champêtre* by Titian (c. 1485-1576) in the Louvre collection.

FIGURE 13. The *Pala* of Giorgione: *The Virgin and Child with St George and St Francis*, in the cathedral of Castelfranco Veneto.

development of Nazi ideology. Darwinism combined with researches into the origin of the Aryan race, into its prehistory and etymology, helped to produce the theory of the master race and the justification of German superiority by right of blood. All this was despite the much earlier warnings of the noted scholar Max Müller, who had deplored 'the unholy alliance between philology and physiology' and who maintained that the term 'Aryan' applied wholly to language and not to race.[23] The Nazis were also skilful in adapting to their cause earlier movements in the arts and scholarship such as Wagner's retelling of Norse mythology in his Ring cycle, Nietzsche's turning to the largely unknown figure of Zarathustra from Zoroastrian mythology for his doctrine of the Superman, and the historian Heinrich von Treitschke's adaptation of Hegelian doctrine to prove that the highest manifestation of the human spirit was to be found in the state of Prussia and by his celebration of Prussian military glory as a jewel as precious as the masterpieces of German poets and thinkers. As history was reinterpreted, so was science: Goebbels once said that if science failed in any way to support the ideology of Nazism, then Nazism would lead and science would have to follow in its footsteps. Though Hitler drew much of his historical justification from thinkers like Houston Stewart Chamberlain, his own appeal to the past, in addition to his obsession with racial purity, was centred on *Lebensraum* – living space – and the memory of the conquest of the Slav lands by the Teutonic Knights. 'We are where they were six hundred years ago. We stem the Germanic stream towards the South and West of Europe, and turn our eyes eastwards.'[24] Debased notions from theosophy also made their contribution: Hitler took the swastika, or *Hakenkreuz*, believed to be the symbol of the wheel of life to the ancient Aryans and he turned it into the wheel of death. The ideal Aryan was again a physical type: blond, tall, slim, muscular, ruthless, the type celebrated in Leni Riefenstahl's films and the decorations of Nazi stadia and official buildings. Massive naked men expressed naked power and when they were shown leading obedient horses they signified the leader empowered by will to guide the race or people.

Both Fascism and Nazism drew much of their support from the fact that they were reactions to another, older and in many ways more powerful image of man, the image underlying international communism. They differed from communism in its international aspirations – though not as communism became under Stalin – in that they were each centred on the races or countries of their respective births. They also differed from communism in that communism appealed to the humanitarian ideal of relieving the sufferings of mankind as a whole. Whereas the Nazis and Fascists were limited to their national memories by their sense of racial superiority, the communists could, because of their claims of fraternity with all races, draw on a much wider repertoire of memories and historical researches for justification of their theories. In one of the later editions of *The Communist Manifesto* Engels exultantly annotates the famous sentence 'The history of all hitherto existing society is the history of "class struggles"' by saying: 'that is, all *written* history'. At the time of its composition, in 1848, he says prehistory was unknown but by 1888 he could claim that it had been proved that the inner organization of all primitive societies from India to Ireland was communistic.[25] Therefore the communist movement was seeking a return to this primitive harmony. In developing dialectical materialism, Karl Marx had all the astonishing discoveries of the nineteenth century at his fingertips: the realization from Darwin that the evolution of man could be accounted for in terms solely of physical descent and the influence of the environment, the accounts from early anthropologists from which could be deduced the state of primitive man, the researches of historians into the origins of the Italian city-states which showed how bourgeois societies came about, the reversal of Hegelian dialectic to show that matter and not the spirit was the outcome of thesis, antithesis and synthesis. To him and his followers his theories formed a complete philosophy, founded on scientific truth and accuracy, so accurate, in fact, that the future could be predicted from it. That future lay in seizing power, in establishing the dictatorship of the proletariat and eventually in bringing about an earthly paradise when the state would wither away. The revolution did come and the dictatorship was established, not in Germany or England, the countries most advanced in capitalism, as Marx had predicted, but in backward Russia. The symbols chosen to represent the new state were the hammer and sickle, supposedly the union of the factory worker and the peasant to create socialist society, the one, in fact, a symbol of repression and the other of death. As for the ideal human being that the Soviet state promoted, it was that of the proletarian worker, muscular, hammer-wielding, the spearhead of mankind, and, like the Fascist and Nazi ideals in this, mindlessly single-minded.

These three ideals were brought together at the Paris Exhibition of 1937 (figure 14) in an extraordinary confrontation. For these three ideals, all based on the physical and biological aspects of man, men and women have died in their millions, in heroic acts of self-sacrifice in support of them, as conscripts, as helpless civilians, or as victims of the regimes they represented. There was, and still is, a power in them that is immense. They attract because they offer alternatives to the imperative to freedom in the individual human soul and the fear of the soul's loneliness and responsibility. They attract also because they are against creativity, appealing to the black jealousy that the creative spirit can evoke in mean and mediocre minds – as the Nazis burned the works of Heine and the scores of Mendelssohn, as the Bolsheviks had the poets such as Gumilev and members of the intelligentsia shot or drove even those who had supported them, such as Mayakovsky and Esenin, to suicide.

Looking at the power behind them gives us more insights into aspects of the Great Memory as the repository of accumulated emotions, the wounded pride that lay behind Fascism, the virulent hatred coupled with the need to blame that still shocks from the pages of *Mein Kampf* and which can be traced far back into German history, and the fear and terror that characterized the leaders of communism. The very first sentence of *The Communist Manifesto* reads: 'A spectre is haunting Europe – the spectre of Communism.'[26] Elsewhere Marx was to say that the terrorist is what he is because he is terrified. At the very outset of their movement Marx and Engels took an image, not of life or of hope, to characterize their ideal but one from the superstitions of the past they would in all other circumstances have condemned. Communism was a ghost, a revenant, a spirit unappeased from the past, demanding blood vengeance for the crimes of forgotten generations. It was a manifestation of ancestral anger. The images of the crushed, starved and exploited peasants and workers of the past were like a vast crowd anticipating the tumbrils and the executions that would follow revolution, adding their presences to the new international audience of the proletariat. It is the awakening of this international awareness across a great part of the inhabited globe that may turn out to be the chief achievement of communism. It created the audience that, having been made aware of what was happening in the rest of the world, brought it down.

What all three of these political philosophies share is that in their expressions of a human ideal, they draw on another dominant image of man in our century, one that owes most to influences from the past and the reinterpretation of history and prehistory: this is the scientific image of man, a strange, incomplete, dualist phantom that has immense influence on our society and our education.

5

Time and the scientific images of man

S t Augustine said that the world was made, not in time, but simultaneously with time.[1] In Indian thought each universe is said to be an
exhalation of the breath of Brahma: it dissolves and is reabsorbed on the
inhalation, to be re-created on the further outbreath. Both conceptions
depend on a creator deity who transcends time but the development of
these conceptions has been very different in West and East, as these two
following illustrations may show.

Our parish church, tucked under the Sussex downs, possesses one of
the earliest masterpieces of English medieval wall painting. Perhaps only
twenty or thirty years after the Norman Conquest in 1066, an artist whose
style is recognizable in fragments to be seen in other churches painted above
the chancel arch Christ in glory supported by angels and accompanied by the
twelve apostles. The side walls depict the good and the bad all judged by the
supreme image of man, which is Christ. The colours are reds, browns, ochres,
creams and whites and the painting is executed with special attention to
the robes of the figures and the looping rhythms of the wings of the angels.
Were the sermons ever dull in the church, there would always remain this
sermon to attend to. It is a sermon about time, the use we make of time,
and the ending of time, about the majesty of humanity redeemed by God
incarnate, and about the imagination of western Christianity.

Christ and his angels are restoring the memory of the life experience
of every human being that has ever lived. This is one interpretation of what
the Last Judgment means: the instantaneous recovery of all the experiences
of the past or, in other words, the return of the Great Memory in its fullness.
It is disturbing enough to think what this would mean in terms of our own
individual souls: that we should relive in an instant the compressed thoughts,
feelings and impressions of a lifetime, together with the searing knowledge of
the causes and consequences of everything we have done or omitted to do.
It is even more disturbing to suppose that it also means the instantaneous
recovery of the memory of all created things. This, on a mercifully slower

scale, is an analogy for the process of the recollection of the past brought about by the scientific age.

Western science has grown out of the paradigm of the Christian conception of time as a linear sequence from creation and the Fall of man, intersected and given meaning by the Incarnation and ending in the Second Coming and Last Judgment. This conception owes most to the earlier Judaic view of time established on the basis of prophecies foretelling a messiah and the coming of a kingdom of the righteous. The concept of causality as developed in western science is intimately bound up with time as a linear sequence in which causes always precede temporally their effects. In contrast, most ancient Greek theories of time were cyclical, like Plato's recurrent Great Year and the theories of the Stoics. Most eastern cosmologies, whether Hindu, Buddhist or Taoist, are also cyclical. There are indeed many references in the Gospels to time as a cycle but these were ignored or reinterpreted, partly through a ferocious desire to make punishment in the afterworld not just for a cycle of time, the *aion* of the Gospels, but for ever and ever, and partly to establish the Incarnation as a unique event which could never be repeated. One curious corollary of the establishment of this linear concept of time was that, in contrast to Greek thought and to other current ideas, time was compressed into a very short period. By working back through the genealogies in the Old Testament, Eusebius came to the conclusion that creation began in 4,500 BC under the sign of Aries. This was later corrected in the early seventeenth century by Johannes Kepler and Archbishop Ussher to the year 4,004 BC.

I want to contrast this short time span with a story from Hindu mythology retold by Heinrich Zimmer.[2] The story concerns the chastening of the pride of the god Indra. A certain dragon had caused general destruction on Earth and in the heavens by absorbing all the waters into its body. Indra did battle with the dragon and killed it, releasing the waters and thereby earning the gratitude of the other gods. He determined to rebuild his own palace and the palaces of the other gods that had been destroyed as a result of the dragon's activities. He gave orders to Vishvakarman, the architect of the gods, to start building and he never stopped giving orders for more and more towers and pavilions. Vishvakarman became so burdened with Indra's demands that he went in secret to the creator god Brahma for help in controlling Indra. Brahma promised to help. When Vishvakarman had left, Brahma went to Vishnu, the highest of the gods, who signified that something would be done.

The next morning a ten-year-old Brahmin child of exceptional beauty, his voice 'deep and soft as the slow thundering of auspicious rain clouds', visited Indra in his palace. Indra received the child with the respect due to his caste and was surprised by the child's first questions to him.

'How long will it be before Vishvakarman will finish this palace? No Indra before you has ever succeeded in completing such a palace as yours is to be.'

Indra asked the child mockingly if they were so many, the Indras and Vishvakarmans he had seen or heard of.

'Many,' says the child, who speaks of the immensity and the numbers of the universes known only by the Knowers. 'Who will count the universes side by side, each containing its Brahma, its Vishnu and its Shiva? Who will count the Indras in them all? . . . The universes – like delicate boats they float on the fathomless pure waters that form the body of Vishnu. Out of every hair pore of that body a universe bubbles and breaks.'

While he speaks, a procession of ants in a column four yards wide crosses the hall. The child looks at the ants and laughs. When Indra asks why he laughs the child refuses to say. As Indra presses him and shows himself to be more humble, the child relents, saying:

'I saw the ants, O Indra, filing in long parade. Each one was once an Indra . . .'

A newcomer appears in the hall. It is a hermit, and the hair on his chest forms a circle bare in the centre. Asked about himself the hermit says he is so short-lived, he will never have a livelihood or marry. Asked about the curious circle of hair on his chest, he answers: 'With the fall of one Indra one hair drops.'

At that both hermit and child vanish. The hermit is Shiva and the child is Vishnu.

Overcome with remorse, Indra sends for Vishvakarman and loads him with presents and expresses his gratitude. He decides to retire from his palace and his duties to live as an ascetic – to the horror of his wife, who, with the help of the priest Brihaspati, manages to persuade him to stay.

Although we do not know how many ants there were in that column passing through the hall, we know the length of the cycle of Indra which each one represents. It is 71 and a fraction times a great cycle of time, or *mahāyuga*, which lasts 4,320,000 years – well over 300 million years. A thousand *mahāyugas* represents one day of Brahma – 4 billion years.

Against such immensities, what is the worth of the individual human soul and what becomes of the uniqueness of the Incarnation? In the fullness of Indian thought the uniqueness of humanity is redeemed by the conception of the atman, or Supreme Self, which subsumes all the gods, all the possible universes, and all periods and cycles of time and is present in every human being. In earlier Christian thought the paucity of time was redeemed by the sense of the immensity of the eternal worlds, a new understanding for the Mediterranean world. The shortness of created time was paralleled by the shortness of man's physical life and the glory and the everlastingness of eternal life in the bosom of God counterbalanced the transience of mortal existence. Philosophy spoke to Boethius of eternity as 'the complete, simultaneous and perfect possession of everlasting life'[3] and from the Book of Revelation onwards Christian writings are full of the splendid immensity of the heavenly worlds.

With such conceptions of eternity the early Fathers of the Church were very successful in suppressing cyclical theories of time from pagan antiquity and in excluding them from any current western system of thought. The earliest Christians were convinced that the Second Coming, as prophesied by Christ who would appear to make 'all things new', was imminent. Their successors, who had to survive the crisis of disappointed hopes when the Second Coming failed to happen, had to fight doctrines of reincarnation and metempsychosis made popular by the mystery religions which were linked to cyclical theories of time. The later rise of Islam, which, like Christianity, owed its conception of time to the Judaic traditions they shared, was to create a buffer insulating the West from these ancient and eastern conceptions.

Cyclical theories did, of course, survive, chiefly where Neo-Platonic ideas were fostered. They also survived in the myths of the ages of gold, silver, brass and iron. These myths, divorced from the religious context of Christianity, did not have the force of the *yugas*, the comparable four ages, of Hindu thought. Nevertheless, they recur at certain crucial times in the history of western civilization. The most influential accounts of the Golden Age were in Virgil's fourth eclogue and in Ovid's *Metamorphoses* and these were the sources on which thinkers and poets constantly drew. Thus the ideal of the Golden Age returning appears in the school of Chartres at the same time as the beginnings of the Gothic style; it is a running theme in Dante's writings; it occurs in the rebirth of philosophy in fifteenth-century Florence; and it was particularly important in the ideas of Francis Bacon and the founders of the Royal Society. Francis Bacon said in his *Valerius Terminus*:

it is not the pleasure of curiosity, nor the quiet of resolution, nor the raising of the spirit, nor victory or wit, nor faculty of speech, nor lucre of profession, nor ambition of honour or fame, nor inablement for business, that are the true ends of knowledge; some of these being more worthy than other, though all inferior and degenerate: but it is a restitution and reinvesting (in great part) of man to the sovereignty and power (for whenever he shall be able to call the creatures by their true names he shall again command them) which he had in his first state of creation.[4]

It is a theme particularly linked to memory and the creative possibilities of humanity. It implies that we all have a memory in us of the lost paradise of the Golden Age or what mankind was in Adam and Eve before the Fall, and that the creative urge is inspired by that memory to recreate its joys and depth of knowledge. It also suggests that the experience of creativity would be different in each of the four ages: in the Age of Gold, a time of benign climate and an all-providing nature, there would be no need to invent machines to overcome inertia or to build against the cold: all creativity would be a spontaneous response of praise and enjoyment and all knowledge would be an immediate intellection of the natural laws which inform nature and humanity. The progressive decline towards the Age of Iron with its wars, natural catastrophes and extremes of climate imposes on man an ever-increasing need to create and invent for his own protection as much as to preserve the diminishing memory of the Golden Age. The thought that the Golden Age could come again and the conviction at certain periods that it had actually returned was nevertheless a fruitful conception. In cyclic time the Golden Age is as much a memory of our future as it is something that occurred in the past.

When eastern ideas began to filter through in the sixteenth century with the opening up of the trade routes to the East, it was the extension of time and of creation backwards in the greater scale of Hindu thought rather than the cyclical nature of time that impressed freer thinkers. Thus in the deposition of Christopher Marlowe's heretical and blasphemous sayings made by an informer after his death in a tavern brawl, the first saying attributed to Marlowe to establish his depravity was that the Indians and other nations had records going back 16,000 years, far longer than the mere 6,000 years since the time of Adam authorized by official doctrine.[5] For long after Marlowe's time serious thinkers kept to the biblical chronology though some had ingenious ways of fitting the immense task of creating the world into the narrow time scale. Thus Sir Isaac Newton suggested to Dr Burnet, the author of a notable work on the creation of Earth and its rocks, that God in His wisdom may have made the Earth rotate at a slower pace during the six days of creation in order to achieve so much. Dr Burnet did not agree.[6]

The difference between the conception of time and creation common to the Christian Fathers and Dr Burnet and the conception of geological time we now possess is brought home to me on each occasion I walk up the path to the porch of our parish church. The path is laid with flagstones which are indented with a pattern of wavy rounded runnels such as you see on sand or estuarine mud flats. Each time I look at them I am reminded of my friend Gordon van Praagh who first showed me such stones, saying: 'Do you realize what you are looking at there? You are looking at the moment when the tide of the Wealden Lake went out *for the last time!*' The region north of us, the Weald, was once covered by a lake so vast it was subject to tidal influence. The sand of its beaches was corrugated with these patterns as the water withdrew and what is preserved in the stones of that path is the record of what happened over a period of a few hours in prehistory.

Everything he told me derived from the impact of the discovery and acceptance of geological time in the course of the last two centuries – the discovery that extended the memory of the Earth backwards by millions of years.

Up to this point I have been putting forward the theory of the Great Memory with examples drawn from human history and prehistory. In turning to the relationship of the scientific image of man and the Great Memory, we are forced to consider the Great Memory as relating to the past of humanity but also to the past of the Earth and of the universe. This brings me to the crux of my argument for this part of the book.

The crux is this:

For the past two hundred and fifty years we and our closer ancestors have been living through an ever-intensifying process of recovering knowledge and information about the past. The Great Memory has been giving us the impressions and psychic energy to make a new culture but we have been unable to assimilate the mass of material. The means employed for this giant act of recovery include art, religion and scholarship but it owes far more to science.

Memory provides the raw energy of inspiration and creative endeavour. To be converted into civilized arts and forms of knowledge its contents require assimilation, interpretation and conscious purpose. Science has not yet found its true purpose because it is still at the stage of the recovery of the past, of the Great Memory. Science will not discover its true purpose until it is guided and controlled by an image of humanity huge enough in its conception, simple enough in its message and attractive enough in conveying a sense of unity, to satisfy the aspirations and needs of humanity as a whole. Science and its applications have created the means whereby humanity can have an unprecedented awareness of the globe and its happenings but we, the beneficiaries of science, do not yet know how to use those means of communication.

One of the ways in which the Great Memory releases its hidden treasures is through our dream lives. Just as the pulsations of deep undersea waves are said to have an effect on climatic changes, so alterations in the Great Memory at unconscious levels may be bringing about changes in the climate of opinion. Another way in which it works or through which it brings up its gifts is more surprising but, I think, less contestable. It works through the applications of new technology, as can be seen by developing further some of the examples I gave in chapters 2 and 3, such as the technological introductions of the late eleventh and early twelfth centuries. The heavy plough was one of many technological advances during the Dark Ages that were to make western Europe by 1100 a wholly different society in terms of its command of machines beyond anything known in the classical world or before and probably, by that date, equalling China. The heavy plough released the energies contained in the deep alluvial soils of northwest Europe that light Roman ploughs had never been able to touch, thus providing the wealth from agricultural surpluses for the rebuilding of cities and the construction of the great cathedrals. The heavy plough also uncovered the Roman cities the barbarians had laid waste and the worm had buried, revealing sculptures, capitals and artefacts that inspired artists anew and unsealing the caches of Roman glass which, melted down, made the first stained-glass windows.

Another introduction, the stirrup, brought about the training of the heavy cavalry that, against all the odds, fought its way to the capture of Jerusalem and the success of the First Crusade – a venture that was to lead to the recovery of the works of Aristotle and the discoveries of earlier Arab philosophers and scientists.

Yet another crucial innovation was in the tools made possible by improvements in metallurgy. Among these were fine chisels, strong enough to take hammer blows without shattering or spoiling the stone. The monks of Canterbury in the 1180s were amazed to see William of Sens's workmen carving with chisels instead of axes.[7] It was the use of the chisel that helped to release the new range of emotional expression in the carvings from the Royal Portal of Chartres (1150) onwards that created the new Gothic image of man about which we spoke in the last chapter. Here again that image arose from the need to make new images of the past, new visual portrayals of Christ and his Apostles, of the characters of the Old Testament, and of the saints and doctors of the Church. The realistic portrayal of contemporary men and women only came after the creation of the new image of man through the reinterpretation of the past and then, initially, they had to be dead because that image was transferred in the first place to tomb sculpture. Only later does it come to be applied to the representation of the living.

As the technology of western Europe and North America has advanced in power, range and sophistication, so it has provided part of the means whereby, on a greater scale than ever before, the Great Memory has been releasing forgotten and undreamed-of knowledge about and from the past. The practical use of geological knowledge in the search for coal and minerals in the eighteenth century led to the establishment of geology as a branch of science. From geology came the first evidence that the world had been in existence far longer than the date of 4004 BC. The new geological timescale permitted the interpretation of the fossil record, leading in turn to the general acceptance of Darwin and Wallace's theory of evolution. The past of man and of the animal, vegetable and mineral worlds was reinterpreted wholly. Thus the old paradigm was destroyed and the way made open for new sciences such as palaeontology, archaeology, palaeobotany and astrophysics, all of which made new and revolutionary contributions to man's image of himself and of his origins, thus affecting cultural, social and political life, as in some of the instances already given. The search for fossil fuels was extended to oil and natural gas. The discovery of new elements led to the release and use of nuclear energy and also, through the technique of spectral analysis, to the study of the composition of the planets, our sun, the stars, the interstellar dust clouds and the galaxies. From this have come new ideas about the past of the universe to which I turn again in the next chapter.

Modern man finds the energy for his needs in fossil fuels. As a result of his search for fossil fuels, he has unleashed on a scale unknown before in recorded history what may be called by analogy the fossil fuels of the Great Memory, not only the buried, sedimented psychic energies of past art, thought and belief, but of all forms of life that have ever existed on this planet.

The rediscovery of the past through the methods and researches of scientists are only one part of the release of knowledge from the Great Memory into the common store of information available to educated men and women of most nations. Through the superior technology of the West, India was conquered, China was subjugated, and the Islamic countries were either made colonies or protectorates or client states. Through the efforts of missionaries, of learned judges such as Sir William Jones and scholars such as Max Müller, the religious scriptures and philosophical writings of the important eastern civilizations were made available to the West during the very period when science was weakening the hold of the Judaeo-Christian tradition on social and intellectual life. Conceptions of limitless time beyond the calculations of western scientists, of the universe constantly being destroyed and recreated, of matter as a dance of energies, echoing the theories of quantum physicists, are only some of the ancient ideas that were brought to the West and that are still slowly being assimilated.

From the standpoint of the hypothesis of the Great Memory, we and our immediate forebears have been living through an act of recollection of the past without parallel in recorded history. If, as the hypothesis states, emanations from the Great Memory precede or accompany most major changes in the life of large groups of humanity, then this act of recollection on the part of science and scholarship is of a scale both in extent and in potential release of energy that makes one tremble to contemplate. A possible corollary to the hypothesis is this: the further back in time the recollection from the Great Memory goes, the greater the effect it will have upon the future. Even now scientists are investigating the events that took place at the start of the Big Bang, events that occurred in divisions of time so small there is as yet no name for them. The parallel in our terms to finding the origin of creation would be to discover the sources of human creativity.

The third part of the hypothesis states that the energies released from the Great Memory bear fruit or become destructive according to the ideal or image of humanity guiding the society into which those energies enter. If we look at the scientific images of man, we find several strange creatures, none approaching in grandeur of spirit or imaginative conception the task of assimilation and direction that lies before us.

The images make a neat dualism, between the scientist as wizard, magus, healer, revealer of hidden knowledge and explorer of the future and the scientific image of man as a creature evolved from a branch of the primates, successful in the evolutionary sense owing to his ability to master his environment, but whose thoughts, drives and emotions are the effect of his body chemistry. The dualism is therefore between a man of will and a man incapable of will.

The first is the archetype of the wise old man, the Uranus figure whom the popular imagination found embodied in Einstein. The popular imagination also sees another aspect to this figure, the loopy professor, the Dr Who, the dotty savant who is, in general, on the side of the good. His dark shadow is the wicked but brilliant scientist, Dr Moreau in fiction and Dr Mengele in all too real life. A subspecies of the 'good' aspect of this type is an image of themselves popular among many scientists who see the advance of their various subjects as the natural consequences of their education, of their provision with the right equipment and with a sufficiency of research assistants, and of the esteem of society. Encapsulated against ideas from outside their disciplines, they are distrustful of intuition, inspiration and the other means by which great creative impulses come. Another figure in the popular imagination is a younger version of the wizard scientist such as the hero of *Raiders of the Lost Ark* or the hero such as Superman who is the child of another planet and who is an athlete of science. The knowledge of how to apply the principles of physics is built into his muscles as he leaps over skyscrapers, repels bullets, and flies through the air. With his extraterrestrial origins, his ability to fly, and his concern to help humanity, Superman is an angel in disguise. Jerry Siegel, who invented him as a hero for comic books, originally thought of him as one of the bald mad scientists characterized by the first part of our dualism.[8]

The second side of this dualism is man as beast. All over the world biologists of blameless life have for years taught this view of early man as a brutal cave dweller, as an animal without intellectual curiosity, morals or aesthetic sense – all without taking into consideration the evidence from remains and excavations for belief in an afterlife, the existence of forms of social life which would have required rules, rituals and emotional conformity, and the ability to devise and respond to symbols as a means of communication.

If we look at the two aspects of the scientific image of man, we find that one, the magus scientist, is all head and the other, the caveman, is all loins. We also find that both are predominantly masculine. There is no heart, no emotion, no place for the feminine, except for the first as a helper or secretary and for the second as another body to be clubbed and violated. As images of true human beings they are both lacking and unbalanced.

This attitude to the feminine is not only a presupposition of nineteenth century and modern science. It is embedded in the metaphors of many of the founders of the scientific age – as Mary Midgley points out.

The literature of early modern science is a mine of highly-coloured passages that describe Nature, by no means as a neutral object, but as a seductive but troublesome female, to be unrelentingly pursued, sought out, fought against, closed into her inmost sanctuaries, prevented from escaping, persistently courted, wooed, harried, vexed, tormented, unveiled, unrobed and 'put to the question' (i.e., interrogated under torture), forced to confess 'all that lay in her most intimate recesses', her 'beautiful bosom' must be laid bare, she must be held down and finally 'penetrated', 'pierced', and 'vanquished'.[9]

Francis Bacon is one of the prime sources for this imagery. He said that men ought to make peace among themselves so as to turn 'with united forces against the Nature of Things, to storm and occupy her castles and strongholds'. By these means scientists would bring about the 'truly masculine birth of time' by which they would subdue 'Nature with all her children, to bind her to your service and make her your slave'.[10]

In one of the first works of science fiction, *Frankenstein*, Mary Shelley describes how, having created a monster who is the shadow or the projection of all the darknesses in his own nature, Victor Frankenstein breaks his word to the monster who brings about the final tragedy. The monster has begged Frankenstein to create his female counterpart, to console his loneliness and redeem his violent nature: Frankenstein started on this work and then, overcome with revulsion, destroyed the female he began to create. When Frankenstein marries his adopted sister, the monster murders her on the bridal night. Scientist and monster end pursuing one another through the frozen north. The extraordinary popularity of this story, including the making of over twenty films based on it, points to invidious truths about the course science has taken in the general mind.[11]

Just as the scientific images of man have had their influence on the dominant political philosophies of Fascism, Nazism, and communism, so we find that what science lacks – a civilized expression of the feminine – is also lacking to a great extent in these philosophies. In Fascism and Nazism there were ideals of womanhood but chiefly as breeders of warriors and as the mothers and mates of heroes – and these ideals, under a guise of equality, are what largely applied in countries under communist rule. The qualities of the Eternal Feminine, calm, mercy, stillness of the soul and compassionate wisdom, could have no place in such philosophies which would have seen them simply as weaknesses.

The view of man as brute or animal is one of the consequences of reductionism, a mental attitude necessary in science for establishing the causes of phenomena on the physical or material level. What has been a necessary discipline in logic for the successful interpretation of experimental work has turned into a dogma expressing the belief that causality is entirely material and that the understanding of matter is the only object of truth. The extent to which it is dogma was recently revealed to me at a conference on reductionism at which speaker after speaker, each wearing the comfortable smile of the saved, began their contributions with affirmations of their atheism and their complete trust in mechanistic explanations. The conference had its meetings beneath the carvings of Green Men on the beams of a medieval room in Cambridge where in the fifteenth century theologians would also have begun their disputes with assertions of their orthodoxy.

Just as those theologians would have been guided not a little by fear of persecution and of exclusion from their group, had they not asserted their orthodoxy, so, I felt, I was in the presence of similar barely masked fears, fears which also have a dominant effect in current scientific philosophies such as the fear of teleology, or the ascription of purposes to natural processes, or the fear of anthropomorphism in the biological sciences. What the fear of anthropomorphism has led to in descriptions of animal behaviour is a proscription of all reference to higher human positive emotions as analogies for how animals feel or behave: the proscription does not apply to analogies drawn from human aggression or negative behaviour. The robin sings to assert his territorial dominance, not because he enjoys singing; the lark carols high in the air to distract attention away from her nest, not because she is possessed of a talent supremely to be manifested; the starlings, mustering for balletic displays in October, perform their dances in the air, either because they feel safer in groups or to train for emigration, but not because of delight in a shared artistic creation. Thus purpose is allowed, but only in relation to aggression or fear; and anthropomorphism is allowed, but only when it is a matter of survival.

This limited anthropomorphism has been reflected back on the nature of human beings themselves – particularly in relation to the teaching of human reproduction in schools until recent years. The biologists, trained to look for resemblances between human and animal behaviour, started from the copulation of animals, generally leaving out the courtship rituals and behaviour that differ so much between species, and led from that to the mechanics of human mating. The stress was on male dominance.

How much current and nationalist preoccupations affected conceptions of human life in prehistory may be seen from studying figures 15 and 16. The first shows the English conception of Stone Age life as reproduced in a Nuffield biology text for schoolchildren in 1966. In the Japanese translation of this same text the editors substituted figure 16 as being quite clearly much closer to the truth. Instead of the incompetent hunters as Swanscombe Man was depicted, the Japanese editors insisted on early human beings with Japanese facial characteristics.

The popular images of our remote ancestors as barbaric in nature, although often unscientific in fact, have been used to reinforce the neo-Darwinian gradualist theory of evolution with its denial of consciousness and its gross and distorting effect upon political philosophy, politics and the wars of the twentieth century. Instead of the grandeur and beauty of man and woman in the primeval state as presented in most founding myths, we have repeatedly been told that we are in our ancestry and in our essential natures unredeemed barbarians. It is a secular form of original sin, without the hope of redemption. But if there was no golden past, there would certainly be a golden future, a myth promulgated by influential scientists deeply attached to Marxism such as J. D. Bernal and J. B. S. Haldane. Bernal foresaw a possible future when people would lead 'an idyllic Melanesian existence of eating, drinking, friendliness, love-making, dancing and singing'.[12] They would be ruled by scientists who would have found 'the means of directing the masses in harmless occupations and of maintaining a perfect docility under the appearance of perfect freedom'.[13] The scientists would then start to mechanize their bodies to secure immortality for themselves and would explore space. They would become completely aetherialized into an immortal multiple individual 'becoming masses of atoms in space communicating by radiation, and ultimately perhaps resolving itself entirely into light'.[14] '. . . From one point of view the scientists would emerge as a new species and leave humanity behind; from another, humanity – the humanity that counts – might seem to change *en bloc*, leaving behind in a relatively primitive state those too stupid or too stubborn to change.'[15] If there is a reaction against these plans he says that the old mechanism of extinction will come into play and that the better organized beings will be obliged in self-defence to reduce the numbers of the others, until they represent no inconvenience. Bernal was, in fact, proposing rule by a future politburo of scientists who would use the methods of Stalin that he and thousands of other Marxists in the West condoned in the belief they were necessary for the greater good of humanity – namely methods of control through terror and extermination. 'In a Soviet state . . . the scientific institutions would in fact gradually become the government, and a further stage of the Marxian hierarchy of domination would be reached.'[16] Somewhat similar futures have been foreseen by other prominent scientists such as the physicist Freeman Dyson.

In the passages from Bernal, who, it must be stressed, had a wide influence on the general culture of scientists and on intellectual life over a period of thirty years, we find quite clearly – if unconsciously on his part – the dualistic images of man: the wizard scientist who can create his own immortality through physical means and the descendants of the primeval brutes who will be forced to accept the happiness designed for them or be extinguished.

What has helped to preserve the worth of woman and the ideal of the Eternal Feminine from these cruel masculine imaginings and the criminal dictators that have made use of them for their purposes of conquest and domination? First, it is the stubborn, patient and nonetheless glorious determination of people to get on with their lives and to conserve their private thoughts and visions while agreeing outwardly with whatever political philosophy is in power – and half or more of any society is likely to consist of women. We get glimpses of those stubborn thoughts from the Second World War: in Russia Stalin had to appeal to the ancient image of Holy Mother Russia, not to the achievements of communism, to rouse the patriotism necessary to drive back the Nazi invaders. In Great Britain, early in the course of the war, investigations were conducted by Mass Observation to find out what people really thought they were fighting for.[17] It turned out not to be King and Country or the British Empire or the defeat of an evil enemy: it was an ideal rural England centred on the image of a village of cottages round a parish church, cottages where lived mothers, sweethearts and wives awaiting a happy return and a contented life that would end quietly in the maternal earth of the village churchyard. This is all the more extraordinary if we consider that most of the servicemen and women would have come from urban backgrounds, but it was an image given the widest circulation in popular culture of the 1930s and 1940s in films and popular songs, through radio programmes and the symbols and graphics of advertising as well as in the art of the painters and sculptors now known as the Neo-Romantics.[18]

In other ways the ideal of the Eternal Feminine has been preserved through the poetic imagination – a theme I return to in the next chapter. One of the greatest advocates of humane directions that science could take other than the ones scientists have in the main followed was Goethe. He was also responsible in the ending of *Faust Part II* for one of the most memorable celebrations of the ideal ever uttered. Faust, under the guidance of Mephistopheles, who exhibits all the limitations of thought and feeling characterized by living entirely on the horizontal line of time, is saved at the last by the intervention of Gretchen, whom Faust betrayed and abandoned, and by the mercy of the Virgin Mary. The final chorus sings:

Alles Vergängliche
Ist nur ein Gleichnis;
Das Unzulängliche
Hier wirds Ereignis;
Das Unbeschreibliche,
Hier ists getan;
Das Ewigweibliche
Zieht uns hinan.[19]

All that is passing
Is but a parable;
Here is accomplished

What was unreachable;
Here is achieved
What is ineffable;
The Eternal Feminine;
Draws us above.

In a London production in 1988 this last scene was performed by all the actors entering in darkness, holding candles that illuminated only their faces. They all spoke together the final chorus which had, as a deliberate reinterpretation, these last two lines:

Woman in all of us
Shows us our way.[20]

6

Freedom and creativity

When the old cathedral of St Paul's was left a dangerous ruin after the Great Fire of London in 1666, Sir Christopher Wren was commissioned to build a completely new cathedral in the current Baroque style. After many discussions and the construction of several models it was decided that the new building should follow the pattern of the cross set by its Romanesque and Gothic predecessor and, in effect, be based upon the form of a man. When on a June day in 1675 Wren and his master mason stood among the debris of the burnt fabric – so he later told his son – having decided the exact place over which the centre of the dome was designed to rise, they ordered a workman to bring a stone from the rubble in order to mark the spot. The workman chose a stone at random. It had come from a tomb and when they looked at it they read the one word *Resurgam* – I will rise again.[1]

It was a chance affirmation of the symbolism that was inherent in the design he had already made for the dome: that the dome should rise from eight massive piers – eight being the number of resurrection because Christ rose again on the eighth day of Holy Week. It also symbolized here not only the rebirth of the cathedral but also the return of the Golden Age which poets and natural philosophers among Wren's contemporaries saw as the significance of their time (figure 17).

Above that stone incised with the promise of the resurrection arose the famous dome which in its internal and external dispositions is one of the most remarkable statements about the nature of man of its period – the creation of an architect who was also a mathematician, scientist and a founding member and president of the Royal Society, the establishment of which more than any other event marks the arrival of the Scientific Age. It was a time when in literature, philosophy and portraiture much new thought was given to the nature and purpose of man, to character, personality and right behaviour, through the early novel and the renascent drama and in the deliberations of scientists and thinkers. Through these varied means there arose the ideal of the man of reason or, in France, *l'honnête homme*, a man who is chiefly judged by his consistency in living and expressing himself in a humane and reasonable manner. This consistency is analysed keenly by La Rochefoucauld in his *Maximes* and is tested, generally by shrewd and witty women, in the comedies of Molière. The man of reason was also a man of religion and the accord between his right behaviour and his mystical longings finds its patterns in authors such as Bishop Jeremy Taylor for English and Irish Protestants and Archbishop Fénélon for French Catholics. The influence of Jacob Boehme in founding faith on direct mystical experience was also strong, as were the continuing influences of Rosicrucian and alchemical writings with their themes of the perfection of man. The ideal had its feminine counterpart in the lively, educated and emancipated women known as the *précieuses*. Where we find so many of these qualities brought together in a single artistic unity is in the dome of St Paul's. If we stand at the union of the nave with the crossing and look up, we find gifts from the Great Memory – the proportions and ornament of Hellenistic and Roman imperial architecture – transformed into a fresh vision of the nature of man as a rational being, the complexities of his thought, the reticulations of the images through which his higher emotions are expressed, the canon by which his body is formed, rising up to the cosmic symbol of the dome, the universe of which he is part.

In the later eighteenth century four statues celebrating ideals of human achievement were set in the recesses formed by the arches linking the cardinal openings of the crossing. They are Sir Joshua Reynolds for art, Dr Johnson for literature, John Howard, the prison reformer, for humanitarianism, and Sir William Jones for scholarship and the law. The first two we could expect to find there: they were acknowledged as pre-eminent in their fields in their time. The other two bespeak a wider and greater influence on the future: the presence of John Howard indicates the appearance of a new ideal of practical Christianity and of humanitarianism which was to influence scientists and social reformers and the general climate of opinion. The presence of Sir William Jones (1746–94) is possibly of even deeper significance. A brilliant lawyer and scholar, he was barred from advancement in England because of his outspoken support of the American colonists in the War of Independence. He was appointed a judge in Calcutta, where he studied Indian languages and learned Sanskrit. He broke down the mistrust that many Brahmins had of European enquirers into their sacred writings and early texts and he was one of the first scholars to bring to an eastern literature the skills of textual analysis that had been developed from the study of Greek and Latin classics. Among his translations were the Laws of Manu, the legal system of the ancient

Hindus, and the *Shakuntala* of Kalidasa, greatest of Sanskrit dramatists. Goethe knew and profited by his translations and his work inspired the new generation of scholars in England, France, Germany and the United States who explored the common roots of the Indo-European languages, a discovery first made plain by William Jones.[2] Thus he helped to initiate one of the most important effects of all the gifts of the Great Memory we have so far considered – the hitherto unrealized cultural ancestry that linked the Vedic, Greek and Celtic civilizations.

The combined effect of western ideas and technology with the respect and interest shown in Indian culture by scholarly administrators such as Jones and Charles Wilkins, who translated the *Bhagavad-Gita* into English in 1783, was to awaken the interest of young Bengalis in their heritage. Most notable among these was Rammohun Roy (c. 1772–1833), who believed that reason as expressed in the Upanishads was the foundation of Hindu religion and that where outside and western ideas were consistent with the spirit of reason they should be welcomed and introduced. A scholar, religious and political reformer, translator into English of the Upanishads, feminist and publisher, he was the founder of the Brahma Samaj, the first of the Indian religious and reforming societies that nourished the new intelligentsia of India who were eventually to win independence for their country.[3]

Jones's statue (by John Bacon the Elder) shows him holding the Laws of Manu with one hand while his other hand rests on the plan for the Asiatic Society which, with Warren Hastings, he helped to found. On the plinth of the statue is a carving in high relief showing a half-naked angel with a torch and a bearded philosopher with a lamp. Youth and age, divine knowledge and human reason, share the task of unveiling a disc on which is portrayed India or, rather, the wisdom of India – as a beautiful young woman with her right breast bared. Her right arm enfolds a statue of the Hindu trinity and her left arm supports a representation of Vishnu saving the gods by providing them with the *amrita*, the elixir of immortality. He makes the gods and the demons come together in order to churn the ocean so that it gives up a series of gifts that are essential to civilization. These include his bride Lakshmi, the goddess of beauty, love and prosperity, as well as the elixir. Vishnu is present in the scene seated on top of a mountain which he has provided as the churning stick. The demons and gods rotate the mountain by pulling at each end of a great snake wrapped round this extraordinary churning stick. The demons pull from the snake's head and the gods from its tail. The mountain needs a base on which to rotate and Vishnu provides this by placing himself in his incarnation as a turtle in the ocean underneath the mountain. His name as this incarnation, 'courma avatar', is inscribed on the side of the disc in the carving.

In this male pantheon the portrayal of the wisdom of India is the only female presence – yet she looks out on the fundamental female symbol of the circle from which the dome rises, the heart of the cathedral and the centre from which the feelings of the spectator are expanded to the universal.

The wisdom of India is here a prophetic image: she foretells the influence that eastern philosophies and art will have in their contribution to a universal culture. The struggles and the interchanges between England and India have been like the churning of the ocean of history in order to bring forth from the past the elixir of immortality contained in the Upanishads and the *Bhagavad-Gita*.

The choice of those four men and the modes of knowledge and achievement they represent point to a unity of culture that was still accepted and understood. The period when their statues were erected was possibly the last time in which an educated person could expect to have a grasp of what was happening in the arts and sciences equally. Not only poets and intellectuals such as Coleridge but much of fashionable London would attend Humphry Davy's lectures at the Royal Institution. Goethe is the supreme example from this time of a man to whom no branch of knowledge was shut – but one has only to pick up volumes of the *Gentleman's Magazine* or comparable publications in France and Germany from the early nineteenth century to see what the landed and middle classes were interested in and to be ashamed by the contrast in the meanness of thought and the narrow scope of our present intellectual journals and papers.

On the other hand, why are we not more barbaric than we are? Why have the political economists, the technocrats and the wizard scientists so far failed to eliminate the cultivation of the higher emotions entirely? To put it another way, what has preserved the ideal of the Eternal Feminine and the wisdom of the 'woman in all of us'?

I suggest that it has been kept alive by the spirit of humanitarianism as exemplified by John Howard, by the greatness of our inherited traditions, by the opening-up of the western mind to the mystical traditions, religions and myths of other cultures, by music, and by the poetic imagination which is fundamental to the appreciation and experience of our regard for others and our capacity to be influenced by myth and music. The poetic imagination has always had a special connection with cosmology and the comprehension of worlds and it is also concerned with the inward life of things and creatures. Speaking of poetry as a process more general and primary than the art of writing verses, the philosopher Jacques Maritain called it 'that intercommunion between the inner being of things and the inner being of the human Self which is a kind of divination . . .'[4] The poetic imagination is the power of imaginative sympathy with which we enter into the lives of our fellow human beings, of animals, plants and the works of nature. It is that world we live in when we rejoice in the sight of birds feeding their young and are touched by the beauty of autumnal cherry leaves. It is by definition the 'making' imagination as the original meaning of poetry is a 'making'. It subsumes the creative imagination because it makes the atmosphere and the unity within which the creative imagination works. It is the conscious zest for life and the experience of wonder. It is what Shakespeare expresses through the mouth of Proteus:

> For Orpheus' lute was strung with poets' sinews,
> Whose golden touch could soften steel and stones,
> Make tigers tame, and huge leviathans
> Forsake unsounded deeps to dance on sands.[5]

None of us lives in the world we are taught we live in: the Gradgrind universe of facts and vacuities. We may often exist in that universe but we do not live there. We live in our imaginations, because, as Blake said, imagination is the human existence itself.

Our imaginations may construct for us worlds that are tiny and circumscribed nests but they are still worlds for us as experiencers. Most of us have to construct universes because our children ask us immense questions about the origins of things; most of us have some private way of explaining to ourselves our existence in a world in which the grass grows and the child dies. Going by the evidence of many surveys of religious experience and belief, it is probable that most people believe that there are worlds beyond or including this world of our physical existence, states of existence or future lives to which we go and the quality of which is determined by how we live our lives in this world. In doing so we imagine worlds that are objectively moral.

Our conceptions of this world and other worlds grow out of our need to find order, reason, sense and unity in our existence. A universe is by definition a unity and a cosmos is etymologically an adorned or ordered universe. It is one of the characteristics of the poetic imagination that it sees the particular within whole contexts: it creates worlds of emotion and intuition that always imply meaningful universes. In this it differs from the scientific imagination, which tends to fragment or to build its wholes from fragments, whether of particles or of pieces of knowledge. The astrophysicist has to follow strict procedures in guiding his imaginative conceptions; so does the poet, but the poet can be taken up to unity when he expresses the universe in the wholeness of an image: as a white rose, in the case of Dante; as a musical octave in the form of a golden chain, in the case of Milton; or as a universal divine human being which is also the imagination of Jesus, as in the case of William Blake.

Once the astronomer and the poet were one and the same; once, perhaps, all our ancestors were poets, naturalists and astronomers because language was uttered only as rhythmic poetry and song and the act of naming, of binding discovery to oneself, was an inspired and creative act that changed and enlarged perception. The beast, the plant, the constellation, could not be wholly perceived until the essence of their being was spoken as a word through the mouth of the poet or shaman and that word or name was linked to the greater wholes of the dream life and the mythic background of their people. Cosmologies were created by the inspired poets, by the bards of the Rig-Veda, the authors of the *Epic of Gilgamesh*, by Homer and Hesiod, by the Quiché Mayan poets of the *Popol Vuh*, the Norse skalds of the *Elder Edda*, and by Moses. You cannot create, each of these would have said, unless you are one with the source of creation.

Is the poetic imagination as a means of expressing a satisfying and complete world picture utterly effete? John Milton could be considered the last poet in the western world to have created a widely influential world picture that absorbed and surpassed the scientific knowledge of his day. There is a great and wonderful world picture implicit in the works of Goethe but he is often considered antiscientific, for all his stress on the experimental nature of his studies. The professional scientists would seem to have taken away all our rights of speculation and imagination and we have to await each barely comprehensible statement from them with our own powers of judgment suspended. This is, culturally speaking, our own fault.

There is, nevertheless, a huge hunger to know about the nature of the cosmos. We intuitively feel that the inner exploration of our natures is linked to the exploration of our planet, our solar system and the wider universe, that there is an identity between our highest selves and the mystery of the intelligence in creation. We have the science and technology we deserve in the sense that what we hunger for and desire determines the climate of opinion in which our scientists and technologists work. Their aspirations and their sense of humanity which decide how they interpret their researches are as dependent on the moods and factions of their wider audience beyond their own community as are those of artists and writers. The current sense of disappointment with science may lead both to a more objective view of what the purpose of science may be, beyond the framework of thought and experiment directed at creating golden futures for us all, and to an awakening of our own responsibility for what we have asked scientists, the chemical industry, the weapons industry and all the other forms of manufacture dependent on science to do on our behalf.

We possess in our endowment of the poetic imagination a means of judging and evaluating the cosmological theories now current because all cosmologies are based on metaphor. We may not understand the mathematics that guide our astrophysicists on their mental journeys but we can grasp and judge the quality of the metaphors and images in which they express their ideas. Past cosmological systems can be seen very clearly at times as projections on to the heavens of social, political and religious preoccupations among the societies that developed these systems. We should be detached enough now to be able to do the same to current twentieth-century ideas.

The belief among the Mayan and Aztec nations that the Sun had to do battle with the forces of darkness every night in order to rise again is indicative of their warlike society. The image expressed in the Rig-Veda of the universe first appearing as a giant tree out of the trunk of which emerged the gods is one proper to a society living close to forests and among people devoted to tree worship. Much of Egyptian cosmology was related to the rise and fall of the Nile. The whole order of the Chinese Empire was seen as a reflection of the Heaven of the Jade Emperor and the Immortals. The philosophers and cosmologists of the Greeks found in the universe the powers of the mind they had so recently discovered in themselves. The Arab and Christian scholastic philosophers who preserved and recreated the philosophies inherited from Greece and Rome similarly saw in the perfection of the spheres of heaven the perfection of the divine mind so that, as in the example already given from Dante, they thought that the spheres of the planets, the fixed stars and the Primum Mobile were kept in motion solely as an effect of the contemplations of the angels responsible for each sphere.[6]

When Copernicus made his suggestion that the Sun was at the centre of the universe, not the Earth, he was directed as much by the tradition of the centrality of the Sun as an image of supreme consciousness and spiritual light in Christian Neo-Platonic mysticism as by his calculations. Kepler, in the long searches that led him to the discovery of the laws of planetary motion and of the elliptical paths of the planets, was also guided by Neo-Platonic thought and the magical philosophy of the Renaissance.

The tendency from the seventeenth century onwards was to devise cosmologies that were self-consistent, that required no further management once the Creator had set them in motion, that were, in fact, perfect machines that worked according to the principles of the machines or technological inventions that were most advanced in their particular day and therefore provided the most vivid metaphors for the explanation of their workings. Often these mechanical metaphors have social and political implications as well, as the following instances in historical sequence show.

The calm regularity of Sir Isaac Newton's solar system with its checks, balances and pendulums reflects the skills of contemporary clockmakers such as Thomas Tompion and James Knibb. Many of its principal features were demonstrated in the astronomical toys known as orreries (after the Earl of Cork and Orrery who popularized them), worked by turning a handle engaging a series of gears which made the planets circulate according to their relative motions about the Sun. The grandeur of Newton's conception was all the more welcomed since Newton became a pillar of the Whig establishment which had brought about the Glorious Revolution. The British Constitution, the creation of that establishment, could be seen as the most perfect form of government because, with its system of checks and balances, it was the one that most nearly reflected the order of the government of the heavens.

Later in the eighteenth century the convulsions of revolution and of the Romantic movement are reflected in the more dynamic Kant–Laplace model of the universe, which had to take into account not only the discovery of new planets such as Uranus but also an awareness of the multiplicity of galaxies. Laplace believed that astronomical and scientific knowledge was on the verge of becoming so complete that all future events could be predicted with utter certainty: as one of the many scientists flourishing under the patronage of the Emperor Napoleon, he was asserting a dominion over the universe as complete as his imperial master destined for the world.

With the rise of the Industrial Revolution the dominant metaphor changed to that of the steam engine and a concentration on the nature of energy, so that the universe came to be regarded as a giant machine running on a vast, calculable but ultimately finite amount of energy, the using-up of which would lead, according to the second law of thermodynamics, to the heat death of the universe. Conservation as a scientific principle was not unallied to conservatism as a political doctrine. The chief authors of these theories, Rudolf Clausius and Hermann von Helmholtz, were both upholders of the Prussian state and their chief publicist in English-speaking countries, William Thomson, Lord Kelvin, received his peerage because of his contribution to Conservative politics.

The metaphors change again with the discovery of radioactivity and investigations into the nature of the atom and, also, Edwin Hubble's discovery of the expansion of the universe in 1929. Stealing their metaphors from cell biology, namely the fusion and fission of cells, physicists applied what they learned of the behaviour of radioactive forces on Earth to the generation of heat in the Sun and other stars. Using the new technology of radio communications, astronomers such as Karl Jansky took the study of the universe far beyond the limits of sight to create a picture of the cosmos that consisted of a series of transmitters and receivers – like the great cities of the Earth that were now in immediate communication with one another. These transmitters and receivers were travelling constantly away from one another, a process described in another metaphor that reflected the contemporary increase in rapidity of travel and communication on Earth – expansion.

Hubble's discovery was to lead to a further metaphor – that of an explosion: the Big Bang. This theory has held sway after the experience of the dropping of the first atom bombs on Japan, over the following decades when the world has lived under the fear of nuclear holocaust and of big bangs on Earth.

The picture given by most of these metaphors is of a frightening immensity, of galaxies rushing away from one another 'like ghosts from an enchanter fleeing', of lifeless and unregenerating cosmic flames that are destined only to extinction, or the hopelessness of the desert and the despair of emptiness. It is wholly at variance with our experience when we sit out on the grass on a moonless and cloudless night and gaze at the arch of the Milky Way, searching for planets in the ascendant and letting the forms of beloved constellations reveal themselves in the wealth of luminaries. We sink back into a happy sense of our own nothingness before the beauty and certainty of the stars. Yet, though we may feel our nothingness, there is about us an aspect of immensity: all those stars and all the invisible worlds beyond them are necessary for us to have come into existence.

Such a thought has helped to bring a fresh image into astronomical and scientific considerations. It is called the anthropic cosmological principle, 'anthropic' coming from the Greek word for man in his wholeness as opposed to *andros*, man as a physical being.

This idea is the direct result of the return to the origin of things by physicists investigating the Big Bang. It has arisen from calculations made on the basis of the boundary conditions necessary for the appearance of life in the universe. These are so narrow, so limited, that on grounds of probability life is a very unusual event to have happened. The implications of this theory have led some thinkers to suggest that the universe is self-aware, that its awareness of itself is written into the laws of nature, that the reality of the universe is tied to us and depends on us as observers, and that the appearance of conscious life points to a guiding intelligence in the universe.

Naturally such a revolutionary idea has been much contested by some. One of the objections to it is that it is not necessary in the sense that physics can get on happily without it. I am not so much concerned with whether the anthropic principle is ultimately true as in the current timing of its appearance in scientific thought and expression.

The anthropic principle can be regarded as an exceptional gift from the Great Memory because it depends on a return to the beginning of all there is to be remembered.

The importance of the appearance of this idea can be estimated by comparing it with the quality of the images used to illustrate cosmological theories from the later seventeenth century onwards, from the clockwork solar system to the nuclear explosion. This is the first time that an image depending on consciousness and will has entered into scientific cosmological discussion since the banishment of the angels from the heavens – apart from the conceptions of the World Soul expressed by German Romantic philosophers and scientists such as F. W. J. Schelling and Lorenz Oken.

There are four current statements of the principle. The first, the weak anthropic principle, states that the values of physical and cosmological qualities are restricted by the requirements for the evolution of carbon-based life forms and for the universe to be old enough for this evolution to have happened. The second, the strong anthropic principle, carries this further by saying that the universe must possess the properties that allow the development of life in the course of its history. The third, the participatory anthropic principle, says that observers are necessary to bring the world into being. The fourth, the final anthropic principle, says that information-processing intelligence must appear in the universe and that, once in existence, it will never die out.[7]

At first sight it is the last statement that is most surprising, the thought so contrary to the doom-laden thoughts of nineteenth-century cosmologists, that life is inextinguishable and will come to dominate the universe. The authors of the final anthropic principle, John Barrow and Frank Tipler, show themselves to be in the tradition of Bernal and Freeman Dyson: the expansion of life will come about through space travel. It is, however, the participatory anthropic principle – that observers are necessary to bring the world into being – that takes the principle far away from reductionist science into philosophy and religion. Thus the scientist Paul Davies has recently said of the fact that the universe has generated self-awareness through conscious beings: 'This can be no trivial detail, no minor byproduct of mindless, purposeless forces. We are truly meant to be here.'[8]

These ideas also bring to mind the ancient belief in many traditions of a Universal Man or Woman out of whom the rest of the creation is made. For example, in the Rig-Veda 'The Hymn of Man' tells the story of how the gods create the world by making the cosmic man, Purusha, the victim in a sacrifice by dismembering him. This man has a thousand heads, a thousand eyes, a thousand feet. In him is contained everything in the past and in the future. He is the ruler of immortality. From his body were made all the beasts, the chants and forms of verse, domestic animals, the four castes and much more:

The moon was born from his mind; from his eye the sun was born. Indra and Agni came from his mouth, and from his vital breath the Wind was born.

From his navel the middle realm of space arose; from his head the sky evolved. From his two feet came the earth, and the quarters of the sky from his ear . . .[9]

The dismemberment of Purusha to make the world has many parallels in other mythologies, including the story of the Norse giant Ymir and the tearing-apart of the primal goddess Coatlicue in Aztec legend. In the first description of the creation of man and woman, as the archetypes of humanity, in Genesis it is said: 'So God created man in his own image, in the image of God created he him; male and female created he them.'[10] From this passage was derived the kabbalistic idea of Adam Kadmon, the universal human being who contains, as does Purusha, the nature of all other living creatures within his limbs, body and form. Implicit in this idea is another conception of evolution: that the various forms of life as they have appeared on Earth in the course of time are a revelation of different aspects of the universal principle of humanity, rather than the effects of random mutations that are successful or not according to how the species adapt to their environments. The same archetype is expressed in another way, that of sound, as in the opening of St John's Gospel where the Logos, the universal Word of creation, is incarnate as man. It is to be found also in the Norse legend of the origins of poetry which is made by the dwarves from the blood of the perfect man Kvaesar.

The thought of man and creation arising out of sound brings back the theme of the Great Memory. We have been looking at the imagery of various cosmologies. What of the imagery associated with memory? In English and in French we call memories back – *nous nous rappelons nos souvenirs* – as though they were biddable creatures. Memory is also associated with the Earth and with spatial conceptions. The Titaness Mnemosyne is an earth goddess and we habitually speak of buried memories and of their waking up, again as though they were creatures capable of resurrection. Memory is also associated with the seal or the matrix, the impression made by a life upon history and conversely the impressions left by experience upon the individual soul. Many of these associations come together in the association of memory with space in Indian cosmology: space, or *akasha*, marks the beginning of all created things, the space that is necessary for the creatures of time to exist within. *Akasha* is also the level of the universal memory, which contains the objective narrative of all that has ever happened. It is what pours forth from the mouth of the Face of Glory. In terms of human experience *akasha* is associated with the human sense of hearing and therefore communication by sound.

Out of the flat vellum pages of a manuscript long untouched in a monastery library, the musicologist recreates the score of chants and antiphons that have not been sung for seven hundred years. The music is performed again and the words of the music turn out to be full of the concept of *viriditas*, greenness. Thus the recently discovered music and poetry of the Abbess Hildegard of Bingen have been restored and given to audiences millions greater in number than could have heard it in her lifetime – and received with all the more enjoyment and understanding because her message of celebration of the divine spirit alive in the works of nature is one that is received with the deepest sympathy by a generation waking up to its divorce from nature.

It has been by studying the background radiation of the universe, the residual ripples of the primal explosion of the Big Bang, that astrophysicists have been led to trace the events of the first moments of the creation of our universe. It is through the studying of the signals sent across the immense spaces of the universe that the theory of the Big Bang arose in the first place and it is from that theory that, in turn, the theory of the anthropic principle has emerged.

It has also grown out of another metaphor used in modern cosmology, the spatial metaphor of expansion. Earlier I related the theory of the expansion of the universe to the expansion of travel and communications in the early twentieth century, but 'expansion' is a word rich in meanings. It is associated with conquest and therefore with the pride of man in his domination of nature but it also has the grander and yet humbler associations of the expansion of the mind and the spirit and, above all, the expansion of consciousness.

If I am right in my thesis of the role played by the Great Memory in providing the stimulus and the psychic energy for the appearance of the new and for the introduction of new civilizations, then we require a concept of our own humanity that takes into account the potential of our capacity for consciousness and creativity in order to direct and use what the Great Memory is giving us. Such a concept cannot be realized through science alone: it needs, as the Russian philosopher P. D. Ouspensky said in 1912, the convergence of the four major modes of human cognition; science and philosophy, art and religion.

He wrote of science and philosophy as the organized forms of intellectual knowledge and of religion and art as the organized forms of emotional knowledge, and he said that all four really begin to serve true knowledge only when they begin to serve intuition – 'the sensing and finding of some inner qualities in things'. He went on to assert that the aim of even purely intellectual scientific and philosophical systems is not only to provide certain information but 'to raise man to a height of thought and feeling where he himself can pass to the new and higher forms of knowledge, to which art and religion are closest'.[11]

What we have been given from the past and from the study of the natural world is still largely at the level of information. One of the features of the creative experience, as we shall see in the next part of the book, is the way in which information can be assimilated and transformed by the awakening effect of consciousness on experience and memory. Therefore to pass beyond the transmission and receiving of information is one of the great needs of our time just as we have to pass beyond the dual scientific images of man as wizard-scientist and as primate beast.

The idea of the anthropic principle is a thought that may not be unthought even though the theory of the Big Bang from which it arose may itself be displaced. The anthropic principle may, though it arose from the investigation of the remote past, find its fulfilment in the understanding of the present moment and of the nature of consciousness that is coming to us through quantum physics and its gradual approach to the thought that consciousness and the physical world are complementary aspects of reality.

It is not the only indication that science is turning to images of humanity so as to comprehend levels of organization in nature. Even if he was employing the phrase in a general or metaphorical way, Stephen Hawking has brought back into popular scientific discourse the idea of the mind of God. The feminine image has returned in the conception of Gaia, the name of the Greek goddess of Earth, now given to the self-regulating organism of the biosphere. It is an image that has caught the imagination of a world that needs to comprehend itself. Whenever the goddess image has returned in the past, then the Green Man or the Face of Glory has also returned – and this, as we have already seen, has happened.

Those are not in themselves the new images of humanity implicitly needed by the line of argument I have been developing. They are signs of the recurrent power of the poetic imagination still at work in our society today. They have come to help, not to rule. What will as much drive us towards new understanding and new ways of living together in the light of fresh ideals will be the twin forces of pity and fear. These are among the challenges presented to us by the Face of Glory as he invites us to share in his divine creativity in helping us to come to grips with problems so painful, so unendurable that new means of overcoming them will have to be found. Chief of all the challenges is that of freedom, the state of the liberated imagination that we often fear as much as we desire it. Our creativity and our urge towards freedom are two aspects of our central characteristic as human beings – our capacity for consciousness. Just as circumstances, threats and the challenge of the unknown and the difficult impels us to develop our creativity, so the same forces drive us to value and defend our freedoms.

Freedom is now a concern of the whole planet. What is new about our awareness of events of the scale of the planet is that we know about them through the images of the camera in a way that was impossible two hundred years ago and possible only through written reporting often delayed in transmission a hundred years ago; and as we know about them in this immediate way, so we *feel* about them with a depth that is both more informed and more intense.

Can the future ever be quite like the past again when the whole world has seen what a dictator's eyes look like when he realizes that the game is up and no terror he can threaten will quell the crowd raging beneath his palace balcony? 'World history is the judgment of the world,' said Schiller,[12] and through the immediacy of television reporting and video films we through our eyes and ears are forced to become the conscience and the judgment of the world as it is in the immediate present.

In film and video the memory remains to be recalled with an intensity never possible before the invention of cinematography, as my wife and I experienced recently on a visit to the new museum at Caen devoted to the Normandy landings of 1944, Le Mémorial. It is a sombre experience to pass through all the evidence of occupation, bombardments, executions of hostages and members of the Resistance, but more telling and shocking than anything is the film shown there of the landings. From the outcome of the Normandy landings and the battle that followed has ensued the present political configuration of Europe and the world authority of the United States. Future historians will probably see it as equal in importance with the Battle of Salamis for stopping Persian domination of the Mediterranean or the Battle of Tours in preventing the Muslim conquest of western Europe.

On a huge curving screen we see at the same time two sequences of film – one the preparations for the invasion by the Allied forces and the other the preparations against the possibility of invasion by the German occupying forces. What we see is largely the young men of both sides who are to fight the battle. In one sense it is as though we are witnessing the training of two teams for a forthcoming football match; there is a vigour and a cheerfulness about the participants that cannot always have been for the camera as we see one side constructing the Atlantic Wall and the other side practising for the landings. They seem to be young people who are essentially the *same*. It is the vigour and cheerfulness, however, that intensify the sense of drama and tragedy·as we set sail on the night of D-day with one side and wait in nervous ignorance of what may come at us with the other. The ignorance disappears, for we look down on the parachutes of the US Airborne Division floating in the night sky as they begin the invasion and we see the guns in action as the Royal Navy bombards the Normandy coast. We climb into the landing craft with the Allied forces, we leap into the waters of the Channel as the landing craft lower their bows and we wade with the soldiers ashore on the beaches of Normandy while at the same time we hurry to action at the sirens and orders summoning the German army and run with them to the gun emplacements, the tanks, the cliffs and beaches to repel the invasion. Though we know what the outcome of the fighting will be in six weeks' to two months' time, just as we know what will happen to Oedipus when he boasts that the prophecies foretelling doom cannot possibly refer to him, though we know there will be 'a famous victory', as in Robert Southey's poem, it is the awareness of what is happening to the individuals, to the cheerful faces, to the healthy bodies and intelligent minds, that overwhelms us. We are on the beaches, we are under the cliffs at Omaha, we watch the scaling ladders being catapulted up to the top of the cliffs: in a few minutes we are given the hours of climbing, fighting, climbing again, fighting again and again that won those cliffs and therefore the Cotentin peninsula, and then we are off to a great beach just southwest of where we are watching the film.

The two sequences – German and Allied – have become one wide-angled film. We are in the cockpit of a German fighter skimming over the broad, unprotected beach machine-gunning the Allied soldiers below us on the sands.

A moment later we are skimming over the beach in a light aircraft at the same height. It is the same beach filmed at the same time of year and it is entirely empty. We also see it in full colour – nearly everything preceding has been in black and white. The sense of extinction, of unity in death, is almost more shocking than anything we have so far witnessed and with that flight the film ends.

For the individuals forming the largely conscript armies engaged in that battle there was no choice but to be there, no choice but to kill or be killed. They were there because their fathers had fought another war thirty years before, also largely on French soil, they were there because Lazare Carnot had invented the conception of conscription in France a hundred and fifty years earlier, they were there because the old order in Russia and Germany had collapsed as a result of that other war and ideologues and terrorists were able to seize power in both those countries. These ideologues and terrorists acted in the name of two political philosophies that both drew on the revival·of knowledge, ideas and images from the past though these were interpreted in contrary ways, that both asserted ideals of man that were established on the scientific images of man, and that both aspired to domination of the world. The combatants were supported by all the most modern devices for inflicting destruction, for communication with their own side, for the bafflement of the enemy and the practice of deceit, and for transport, supplies and logistics, that the ingenuity of scientists, engineers and designers could invent.

Is this what science and human creativity are truly for? The young men of the Allied forces were told they were fighting for freedom and the young men of the German army were told they were fighting for the rights granted them by their racial superiority and to avoid enslavement. The success of the Allies certainly led overall to the recovery of political, social and intellectual freedoms for many peoples and nations. But those freedoms always decay unless they are renewed by the spiritual forces of creativity and civilization.

The ultimate purpose of our creativity is the gaining or recovery of freedom – freedom from hunger, ignorance and pain with the help of science and medicine, freedom to use our powers of reason with the help of philosophy, freedom to expand our imaginations and emotional responses with the help of art and freedom to become our true selves with the help of religion. Beyond all those is the freedom that surrounds us and imbues us potentially, which is in consciousness, the quality which with the poetic imagination we all share with our fellow human beings and on which all our other freedoms depend and from which all our different creative powers flow. It is the freedom of joy in being alive and when that freedom is linked to a new poetic conception of the universe, then a new art will find expression through us, an art of spontaneous dance, song and music that will blow through us like the wind through a hedge of roses in the sun.

Part II

*Inspiration and the
image of conscious humanity*

7

The intellect of love:
creativity as the moment of knowing

Surya, the god of the Sun, advances through the sky, drawn by the seven horses of his chariot. He is attended on either side by dawn and twilight. In the aureole above his head is the Face of Glory whose mouth pours out the leaves and decoration of the background of the statue. The Face of Glory symbolizes the energy and the power of the god extending into the world. The figure of the god, much greater in size than any of his attendants, is an image of divine power realized in human form. His face radiates a subtle smile, conveyed as much by his calm young eyes as by the curve of his full lips. His body stands firm and confident like an unquestioned and benign conqueror. He conveys at once the bounty and life-giving force of the Sun in the sky and the power and peace of the Sun in the universal mind as the bearer of consciousness and creativity.

I am describing a statue from the thirteenth-century temples of Konarak (figure 18) and therefore contemporary with the sculptures of the north and south portals of Chartres and the west front of Rheims. It comes from towards the end of a long succession of masterworks that precede in their origins by at least two centuries the revival of sculpture in the West. Time and again in seeing the sculpture of this tradition we experience its vitality and power as a physical sensation: as we look at the gods and goddesses and the plastic forms their bodies have been carved into, we feel our own bodies come to life. Watching Surya, we feel our feet move upon the ground with his strength and confidence; we are aware of a finer glow upon our skin as a response to the texture of the carved stone; and we see with sharper vision as though the vitality of Surya's spiritual light has the power to enhance the capacity of our eyes to harvest the beauty before us.

Just as in western cathedrals Christ was set in the light-radiant mandorla, holding the book of the Logos, or at the centre of the radiating rose windows as the ultimate source of life and light, the spiritual sun of righteousness, so Surya appears here as the illuminator and blesser of the world and of all human intellects. According to Indian aesthetic theory, the unknown sculptor who carved him would have seen the origins of the statue, not in his private dreams, but in a state of unified consciousness that precedes the awareness of the ego and in which the Lord of creative work, Vishvakarman, would have given him the image to be carved. This he would then have worked upon guided by his sense of discrimination and his memory of the inspiration. So much is given in that state of unified consciousness that the sculptor on completing it might have exclaimed in amazement, like the sculptor of one of the temples at Elura: 'O how did I make it?'[1]

The sculptors of Chartres were giving the first expression in plastic art to the western concept of the worth of the individual within the ambience of eternity and not yet divorced from communication with the divine and with the angels. They were concerned with the perfection of the resurrected body. The sculptors of Konarak on the other hand were raising their hearts and minds up to a conception of humanized divinity so vast and all-inclusive that their individualities vanish in every way – except one, which is in the skill that only people of inborn genius and ceaseless training could bring to the execution of such masterpieces. They were also concerned to show another kind of perfected body, the freedom of the subtle body brought about by the practice of yoga.

The religions, the traditions and the historical settings are totally different and yet what links this statue of Surya together with the sculptures of Chartres – beyond the remarkable similarities between the craft organizations of the western and Indian masons and sculptors, and beyond even their use of the symbol of the Green Man or the Face of Glory as the divine creative power they had to manifest – is the feeling for light as the height of universal consciousness. To this consciousness every true artist should aspire for illumination so that he *knows*, indelibly and absolutely, what it is he has to express.

The creative moment is when we know that we know and what it is that we have to do. In many cultures of all ages the appearance of that moment is described in terms of light and of energy linked to light. Sometimes it is shy and glimmering as when, in the decay of their civilization, the Aztecs described their chief source of consolation, their songs and poems, as 'fireflies in the night'.[2] In other cultures it is bold and assertive, as in the triumphant announcement in Haydn's *Creation* of the making of the Sun or the description in the *Bhagavad-Gita* of the Universal Self as 'the radiance of a thousand suns'.[3]

The characteristics of this moment are the different ordering of consciousness apparent through enhanced awareness of the present, a sense of unity and, very often, the experience of impersonal joy, together with an alteration in the experience of time.

In starting this enquiry into the nature of creativity and the sources of new ideas and images, I have suggested the Great Memory as one source on the scale of civilizations and great social and political movements. This has an analogue with the experience of many creative artists, thinkers and scientists who often return to, or find that they are given back, intense memories of their childhood. The course of their future creative lives has been set for them in the experiences of childhood and these experiences, often linked to specific incidents, emotions or personal discoveries, have the quality of mystical illumination. The reason why they recur so powerfully is that they have sealed an indelible imprint on the memory, the imprint of awakened consciousness. In recalling such memories we seem to see ourselves then as we are essentially now: the differences of age, growth, decay, learning and forgetting are trivial compared to the identity of individual selfhood with what it was in the past and what it is now. To put it another way, it is a linking of present moments, or it seems like a linking when in fact there is only one present moment manifesting at different stages in life. Such experiences point to consciousness as having independence of time and locality. It is indeed 'non-local', as some neurophysiologists, drawing on ideas in quantum physics, are now describing both consciousness and memory.

Some artists and poets have described this period of their early lives as one when they were in conversation with angels: thus said William Blake in the eighteenth century and the Sufi mystic Shams-i-Tabrizi in the thirteenth century.[4] The experience of meeting Beatrice when he was almost nine years old determined the creative direction of Dante's life and her influence and the glory of the moment of that first meeting recurred again and again throughout his writings. Goethe was profoundly affected by a similar experience with the original Gretchen in Frankfurt when he was a boy. For two of the most famous examples of writers who found their great themes when they turned back to the impressions of childhood we have only to mention Wordsworth and Proust. The emotional drive to question and discover is also established very early in life for many scientists. Faced with any machine, the infant James Clerk Maxwell always asked 'What's the go of that?' and recently Rupert Sheldrake has described the effect on him at the age of five of seeing willow stakes planted to make a fence that had turned into trees.[5]

Nikola Tesla, one of the chief makers of the technology of the modern age, believed that nature was a reservoir of energy which could be tapped if the right means of resonance could be found to release the energy. As a small child in the Croatian village where he was brought up he watched the arrival of a new fire engine bought by the village. When the fire engine was demonstrated to the villagers beside a river, the firemen worked the pump but nothing came out. No one knew what to do. Tesla waded into the river, where he found the hose had collapsed. He reinflated the hose and spray poured out of the nozzle, drenching the crowd. This experience is said to be one of the crucial experiences in his early life for arousing his interest in potential energy.[6]

The knowledge that we are capable of doing something that hitherto we thought ourselves unable to perform often strikes home with such resonance that we always remember the time and place of the realization. For example, I have a very clear memory of the moment when I realized I could read. I was five, sitting at a desk in a large schoolroom with high windows at the Land's End in Cornwall. I could tell that something had happened to the formerly separate letters and words on the page before me. They had begun as though of their own accord to be connected with one another and to communicate sense to me. It was an exhilarating moment always associated in memory with those high windows through which the light, filtered by the clouds over the Atlantic Ocean, poured in like a symbolic awakening to the worlds of exploration that would follow my realization.

It is likely that everyone reading this will have similar experiences both from their earliest childhood and from later periods of life. The most familiar examples probably come from the attainment of some new physical skill or coordination. Whenever we very much want to do something or are being trained or educated to do something, there comes a point – if we are not constitutionally unable to fulfil our desire – when we are aware that we are doing what we were incapable of doing last week or even that morning. In learning to swim, we flounder for months rarely getting both feet off the sand or the bottom of the swimming pool; then all at once we realize we are swimming. We are learning to ride a bicycle, constantly falling off, and the unexpected moment comes when we see with wonder that we have achieved balance and do not fall off. We learn to drive and live in a state of miserable confusion and fear, having to learn new spatial perceptions such as being able to see out of the back of our heads as well as sideways and frontwards while performing a series of unrelated actions with our hands and feet. Incalculable in its approach, the moment comes when the fear is gone, the machine goes safely in the directions we intend and a new fluidity coordinates all our movements and perceptions into the act of driving.

The same experience can be known from intellectual activities and emotional development. One day in my youth I idly picked up a copy of *Le Père Goriot* and found myself, though certainly not knowing all the vocabulary, deep in the description of Madame Vauquer's lodging house. As I was led to the phrase in which Balzac summed up all the accumulated impressions of that dingy establishment – *'l'odeur de pension'* – I was responding to the atmosphere and the emotions in the novel. It was the arousal of my emotions that enhanced both my fluency in reading French and my comprehension of it. Such experiences of the sudden grasping of an idea or a mathematical technique are very common. There would be no real education without it because it marks the point when the knowledge in the book or the mind and words of the teacher have become the possession of the pupil.

With maturity we often learn to trust and to wait for the solution or instruction that will enable us to solve a problem in a personal relationship at home or at work – or, if it is insoluble by direct means, to create an attitude in ourselves that will lessen the harm the problem is causing. Nearly always unexpectedly, answers that will settle or ameliorate the situation flash into the mind or are presented to us in dreams. Such moments of awareness change the future, opening up new possibilities for ourselves and, sometimes, for others. The solution seems to come in a moment of opened consciousness.

There is a Greek word for the moment of appropriate action or the appearance of the creative solution. It is *kairos*, a word with the meanings of proportion and of times or actions that are in season. It was used in the Greek version of the Old Testament, the Septuagint, most notably in the translation of the passage in Ecclesiastes where the preacher speaks of 'a time to be born and a time to die; a time to plant and a time to pluck up that which is planted'.[7] Shakespeare was speaking of the same capacity to act rightly and at the appropriate time when Edgar comforts his father Gloucester in *King Lear* with the words:

> Men must endure
> Their going hence even as their coming hither.
> Ripeness is all. Come on.[8]

Just as we, thinking ourselves perhaps uncreative, actually depend upon the gift of the creative moment, so many artists and scientists learn to depend upon this moment as their chief means of insight and inspiration. Paul Valéry took the image of the palm tree waiting patiently with its unseen mat of roots searching under the desert for moisture, working their way into the bowels of the earth in pursuit of the deep water that the summit of the tree requires. Then one day a gust of wind, the fluttering of a pigeon, a woman leaning against its trunk, will cause the fruits to fall.[9] The chemist Linus Pauling said this of one of his methods of working:

For solving problems that initially defeat me I deliberately make use of my unconscious mind. I think about the problem for about half an hour in bed and then go to sleep still thinking about it. I do this, perhaps, for several nights, and then forget about it all together. Months or sometimes years later, as with the structure of α-keratin, the answer pops into my head.[10]

This indicates a deliberate or conscious application of the incubating capacities of the mind which would never work so efficiently if they were not given directions for their work.

As for 'the answer pops into my head', this accords with the innumerable accounts of the moment of inspiration which mention the suddenness with which an image or an insight appears. Many of these descriptions have the flavour or characteristics of moments of mystical insight or illumination. Above all they are unifying experiences: they seem to bring together the waking and the dreaming sides of human nature, the left-hand and right-hand hemispheres of the brain, and, as a consequence, the information from past thoughts and experiences is reorganized and given new significance as the mind works with more than usual efficiency and speed as though it were raised into a different time world.

The ways in which inspirations come to gifted recipients are common to all mankind and we can understand a great deal of what they tell us about their creative processes because we too possess those creative processes. We all dream, we all express ourselves in similes, metaphors and images, we all have powerful feelings, we all experience the brilliant sudden solution; great numbers of us have had mystical experiences, moments of illumination, visions, and gifts of unaccountable happiness. All such experiences, which are common to most people, will figure in the examples of creativity to which we will come. Yet another similarity is in the experience of time and the enlarging of potentialities in another world of enhanced awareness.

What is that different time world, that set of other dimensions out of which we receive instructions and help in a way that coordinates our minds and emotions into an experience of unity? One of its characteristics is that it is a state of great simplicity: the problem that seemed so confused and so chaotic, so immalleable to reason or form, is resolved into clarity. We *know* what to *do*. Another characteristic is that the state brings together parts of our memories and experience that never to that moment we would have dreamed of putting together and associating. In other words, it brings about the leaps of thought that create metaphor and the discovery of new forms of knowledge.

We are so accustomed through the influence of psychoanalytic theories to think of creativity as being caused by the unconscious or subconscious workings of the mind that we are blinded to what is in fact in the experience of all of us, the moment of knowing and all that implies. The moment of knowing, by definition, is a conscious experience. We would not know what we know unless we were conscious of knowing. In that moment we are freed from the unconscious when it is the prison of ignorance. Here I turn the accepted notions upside down by stating this: *Conscious experience sets the creative process in motion.* By this I mean that inspiration, insight and intuition result from the moment of knowing or conscious experience. Furthermore, the synthesis of different elements of past experience which are brought together in a moment of consciousness is caused *in* the moment of knowing, not by the incubating or preparatory unconscious stages. They are the preparation of the various ingredients of the dish, not the making of the dish itself. What are waiting in the memory or unconscious for synthesis are the traces of earlier moments of conscious experience, the striking visual impressions that will make the images of the poem to be or the questions aroused by earlier experimental work that will feed the crucial observation. The unconscious is made up of dormant consciousness. We know most about those unconscious stages through dreams and, for those of us who experience them, hypnagogic images. Another characteristic of the moment of knowing is that it brings the dream levels more clearly into awareness and in fact joins them to the awareness of the waking state, and the unity through which new conceptions and images arise is owed to the marriage of the waking and dreaming states but with an efficiency and power of coordination far beyond the sum of possibilities of the conjoined states. Because our ordinary state of awareness works so slowly, it is difficult for the mind at this level to accept the speed at which the creative moment carries out its syntheses.

We are also accustomed to think of ourselves as living in a four-dimensional continuum of space-time. It is linear and inexorably sequential. We cannot step in the same river twice, according to this habit of thought. That habit of thought vanishes, however, before the experience of the moment of knowing, the moment when the future is changed almost, it seems, by the future itself because the possibilities of the future are opened up to us in a wholly new way.

We can look at these ideas from two different ways. One is the overall creative life of an artist or scientist when the directions of their themes or researches are clearly apparent from their childhood and can appear in hindsight as the fate or destiny they are given. The second is to look at reliable descriptions of the creative moment from many cultures and disciplines.

Rilke once said that it seemed to him that he had only one poem to write and that each successive poem was a more adequate version of that one poem.[11] When we look at the life of Dante, we find the germs of *The Divine Comedy*, especially indications that he will see Hell and Heaven, in his earliest poems, written before the age of twenty-four. In the case of Goethe, the whole of his vast oeuvre may be seen as what was necessary to the completion over a period of nearly sixty years of the two parts of *Faust* from its inception in the *Urfaust* of 1774 when he was twenty-five. In all Pushkin's longer narrative poems from the early *Prisoner of the Caucasus* onwards, the same pattern of the superfluous man and the rejected heroine may be found, up to and including its fullest representation in *Eugene Onegin*.[12] I have already given a similar example in speaking (Chapter 2) of the continuity of the theme of civil war and its resolution in marriage throughout the creative life of Shakespeare. Sometimes we see similar patterns in the works of artists and sculptors where certain primordial forms possess them with a fascination that never ceases, such as the 'S' shape in the works of Michelangelo. Sometimes such shapes come from the artistic and religious traditions within which the artists are trained, such as the triangle shape of the Madonna and Child, to which successive painters and sculptors give their individual interpretations.

In all these cases it is as though the great theme or obsession of an artist is independent of the linear sequence of his life. The linear sequence is necessary for its manifestation as a physical artefact or for its communication to others but its cause does not lie within the sequence. It is at right angles to the direction of time, always immanent, and sometimes, when the *kairos* flowers, taking the artist up into this different continuum of understanding and illumination.

These moments of illumination have certain characteristics, beyond what they all share in that they are moments of knowing. The three main characteristics are that they are realizations of truth, of expanded consciousness and of impersonal joy. One of these will often be preponderant over the others, as in the case of scientists reporting on their initial period of discovery – where the emphasis is on the realization of truth. Other characteristics include the suddenness with which they appear and the awareness of new possibilities.

William Blake, describing this moment of illumination, says in his *Milton*:

Every Time less than a pulsation of the artery
Is equal in its period & value to Six Thousand Years,
For in this Period the Poet's Work is Done, and all the Great
Events of Time start forth & are conciev'd in such a Period,
Within a Moment, a Pulsation of the Artery.[13]

Dante, in a passage Blake probably did not know at the time of writing *Milton*, speaks of a single moment, *un punto solo*, of his vision of Paradise as containing within it more knowledge and experience than the two and a half thousand years of human history that had passed since the journey of the first ship, the *Argo*, made Neptune wonder at its shadow passing over his head.[14]

A Chinese poem, describing the moment of enlightenment, sums up the sense of new energies and possibilities thus:

Last night the spring rains came rushing to the river.
Today the huge ships float like clouds upon the stream.
Vessels that could not stir before
Now travel freely in the middle of the current.[15]

Richard Wagner tells in his autobiography of how the inspiration for the Prelude to *Das Rheingold* finally came to him after much trouble and grief.

After a night spent in fever and sleeplessness, I forced myself to take a long tramp the next day through the hilly country which was covered with pine woods. It all looked dreary and desolate, and I could not think what I should do there. Returning in the afternoon, I stretched myself, dead tired, on a hard couch, awaiting the long-desired hour of sleep. It did not come; but I fell into a kind of somnolent state, in which

I suddenly felt as though I were sinking in swiftly flowing water. The rushing sound formed itself in my brain into a musical sound, the chord of E flat major, which continually re-echoed in broken forms; these broken chords seemed to me melodic passages of increasing motion, yet the pure triad of E flat major never changed, but seemed by its continuance to impart infinite significance to the element in which I was sinking. I awoke in sudden terror from my doze, feeling as though the waves were rushing high above my head. I at once recognized that the orchestral overture to the 'Rheingold', which must long have lain latent within me, though it had been unable to find definite form, had at last been revealed to me. I then quickly realized my own nature; the stream of life was not to flow to me from without, but from within.[16]

This passage might be taken as a contradiction of my insistence on regarding consciousness as the prime source of creativity. I set it here, however, to emphasize the thought that consciousness in the universal sense *includes* all other states of awareness, dreams or sleep known to human beings. Wagner could have gone on with his doze and dropped off into deep sleep for the next twenty-four hours and awoken only with a hazy feeling of a lost dream. It was the moment of awakening and of realizing what was flowing through him, the act of recognition of the significance of the rushing sound that was the creative moment in which he *knew* what he had to do with the gift. Consciousness of this order seems to connect the dreaming sides of our natures with the waking sides, standing above both. Pushkin described his creative processes as having two aspects. One of these he called 'enthusiasm': this was the rush of ideas, images, words and thoughts which passed through his awareness. The other aspect was what he called 'inspiration' and this he thought of as the higher quality. He meant by 'inspiration' the faculty of choice with which, with lightning speed, he selected among all the choices of words and images aroused by his theme and his emotions and which determined what he set down.[17] The very fact that he was aware of the two complementary processes in action simultaneously points to a state of consciousness above these processes from which he could observe them.

I realize also that some consider the directing of awareness on to active processes of the mind as destructive or limiting to creative powers. Valéry spoke of some functions as preferring the darkness to the light, saying of the modesty of the automatic functions that he could draw from it an entire philosophy summed up in the phrase: 'Sometimes I think and sometimes I am.'[18] Immanuel Kant said that when the powers of the mind are in action, one does not observe oneself, and when one observes oneself, those powers cease to work, pointing also to the ways in which persons observed by others become embarrassed or try to disguise themselves.[19] This is like a negative acknowledgment of what I have been saying about the role of consciousness in creativity: that things and mental functions are changed when consciousness is directed on them. It is true in this negative sense if the attention of the mind is diverted from the object of creation or discovery on to the functioning of the mind, but, as is shown by the several examples that follow, there is a kind of attention that does not interfere, that does not pull up the plants before their roots are set or introduce doubts and fears into a confidently working process. Here we see, as part of the effects of consciousness, the observer who notes and remembers the inspiration, the knower who knows the knower. The characteristics of the realization of truth, of expanded consciousness and of impersonal joy which I ascribed to moments of inspiration and knowing are to be seen in these following examples – which we hear about only because in the recipient of each of these inspirations there was a calm, deeply set observer who registered in memory the various experiences.

For an example of inspiration coming suddenly as a realization of truth, this is the remarkable account by Sir Lawrence Bragg of how, in 1912, he discovered X-ray crystallography, the means of analysing the positions of atoms in crystals which brought about a major breakthrough in the understanding of the nature of matter. He and his father had been puzzling about the nature of spots that showed up in X-ray photographs taken by the German scientist Max von Laue. Bragg was only twenty-two at the time, a young postgraduate student at Cambridge.

It is worth while describing this inspiration in some detail because it shows how scientific ideas often arise. They come because one hears about a piece of knowledge from one source and happens to have a quite separate piece of knowledge from another source, and somehow the two just click together and there is the new idea. First, J. J. Thomson had lectured to us about X-rays, and explained them as a wave-pulse in the ether caused by the electrons hitting the target in the X-ray tube and being stopped suddenly. Second, C. T. R. Wilson had given us very stimulating lectures on optics, including an analysis of white light which showed that one could think of it either as a series of quite irregular pulses or as a continuous range of wavelengths. Third, we had a little scientific society in Trinity, and at one of our meetings a member had read a paper about a theory, that in crystal structures, the atoms were packed together like spheres whose volumes were proportional to the combining power of the atoms . . . Hearing this paper, I realized that the atoms in crystals were arranged in parallel sheets . . . So these three bits of knowledge were part of my background. When I was walking one day along the Backs at Cambridge – I can remember the place behind St John's College – suddenly the three bits came together with a click in my mind. I suddenly realized that von Laue's spots were the reflections of the X-rays in the sheets of atoms in the crystal.[20]

The way in which physical surroundings can affect discovery appears very strongly in my next example, which brings together inspiration as a moment of truth with inspiration as a moment of conscious knowing. The French doctor and bacteriologist Charles Nicolle was working at the Muslim Hospital in Tunis in 1909 at the time of an epidemic of typhus. He, like other doctors, was puzzled by the fact that though typhus is a contagious disease, typhus sufferers in the hospital in beds next to patients suffering from other diseases did not transmit typhus to them. Outside the hospital, however, Nicolle would diagnose contagion in the town and among hospital staff dealing with the reception of patients.

One day, he entered the hospital and saw a body at the bottom of a passage. This was not unusual: typhus sufferers would find their way to the hospital and collapse on the last steps. Nicolle strode over the body. 'It was at this very moment the light struck me. When, a moment later, I entered the hospital, I had solved the problem . . . This prostrate body and the door in front of which he had fallen had suddenly shown me the barrier by which typhus had been arrested . . . the agent of infection had been arrested at this point.' The reason why typhus sufferers in the hospital were not passing on the disease to other patients was that, on reception, they had been stripped of their clothes, shaved and washed. They no longer carried on them the agent of infection which Nicolle saw instantly was a flea. He was so certain of his intuition that, though he carried out two months of experimental work to test it, this work neither excited nor surprised him. It was in fact so boring at times that, as he says with charming frankness, 'it was because of vanity and self-love that I continued'.[21] What is of further interest in his description is the powerful symbolism of the dead or dying sufferer and of the door with its double meaning of barrier and entrance, together with the familiar imagery of light in the moment of inspiration.

For an example of expanded consciousness we go to the twelfth-century German abbess Hildegard of Bingen who described the two stages of awareness in which she saw her visions and from which her music, her poems and her prose writings derived. She describes these stages as 'the cloud of living light' and 'the living light itself'.

From my infancy up to the present time, I being now more than seventy years of age, I have always seen this light in my spirit and not with external eyes, nor with any thoughts of my heart nor with help from the senses. But my outward eyes remain open and the other corporeal senses retain their activity. The light which I see is not located but yet is more brilliant than the sun, nor can I examine its height, length or breadth, and I name it 'the cloud of the living light'. And as sun, moon, and stars are reflected in water, so the writings, sayings, virtues and works of men shine in it before me. And whatever I thus see in vision the memory thereof remains long with me. Likewise I see, hear, and understand almost in a moment and I set down what I thus learn . . . But sometimes I behold within this light another light which I name 'the Living Light itself' . . . And when I look upon it every sadness and pain vanishes from my memory, so that I am again as a simple maid and not as an old woman. And now that I am over seventy years old my spirit, according to the will of God, soars upward in vision to the highest heaven and to the farthest stretch of the air and spreads itself among different peoples to regions exceedingly far from me here, and then I can behold the changing clouds and the mutations of all created things; for all these I see not with the outward eye or ear, nor do I create them from the cogitations of my heart . . . but with my spirit, my eyes being open, so that I have never suffered any terror when they left me.[22]

For an example of impersonal joy we have Dante describing the moment when the opening of his first great poem came to him:

It chanced that as I was walking one day along a road beside which flowed a river of very clear water, such a desire to speak came upon me that I began to think about the style that I should maintain; and it struck me that it would be wrong to speak of her [Beatrice] unless I addressed myself to other ladies in the second person; that is to say not to *any* other ladies, but to those who are noble and not merely women. At that moment, I say, my tongue spoke as though moved by itself and said 'Donne ch'avete intelletto d'amore.' [Ladies who possess the intellect of love.] I laid these words up in my mind with great joy, intending to make them my beginning; then after returning to the already mentioned city and reflecting for several days, I started a poem with this opening . . .[23]

We can find other instances in which the characteristics are more generally mingled. The mathematician Sir Roger Penrose describes how he had been reflecting on whether there might be a precise mathematical theorem to be proved to show that space-time singularities are inevitable. (This was in relation to speculations about the nature of quasars, recently discovered in the 1960s.) He had been visited by a colleague who engaged him in voluble conversation as they walked down the street. They had to cross the street and in the break in the conversation an idea came to him. This was blotted out by the resumption of the conversation. Later, when his colleague had left, he was surprised by a feeling of elation he could not account for. When he went over the events of the day, he brought to mind the thought that had come while crossing the street:

a thought which had momentarily elated me by providing the solution to the problem that had been milling around at the back of my head! Apparently it was the needed criterion – that I subsequently called 'a trapped surface' – and then it did not take me long to form the outline of a proof of the theorem that I had been looking for . . .[24]

He is particular interesting on the immediate aesthetic judgments – rather like Pushkin's 'inspiration' – that are made in the experience of inspiration.

It is these judgements that I consider to be the hallmark of conscious thinking. My guess is that even with the sudden flash of insight, apparently produced ready-made by the unconscious mind, it is *consciousness* that is the arbiter, and the idea would be quickly rejected and forgotten if it did not 'ring true'. (Curiously enough I *did* actually forget my trapped surface, but that is not at the level that I mean. The idea broke through into consciousness for long enough for it to leave a lasting impression.)[25]

Implicit in the examples I have given and in my own comments are questions about the status and scale of consciousness. When an answer pops out or an idea breaks through or when we are granted a vision as a gift, where are these answers, ideas and visions coming from? According to what I have been saying, they are the product or effect of consciousness in the moment of awareness. For many examples of creativity I could say that the enhanced consciousness that brings about these instantaneous breakthroughs or understandings is a rare, transient but fruitful mental condition which has no universal significance. Much of the art of this century could be regarded in this way because it is the expressionism of private worlds and individual psychologies.

I think it worth while, however, to look at consciousness on a much wider scale. Consciousness is the awareness of the self through which we participate with the world and by which we know our bodies, feelings and inner natures. On the wider scale it subsumes everything: our sleeping, our dreaming, our daydreaming, our daytime awareness and also our moments of enhanced perception, intuition and creative thought and action. Without consciousness there is no world: thus it subsumes space and time, language, prehistory and the future, the latency of life in matter and the appearances of life in matter and death. We can imagine a world without consciousness – which is what we are required to do in general and popular scientific thought. What we cannot do is to undertake the act of imagining such a world without the help of consciousness.

For the exercise of all the other functions on which our creativity depends, in addition to imagination, such as will, discrimination, coordination of faculties, consciousness is essential. What the study of creativity helps us to appreciate is that consciousness is limited and restrained when regarded simply as fluctuating states of awareness, but liberated, or rather the source of liberation itself, when it is seen as the continuum of existence, in other words as universal consciousness. In this case the fluctuations in our states of awareness are fluctuations in our apprehension of truth. The Sufis spoke of the eye of the heart, the opening of which is the true aim of religion, art and education. Dante and his friends spoke of the noble heart through which they learned of 'the intellect of love', the awakening of which made manifest the inner beauties of the beloved and of creation. The discoveries scientists make in the moments of consciousness we have been studying are not private delusions but insights into nature and universal truth. Can universal truth be appreciated fully by anything less than universal consciousness? And should we not accord to artists and writers and composers the acknowledgment we give to scientists: that what they know and tell us is objective in the sense that it comes from a greater mind, a greater imagination, a greater memory than the ordinary inefficient faculties of the brain?

This is the picture I am evolving of the relationship between consciousness and creativity. Consciousness is one and available to all of us. How it shines through us and what we do with the gift of its light, both of these depend on the niche or window of history in which we are placed – and over all that we have little control or choice. The extent to which the eye of the heart is opened within us or to which we can know on the level of the intellect of love, all that is much more amenable to our will and our understanding, in proportion as we are amenable to the light of consciousness itself.

Science often depends on hypotheses so huge in their scope they are unprovable; gravity and evolution are two such hypotheses. They are working modes of thought. So too in the wider field of culture and civilization the hypothesis of universal consciousness has also been a fruitful mode of thought: thus it was to the sculptors of Konarak as it was to the sculptors of Chartres, to Dante and to Blake, to the German scientists of the Romantic period, to Einstein and to Tesla.

So it was also for Schiller and Beethoven and I turn again to the writing of the ode 'An die Freude' and to the composition, based on the ode, of the cantata which makes the last movement of the Ninth Symphony. Both Schiller and Beethoven believed in the existence of a universal consciousness and in their artistic lives acted in that belief and worked according to it. Beethoven wrote out and kept on his desk this quotation from Schiller's story 'Die Sendung Moses': 'I am that which is. I am all that is, that was and that will be. No mortal man has raised my veil. He is solely from himself, and all things owe their being to Him alone.'[26]

The creative act is an act of incarnation, a drawing-down from spiritual and mental worlds of images and tones that demand manifestation. As in cases already cited, sometimes the work comes seemingly ready formed: this was probably the case with Schiller when he wrote 'An die Freude' in the summer of 1786 for his friend Körner to set to music. In other cases often the artist may receive a preliminary inspiration, a nod to him from beyond, that at some time he will need this or that thought, theme or idea: it took Beethoven nearly thirty years to find the right form into which he could set the 'Ode to Joy'. For constant and barely remitted production of work, the poet and composer both need to find that place in their natures where they can live nearest to the communications that come from their deeper selves. Schiller's and Beethoven's descriptions of their creative processes are curiously complementary and almost interchangeable for their respective arts. Schiller said that, before he composed, he experienced not a logically connected series of images but rather a musical mood. 'With me emotion is at the beginning without clear and definite ideas: those ideas do not arise until later on. A certain musical disposition of mind comes first, and after follows the poetical idea.'[27] Beethoven said that he never composed without having an image in his head.

They were complementary in other ways, especially in their lifelong support of ideals of freedom and in their attachment to the ideal of the Eternal Feminine. For Schiller the thought of freedom was always attached to *das Ewigweibliche*: Joy to him in the ode is a woman. Later in life, happily married, he was to express through a series of historical women in his plays the theme of how they achieved a moral freedom by rising above their sufferings and their physical circumstances. Frequently in love and never to be married, Beethoven was to express again and again his adoration and need for an ideal woman, both in his private writings such as the letter to the Unknown Beloved and in his compositions such as the slow movement of the Fourth Symphony, the song cycle *An die ferne Geliebte* and, above all, in the characterization of Leonore, the heroine of *Fidelio*. *Freude*, the Joy of Schiller's ode, becomes for Beethoven Leonore returned on a planetary scale: this time she releases not just the prisoners in Pizarro's fortress but the whole of imprisoned humanity.

The originality of Schiller's poem for its time was astounding. It was written three years before the French Revolution. Its originality lies partly in its new conception and feeling for the whole of humanity. Such ideas had become current through the works of Rousseau and the Marquis de Mirabeau but no one else had ever so concisely and so powerfully said: 'Yes, everyone, every human being can experience this divine joy and be perfected through love.' It owes much in its imagery and influences to the rediscovery of Greece in Germany in this period, an aspect of the Great Memory to which I have already referred. In 96 lines of pounding trochaics Schiller takes us, his fellow human beings, into the hallowed place of Joy. All men will become brothers where her wing passes over. The universal embrace is felt through all individual relationships of love and affection. The scope of Joy's influence is cosmic. 'Everything good, everything evil follows in her path of roses.' From the lowliest to the highest her influence extends. the worm was given pleasure and the cherub stands before God. It is God, the loving Father beyond the stars, that the millions on Earth must recognize as creator. Joy releases suns from the firmament as she does flowers from their buds. She smiles at the seeker from the burning glass of truth, she points the sufferer's path to the steep hill of virtue and we see her banners on the sunlit hill of faith. We cannot pay back the gods; we can become like them. Our ledger of debts is cancelled. In a flurry of images of drinking and toasting, Joy is revealed as the sparkling wine of heaven: indeed the whole universe is a goblet overflowing with her foam.

Every vice that divides humanity flees before courage, truth and pride in humanity.

Beethoven said: 'What is new and original appears of its own accord without one thinking about it.'[28] Taken in the context of his other remarks about the sources of his inspiration, it means that the artist is the vehicle for what comes to him from his higher self acting on his particular physical, psychological and mental identity. In the case of Schiller's state at the time he wrote 'An die Freude' we can point to all kinds of influences that affected the writing of the ode, not least the freedom he was experiencing for almost the first time in his life after a long, repressive education under the daily eye of the Grand Duke of Württemberg who locked him up for eight years in his academy, deciding first of all that he should be a lawyer and then a regimental surgeon. We might have predicted that he would have written an ode to freedom but never an ode to joy.

It is the unpredictability of what may come through inspiration that to my mind defeats most of the explanations of creativity that are based on scientific theories, whether they are genetic, chemical, environmental or psychoanalytical. The same unpredictability often applies to the appearance of creative personalities. The explanations are both too partial and too general: no one could have predicted that Schiller as a great writer would have come from his father's military background; Beethoven's father was a musician but his drunkenness and violence could have put the young Ludwig off a musical career far more than his father's mediocre talents might have inspired him to emulation.

What these theories all account for are necessary contributory factors – even the neuroses and the illnesses may be necessary – but they do not account for the freedom of the spirit in creation and the state of being in the creative moment and of constantly returning to it, any more than they can satisfy ourselves as explanations of the times we approach and exist in that freedom and that state of being in the presence of art.

It was equally unpredictable that Beethoven would break all the accepted rules of symphonic composition by incorporating a cantata within the Ninth Symphony. It was certainly unpredictable to himself until quite late in the composition of the work. He had thought of setting the 'Ode to Joy' in 1793; later he thought of incorporating it in an overture. The first sketches for the Ninth Symphony indicated an orchestral finale; he was, however, working on the never to be completed Tenth Symphony at the same time, for which he did propose the inclusion of a chorus based on another text. The Ninth Symphony made slow progress while he laboured with the Missa Solemnis; the return to sacred choral music and to a more specific concentration on Christian themes and doctrine provided an experience which is thought to have influenced his interpretation of Schiller's ode. By 1822 he had made the discovery that it was in the Ninth Symphony that he was to introduce the chorus and that the text he would set for it would be the 'Ode to Joy' which had fascinated and tantalized him for so long. One of his chief struggles was to make the link between the slow movement and the purely instrumental part of the symphony with the cantata. He found himself forced to write the introductory text and one day, Schindler reports, 'he entered the room and called out to me "I have it, I have it." And he showed me his sketchbook where he had written: "Let us now sing the song of the immortal Schiller 'Freude'" . . .'[29]

The first performance, on 7 May 1824, was given before a packed audience. Beethoven stood in front of a conductor's stand and flung himself backwards and forwards 'like a madman'.[30] The musicians in fact followed the conductor Umlauf. The audience applauded not only between the movements but, apparently, at times during them. Differing accounts speak of Beethoven continuing to leaf through the score either after the scherzo or after the end of the last movement and of how the contralto soloist had to tap his shoulder and turn him round to the applauding audience his deafness prevented him from hearing. Though at times some of the weaker string players had to lay down their bows at the unfamiliarity and difficulty of the music and the sopranos did not sing when they could not reach the high notes, in terms of its reception the first performance was a triumph. When Schindler got Beethoven home to his house, Beethoven, learning how small the box-office returns were, collapsed.[31]

It was his prestige in Vienna that had at least aroused an enthusiastic response. The first performance in London in 1825 was received with respectful rudeness: the repetitions should be omitted and the chorus removed. This response was echoed in other cities. Fanny Mendelssohn, when her brother conducted the work in 1836, was horrified by the symphony, which she heard as a gigantic tragedy which in the last movement collapsed into burlesque.[32] The subsequent history of the work illustrates how, in the case of great originality and the imposition of new demands on players and performers, creative work may continue long after the originator, the playwright or the composer has finished his own work. It required a long sequence of composer conductors such as Wagner and Mahler and other conductors famous for their powers of interpretation to realize Beethoven's intentions, and to bring about the special place the symphony holds on the international scale. In their interpretations they sometimes improved on Beethoven with contentious additions or changes. Leonard Bernstein also managed to improve on Schiller, with his change of *Freude* to *Freiheit* in the performance he conducted in Berlin in 1989 to celebrate the reunion of Germany.[33]

What Beethoven did in setting Schiller's poem was in a novel sense to translate it: from the language of the German-speaking regions to the universal language of music so that the millions Schiller writes of who will be embraced by Joy could hear and understand it without the barrier of an unknown language. Beethoven set only eighteen lines of the ode: yet it is as though the images and cosmic messages of the other, unset stanzas are present and alive in the vibrancy and life of the music. Schiller had in this poem made the spirit of Greece cover the whole world; Beethoven infused his setting through the oratorio-like associations of the cantata with a spirit of Christian humanitarianism and love unlike anything that can be thought of in the Christian churches of his time, though in the passages of cosmic adoration he echoes, and excels in the echoing, the worship of the divine in nature common to so many contemporary poets and artists, from Novalis to Caspar David Friedrich. In this last movement of the Ninth Symphony the two sides of Beethoven's nature – the aggressive Dionysiac power and the incomparable feminine tenderness that we hear contrasted so often in the other symphonies and the piano sonatas and chamber music – are brought together as never before in the spirit of the Eternal Feminine and the image of millions of his fellow human beings he must have held before his eyes as he composed the cantata.

8

Manifestation and the individual

The Green Man challenges us to discover the freedom of being ourselves as individuals. What our forebears saw instinctively in him, the principle of life that we share with the world of plants, we can understand in our scientific age through the concept of photosynthesis. When we see him with the vegetation of spring pouring from his mouth, he is like a fountain giving out the waters of creativity. He is an image of manifestation, of the appearance of the new and the reborn in the world. He entices us with thoughts of the invisible powers that are the source of his bounty and his eyes shine with the light of the consciousness immanent in all created things of which he is the emblem.

Water, like light, is an image anciently associated with consciousness and creativity. In the concept of photosynthesis light and water are brought together to give us an analogy between what is the most important biological process on our planet and the creative process in humanity.

Photosynthesis is the process whereby, through the action of photons of sunlight on the chlorophyll in the cells of vegetation and plankton, the nutrients received by the plant through the medium of water from its root system in the soil and from the carbon dioxide in the air are split up into oxygen, which is released to the atmosphere, and into carbon compounds on which the plant cells feed and of which they themselves are made. The surfaces of the leaves harvest the light and this sets off a continuous series of chemical reactions, each lasting a few milliseconds, bringing about the process on which all other living creatures depend for breathing and nourishment. This process in turn depends on the sun as the source of the light that brings it about. What comes from the sun, the air and the water is general to all plants: what makes a plant an example of its particular species is its ancestry: what decides whether its growth is stunted or full is the environment into which its seed fell or was planted.

The analogy is this: consciousness is the universal energy, the continuum for humanity which has no inner and no outer sides. How it is manifested in creativity depends on the abilities of an individual which arise from the genetic inheritance, family and social environment, the climate of opinion and taste in which the individual is raised, and the subtle and powerful forces of tradition, religion, myth and the Great Memory. Like the plant cell that could never be activated into photosynthesis without the power of the sun, so the individual human being could never *be* a human being, let alone create and communicate, without the light of consciousness. The light of consciousness, therefore, can be regarded as bringing about the equivalent in the psyche of the process of photosynthesis – photopoeisis, to make a neologism. The sun of consciousness rises on the night forests of the imagination and awakens the sleeping images and archetypes in the soul to new life and new expression, marrying impressions in the physical world to these images and re-creating the experience of the living myth.

Where does our individuality come into this? The individuality that can tell us from a few bars of music that what we hear is Handel and not Bach or that, from a small detail of a painting, can make us say Rembrandt and not Hals, that can make one nineteenth-century French scientist pursue the origins and nature of life (I mean Pasteur) without ever hurting anything beyond bacteria while another – Magendie – relentlessly and without feeling cuts up hundreds of dogs while they are still alive in order to study the nervous system. The individuality that enables us to identify the work or mood of others expresses itself through self-images. The plant has a self-image of what it has to be like at each stage of its development: it is there not only in the seed but present in every part of it, as can be seen when we take cuttings. It is encoded to send out twigs or fronds at certain intervals, to change the shape and colouring of its leaves, to flower at the best time for pollination, and to die. We too grow out of cells encoded with self-images that ensure our physical individuality. The technique of genetic finger printing has established that we as physical human beings are all unique creatures, each given combinations of features and tendencies that no other human being possesses.

Much has been made of the influence of physical individuality upon creativity – with surprising results, such as the suggestion that by superimposing Leonardo da Vinci's self-portrait upon the features of the Mona Lisa it can be seen that Leonardo was painting in the Mona Lisa a feminized portrait of himself.[1] It has even been suggested that what is special and unusual about van Gogh's landscapes is derived ultimately from his physical appearance, his blue eyes and spiky stubblelike orange-yellow hair.[2] Such theories may trivialize and take attention away from the achievement of great creators, but it is also clear that physical abilities and disabilities have had important effects on bringing about collaborations in both the arts and the sciences. Fritz Haber, who invented the method of extracting nitrogen from the atmosphere at the time just before the First World War when the chief natural supplies of nitrogen from guano in South America were starting to run out, was as an experimental chemist a hopeless butterfingers, according to his son.[3] He needed the help of his friend and colleague, the far more adept Carl Bosch, who had been a plumber before he became a chemist, to make his idea into a practical working system that could be applied on an industrial scale. The discovery of electrical applications and of radio and its relationship to the electromagnetic spectrum similarly depended on the work of a series of scientists, some more gifted theoretically, and some more gifted in experimental work: Faraday demonstrates the relationship between magnetism and electricity, Clerk Maxwell works out its theoretical basis, Heinrich Hertz produces the experimental proof, and Marconi applies Hertz's work to the invention of radio.

The importance of combining different skills requiring their own special kinds of physical coordination can be seen at their clearest in a team game or in a performance of an opera or ballet. Those taking part in the performance have their roles decided first of all by their physical constitutions and their training, but no amount of training will turn the pigeon-toed leader of the orchestra into the *prima ballerina assoluta* or even the fat tuba player into the fat leading tenor.

Good health, bad health and the disabilities of age can all affect an individual's creativity. Housman was most likely to write poetry when he was out of sorts. Before Wagner had the experience quoted in the last chapter of being given the Prelude to *Das Rheingold*, he had been suffering from dysentery brought on by eating too many Italian ice creams; this had been followed by violent seasickness on the journey to La Spezia. He had probably been forcing himself to create with the wrong part of his mind and he needed the relaxation brought on by illness and physical exhaustion for him to become aware of what was being given him to happen. Similarly Housman, with his savage analytical scholar's mind, needed to escape from that mind in order to compose. Much debate has been given to what gave rise to Titian's late style, when he was painting with very thin layers of paint and often reworking themes from his earlier days with an almost impressionistic technique: it has been suggested that he harboured his strength by painting with lightly loaded brushes.

The physical conditions required by different individuals are as varied as their temperaments. The sociable Goethe needed complete solitude when he composed; Raphael, on the other hand, could paint while carrying on a stimulating conversation with several people. The sickly Schiller kept a drawer of rotten apples in his desk and would revive himself by sniffing them when he was exhausted by his labours. Pushkin, while experiencing the flow of enthusiasm and inspiration, would sit stark naked in his fiercely heated study, taking spoonfuls from a large jar of marmalade to refresh himself as he wrote. Some need wine; some need music and wine; some have to avoid wine but need tobacco; others have to keep away from both; some need sex and some avoid sex. Balzac wore a monk's robe while writing and he believed he lost a novel every time he had an orgasm. Victor Hugo needed sexual intercourse daily into his eighties.

One could fill several books with the eccentricities of artists; what may seem like fads or caprices or derangement may often have been forms of self-protection or the result of certain knowledge about what is necessary to keep the flow going. Beethoven, walking along a street, unshaven, scruffy, talking to himself, laughing out loud, stopping to scribble something down in his notebook, may have seemed just a mad peasant: what he was actually doing was composing in his mind music that would sound to later hearers the essence of normality in the sense that the norm of humanity is wisdom and an understanding heart. He was, of course, for the second half of his life almost entirely deaf and he is one of the supreme examples in our culture of a creator who advanced far beyond his earlier achievements despite or perhaps because of his disability. One thinks of Heine confined in his last years to his 'mattress grave' composing his finest poems, and especially of Milton. Milton was as visually gifted as Beethoven was aurally gifted. His blindness forced him out of public life and in fact forced him to return to poetry and his early desire to write a great epic poem, saving him also perhaps from the execution or imprisonment that was the fate of several notable supporters of the Commonwealth at the Restoration. Deprived of the sight of the physical world, he had to create other worlds in his imagination: sometimes lying awake all night without a single verse coming and at other times feeling such an impetus that he would ring for his daughter Mary whatever the hour. In the daytime he would lean backward 'obliquely in an easy chair with his leg flung over the leg of it and dictate up to forty lines at a time'.[4]

If the purpose of our creativity is to gain or increase freedom, the means by which it achieves that purpose is through manifestation in the physical world and through the transformation of the physical world. There is a two-way flow in the creative process: the gift of freedom from above and the search for freedom from below. All creative persons, once they have been taught or learned the tradition or skills of their art, science or craft, have to find again and again that place within themselves where they can receive the gift from above and they can only find it through the force of their desire and yearning for that place.

The image that arises naturally in the language and discourse of the creative process to describe the flow of inspiration is that of water. Down the steep mountainside from heights invisible to the eye falls the cataract that feeds the tributaries of rivers that wash the walls of cities. From the depths of invisible rocks wells the spring coloured with the salts and minerals gathered on its way to the light. The rhythm of the waves champing on the beach, throwing up the sand and dragging it back again in their constant work of sculpture of the coastline, is a paradigm of the inner vibration in the soul. The repetition of the breakers sets up the rhythms and patterns of work to be manifested which come about as the suddenness of a single wave shot through with sunlight on its curving back signifies the breaking-out and the swamping of our ordinary minds by the moment of awareness that is the moment of inspiration. Water is the medium of interchange: its condensation signifies the descent into matter and its evaporation the return to the finer physicality of the atmosphere. It is the means of transport through sap in plants for the process of photosynthesis to take place and it brings about the rebirth of life in deserts as it maintains the vigour of life in jungles. In myth it is the ocean churned at Vishnu's direction to bring forth the treasures of civilization and the elixir of immortality and it is the well of Mime from which Odin gained his wisdom. It is the pool of the goddess Dana at the source of the Boyne where swim the salmon who eat the hazels of knowledge that fall into the water: one only has to eat a single scale of one of those salmon to become a bard. It is the Castalian spring at Delphi, once the waters where murderers purified themselves before they could approach the oracle and later, by association with the Muses, the fount of poetry.

This is the Netsilik Eskimo poet Orpingalik speaking of how poems are born:

Songs are thoughts, sung out with the breath when people are moved by great forces and ordinary speech no longer suffices.

Man is moved just like the ice floe sailing here and there out in the current. His thoughts are driven by a flowing force when he feels joy, when he feels fear, when he feels sorrow. Thoughts can wash over him like a flood, making his breath come in gasps and his heart throb. Something, like an abatement in the weather, will keep him thawed up. And then it will happen that we who always think we are small, will feel even smaller. And we will fear to use words. But it will happen that the words we need will come of themselves. When the words we want to use shoot up of themselves – we get a new song.[5]

143

The imagery of water and of related themes of drink, wine and milk and of sailing, navigation and swimming returns again and again in accounts of creative moments from many cultures. Dante in one of his Latin eclogues written at the time of the composition of *Paradiso* writes of the ewe who comes to him of her own accord, never to be forced, to be milked of verse[6] and in the opening of *Paradiso II* he dares his readers to follow his boat across the untraversed seas his vision draws him to cross. The ocean, especially in the centuries of western exploration, was a great image of the unknown: the elderly Newton looking back on his career said he had been 'only like a boy playing on the seashore, and diverting myself in now and then finding a smoother pebble or a prettier shell, whilst the great ocean of truth lay all undiscovered before me'.[7]

The imagery of water and of flowing is not dead metaphorical language: it recurs so often because it is closest to actual experience, as we have seen in the case of Wagner and the beginning of *Das Rheingold*. The German-American writer on music Arthur Abell conducted a series of interviews with many of his most prominent contemporaries at the close of the nineteenth century. Some of them spoke to him with such a dread of what might be thought of them if their experiences were generally known that they imposed a ban of fifty years after their deaths on the publication of their interviews. Thus Brahms told him:

When I feel the urge I begin by appealing directly to my Maker . . . I immediately feel vibrations which thrill my whole being . . . In this exalted state I see clearly what is obscure in my ordinary moods; then I feel capable of drawing inspiration from above as Beethoven did . . . Those vibrations assume the form of distinct mental images.

Straightway the ideas flow in upon me, directly from God, and not only do I see distinct themes in my mind's eye, but they are clothed in the right forms, harmonies, and orchestration. Measure by measure the finished product is revealed to me when I am in those rare, inspired moods . . .[8]

Tchaikovsky, writing to his patroness Nadezhda von Meck, said:

Generally speaking, the germ of a future composition comes suddenly and unexpectedly . . . It takes root with extraordinary force and rapidity, shoots up through the earth, puts forth branches and leaves, and finally blossoms. I cannot define the creative process in any way than by this simile . . . I forget everything and behave like a mad man; everything within me starts pulsing and quivering; hardly have I begun the sketch, ere one thought follows another . . . If that condition of mind and soul, which we call *inspiration*, lasted long without intermission, no artist could survive it. The strings would break and the instrument be shattered into fragments.[9]

There are clusters of imagery that recur in accounts such as these: they are of lightning flashes, waters undammed and flowing, and the eruption of spring as in Tchaikovsky's account. From the tiny point of concentrated and absorbed attention the mind is expanded into the universal. As Blake says in *Milton*:

Thou percievest the Flowers put forth their precious Odours,
And none can tell how from so small a center comes such sweets,
Forgetting that within that Center Eternity expands
Its ever closing doors that Og and Anak fiercely guard.[10]

Where do the content and the assimilation and the understanding come from? According to this passage from Blake, they expand from the centre of the flower which is the individuality of the poet. And how does it appear in such a young age as in the case of many artists, musicians and mathematicians? When one contemplates the achievements of the infant Mozart or comes away from the Picasso Museum in Barcelona having seen what Picasso was capable of in his early boyhood, one feels the need of a theory that encompasses and subsumes all the rival explanations, including an explanation that accounts for individuality.

The simplest explanations are, in many ways, the traditional ones. These depend on some form of pre-existence for the individual human being. In Buddhist and Hindu belief the pre-existence is in the form of previous lives so that the reincarnated soul, in moments of inspiration, draws on the memory not only of this life but of many earlier lives. In the Neo Platonic tradition, there is the doctrine of reminiscence: the soul remembers a state of purity and bliss in pre-existence when it lived on the plane of the good, the beautiful and the true. Dante expresses this as the soul remembering its contact with God at the moment of its creation and retaining the traces of universal love and knowledge from that moment

– and that would include the imaginative sympathy with which he was so supremely endowed. In Dante's case also he speaks of communication from the dead: Beatrice in *Purgatorio* tells him that she is the true source of his inspiration.[11] Similarly Blake believed he was inspired by the dead, chiefly his brother Robert. In many cultures the power and authority of the poet derives from his special ability to communicate with spirits who utter verses through him.

The Neo-Platonic theme appears in a sonnet by Canon Dixon, the friend and correspondent of Gerard Manley Hopkins:

> There is a soul above the soul of each,
> A mightier soul, which yet to each belongs:
> There is a sound made of all human speech,
> And numerous as the concourse of all songs:
> And in that soul lives each, in each that soul,
> Tho' all the ages are its life-time vast;
> Each soul that dies, in its most sacred whole
> Receiveth life that shall for ever last.[12]

At much the same time as Dixon wrote this poem, Hopkins wrote in a sonnet of his own an evocation of the inner voices of all things created:

> Each mortal thing does one thing and the same:
> Deals out that being indoors each one dwells;
> Selves – goes itself; *myself* it speaks and spells,
> Crying *What I do is me: for that I came.*[13]

The two poems contrast a seeming paradox; on the one hand the universal soul; on the other hand the individual mind or ego – how can the one express or comprehend the other? It is resolved through another paradox, that of the creative personality. What is most necessary for Mozart to be Mozart or Picasso to be Picasso is not so much their special combinations of skills but the wholeness of their individualities. It is through their individualities that the universal sympathy and inventive genius that we love and admire and are awed by in their work are manifested.

Individual, conversely to current usage, means in its original sense something that cannot be divided. Both meanings – the separated and the unseparated – come into play whether the term is used of our physical nature or our mental lives and our souls. In the physical sense it conveys our sense of special separateness, each being a creature whose awareness of self ends at the interface of skin with air and whose health depends on the defences of an individual immune system; it also conveys the sense of creatures that, if divided, if hanged, drawn and quartered, would no longer be those special creatures. On the other hand we are, physically, undivided from the cell world of the biosphere, from the air of the atmosphere and the energies of matter.

We would, however, *know* nothing of our individuality without the possession of the qualities of emotion, thought, memory and consciousness with which we are endowed and our capacities for observation, explanation and communication. The uniqueness of our experience, of our viewpoint of the world, is paradoxically what we need in order to share and to communicate. Our sense of ourselves is, similarly, what we need in order to learn what it is that we are undivided from at the level of the psyche or the subtle world. This is what with our families, communities and countries we share in the way of assumptions, social mores, language and common culture.

If we look further inwards, still tracing what we are undivided from, for the sources of music, art, poetry, ideas, images and archetypes, and for the essence of mathematical and scientific laws, for what we share with the rest of humanity, dead, living now, and to come, we find ourselves in a world dark in its potentiality, a world above and including time, the world of the unmanifested angel. We come here even more fully to our sense of ourselves and to whether we feel ourselves as sharing a greater awareness or connectedness or as shut in and separated. We can test the contrast by comparing what we feel like when, as creators or enjoyers, we are most fully aware, happy and capable and know ourselves to be the vehicles and the appreciators of the fresh, the new, the original, with the times when we are arid and incapable of creation or enjoyment. In the first case, in common with so many accounts of the creative process, we are most fully ourselves. We say with the plucked string and the swung bell: 'What I do is me; for that I came.' In the second case we feel insufficient, inadequate, and ashamed and untrusting of ourselves.

In relation to creativity, how the artist or thinker sees his individuality and its purpose may affect profoundly the work both in its manifestation and its interpretation. Where there is the sense of sharing, the individuality is itself an instrument, perhaps the chief creative instrument. Most of us barely use the full potentiality of our minds and that is probably not because we are stupid or ungifted but because we do not empty our minds enough to open up their capacity for receiving the intelligence of universal mind and consciousness. This is what I mean by individuality being a creative instrument, a true mirror of the consciousness of the primal and universal human being.

To understand both manifestation and interpretation we have to look at what lies beyond all preparation, skill and hereditary predisposition, and that is the desire to make and to understand. This again depends on the creative personality and the wholeness of individuality. Put in traditional terms, that desire comes from above the level of the angels. The Sufi poet Ibn Arabi writes of a high spiritual state called 'the sadness of the Divine Names'. What he says arises from consideration of the traditional saying of the Prophet in which God explains his reason for creating: 'I was a hidden treasure and I yearned to be known. Then I created creatures to be known by them.'[14] The sadness of the angels is owed to the fact that, though they can see and admire so much of the wonders of creation, they still know that there are infinitely more secrets to be revealed and their longing to know seems never to be satiated.

The desire to reveal a hidden treasure is what impels the creativity of many gifted people. The excitement of the process of creation is that after the initial inspiration the revelation of the treasure is as much a discovery for the creator as it will be for its audience or recipients. Such excitement feeds desire and impels the dreams of the artist ever further into the future. Boris Pasternak once said that the point of literature was to 'seize something of that magic, the future'.[15]

The desire to create is sometimes so powerful that it is the initiatory force. It is as much the desire to be in the state of creating, of connecting with the hidden greater mind or consciousness, as the desire to produce something or to convince others, that arouses the creative forces. Just as, in the examples I give in Chapter 13, what drives us to music, to reading, to the enjoyment of art is the desire to change our sense of ourselves, so the creative act can be an act of redemption of the sense of individuality.

The need to change the sense of the self is characteristic of the accounts of many Chinese painters and calligraphers. The seventh-century calligrapher Yu Shih said that when a man is about to take up the brush, he 'must draw back his vision and reverse his hearing, discard all thoughts and concentrate on spiritual reality. When his mind is tranquil and his breath harmonious his brush work will penetrate into subtlety . . . Tranquillity means harmony in thoughtlessness.'[16]

The same cleansing of the mind as a preparation for writing is described in Lu Chi's 'Essay on Literature' written in 302 AD. First he describes the motive or desire to write arising in the poet as he surveys the whole of the

universe, and as his spirit is touched by ancient writings, by the feelings
aroused by the seasons and the forms of nature, the deeds of the virtuous
and the forests of letters and the treasuries of poetry. Next comes the
stage of meditation before writing, when all external vision and sound
are suspended. Then emotion, first glimmering and then growing to full
luminosity, lights up the images:

Now one feels blithe as a swimmer calmly borne by celestial waters,
And then, as a diver into a secret world, lost in subterranean currents,
Arduously sought expressions, hitherto evasive, hidden,
Will be like stray fishes out of the ocean bottom to emerge on the
angler's hook;
And quick-winged metaphors, fleeting, far-fetched
Feathered tribes, while sky-faring are brought down from the curl-clouds
by the fowler's bow.
Thus the poet will have mustered what for a hundred generations awaited
his brush,
To be uttered in rimes for a thousand ages unheard.[17]

This seeking for contact with the source of ultimate knowledge within
oneself, this willing surrender of the ordinary concerns and desires of
day-to-day life in the hope and trust that new understanding will be
revealed is quite at variance with our western pictures of the artist
expressing his ego and the scientist conquering nature. Seen from the
viewpoint of universal consciousness in which the desire to make and
understand first arises, the images that come to mind to help explain our
creativity to ourselves are not those of sieges, taking by storm, conquest
and domination but those of incarnation, seeding and conception, birth
and growth.

There are complementary images to those of water, also concerned
with creativity and they are those of the lightning flash, fire, the heat of
the sun and the being of light which we call the angel, or the messenger of
the divine will. Graham Wallas, a philosopher writing in 1926, set out the
processes of creativity in four stages: (1) preparation, or the acquisition of the
knowledge, skills, and experience necessary for the future; (2) incubation,
the assimilation of impressions, images and thoughts into what Henry James
called 'the deep well of unconscious cerebration'[18]; (3) illumination, the
moment or period of understanding and of knowing that one understands;
and (4) verification, the work of the proof of a theory or the execution of

a work of art.[19] With the imagery of fire and of the angel we are concerned particularly with the stage of illumination.

Fire and angels come together in Isaiah's description of how he received his gift of prophecy. He saw a vision of the Lord and was made aware of the impurity of his lips and of those he lived among. A seraph flew to him with a live coal. Placing the live coal on Isaiah's lips, the seraph told him that, as it had touched his lips, the impurity was removed and he was purged of sin. Then, when the Lord asks who will go and speak on his behalf, Isaiah is ready to say: 'Here am I: send me.'[20] Pushkin, in his adaptation of the story in his poem *Prorok* (The Prophet), tells how the angel tears out the lying tongue of the prophet but also how the prophet's perceptions and understanding are transfigured to degrees of sensitivity and comprehension beyond all experience so that he is made into a worthy vehicle for the voice of God.

Prophet and poet both portray a man seeing his divine possibilities, infinitely beyond the limitations of ordinary thought and feeling and having his passionate desire to be cleansed and his mind replaced by the divine mind and imagination fulfilled. It has much more ancient forebears in the tradition of shamanism where the shaman, generally on behalf of others or of his tribe, undergoes rituals to bring himself into contact with the deepest powers within himself.

The angel tradition similarly is concerned with prophecy and revelation to others and also with the renewal of civilization. Like the many other great themes and images in western civilization and art that I have related to the theory of the Great Memory, it seems to die and then to recur unexpectedly: one of the ways in which one can trace it is to follow the influence of the chief Christian work of codification of the angels, *The Celestial Hierarchy* of Dionysius the Areopagite. Written by a Syrian mystic and monk in the fifth century, it reached France in the ninth century, when it was translated by John Scotus Eriugena, the Irish scholar who revived the study of philosophy in the West. Abbot Suger at the turn of the eleventh century and the beginning of the twelfth was inspired by the light mysticism and the angelic themes of Dionysius to become the chief patron of the architects who created the Gothic style. In his prayer with which he concludes his account of the consecration of the new choir of St-Denis, he beseeches Christ that:

by these visible blessings and others, thou mayest invisibly restore and miraculously change our present condition into the Heavenly Kingdom. Thus, in delivering up the Kingdom to God, even the Father, thou mayest in strength and mercy join us and the nature of the angels, Heaven and Earth, into one State; thou who livest and reignest as God for ever and ever. Amen.[21]

Concurrent with the rise of the Gothic style and perhaps arising from the same impulse came the rediscovery of the powers of the human mind through scholastic theology and philosophy. One of the aims of these rigorous disciplines was to reach the level of understanding, the shared and immediate intuition of truth, known as *intellectus* which is the property of the angels and which is above the ordinary human processes of thought, known as *ratio*. Many of the most prominent scholastic philosophers, including Aquinas, wrote commentaries on *The Celestial Hierarchy* and the emphasis on the angels as cosmic intelligences is reflected in the expressions of the faces of angels as depicted in Gothic sculpture.

The angel is an emblem of creative inspiration, of higher intelligence and of the highest art, which is the art of praise. The angel is also connected with important changes in the enlargement of the human capacity to think. The portrayal of winged heavenly bodies arises as a consequence of what happened in the many unconnected cultures in the fifth century BC when almost synchronously a new understanding dawned of the powers of the mind: in the band of Earth that stretches from China across the central plain of northern India to the Mediterranean, we find in the art or literature that was to arise from these new religions and philosophies the floating immortals of Taoism, the winged *apsaras* associated with Buddhism, the winged bulls and intelligences associated with Zoroastrianism, the seraphim and cherubim of the major Hebrew prophets, and the winged Victories and the other winged beings, such as Iris, the messenger of the gods, appearing in Greek art at the same time as the wakening of Attic philosophy. The liberty of the upper regions of the air was for all these cultures a symbol of the freedom of human thought in its mode of expansion.

The angel is also an emblem of the descent of divine messages – most famously in Christian tradition in the Annunciation of the Archangel Gabriel to the Virgin Mary. In Islam it is the same archangel who dictates the Koran to the Prophet Mohammed. In both traditions also the angel is the recorder or the divine remembrancer: so St Michael inherits the role of Minos and of Egyptian gods as the judge of souls. As the repository of all acts and thoughts he may be thought of as the Great Memory.

In the Renaissance period the work of Dionysius is taken up again and incorporated in the magical philosophy of the period, most particularly in relation to creativity by Marsilio Ficino. Though, following the Reformation and the rise of mechanistic science, the angels were increasingly excluded in any part of the running of the physical universe, they survived in the art of both Catholicism and Protestantism, particularly where music is concerned, and in the never-dying thought that our earthly music is a reflection of the heavenly hymnody and of the realms of pure sound heard by the composers in their states of pre-existence. They are particularly present in the mystical poetry of the period, in St John of the Cross, in George Herbert, Henry Vaughan and Thomas Traherne and in Angelus Silesius, rightly so named.

The angel was a necessary image to many of the Romantic poets and though it became debased in the art associated with the Victorian cult of the dead – which is why both the religious and the unreligious have fled from the consideration of angels – the theme of the angel and of the angelic hierarchies returned in a most extraordinary way in the years preceding and including the First World War. New translations of Dionysius the Areopagite appeared and new interest in mystical traditions helped to revive the theme. It returned in popular belief in the mass hallucination of the Angel of Mons, the story of the angel that appeared to wounded soldiers after one of the first battles of the war and which, fanned into circulation by the popular press, was an image of consolation in the midst of suffering that millions of people wanted to believe. It had also reappeared in the current influential theosophical movement and most of all in an offshoot of theosophy, the anthroposophical movement started by Rudolf Steiner. The cosmology of Steiner's thought, his development of evolutionary theory, and his account of individual human psychology, all owe much to *The Celestial Hierarchy* of Dionysius the Areopagite. His thought, with its emphasis on the action of the spirit on matter, and his teaching on the proper relationship of man with the soil will probably in the eyes of future historians turn out to be one of the most important precursors of the environmental movement and the change in thinking that this movement is bringing about.

My third example of the return of the angel in this period is also one of the supreme accounts of the suddenness and unexpectedness of the moment of inspiration. In the winter of 1911–12 the poet Rainer Maria Rilke, bothered by an awkward business letter, went for a walk on the bastions of the Castle of Duino, near Trieste, where he was staying at the time. A storm was blowing and the sea was raging two hundred feet below: as he paced up and down, trying to calm his thoughts, it seemed as though a voice called out to him: '*Wer, wenn ich schriee, hörte mich denn aus der Engel Ordnungen?*'[22] ('Who, if I cried, would hear me among the angel orders?') That line of verse, transcending and yet including all the poetry he had written to that date, was to become the opening of the first of his *Duino*

Elegies, the rest of which, apart from certain passages, was given to him in an intensive period of inspired work – which also included *The Sonnets to Orpheus* as an extra gift – shortly before he died in 1922.

Rilke saw our task on Earth in this way: we are 'to stamp this provisional, perishing earth into ourselves so deeply, so passionately, that its being may rise again "invisibly" in us'. We are bees, storing the honey of our experience in the hives of the Invisible. 'The Angel of the Elegies is the creature in whom that transformation of the visible into the invisible we are performing already appears completed.'[23]

The theme of the angel appears in the work of other poets in this period, for example in Paul Valéry, but the most notable counterpart to Rilke's use of it, that I know of, is in the collection of poems entitled *Sobre los angeles* of 1927 by Rafael Alberti. The angels of Alberti are emblems of mental and psychological states that are in himself but are also portrayals of the inner side of the faults and inconsistencies in society that were to lead to the Spanish Civil War. Thus the greedy angel is a man who does not know he is dead: he is capitalism believing it is able to buy anything, even the sky. On the other hand Alberti says to the hideous angels who are the poor that they are the reason for the journey of history: that they sleep in the marshes in order that a miserable dawn may wake them to the glory of dung – the dung being the alchemical state of putrefaction which is the beginning of new life. This is Alberti's description of his state when writing *Sobre los angeles*.

A 'guest of the clouds', I fell to scribbling in the dark without thinking to turn on a light, all hours of the night, with unwonted automatism, febrile and tremulous, in spontaneous bursts, one poem covering the other in a script often impossible to decipher in broad daylight ... Rhythms exploded in slivers and splinters, angels ascended in sparks, in pillars of smoke, spouts of embers and ashes, clouds of aerial dust. Yet the burden was never obscure; even the most confused and nebulous songs found a serpentine life and took shape like a snake in the flames.[24]

All these poets found themselves drawn by the theme of the angel even though they were alienated from or opposed to the Christian traditions from which they had in the first place received the image. Like Alexander Blok, who spoke of a comparable image, the Spirit of Music, to account for the apocalyptic state of society in revolution, the forces of history, in their own souls and around them, drove them to seek the image of a suprahuman being that was both judge and patron, a state of consciousness untouched by but observing and including the baseness and the violence of human imaginations given to murder and war.

The theme of the angel also appears in the art of the twentieth century and not only in works of commissioned sacred art, such as Jacob Epstein's *St Michael* at Coventry Cathedral, but in artists so different in their traditions and antecedents as the Russian-Jewish Marc Chagall and the Cornishman Cecil Collins. The Angel is one of the three main symbols in Collins's work, the others being the Lady or Anima and the Fool, who for him stood for purity of consciousness. He spoke of the Angel thus:

> the angelic intelligence is that which connects all the worlds and very often visits this world and enters into the world, into the battlefield of this world . . . They exist to help transform our consciousness . . . Angels are living at a higher speed than we are and because they are at a higher speed we don't see them . . . They are here as part of the transforming process of the universe and, of course, the Fool and the Anima . . . are two instruments of their transformation . . . They are the vision of God, the winged thoughts of the Divine Mind.[25]

To regard Collins's words as the remarks of a benign eccentric with whom the generality of the population disagreed would be wrong. There is a deep divorce in our society between what is allowed to be expressed and what people actually live by. Surveys of religious experience record not only a far higher number of mystical experiences among the population than was ever suspected but also a widespread belief in the presence of a guiding spirit or guardian angel, not to mention cases of seeing an angel. The records of those who have undergone the near-death experience include a high proportion of out-of-the-body experiences; that is, of receiving the liberty of the air and of visions of angels.

I am writing this in a millennial decade when many interests are proclaiming the coming of judgment and apocalyptic events. These in themselves would be enough to bring back the images of angels as instruments of judgment and punishment. Some, however, have predicted bigger changes on a quieter scale.[26] The angel can also be another image for the state of awakened consciousness for which the Green Man, the Face of Glory and Khidr may also stand. This change is a change of mind which must depend on the widening of consciousness throughout humanity and which will bring great changes in society through all individuals discovering a new sense of themselves, a sense of their individualities as instruments of knowledge, experience and communication and not only as mouths to be fed or eyes to be sated.

It has also been said that we are about to undergo a transformation of human mental powers that will be even greater in its expansion of thought and creative abilities than the discovery of the powers of the mind that took place in Asia and Europe in the sixth and fifth centuries BC.[27] The first forms of the angel appeared in association with that earlier transformation and, as we have seen, the angelic hierarchies and images have recurred at many important stages in the development of new civilizations ever since. To dare a prediction based on the hypothesis of the Great Memory for the first time in this book, I predict that the angel will return as a necessary image in many forms of thought and art – and in forms of thought and art still to come into being. I think it will return not only to art and religious thought as a universal archetype but with the acceptance of the idea of universal consciousness it will arise first of all in the exploration of the ecology of the spirit (of which we spoke in Chapter 2) and then in the study of dynamic and creative order in nature as in ecological relationships and in the overriding ideas and forms of species.

I also predict that the image of the angel will be of increasing importance as an emblem in these ways: in accounting for the speed and powers of organization brought about by consciousness in the creative moment; in signifying the mind that knows the future, that comprehends the natural law or the form of a work to be created, and as the messenger between the deepest, truest self and states of ordinary awareness; and in understanding the ways in which our minds and understanding are expanded through metaphor, analogy and the phenomenon of synchronicity. In using the habitual imagery of creativity I am following the example of a German scientist of the nineteenth century, Gustav Theodor Fechner, whose name is given to the law of psychological impressions. Fechner is an example of those who have triumphed and learned from severe physical disabilities: he was virtually blind for three years, a period during which he was unable to endure any contact with sunlight. He was possessed, however, of great gifts for analogy and metaphor and when he recovered his health and sight he devoted much of his work to the thought that science should be based as much on analogy as on the experimental method and that the analogical method was particularly suited to what he called 'the daylight view': this is an approach to the world based on seeing the spiritual as the rule instead of an exception in the midst of nature. The method was based on many direct experiences, including his remarkable description of what he saw when his sight was restored to him. This is one of those experiences:

One spring morning I went out early. The fields were greening, the birds were singing, the dew glistening, smoke was rising, here and there and here and there appeared a man: there fell on everything a transfiguring light; it was only a tiny fraction of the earth, only a tiny moment of its existence and yet as I comprised more and more in the range of my vision, it seemed to me not only so beautiful but so true and so evident that it is an angel, so rich and fresh and blooming, and at the same time so stable and unified, moving in the heavens, turning wholly towards heaven its animated face and bearing me with it to that same heaven – so beautiful and so true that I wondered how men's notions could be so perverted as to see in the earth only a dry clod, and to seek for angels apart from earth and stars or above them in the vacant heaven, and never find them.[28]

9

Metaphor, dream worlds and vision

The Green Man as the radiant face of the biosphere gives us the air by which we live and breathe. As the mouth of the creative force within our souls he blows towards us unremittingly the winds of myth, stories, fugitive visions, symbols and images in our dream lives and our waking existences, in that inner breath of the spirit which is the awareness of life. The wind drives the waves and the rain clouds and it blows the embers of ardour into flame. 'As free as the wind', we say; 'a wonderful atmosphere', we acknowledge in a gathering of like-minded people or in a holy place as though both were surrounded by a special kind of air. Thus we derive the use of 'atmosphere' as a synonym for mood from the envelope of air which embraces Earth; we call the creative moment 'inspiration' as though in that moment we breathed in the finer air of Heaven; at the sight of beauty we catch our breath and as it passes we sigh with longing for it to return. The whole of creation is a single exhalation of Brahma. In Eden God breathed upon the clay and so made Adam, who on waking saw his maker as his first perception and who, expelling the breath breathed into him, shouted the first word, the name of God, as an exclamation of joy.

I turn the earth with a fork and the earth smell, the *petrachor*, hits my nostrils. It is the sweat of the Green Man, being the residue of the volatile oils released from plants over millions of hot summers that travelled in the currents of the atmosphere and dropped into the soil. Air is the element of touch: I know it in the slightest breeze that, touching my skin, marks the limits of my earthbound physical body. It is the element of freedom: when I look up at the flight of birds I see not only their freedom in the element of air but images of freedom in my mind. There is an ancient association of the air with the carriage of metaphors, similes and images into our thoughts. Through the mouth of Theseus, Shakespeare says:

The poet's eye, in a fine frenzy rolling,
Doth glance from heaven to earth, from earth to heaven;
And, as imagination bodies forth
The forms of things unknown, the poet's pen
Turns them to shapes, and gives to airy nothing
A local habitation and a name.[1]

His contemporary Sir John Davies in his poem *Orchestra* develops a further
association of air with the art of the dance:

And now behold your tender Nurse the Ayre
And common neighbour that ay runns around,
How many pictures and impressions faire
Within her emptie regions are there found
Which to your sences Dauncing doe propound?
For what are breath, speech, Ecchos, musick, winds,
But Dauncings of the Ayre in sundry kinds?[2]

It is the appearance of images out of nothing, out of 'thin air', that inspires
the association of this element with metaphor. Who has seen the wind? And
yet we see the effect of the invisible, the pulses of the wind in the dancing of
waves and leaves, in the patterns of bird flight and the rapidly changing faces
of clouds, so that we also associate air with breath, rhythm and dance.

In dance and its related art of mime we see at its clearest and simplest
the way in which the body can be controlled so that every part is used
to communicate a meaning through gesture, stance, and rhythm. We see
this in most forms of dance but it is in what remains of sacred dance – in
Buddhist monastery dances and in the temple dances of the Hindus – we
are witnesses to the most complete union of feeling, thought and narrative
action expressed through the body. A similar union is to be seen in the
ceremony of the Mevlevi dervishes.

Metaphor is a game, an attempt to make temporary captures of chaotic
impressions and experiences and to bring them under control, and yet if we
look for the chief sources of metaphor we find them in what seems at first
the part of our natures least pliant to control; our dream life.

Metaphor is a necessity of the human spirit. Pasternak says it is
necessary because we are so short-lived we need it to compress and contain
our experience.[3] It is our chief means of stepping from the known to the

unknown, of explaining the unfamiliar in terms of the familiar. The word means 'the bearer beyond'. Metaphor can be thought of as encapsulated myth because it answers to the same need of bringing the inexplicable into sight if not into grasp. Our language is as stratified with metaphor as is the soil beneath our feet with the overlappings of geological ages and the middens of prehistory.

As metaphor draws on the past to explain the present or the unknown, so it is an aspect of memory. Our memories are often, or perhaps always, metaphors: we have a particular picture in our minds of a house in our childhood which stands for many years of experience of family life; we sum up the dead in certain intense images from the past. Unless we want to become like the mapmakers in Jorge Luis Borges's story 'Del Rigor en la ciencia', who were so driven by the desire for accuracy that they were impelled to make a map that was exactly the size and with all the details of the empire where they lived, we are forced to condense the past into images that become metaphors of our present identities. Thus the gigantic images of the Great Memory can be regarded as metaphors: a heroic past recovered by a people seeking or fighting for independence is a metaphor of how they wish to act and what they wish to become. The use of the phrase 'the Great Memory' is itself a metaphor, the attribution of a faculty observed in human experience to a process in history and in nature, or, to put it another way, it is a metaphor for a reality that imbues and has effects upon physical reality.

Aristotle says in the Poetics that the capacity for finding or making metaphor is one talent that can never be acquired: it must be inborn and is the token of genius.[4] Perhaps he is right in the sense that the great poets and dramatists with whom he was concerned were exceptionally gifted as makers of images and similes. On the other hand we could all be said to be born with that talent, first because we could never understand and use metaphor ourselves unless we had some capacity for it and second because in our dream lives we are constantly making metaphors out of our experience to explain our lives to ourselves.

We all possess in our dreaming natures a hidden magician who rearranges our thoughts, emotions and impressions into films and dramas such as we could never invent in our daylight awareness.[5] He can be thought of as our guardian angel who sends the messages we are deaf to hearing in other ways. To take the simplest examples, many, if not most, of our dreams are metaphors of our physical state while asleep. You dream that you have been buried alive and you wake up in order to escape from the terror to find that the sheet is wrapped close round you like a shroud. The hidden magician has rushed to give you a metaphorical explanation of the sensation of being wound round like a corpse. The extent to which the hidden magician transposes the messages from the body into images was once made very clear to me when, after an operation, I had been given painkillers. I felt nothing in the way of physical pain: my sleep was tortured, however, with dreams and hypnagogic images of violence, of brilliant but savage colours, of leering and cruel faces, of slashing knives and battles, of a temple that started vibrating in all its stones and whose columns began to jerk up and down as though they were springs and then turned into Roman legionaries marching off to fight. It was more painful to endure in some ways than the illness that had led to the operation: madness seemed to follow physical sickness. Yet there was someone awake enough in me to see that all the messages from my body, outraged at the necessary violation of the surgeon's knife and unable because they were blocked by morphine drugs to use their normal pathways of communication, were funnelled to the hidden magician who interpreted them to me in images of civil war.

If the hidden magician and his sometimes less competent apprentices can make so much out of physical sensations, how much more can such talents give to more positive and creative ends! There is no part of our natures, our sexual desires, our emotions and our thoughts that he cannot play games with and force at some time or another into our attention. He has access to all the locked cupboards in the libraries of our memories and he can play reels and videos of our past we thought forgotten for ever. What is more, and what makes his activities so akin to the examples of the creative moment I have given in earlier chapters, is the speed with which he coordinates and directs memories and impressions into new syntheses and fantastic worlds. How do we make friends with him, how do we entice him into making his games the games we want to play?

The answer seems to lie, where enhancing creativity is concerned, in what we love, what questions, mysteries or images we habitually turn our minds to, what, in effect, we dream about. He responds to unremitting desire, the kind of desire that is made apparent in early childhood, as in the instances I gave on pages 121–2 and page 145, or to what is the subject of our daydreams. This is a story of Einstein as a small boy. When he was four or five, lying ill in bed, his father brought him a magnetic compass. He was fascinated by the way the needle was always drawn to the north whichever way he turned the compass. In his *Autobiographical Notes* he said: 'I can still remember – or at least believe I can remember – that this experience made a deep and lasting impression on me. Something deeply hidden had to be behind things.'[6] It is thought that his experience awakened in him what was to be a constant in his thought throughout his life, the idea that there is a fundamental 'invariance' in nature. We will come to this story again when we consider the part played by experiences in childhood that determine the *themata*, or guiding thought forms that affect the interpretation of inspirations. Thus dominant emotions, aroused early in life, can be focused on objects such as a magnetic compass so entirely that the object itself becomes a metaphor or a source of metaphors, bearing the child beyond his visible surroundings, awakening the capacity for daydreaming that will sink into his deeper dream levels, and setting the course of his future career.

Poems, the seeds of novels, the design of buildings and of cities, music, new ideas in philosophy: there are numerous examples of these appearing first of all in dreams. As we have seen, Mendeleev dreamed the form of the Periodic Table that bears his name and had to make only one slight correction after he had woken from sleep and written out what had been given him. Not only ideas and images come through dreams: the hidden magician can be immensely practical as well. The inventor of the sewing machine, Eli Howe, was held up for years in making a successful machine because he set the eye of the needle in the middle of the shank. One night he dreamed that he had been captured by a savage tribe. The king of the tribe ordered him to finish the machine on pain of death. He was being taken to execution when he saw that in the spears carried by his guards there were eye-shaped holes close to the spear blades. He realized that what was necessary was a needle with an eye near the point. He leaped from bed and quickly made a model of the needle with the eye at its point and that enabled him to make a sewing machine that worked.[7]

An eighteenth-century Chinese artist, Kao Ch'i P'ei, had a dream in which he was taken into a cave by an Immortal and shown paintings more wonderful than anything he had ever seen. Desperate to copy them, he had no brushes with him but there was some water in a hollow of the cave wall. So he used his fingers to copy them. When he came out of the dream he realized he had discovered a new technique, that of finger painting, which he employed to great effect in his own work and which was taken up and used by many other artists.

Experimental techniques have been given to scientists in dreams. Otto Loewi won the Nobel Prize in 1936 for his discovery that the nerve impulse is both a chemical and an electrical event. He had had an intuition early in his career that this might be the case but could think of no experiment to test his idea. Seventeen years later this happened:

The night before Easter Sunday of that year (1920) I awoke, turned on the light, and jotted down a few notes on a tiny slip of this paper. Then I fell asleep again. It occurred to me at six o'clock in the morning that during the night I had written down something important, but I was unable to decipher the scrawl. The next night, at three o'clock, the idea returned. It was the design of an experiment to determine whether or not the hypothesis of chemical transmission that I had uttered seventeen years ago was correct. I got up immediately, went to the laboratory, and performed a simple experiment on a frog's heart according to the nocturnal design. Its results became the foundation of the theory of chemical transmission of the nervous impulse.[8]

Perhaps the most influential dreams in the history of scientific thought were the three dreams René Descartes experienced on the night of 10 November 1619 in Ulm. He was then a young officer taking part in the early campaigns of the Thirty Years' War. First he dreamed that in a strong gale he was trying to reach the church of the Jesuit college where he had been educated. At the moment when he turned to greet someone the wind blew him away violently against the church. Then someone else handed him a melon. At this he woke up in pain and he prayed for protection. He dreamed a second time: a noise like a bolt of lightning terrorized him and a shower of sparks filled the room. In the third dream he saw on a table a dictionary and an anthology of the poets open at a passage of Ausonius: *quod vitae sectabor iter?* ('What path shall I follow in life?') An unknown man handed him verses in which the words '*Est et Non*' caught his eye. At the end of this dream he dreamed first that the second dream of the shower of sparks was a dream and then he was given the interpretation of the dictionary, the poem and the Latin phrase. He saw the dictionary as the future unity of all the sciences, the poems as the union of philosophy and wisdom and the phrase '*Est et Non*' as truth and falsity in human attainment and in secular sciences. The first two dreams he took as warnings about his past life – the melon, for example, means his love of solitude that he had sought for selfish reasons. The lightning is the spirit of truth and it was this that indicated in the third dream his task of unifying the sciences. He immediately began writing the work later published as *Discours sur la méthode*. The account of his dreams offers a succinct example of the creative moment as being a moment of simplification, of making clear what the tasks are that lie ahead.[9]

The images of dreams do not come to us only as startling interruptions to our sleep or in the intermediate state between sleep and waking. It was shown a few years ago that the alternating states of deep sleep and REM (or rapid-eye-movement) sleep – the latter being the state in which we normally dream – are related respectively to the left and right sides of our brain and that in REM sleep we are centred in the right-hand hemisphere, which is the domain of emotion and visual experience. Later it came to be seen that a similar ninety-minute cycle of alternating between the two sides of the brain continues throughout our waking state in the daytime and therefore there are times in the day when we are closer to our dream life and consequently more open to the gifts of the hidden magician.[10]

There are at least two other ways in which our dream life manifests itself to us. One is the hypnagogic state in which *before* we go to sleep we experience brilliantly coloured scenes presented to us by the hidden magician. Most children, it is thought, experience hypnagogic images but only about 10 per cent of adults retain the capacity to experience it into later life. What is different about the hypnagogic experience is that one is an observer of the dream images, able to influence them subtly at times, and not, as in a dream, an actor or performer in a drama. It was in this state that Kekulé had the two famous experiences, one of which showed him how molecules combine and the other of which gave him the structure of the benzene ring. Though Kekulé's experiences are spoken of as dreams, they are quite clearly hypnagogic experiences because of the quality of observation he mentions in his descriptions. In my own experience of hypnagogic visions, though they could be frightening when I was a child, they are not so much directly creative messages as 'threshold images', indications that something new and stimulating is about to appear. A recurrent example of a threshold image for me is a hypnagogic image of sunlit water in a stream running over stones that are lit through the water's transparency. It is in itself beautiful and calming – and a message indicating that I have to look out for something else that will be communicated. One of the most delightful and yet sombre accounts of the experience I know of is Keats's 'Epistle to John Hamilton Reynolds':

> Dear Reynolds! as last night I lay in bed
> There came before my eyes that wonted thread
> Of shapes, and shadows, and remembrances,
> That every other minute vex and please:
> Things all disjointed come from north and south, –
> Two Witch's eyes above a Cherub's mouth,
> Voltaire with casque and shield and habergeon,
> And Alexander with his nightcap on;
> Old Socrates a-tying his cravat,
> And Hazlitt playing with Miss Edgeworth's cat;
> And Junius Brutus, pretty well so so,
> Making the best of's way towards Soho.[11]

The poem follows a pattern familiar to those who have let their fascination with hypnagogic experiences carry them into strange polarities and reversals of accepted thoughts. He leaps to a description of a scene of sacrifice from ancient Greece, which must be a preparation for the 'Ode to a Grecian Urn', and then makes a fantasy out of Claude's painting *The Enchanted Castle*. Then comes doubt and finally despair:

O that our dreamings all, of sleep or wake,
Would all their colours from the sunset take:
From something of material sublime,
Rather than shadow our own soul's day-time
In the dark·void of night . . .[12]

He asks if imagination 'brought/Beyond its proper bound' and 'lost in a sort of Purgatory blind/Cannot refer to any standard law/Of either earth or heaven?' And then he describes himself looking at the sea. He was at home 'and should have been most happy'

                    but I saw
Too far into the sea, where every maw
The greater on the less feeds evermore –
But I saw too distinct into the core
Of an eternal fierce destruction . . .[13]

Keats is quite aware of many of the sources of his hypnagogic experiences. His description helps us to see in them the origins of many of his most famous and best loved images and passages: the hidden magician within himself who is constantly reorganizing the experience of life, art, nature, and reading into new wholes of imagery and presenting them as messages or instructions. In this poem we catch glimpses of the dicotyledonous leaves that will grow into the saplings of his other odes as well as that to the Grecian urn.

With the hypnagogic experience, powerful and seemingly unwanted emotions may also come through. 'Away, ye horrid moods,' Keats says at the end of the epistle. It is these eruptions of emotion as well as the fear of delusion and hallucination that cause writers in many mystical traditions to give severe warnings against hypnagogic and similar experiences. They are condemned as 'glamour' in Orthodox mysticism and treated most warily in western traditions. However, what may be a severe danger to the fledgling monk or, at best, a distraction from the object of his contemplation, may be to the artist, poet or scientist the breakthrough to the image or synthesis of information that is necessary for present or future work. The monk does not have the training needed to control and guide the image for the purposes of beauty and usefulness and could only turn it into vainglory. In other traditions these experiences are regarded as signs on the way, threshold images to indicate that a certain advance has taken place. The Svetasvatara Upanishad tells how the meditator will see forms resembling snow, crystals, smoke, fire, lightning, fireflies, the sun and the moon and that these are signs on the way to Brahman.[14] Later (in Chapter 15) we will see how Hugh of St Victor makes use of the image-making faculties as a spiritual exercise for deepening the understanding of scripture.

The next way in which our dream life can impose on our awareness is what I have called 'the waking dream' and what Coleridge calls 'ocular spectra'. This is the interposition of an image or scene seemingly between our eyes and the world perceived before us. Coleridge was quite accustomed to this phenomenon, describing instances of it in his letters and notebooks. It happened to him while he read, while he wrote and simply in the business of living.

I bent down to pick something from the ground . . . as I bent my head there came a *distinct vivid* spectrum upon my eyes; it was one little picture – a rock, with birches and ferns on it, a cottage backed by it, and a small stream. Were I a painter I would give an outward existence to this, but it will always live in my memory.

So he wrote to William Godwin in 1801 and on another occasion he told Humphry Davy that while he was writing a poem 'voluntary ideas were every minute passing, *more or less transformed into vivid spectra*'.[15] One of his finest poems and one in which his powers of conveying graphic scenes with intensity into the reader's mind are most vigorously employed, is his 'Hymn before Sunrise in the Vale of Chamouni' of 1802. He never went there. Its vividness is the creation of his ocular spectra from his reading and, more than that, he incorporated into the poem, without acknowledgment and with a seamless join, some twenty lines by a German woman poet, Friederike Brun, addressed to Klopstock. This German poem must have impressed him and sunk into his dream levels to be given back to him by the hidden magician together with the ocular spectra. As many writers know, the hidden magician is an unconscionable plagiarizer and he is party to no copyright conventions.

Whereas when we experience hypnagogic imagery, we are generally free from distractions – we are in bed, our eyes are shut or we have gone apart for peace or meditation – and whereas we can sometimes predict that it is going to happen, in the case of the waking dream it is quite different. It is quite unpredictable: it may come upon one in the midst of conversation or while travelling surrounded by other people just as much as when one is alone.

To give an instance from my own experience, some years ago, I was walking up the staircase of the house in London where we had a flat on the top floor. It was an early-nineteenth-century house and the half-landings of the staircase were lit by windows looking out on to gardens and trees. The atmosphere of the staircase always reminded me of houses in my childhood and it may have been an emotion recovered from my earliest youth that triggered off what happened. Without any warning I saw with my eyes open a scene from the Middle Ages: I saw a city square where it had recently been raining in front of the west front of a cathedral in the process of being built. A huge lizard was suspended in the air from ropes which were hauling it up the west front of the cathedral. The sun broke through the clouds and illuminated the puddles, the building and the creature in the air. The whole experience, myself, my body, the waking dream, the light on the staircase, were all contained within an almost unbearable feeling of delight, mystery and wonder. Though the immediate experience faded from me, it was left impressed most forcefully, by the emotion as much as the brilliance of the visual detail, upon my memory like an imperative question, a question whose answer could only be made in the form of a poem. The poem had to explain what the creature was doing hanging in the air in front of the cathedral: it came to me rapidly that the lizard was a salamander, the principle of fire that the masons had to incorporate into their unfinished cathedral so that its towers and spires and pinnacles still to be built would rise to heaven with the levitating power of fire. As I wrote the poem, concentrating and always trying to return to the original waking dream, so I was given further intense visual images that unfolded other elements in the story to make it into a coherent narrative. Thus the poem that came entirely from this fleeting waking dream was written and published.[16]

It could be said that what I am speaking of is hallucination but there is a simple test to apply to this experience: it is to say: 'By their fruits shall ye know them.' The kabbalists used to say that dreams are the unripe fruits of prophecy. The instances I am giving all had results: they ended in a sculpture, a symphony, a poem, a theorem or an equation. They are the ripe fruits that have fed others.

It should also be asked why, as everyone dreams, as many people have hypnagogic experiences and as, probably, large numbers experience at times visions or waking dreams, not everyone is creative in the generally accepted sense. The answer probably lies as much in desire as in talent. They do not have the genetic endowment or the cultural nurturing but also they do not have the drive of the desire to make. This does not mean that they do not possess the desire to understand or to appreciate and it is the urgent message of my theme that understanding and appreciation are also talents and arts to be cultivated and that understanding and appreciation also depend upon how our dream life is fed and nurtured.

What is it then that makes the dream or the vision *usable*, capable of interpretation and of expanding understanding? Pasteur said: 'In the field of experimentation chance favours only the prepared mind.'[17] In addition to the inborn and acquired skills that are necessary to expression and to the desire to make or discover, I think it is a particular purity of conscious emotion, a state in which knowing and feeling are unified. There is, as I have said by inference, in the making of dreams and symbols a level of organization, a hidden magician at work constantly reorganizing our experience, knowledge and emotions, and sometimes able by the brilliance of his work to interrupt our sleep and waking life so that we are enticed into becoming the actors in his productions or his audience. Beyond what he can give us is another level of organization, which unifies our waking and our dreaming lives. This is the expansion of our conscious awareness to encompass and marry again the divorced sides of our natures.

The closest analogy to the experience of this state I can think of is that of sound or music. It is as though a chord of consciousness resonates through us, pulsing into rhythms that instantaneously reorganize our dream life, which it brings closer to the levels of awareness, and with a healing suture binds those rhythms to the scattered words and thoughts that also acquire simplicity and coherence from the resonance.

The waking dream as an interposition of the symbols and images of our dream life between the waking self and the world normally perceived by our senses, may seem not to be within the recognizable experience of many people. It is comparable, however, to the ways in which a landscape, a place, a building, a tree or a bird awakens our dream life and brings it more fully to the levels of awareness. This includes the almost universally experienced recognition of atmosphere in a place, often a place with ancient or sacred associations. One of the characteristics shared by the waking dream and the heightened awareness aroused by the atmosphere of a holy place is that they both convey a sense of coming closer to the truth.

In visiting a holy place, expectation and association must often play a part in preparing us for what we may experience: if we are to go on pilgrimage we have to know that there is a goal for our pilgrimage even if that goal is unknown. Too much expectation, anticipating experience, may lead to disappointment but the real test of the special kind of truth we can learn in a sacred place is that sense of being stripped of the old world and of entering a new world which is one we read so to speak with the eye of the heart. Another test of the experience is its memorability: look at the eyes of someone describing a scene or a place of this kind visited years ago and you may find, even if you have not visited the place yourself, an inner picture of the place rising in you created by the unconscious artistry of the conscious experience that is being remembered. There is something else we bring ourselves to these places and that is the intuitive feeling for the symbolism of landscape and water and skies that is part of our archetypal and universal heritage. The ancient abbey enclosed in a valley, the temple set on a mountain peak, the lichenous cross on a windy headland, the chambered tomb, whose slabs are carved with mysterious symbols, set on a lonely island, these resonate with the landscapes of our souls. They are human creations, human additions to the landscape that draw out from us the hidden humanity that is in nature, the indelible anthropomorphism that in secret tells us that everything is alive or is part of a living changing and unchanging whole. Such messages can come as powerfully from landscapes largely untouched by man as these instances show.

In 1816, fourteen years after Coleridge had published his imagined portrayal of Mont Blanc in his 'Hymn before Sunrise', Shelley travelling with his wife-to-be, Mary Godwin, visited the valley of Chamonix.[18] Mary Shelley was to draw on their visit to the Mer de Glâce for the scenes when Frankenstein comes to his interview with his monstrous creation who demands that Frankenstein should make a female companion for him. The ice of their surroundings is the ice of the scientific imagination, as seen in Frankenstein's behaviour. The story arose because she with Shelley, Byron and Byron's doctor William Polidori had entered on a ghost-story competition. She tried in vain to devise a story until one night she went to bed but could not sleep: 'My imagination, unbidden, possessed and guided me, gifting the successive images that arose in my mind with a vividness far beyond the normal bounds of reverie. I saw — with shut eyes but acute mental vision – I saw the pale student of unhallowed arts kneeling beside the thing he had put together.'[19] Mary Shelley thus had a hypnagogic experience into the expression of which she later incorporated impressions of this journey.

Shelley, on the other hand, overpowered by the immediate experience of seeing Mont Blanc from a bridge over the river Arve, was inspired to write his lines on Mont Blanc, a meditation on nature, consciousness, dream states and the source of human thought;

> Some say that gleams of a remoter world
> Visit the soul in sleep, – that death is slumber,
> And that its shapes the busy thoughts outnumber
> Of those who wake and live. – I look on high;
> Has some unknown omnipotence unfurled
> The veil of life and death? or do I lie
> In dream, and does the mightier world of sleep
> Spread far around and inaccessibly
> Its circles?[20]

As the powerful impressions of the visit worked into him, so they evoked the traditional associations of the imagery of the mountain: that the mountain symbolizes unchanging truth, that its interior is the place of the dead, that its summit is the meeting place of man with the gods and that it is also that unveiling of consciousness in which the meeting with the divine can be realized. Gazing at Mont Blanc, 'still, snowy, and serene', he says:

> The secret Strength of things
> Which governs thought, and to the infinite dome
> Of Heaven is a law, inhabits thee![21]

In the visitors' books en route he had affirmed his atheism in an inscription in Greek. Yet here he is attempting to express the hidden consciousness that lies behind mind and matter and includes sleep, dreaming and waking. In this poem the stupendous landscape seems to have shaped the very course of his thought so that we feel the slow advance of new ideas pressing forward like glaciers in the rhythms and counter-rhythms of his sentence structure; these ideas are so massive in their conceptions that to ally himself to any past expressions of godhead or divinity would limit and impede the sense of greatness and of freedom he was inspired to convey.

We do not have to travel long distances to lonely places to experience the merging of our dream lives with our waking experience that characterizes the living myth. It can occur whenever our attention is caught by a natural object and we hold it in ever fuller awareness. During the period I have been writing this chapter a high wind has been blowing boisterously. The wind has been whipping the clouds across the sky, alternating rain with brilliant sunshine while also careering through a normally staid ash tree. It turns all its leaves upside down and reveals the countless yellowing chatelaines of its seed keys which sway from their weight at a slower oscillation than the lighter grey-green cloud shapes of the leaves. The strangeness of its colour contrasts, the wild rhythms of its swaying boughs, and the challenge to its strength and rootedness the wind presents, all give me new images of the tree of life, images that can come only from the dream world the wind brings closer to awareness.

Great landscape painting also depends from this doubling and intensification of visual perception. The many series of paintings by Monet devoted to the discovery of variations of emotion and mood in single subjects – the cliffs at Etretat, the haystacks, the poplars, the west front of Rouen Cathedral in many lights, and the later series of paintings of the flower borders and avenues and of the waterlilies in his garden at Giverny – arise in each case from the mystery and the sense of feelings to be explored in these subjects. The mystery was always too great for one painting alone to convey the range of emotions and the challenge of colours to be evoked. He had to return again and again to the haystacks, for example, in every kind of weather and time and mood of day, sometimes seeing them as rounded, moulded, opaque and shadowed lumps and at other times as shapes whose translucency mocks the seeming opacity of solid things. They become through his attention mythical creatures, beings with souls and individualities of their own. His paintings therefore are mythopoeic explorations of perceived reality and what we respond to in his paintings, far more deeply than we would to a photograph of the same scene or even when we visit his garden at Giverny, is the living myth that is part of our own experience.

In such states of deeply felt atmosphere and of heightened perception we live in a mood in which a special state of self-consciousness arises, purifying our imagination. How does the effect of consciousness on creativity relate to the unconscious working of the dream levels? First of all, in many of the instances I have given of inspiration coming through dreams and visions, there is evidence of long searches and arduous application to experiment, thought and preparation. Second, consciousness of the order I am speaking of unites the dreaming and the waking sides of our natures and it is accessible to both sides. Descartes' three dreams were preceded by two years of application to problems of mathematics and philosophy and his third dream, especially in its close when he is given the interpretation of what the dreams signify, has all the marks of this fuller order of consciousness. He *knew* what he had to do.

The hidden magician is therefore biddable to a certain extent when made the companion to a strong desire. He will often allow his visions and images to come under the control necessary to the execution of a work of art. How that control is first exerted may begin very early in life. The need to gain control may be forced upon a child as an act of courage in facing up the involuntary terrors of the imagination or as a defence against genuine persecution. Rudyard Kipling would be locked up in a mildewy basement by the woman into whose care his unwitting parents had placed him. Inspired by *Robinson Crusoe*:

I set up in business alone as a trader with savages . . . My apparatus was a coconut shell strung on a red cord, a tin trunk, and a piece of packing-case which kept off any other world. Thus fenced about, everything inside the fence was quite real but mixed with the smell of damp cupboards. If the bit of board fell, I had to begin the magic all over again . . . The magic, you see, lies in the ring or fence that you take refuge in.[22]

Robert Louis Stevenson suffered from nightmares from childhood into early adulthood. He discovered a way of transforming them by telling himself stories as he was going off to sleep. This had the effect of calming his dreams and making them less frightening. He called the makers of his dreams his Brownies or the Little People. In his essay 'A Chapter on Dreams' he asked: 'Who are the Little People? . . . And who is the dreamer?' His answer was this:

Well as regards the dreamer, I can answer that, for he is no less a person than myself . . . and for the Little People, what shall I say they are but just my Brownies, God bless them! who do one-half my work for me while I am fast asleep, and in all human likelihood, do the rest for me as well, when I am wide awake and fondly suppose I do it for myself. That part which is done while I am sleeping is the Brownies' part beyond contention; but that which is done when I am up and about is by no means necessarily mine, since all goes to show the Brownies have a hand in it even then . . .[23]

He gives the instance of how the story of *The Strange Case of Dr Jekyll and Mr Hyde* came to him. Needing money badly, he went about for two days racking his brains for a plot.

> . . . on the second night I dreamed the scene at the window, and a scene afterward split in two, in which Hyde, pursued for some crime, took the powder and underwent the change in the presence of his pursuers. All the rest was made awake, and consciously, although I think I can trace in much of it the manner of my Brownies.[24]

Nikola Tesla as a child had to meet a challenge similar to Stevenson's. The way in which he was later able to develop his many influential inventions is probably owed to the way in which he overcame a peculiar affliction which took the following form. His powers of memory of past experiences were so extreme that they could rise up in him in his field of vision as vividly as the scene before him in the present moment. They were often accompanied by flashes of light. These experiences could be terrifying: he could relive all the sadness of a funeral with full perceptive detail returning to him at night and it would persist even though he could punch a fist through it.

He tried by a series of experiments to master these experiences. First he discovered he could replace the sad or terrifying memories with pleasant memories. Since, on account of his youth, he did not have a great stock of memories to draw on, he extended his visualizations by imagining that he was travelling round the world and inventing scenes and people. When he was about seventeen, his mind and interests turned to inventing and he discovered that the visualization techniques originally developed to overcome terror of the unwanted memories could be used for possible inventions. 'Over half a century before the invention of the computer, he discovered what modern programmers know as "modelling and simulation".'[25] He found that he was able to construct, modify and even operate his hypothetical devices, purely by visualizing them.

As an example of what must still lie beyond the most developed powers of visualization, the unitive moment of knowing in creative work, this is the story of how Tesla as a student made his first notable discovery. Shown a dynamo in the classroom, he made suggestions about making a more efficient dynamo. His professor lectured the class on why Tesla was wrong. Stung into intense reflection by the challenge to prove himself right, he spent a long period visualizing different kinds of motor. The problem seemed unsolvable but he still felt the solution lay in the deep recesses of his brain.

One evening in 1882 in Budapest, Tesla and a friend were reciting poetry as they walked through a park. The setting sun reminded him of a passage from *Faust Part I* in which Faust, before he makes his pact with Mephistopheles, laments the fact that as day recedes he has no wings to rise and follow it with his body as he has wings for his mind. As Tesla recited this passage,

the idea came like a flash of lightning and in an instant the truth was revealed. I drew with a stick on the sand the diagrams shown six years later in my address before the American Institute of Electrical Engineers, and my companion understood them perfectly. The images I saw were wonderfully sharp and clear and had the solidity of metal and stone, so much so that I told him: 'See my motor here; watch me reverse it.' I cannot begin to describe my emotions. Pygmalion seeing his statue come to life could not have been more deeply moved. A thousand secrets of nature which I might have stumbled upon accidentally I would have given for that one which I had wrested from her against all odds and at the peril of my existence . . . For a while I gave myself up entirely to the intense enjoyment of picturing machines and devising new forms. It was a mental state of happiness about as complete as I have ever known in life. Ideas came in an uninterrupted stream and the only difficulty I had was to hold them fast. The pieces of apparatus I conceived were to me absolutely real and tangible in every detail, even to the minutest marks and signs of wear. I delighted in imagining the motors constantly running, for in this way they presented to the mind's eye a more fascinating sight . . . In less than two months I evolved virtually all the types of motors and modifications of the system which are now identified with my name.[26]

What had been in Tesla's childhood a technique necessary for him to develop in order to escape from the terrifying recurrences of his memories now came to his aid as a superlative skill enabling him to bring his reasoning powers to act directly upon these gifts from the visualizing faculties of his mind. It is comparable to what novelists and certain historians have said about waiting to write until they hear their characters talking and to the much quoted but questioned letter of Mozart in which he speaks of hearing a work in his mind all at once.[27]

Such states may be looked upon as a form of marriage, between reason and energy, between the left-hand and the right-hand hemispheres, between the masculine and feminine elements in our natures, and between our waking selves and our dreaming selves. The priest at the marriage is consciousness and its child is joy. It may be that the neurophysiologists will find that metaphor may, as it links hitherto unconnected strands of thought and imagery, also bring together and coordinate the energies of different parts of the brain and that the sense of freedom a new metaphor can give us is experienced through this release of energies. In descriptions of these states we see the importance of the transformation of chaotic and often negative emotions into positive and unified attitudes of mind, only through which the powerful energies of the psyche can be made fruitful.

For its greater manifestations it probably arises from the achievement of metanoia, the change of mind and vision constantly mentioned in the Gospels. What Dante describes as the tasks and occupations of the souls in *Purgatorio* is the achievement of the metanoia they strove for too weakly in life. Visions, voices, angels and symbols constantly come to the aid of these souls and Dante participates in these experiences. He makes them real to us because he was drawing on his own experiences of dreams, hypnagogic states, ecstasies and waking dreams which he had earlier described in *La Vita Nuova*. In the central cantos of *Purgatorio* which also mark the numerical centre of *The Divine Comedy*, which I have already referred to in Chapter 3 in relation to the theme of civil war, he relates his waking dreams to one of his own most debilitating faults, which was anger. Led by Marco Lombardo into the black smoke which signifies the blindness of rage, Dante, accompanied by Virgil, experiences three waking dreams, each showing him pictures of the effects of anger; the rape of Philomela, the suicide of Amata and the hanging of Hamaan on the gallows. In the depths of the smoke Marco Lombardo delivers his oration on the creation of the simple soul by God and what the soul needs for its journey through life, the two suns of Church and Empire. Then, as Dante emerges from the smoke, he sees three more waking dreams, this time examples of humility; the humility of Mary before Christ in the Temple, the humility of the tyrant Pisistratus and the humility of Stephen at his martyrdom. As he finishes his description he cries out at the power of imagination, rejecting Aristotle's dictum that there can be nothing in the mind that has not been in the senses. Imagination can rob our senses away from us and what can be the source of visions such as his but the divine? Whether knowingly or not, here he is echoing St Thomas Aquinas, who says that angels can adjust and alter our perceptions so that we can be granted visions. At that point in his journey Dante is well on his way to the recovery of love in the sight of Beatrice, who will take him up to Paradise where one of the chief images within the all-inclusive image of light is the dance. There the blessed souls dance like flights of birds in the free space of Heaven, remaining utterly themselves while in permanent union with the mind of God and forming in their carolling and spiralling movements great images of joy, redemption and salvation. What our dream life gives us at the promptings of our bodies also undergoes metanoia in the dance so that body, dream life, reason and waking life are unified in a paradigm of civilization to perform with others the recreation of myth and symbol that transforms the gifts of the Great Memory and releases new experiences of freedom to performers and audiences. Dante's *Paradiso* helps us to consider another aspect of the origins of metaphor. We often look upon metaphor and its related figures of speech and imagery as the creations of poor humans lighting small torches for their stumbling advances into the darkness. There is another explanation: this is that metaphor is the gift of consciousness to humanity, that great images such as the angel and the lady, as light, as the tree, as the mountain, as the sea are the words or symbols of the divine mind and imagination, implanted in us like our capacity for language and as inseparable from us as our own human natures.

At the other end of the Mediterranean while Dante was still a boy, another poet was writing his masterpiece, the *Mathnawi*, which is for Islam what *The Divine Comedy* is for Christianity. This was Jalalú'ddin Rúmí Mevlana, from whose life and work derives the Mevlevi order of dervishes. The story of the origins of the order provides many illustrations of the fusion of metaphor and vision with life. Rúmí was born in Balkh in Afghanistan in 1207. His family travelled westwards when he was young, thus escaping the later invasion of the Mongol hordes, and they settled in Konya, in Anatolia, then the seat of the sultanate of Rum. He showed early promise of great gifts and as a teacher he drew large numbers of pupils on account of his learning and his spiritual being. He practised and taught monogamy, he practised and taught toleration in religion, and he practised the life of prayer and study which he also taught.

His life was to be transformed by a meeting with a wandering dervish called Shams-i-Tabrizi. One day when Rúmí was with his disciples passing the caravanserai of the sugar merchants in Konya, Shams came to him and asked him a question. A Sufi master had said of his experience of the divine, 'I am the Sultan, I am the Sultan' as though he were fully one with God, whereas the Prophet had said: 'We have not known you as you should be known.' Did this mean that Abu Yezid, the Sufi master, was greater than the Prophet? The question was a shock and a test for Rúmí. He said of the moment that he heard it: 'The seven heavens broke apart and were poured upon the earth. I felt a huge flame mount through my body and issue from the top of my skull. I saw the smoke rise from this point up to the foot of the celestial throne.'[28] With this vision he was given an answer to the question, namely that the light seen by Abu Yezid was proportioned to his window: he had a soul that could be satisfied by a mouthful whereas Mohammed, the Elect of God, could never be satiated.

Shams fainted at the answer. Rúmí had him carried to his house, where they lived in seclusion. Many of Rúmí's pupils became jealous of Shams, who, rather than sow dissension, fled from Konya. Rúmí had him tracked down in Damascus and his messengers persuaded him to return. The rebellious pupils begged Shams' forgiveness for their animosity. After a time the jealousies returned and one day Shams disappeared, perhaps having been murdered and thrown into a well. To console himself Rúmí wrote the *Mathnawi*, dictating the 24,000 verses spontaneously to secretaries while he walked round a pillar holding it with one hand. He also instituted the ceremony of the turning or whirling dervishes, one of the most perfect works of art ever devised for the complete accord of movement and gesture with symbolic meaning. It is founded on the imagery of darkness and light, of motionlessness and action, of death and resurrection. The chief instrument that accompanies the ceremony is the *ney*, or reed flute, and it was about this flute as a symbol of the human soul that Rúmí wrote the opening poem of the *Mathnawi*. It is filled with longing for the reed bed from which it is torn as the soul yearns for its home in God. The sound flowing through the reed is that of fire, not of the wind, and whoever does not burn with this fire will be as nothing.[29] It is only when God breathes through the flute that dawn breaks on the desert and the desert blooms – and only then that we who are dead can rise again to dance, filled with the ardour and the love of God.

10

Interpretation: towards the art and science of praise

Legends and art come to life in the presence of Cretan folk dancers. A man wearing a black cap fringed with bobbles separates from his fellows, his arms extended like wings, and he performs a hopping dance with his right foot tucked round his left calf. Without any seeming bend of the knees, he rises off the ground in a leap that is also a three-quarter turn, with such energy it is as though he has been lifted into the air and held there by the hand of an angel or of an invisible god. As he turns to the audience, his face is lit with a smile so infectious, you feel your face instantaneously turn into a smile. His dance is like that of a proud bird – perhaps Theseus and his fellows performed the crane dance like this on Delos when they escaped from the Labyrinth. To watch such a dance is to feel a link four thousand years back to the long-lost civilization of ancient Crete – and yet to feel that link, to interpret it in the way I have done, is something only possible because of a particularly rich gift from the Great Memory.

It is a hundred years since Minoan civilization was rediscovered on the island of Crete. In 1896 Arthur Evans bought a large and interesting mound outside Herakleion and began his excavations which revealed the origin of the legend of the labyrinth and the Minotaur in the vast palace of Knossos and the evidence of the ritual bull dances. As his work proceeded, so it became clear that Evans was laying bare the remains of the earliest European civilization known to have had its own script and writing, one that had links with Egypt and Asia Minor, but which had its own individuality, its own standards and its own sources of wealth and distribution. What he revealed in the artefacts, such as seals, frescoes and ceramics, and in the architecture was evidence of a civilization that was founded upon the worship and honouring of the Goddess and that was also a celebration of youth such as only a few other cultures, among them the Florentine Renaissance, have ever achieved. Among the many depictions of human beings in the art of the Minoans there are almost no people in middle or old age to be seen: there are instead the bull leapers in fresco and in ivory, the processions of kilted youths, the singing harvesters and the gatherings of young priestesses and fashionable ladies. This is paralleled in another discovery about them, that the pantheon of gods and goddesses we associate with Greece originated with the Minoans and that they honoured the youth of Zeus as they also were the first worshippers of the young Dionysos. Similarly the depictions of the Goddess, on seals, jewellery and in statuettes, full-breasted, wasp-waisted, flounce-skirted and with her arms wreathed with serpents, showing her also in youth as the centre of ecstatic rites, helped to bring about a total reinterpretation of the religious systems of the period when writing, art and astronomy stood on the cusp of transforming prehistory into history. As an instrument of the Great Memory, Evans with the help of his colleagues, unable to decipher the scripts used by the Minoans, analysed the symbolism of Minoan art and architecture and was able to demonstrate the pre-eminence of the Goddess in their culture and therefore set in train a wider realization about the matriarchal nature of our earliest cultures and civilizations – a discovery which in turn, as we shall see later, has profoundly affected our present conceptions of womanhood.

Thus new knowledge affects the interpretation of the past and new interpretations of the past change the perceptions of the present. Interpretation can bind or free the potentialities of the creative moment and here we are to consider what determines interpretation both through preconceptions and originality – in other words, what determines choice.

Every new idea and image offers us choice: to reject or develop them. Then there is the further choice, if we do not reject them, of what we use the ideas and images for. Interpretation is the stage of choice in the cycle of creativity when past experience, reason and discrimination are brought to bear on the initial insight or inspiration. In science, philosophy and mathematics it is comparable to the processes of finding the experimental proof for a hypothesis, of testing by logic and of verification and double-checking.

The word 'interpretation' comes from Sanskrit roots meaning to spread abroad. From this agricultural metaphor has derived a set of meanings, including these: the expounding of meanings in prophecies and texts, translation from one language to another, the exposition and criticism of literature, the estimation of the value of scientific evidence and, most recently, the ways in which dramas, operas and pieces of music are performed. This last and latest meaning reflects a change in attitudes to performance: in ideal traditional terms the performer is the selfless vehicle for the poet or composer who themselves are the selfless vehicles of the gods and the Muses.

FIGURE 14. Images of Fascism, communism and Nazism at the 1937 Paris Exhibition. Seen above a regatta held on the Seine are the Italian Pavilion surmounted by *The Genius of Fascism* by Giorgio Gori in the foreground, and across the river the Soviet Pavilion with a statue by Vera Mukhina of a worker and a peasant woman brandishing respectively the hammer and sickle, and the German Pavilion designed by Albert Speer and surmounted by an eagle.

FIGURE 15. Stone Age life: the English version, c. 1950.

FIGURE 16. Stone Age life: the Japanese version, c. 1967.

FIGURE 17. Looking up into the dome of St Paul's Cathedral, London, 1675-1710.

FIGURE 18. The Sun god Surya: from the thirteenth-century temples at Konarak, India.

FIGURE 19. The
Nightwatch, 1642, by
Rembrandt van Rijn.

FIGURE 20. *Las Meninas*, 1656, by Diego Rodriguez de Silva y Velázquez.

FIGURE 21. *Self-Portrait*, 1661-62, by Rembrandt van Rijn.

FIGURE 22. *Portrait of Eugène Delacroix*, attributed to Théodore Géricault.

FIGURE 23. *Portrait of Baudelaire*, 1847? by Gustave Courbet.

The emotions they express are not theirs personally but those codified and defined as being apt for the mood and themes displayed, just as the creators of the works they perform have a similar knowledge and control of the feelings and nuances they are playing with.

In this I am thinking of systems such as the Indian codification of the *rasas*, or emotional flavours combined in various forms, which are said to have objective effects on audiences[1], or the *Affektenlehre* and *Figurenlehre* in Baroque music (the phrases that indicated specific emotions or passions)[2], or the rules of rhetoric so dazzlingly applied in Philip Sidney's *Arcadia*. Such systems were rejected in the West as their inner intent was lost or as they seemed to limit the bursting energies of the Romantic imagination with its discovery of the voice of the individual. Today the actor and the musician are expected to draw on their own memories, associations and experiences and to bring those to the interpretation of the part or the piece they are to perform. In the older tradition private feelings are of no account and the interpretation is that of the tradition: in the modern mode private feelings are the necessary matter of transformation.

Apart from the influence of traditions and fashions, there is something else fundamental to how we interpret experience. Just as we are born into a tradition, so we are probably born with certain dispositions in the depths of our psyches that determine our habitual choices and our views of the world. There are several ways of describing these deepset tendencies. One traditional way – and still the most widespread in popular culture – is astrology. The conjunctions of the planets at the moment of conception or of birth decide our temperaments, gifts, luck and misfortunes, and our fates. In Dante's time it was thought lucky that it was planetary influences that gave us our individuality because otherwise we would all be replicas of our fathers, our mothers being the mere vessels of our conception and contributing nothing to our physical make-up.[3] In Indian traditional thought our physical and psychological individuality is a joint creation of the burdens and gifts transmitted from past lives and of planetary influences. Psychoanalysis, forbidden speculation about previous lives and celestial influences, has tended to concentrate on the effects of the womb, the birth trauma and early nurturing and attributes the fixing of our dispositions to the period of early childhood. One branch of analysis, the Jungian, puts forward the idea of the collective unconscious, the reservoir of primordial energies and images, the archetypes which we all inherit from the biological antiquity of man and which govern the behaviour both of individuals and of nations. This theory presents another kind of pre-existence for the soul, a tribal or historical dowry bestowed on every individual. Individuals, in order to fulfil the promise of their individualities, have to recognize and come to terms with the archetypal forces in the psyche so that they may achieve full integration of themselves. According to the degree of integration each individual's interpretative faculties will be darkened by an unredeemed shadow or enriched by the energies of that same shadow when brought into the light. This is another way of expressing the need many creative persons feel – Paul Valéry, for instance, among poets – of mastering the inspiration and making it wholly their own. They distrust the seeming irresponsibility of the flow they are given and they need by interpretation, rewriting or reworking and the attention of execution to bring it within the governance and realm of their individuality.

Jung also stated in his theory of compensation that where there is a lack in a society at a particular period a movement will arise to compensate for that lack.[4] Whether it is a civilizing movement or not depends on other factors. The damage to the confidence of the German nation after the First World War was compensated for by the rise of National Socialism. The dominance of the masculine in the warlike society of the Middle Ages was compensated for by the return of the Eternal Feminine both through the cult of the Virgin Mary and the ideal beloveds of the troubadours. The theory of compensation is also related to the hypothesis of the Great Memory because it helps to explain how many of the instances I have already given arose as memories to redress the imbalances of society and climates of opinion. This applies, for example, to the rise of Symbolism in nineteenth-century literature and art – to which we come later in this chapter – as a compensation for the extreme materialism of scientific and social thought.

Memory is closer to our experience than the unconscious, which, by definition, is removed from direct investigation. Where the hypothesis of the Great Memory differs from the theory of the collective unconscious is that it takes into account the return of the particular: the return of buried national memories or the return of the influence of Dionysius the Areopagite, for example. Moreover it does not depend on an unsubstantiated theory of biological transmission, which is a chain upon the acceptance of the theory of the collective unconscious. Though specific types of memory may be located in identifiable parts of the brain, no one has been able to find the store of memory or to place it as a general function in the brain. As was said earlier, to many thinkers today it has to be regarded as non-local, as a field phenomenon, part of the continuum in which we exist. Memory is different from what it recalls: memory is itself a form of re-creation and interpretation of the past as well as the functions of recording and recalling. What Proust's hero Marcel recovers through the madeleine or the rocking paving stone is a simultaneous recurrence of the past interpreted backwards in the light of his present state of awareness and of his experience altered by the passage of intervening time.

On the greater scale the Great Memory is the action of summing up and encapsulating experience as well as the storehouse of what is remembered. It must range from the memory of a people or a nation, the memory implicit, for example, in every word and grammatical construction of a language as it has developed over centuries, to the wider memories of humanity in history and prehistory. It extends into the geological ages when there were no men to observe as it does even further back when there was as yet no planet Earth. Memory on the individual scale is a creative or inventive act in the present as much as, or more than, it is an accurate record of what actually happened: we sum up our shared pasts with our families and friends in symbolic or characteristic incidents just as we encapsulate historical epochs in the persons of representative men and women – the age of Charlemagne or the age of Elizabeth, for example. Again, the further back into prehistory we go, the more likely we are to sum up whole ages in symbolic forms: the Carboniferous Age is a giant equisetum, or marestail; the Jurassic is a zoo of fabulous dinosaurs; the Big Bang is a spectacular rocket soaring into blackness out of blackness. Similarly the prehistory of man has been summed up in a series of sad-eyed apes and hominids and this image has been imposed upon us by a series of sad-eyed biologists and palaeontologists.

Memory must always be partial. It selects from past experience for us and we select in awareness what we wish to keep. The historian selects on our behalf and by what he chooses to investigate and transmit is interpreting just as much by selection as by the particular view he expresses. Selection is therefore part of interpretation. We often use memory to lie to ourselves or to hide unwelcome truths from coming out. We play the same records of the songs of ancient grudges or the hymns of past idealized periods of happiness over and over again in order to justify present failure or to explain current misery to ourselves. In listening to such records we are often at our least aware. In contrast, consciousness changes memory by revealing the continuity of the true self as it was in the seeming past with that same self experienced now. In the light of consciousness memory becomes a source of energy, not of depression, as Wordsworth found when he tells at the opening of *The Prelude* of his return to the Lakes which brought about in memory the recovery of the fair seed-time of his soul.[5]

It is this quality of enhanced consciousness that we sense in many of the accounts of childhood that we have been considering. It is the authenticity of being alive. The state of consciousness of the creator determines the scale and scope of interpretation just as much as it affects the initial inspiration and its flow.

There is another current theory about creativity which throws light on the question of what determines how we interpret our experience and how we express it. It has arisen in the context of the history of science, through practitioners of that subject looking at the guiding themes in the work of scientists and tracing these back where they can to childhood. Gerald Holton suggests that the creativity of scientists is shaped by the preconceptions and assumptions scientists have about the universe and he calls these assumptions or thought forms *themata*.[6] He was led to this idea by the example of ethnologists, mythographers and students of folklore who have studied customs, rituals and legends and traced in them certain fundamental patterns or categories which are comparatively few in number but owe their diversity to the varied societies and environments in which they appear. The themata are also small in number – about a hundred: the variety comes about through the individual experience and the traditions in which the scientists are raised. The themata often come in contrarieties: the continuity or the discontinuity of matter, Einstein holding to the first and Niels Bohr to the second; creation happening once and creation happening continuously, as in the debate over spontaneous generation between Pasteur and his opponents; and gradualism and saltation in evolutionary theory. At various periods in the history of science different clusters of themata have held sway, establishing for their time of dominance the climate of thought within which most researchers and scientists have been content to work. The more innovative and revolutionary scientists seem to bring about changes in that climate of opinion through their dogged insistence on following through the particular themata, often established in early childhood, as in the instance of Einstein and the gift of the compass.

There are many implications to be drawn from this theory: one is to reflect on how little science depends on conventional views of science and on how much it depends on personal convictions about the nature of the world. Another is that it helps us to understand the origins of style. Holton says that the constellation of themata in the work of a great scientist is like a fingerprint and that one can read a scientific paper from which the names have been removed and the thematic fingerprints can be seen in it.[7] Similarly the style of a school of painting or of an individual artist, of a piece of music, of a poem or a novel, all reflect the deeply set themata of their creators. Yet another implication is for the theory of the Great Memory: old clusters of ideas, thought dead and buried long ago, are revived in new forms: Rutherford brings about the transmutation of elements through his experiments with atoms and the dream of the alchemists is reawakened in another way.

We can also extend the suggestions aroused by the concept of themata to the scale of a nation or a culture over many generations. National characteristics, immediately recognizable in terms of phrases, snatches of music, wafts of cooking smells, result from thousands and millions of men and women delighting in the same pleasures or suffering from the same mental or physical ills or fates. It is such characteristics, the accumulation of tendencies in myriads of individuals, that create the audiences of art, the audiences, for example, of seventeenth-century Paris and London and of eighteenth-century Vienna and Prague. The tastes and expectations of such audiences then feed back into the awareness of artists, patrons and performers affecting interpretation and expression in the cycle of appreciation.

The work of Holton and other researchers following similar lines resembles what historians and biographers have been doing for years to historical personages and literary and artistic people: treating them as human beings subject to profound early influences that determine the direction of their thought and creations in later years. The theory does not invalidate the objectivity of what the scientists have discovered but it helps to illuminate how they interpret their findings as it also shows something of the inner importance of the will in creativity.

So far we have discussed interpretation largely in terms of what influences it from heredity, tradition and the past. Now in introducing the concept of will, we consider interpretation as a means of introducing the new and as a source of originality.

The Fathers of the Church were particularly concerned with the nature and validity of prophecy and they looked upon interpretation as a faculty that was higher than prophecy itself. St Augustine divided vision through which man can receive divine truth into three kinds: corporeal vision, spiritual vision and intellectual vision.[8] This was a method for distinguishing the levels of prophecy recorded in the Old Testament. St Augustine thought of intellectual vision as the highest kind of vision because it included the ability to interpret the visions of others. Thus Pharaoh had the dream which only Joseph from his intellectual vision could interpret. Belshazzar saw the writing on the wall but it was Daniel, gifted like Joseph, who told him what it meant. St Augustine's ideas, increasingly shed of their particular associations, have affected European thought and literature, primarily through his influence on Dante. There is another aspect of St Augustine's thought which is also closely linked to interpretation: he said that there was no need for us to be the victims of the impressions that come to us and of the dreams and images that arise in us because we possess the power of will to master them.[9] We can choose to transform them into visualizations that lead to right conduct or to phantasms that lead to damnation. We do not have to be the slaves of our imaginations. Right interpretation therefore leads to freedom.

It frequently happens in science that one scientist may put a completely different interpretation on the experimental work of another. Priestley discovered oxygen but explained it in terms of the phlogiston theory. Lavoisier interpreted his results differently and, by freeing chemistry from the phlogiston theory, gave a wholly new basis for future developments in the subject. Lawrence Bragg gave an original interpretation of the von Laue photographs and so created the new field of X-ray analysis.

In literature and music there are many examples of writers and composers absorbing the imaginative experience of others and turning it into works of art. Thus Coleridge, told by a friend of a dream he had had of a ship crewed by spectres, turned that dream into the story of 'The Ancient Mariner'.[10] Examples such as these show that fully developed powers of interpretation are as much a sign of the exceptional combination of abilities we call genius as the spate and flow of inspiration. I have already quoted Pushkin, who preferred to call the work of interpretation 'inspiration' as opposed to the flow of ideas he called 'enthusiasm', and Keats also speaks of the activity of judgment he was constantly calling on when writing. Thus, in the creative moment, interpretation is part of the great simplification that characterizes that moment. It is part of the knowing. It arises out of the passive observation, the necessary stillness of concentrated awareness of the reorganized experience and images that are offered to the creator. In the knowing, the creator exercises his discrimination and even his discrimination seems part of the unified experience of the inspiration. It enables him to say: 'I know what I have to do, what I have to make, what I have to prove, and I choose to do it this way.' All discrimination can do is to say yes or no, but through decision it offers clarity of purpose and gives order to chaos. It is also part of the wholeness of being and purpose which marks the artist's individuality and which therefore stamps his originality upon his work.

There were further traditions of interpretation much practised by the Fathers of the Church which had a profound effect on the development of western culture. One of these traditions is known as typology: the Old Testament was regarded as a narrative in which the stories prefigured the stories of the life of Christ and the events narrated in the Gospels. Action therefore could be as much a matter of prophecy as the words spoken by the prophets: the achievements and death of Samson were regarded as a prefiguring of the life and death of Christ. Another of these traditions, which goes back at least to Philo of Alexandria, a Hellenistic Jew (c. 30 BC – c. AD 40), was to look for several levels of meaning in scripture. In the development of this method in Christian thought, a story such as the sacrifice of Isaac could be looked at from four levels of meaning; that of the literal truth of Abraham being ready to sacrifice his son at the word of God; that of the allegory of a father sacrificing his son as a prefiguring of God offering his only son in order to save the world; and a further two levels of meaning, the moral and the mystical, concerned with the sacrifice of the soul to God in loving surrender. For centuries it was maintained that only sacred writings had these three or four levels of meaning whereas the poets only had two levels of meaning, the literal or narrative level and the allegorical. It was Dante, convinced of the divine nature of the inspirations he received from Beatrice, who dared to apply to the visions and images arising in his mind the technique of interpretation hitherto only applied to scripture. He adapted a technique meant for the exegesis of scripture into a means of analysing and reconstructing his own inspirations and of finding out how and where they were to be used. These four levels of meaning have a universal and cosmological significance: each level corresponds to an objective reality or world, the highest to the divine world, the mind of God; the next, the moral level, to the world of causes, the mind of the angels and of humanity at its best; the next down, the allegorical, to the soul or mind of humanity as extended in history; and the last, the literal, to the world of action, manifestation and objects. Dante could turn to this classification as a means of objectifying and depersonalizing his inspirations. He saw the possibilities of the four levels in a new way and it is by seeing the world in new ways that interpretation expands experience and releases originality.[11]

As later examples of how interpretation by artists of profound originality can revolutionize and merge past traditions I take two seventeenth-century paintings executed at opposite ends of Europe within ten years of one another. The first is Rembrandt's *The Nightwatch* in the Rijksmuseum, Amsterdam; the second is Velázquez's *Las Meninas* in the Prado Museum, Madrid. The first shows members of the Protestant oligarchy of Holland; the second shows the Catholic court of the monarchs of Spain. They both therefore depict aspects of the power centres in the countries of their respective artists. They both, while drawing on traditions of group portraiture and, less obviously, on religious paintings, introduce a new informality, almost a new sense of democracy and secularization into art that had not been known before. What we see in these paintings are the guiding thought forms, or themata, of both these artists expressed with a vigour and purpose that was unparalleled in the works of their earlier careers. What links them also is that, transcending their formal intention, the central figure in each painting is a young girl: in *The Nightwatch* it is the girl who is the mascot of the Kloveniers Company and wears a chicken hanging from her waist to signify the chicken claws of the company's name;

in *Las Meninas* it is the daughter of the King and Queen of Spain, the Infanta Margarita.

The Nightwatch is one of many examples of group portraits commissioned by Dutch confraternities in this period. The emphasis given to each member of the group would depend on his importance in the hierarchy and the amount he contributed to the cost of the painting. For an artist an invitation to carry out such a commission was an important step in his career, not only financially but because it was a sign of recognition by the Dutch ruling classes of the artist's acceptability. Membership of the Amsterdam City Guard, of which the Kloveniers formed a company, was essential to progress towards power in the city. The City Guard was the closest approximation to a representative body to which the Regents, the oligarchs of the city, could be held responsible. The City Guard had expelled the last Catholic city council some seventy years earlier and their successors remained the guardians of the Protestant cause.

The Nightwatch (figure 19) has acquired not only a wrong name – it depicts a scene in daylight – but also the legend that it was disliked by its patrons. This story seems to be untrue. It was, however, painted between 1640 and early 1642, the period leading to the final illness and death of Rembrandt's wife Saskia, and therefore marks the point of Rembrandt's decline into artistic neglect, social isolation and insolvency. The inner strain and grief may have prompted him to develop further than ever before the themata on which his artistic life was grounded, chiefly the effect of a shaft of light penetrating darkness and revealing the truth of the people or landscape in the light and the shadings of the penumbra. He sees his contemporaries in the same light that he has seen in his imagination in painting the religious scenes of his earlier work – Jesus praying above the shrouded body of Lazarus or the Presentation in the Temple. The light catches, first of all, Captain Banning Cocq as he orders his lieutenant to muster the company. The expression and attitude of the Captain reminds one of the members of the Sanhedrin present but uncomprehending at one of the miracles in the Gospel, a type of the self-satisfied rulers of this world who know how to maintain their power but have no idea of what the real source of power is. Passing deeper and deeper into the darkness we see the bustle of the company as they prepare their weapons – Rembrandt studied the military manuals of the time to ensure accuracy. Where the light falls most strongly in the painting is not on the warlike preparations but on the strange procession in the middle ground of a drummer, a mummer wreathed almost like a Green Man, and the girl mascot with the chicken at her belt. The face of this girl is the emotional centre of the painting. She is both excited and disturbed, and she looks like what Saskia must have looked like as a child. Her dress is painted with bold splays of paint marking the highlights and Rembrandt portrays her face with the attack and simplicity of his later style, as though it breaks through here as an indication of his future path, whereas the militia and their captain are portrayed with the smoothness and polish of his earlier portraits. She is Cassandra-like in that she knows of coming disaster or change but there is no point in telling what she knows because no one will believe her: she is the pained observer of transience. She resembles most clearly his representations of angels or of the Virgin and it is especially in the resemblances to how he had depicted the Virgin that perhaps we will find the clue to why Rembrandt concentrated so much attention upon her. She is the anima, the Eternal Feminine, seen here as a child in need of nurture.

Rembrandt's pupil Samuel van Hoogstraten criticized Rembrandt for making the picture too much according to his own wishes instead of bringing out the individual natures of the members of the company. He nevertheless said that it made the other paintings in the hall of the Kloveniers look like packs of playing cards, preceding this remark by saying that it would survive all its competitors 'because it is so picturesque in conception, so graceful in the placing of the figures and so powerful'.[12] This work, with its long influence including its effect upon the later arts of photography and the cinema, is a new contribution to realism in painting. The realism, however, does not arise from a simple or socially inspired desire to show things as they actually are but as a side effect of Rembrandt's lifelong obsession with the shaft of light striking through darkness.

We now go south to the Prado to consider Velázquez's greatest work, *Las Meninas* (figure 20).

Las Meninas was painted in 1656. It probably depicts an incident at the royal court of Spain when Philip IV and his queen Mariana were giving a sitting to Velázquez for a double portrait. The sitting was interrupted by the arrival of the young Infanta Margarita and her ladies-in-waiting, the *meninas* of the title, together with two dwarves, a nun and the guardian of the maids of honour. The King and Queen are to be seen only in the mirror at the far end of the room, so that any couple looking at the painting from a distance become for a time the king and queen of Spain and are drawn into this moment when the blonde princess appears like a miracle of youth to delight her parents and the artist. Not only do we become the king and queen; we also become the looking-glass on which the artist gazes to paint what we as the looking-glass reflect back to him. We are the witnesses of the interruption. The moment cannot last because a young dwarf runs in and is about to kick the resting hound, which will leap to its feet and shatter the moment with its barking.

The scene is full of observers: the eyes of the King and Queen – or of ourselves as their temporary modern successors – the chamberlain standing on the staircase by the open door at the end of the room, the Infanta and her counterpart in height but not in beauty, the female dwarf, who has her own dignity and grandeur, and the artist himself as he looks from the edge of the huge canvas that marks the first plane in the recession of forms that make one of the most original spatial conceptions ever depicted.

What is the painting about? It is about time and space, a moment in and out of history, it is about the exceptional friendship between Velázquez and Philip IV and his family, it is about the reality of a group of people gathered together in one room at a particular moment, by which I mean the truth about the emotions that they are all experiencing at that moment. It is about the freedom of the soul that is possible even in an environment as rigorously directed as the court of Spain. So fresh and so spontaneous is the execution, it is like a photograph taken two centuries before photography was possible and yet its huge size means that Velázquez must have worked on it for weeks, maintaining the memory of the moment and the spontaneity of his response to it with a liberating ease.

For all its originality it owes much to the past. The device of depicting a couple in a looking-glass comes, most probably, from *The Arnolfini Marriage* by Jan van Eyck, familiar to Velázquez because it was then in the Spanish royal collection (it is now in the National Gallery, London). The big rectangles of the two dimly lit paintings above the mirror on the far wall are of two other paintings by Flemish artists, Rubens and Jordaens respectively. It has something of the rhythms of a sacred conversation, of figures grouped about a saint, only the figure at the centre of the rhythms is the Infanta Margarita.

It also marks a freedom from the past. The freedom is expressed in the different groupings of threes among the twelve personages, grouped both according to their rank and out of their rank. There is the inverted triangle of mirrored king and queen and the Infanta at the centre; the triad of Infanta and her two *meninas*; the triad of the two dwarves and the chamberlain in the doorway; and the triad of artist, kneeling *menina* and the Infanta. The Infanta also becomes part of the triad with the curtseying *menina* and the female dwarf, thus pointing out the parallelism between the Infanta and the regally dressed female dwarf. (There is also a curious resemblance between the expression of the dwarf's face and on the artist's face.) The rhythm sweeps in these other combinations round to the back of the room, to the triad of chamberlain, King and Queen, and then to the triad of King, Queen and artist.

One could analyse the geometry and the rhythms of the painting for a lifetime. Its fascinations have teased artists for three centuries, whether the delightful *Homage to Velázquez* by Luca Giordano (National Gallery, London), Goya's deliberate debt in his *Family of Charles VII*, the Impressionists, such as Manet,[13] or the series of variations on *Las Meninas* by Picasso now in Barcelona, which become more and more barbarously brilliant as he pursued its elusive secrets.

Just as Rembrandt reinterprets the tradition of the confraternity portrait as an image of political and social dominance in *The Nightwatch*, so Velázquez reinterprets the tradition of the royal portrait as an icon of supreme power in *Las Meninas*. Just as Rembrandt incorporates into this secular work striking elements from his religious paintings, so Velázquez gives especially to the Infanta the position of the Virgin and portrays her with the almost painful realism of his sacred works. Here Velázquez's themata – his insight into the way the eyes tell the truth about every human being, whether they are watersellers, cooks, dwarves, monarchs or popes, his fascination with the space that radiates from a human soul, his accuracy playing with his love of impressionism – are all brought together in an act of interpretation that, as in the case of Rembrandt, grants a new impetus to the spirit of realism.

But what is realism, beyond being convincing *trompe l'oeil* and therefore a cleverer lie? It is part of the climate of opinion that had held its sway especially in the western world from the period when these two great works were painted, with the disgodding of the universe and the power of reductionism and materialist interpretations of the world. There is the physical realism of tables and chairs, there is the intellectual realism of the physicists and the economists but there is also the emotional realism of the poet, the novelist and the artist, which is concerned with the truth of feelings, the truth of the invisible. What I see in these two works, in their concentration on the young girls, is the recurrence of the Eternal Feminine, the Virgin Sapientia, emerging as saving forces of life at the very outset of the loss of spiritual vision and of the descent into materialism that was to characterize the coming centuries.

Symbolism is like Nature: the scientists have tried to expel it with a fork and it comes back by other ways. Here I use the term 'symbolism' in a much wider sense than as it is applied to certain literary, musical and artistic movements. I mean by it a tendency for the power within an object or a person when concentrated upon with the attention of art to reveal dimensions of thought and feeling beyond the social and temporo-spatial setting in which they are put and portrayed. It is the experience of the living myth. Part of the drive towards realism came from the past: the examples of still-life painting in Nero's Golden House, copied from Greek originals, together with the reports of the skills of Greek painters such as Zeuxis, whose painting of grapes deceived the birds who came to peck at them, intensified the desire to show things as they actually are and therefore to impel the still-life painting of Spain and the Netherlands towards an ever more convincing realism. In many cases the more deceptive the realism, the greater the impact of immanent symbolism. Thus despite secularization of art and the discovery by artists and patrons that landscapes could be painted and admired for themselves and not as the backgrounds for religious or mythological subjects or that still lives had their own interest beyond their use in depicting the five senses or the seasons or similar themes, there are certain painters, particularly in the French school, whose works possess this power of symbolism. I think particularly of the still lives of Chardin, those depictions of pots and pans in kitchens which are irradiated with a glowing happiness, almost as though the delicious food that has been cooked in them is part of a universal delight that infuses its instruments, or the seascapes of Courbet, the arch-realist, where a single curving wave draws and holds our attention as though it is about to unfold a mystery. The same power of symbolism recurs in the literary form most characteristic of the drive towards social realism which is the novel. Time and again we find in Dickens the accumulation of realist detail used to set a social scene or the atmosphere of a city and creating, not a journalist's description, but a symbolic ambience of gloom or brooding energies.

My point is first that we cannot escape from symbolism and symbolic meanings and second that symbolism offers a world-view allowing interpretation on several levels. Interpretation, as was said earlier, affects selection, whether it is which parts of a landscape that catch a painter's eye or which aspects of experimental evidence a scientist chooses to test or prove his hypothesis. The chief originator of Symbolism, Charles Baudelaire, described his theory of true civilization in his private work *Mon coeur mis à nu*. 'It is not gas, or the steam engine or table-rapping but it consists in diminishing the traces of original sin.'[14] Here he is reviving the older Christian doctrine that original sin restricted and spoiled our imaginations by wounding us in will and intellect. Influenced by Swedenborg and other mystical writers, he sketched his thoughts about correspondences, the means by which Nature can speak to us. The essence of the Symbolist attitude to the world is this: everything that exists has hidden life and hidden meaning. The world is in fact the Land of Enchantment where stones, trees, birds and beasts can all speak. Siegfried drinks the dragon's blood and can understand the language of the Woodbird.

Another version of the distorting effect of original sin is to be found in Hans Christian Andersen's 'The Snow Queen'. The devils have constructed a magic mirror and whoever looks into it sees the world, however bright and glorious it may have appeared before, as ugly, meaningless and boring. They bear it up to Heaven, thinking they at last have the means of getting their revenge, but it slips from their grasp and shatters on Earth. Slivers from that mirror enter the hearts of many human beings and they too, while the sliver remains within them, also see the world as ugly, meaningless and boring. This is what happens to the boy Kay and the story tells of how Gerda made her way to the Snow Queen to redeem him.

We need to have killed the dragon who guards the treasure or to have met Gerda, who is the inviolable beauty of our nature, to recover the true vision. We also have memory, the memory of Eden, the perfect eighteenth century that was Baudelaire's Eden and which he sought through the strange paths of Satanism and the *paradis artificiels* of drugs.

Symbolism as opposed to social realism works as a means of interpretation in this way. You let the world and its creatures speak to you as you learn to translate their language. You listen to the world and let its signs and sounds sink into you. Even the words you yourself use, when held in the mind and allowed to float there, reveal nuances and unexpected meanings. When Rilke came to work for Rodin as his secretary, the sculptor's first advice to Rilke when he found difficulty in writing was to say: '*Il faut travailler.*'[15] He also told him that he should look at an animal in the zoo or at a tree or a stone or a flower, for hours if necessary, until the object began to speak to him. The first result of following this advice was Rilke's poem on the panther.

Symbolism is part of the wider movement of the recovery of myth of which I spoke earlier in relation to the Great Memory, to Wagner, whose works Baudelaire and the other Symbolists greeted with such a sense of joy and recognition, to the scholarly works of investigation into legends and folklore, to the growing interest in mystical experience as the common ground of all religions, and to what all the schools of psychoanalysis are agreed upon, that the imagery of the mind can be interpreted, however much they might fight over what that interpretation should be.

Symbolism has strange children, one of the strangest being Surrealism with its advocacy of imagery and its denial of interpretation, or the philosophy underlying Abstract Expressionism that it should evolve a genuine American mythology free of the Old World and that the way to find that mythology was to deny the use of images from the past.[16] Mark Rothko painted a long series of works that suggest the theme of a door or a window through which he might have passed to an understanding of that new land of myth; and the despair at the end of his life, perhaps at never crossing these thresholds, was expressed in the late canvases where he was painting with black on black.

Symbolism was a reaction against the modes of thought such as positivism, dialectical materialism and reductionism in science which, their proponents believed, were capable of explaining not only all current problems and intellectual riddles but also all that might arise in the future. Any subject that could not be explained, such as consciousness or the mystery of poetry, would be dismissed as not being worthy of mental consideration.

Symbolism possessed its own creative tensions – the chief tension being between the need to expand the means of expression, whether in language, imagery or tones, and a sense of despair at the disparity between the wonders of experience and the narrowness of words to utter experience. It was a tension often felt long before the term 'Symbolism' was invented: Théophile Gautier, according to Baudelaire, used to say '*L'inexprimable n'existe pas*',[17] whereas in the following passage we hear Lamartine explaining that he gave up writing verse because the means at his disposal were too limited to convey the vastness of his conceptions:

When I sat beside the pinewoods on a promontory of the Swiss lakes or when I used to spend whole days wandering on the sounding shores of Italy and as I leaned against the remains of a harbour or a temple to look at the sea or to listen to the inexhaustible babbling of the waves at my feet, whole worlds of poetry used to flow in my heart and before my eyes; without writing them down, I composed, for myself alone, poems as vast as nature, as resplendent as the sky, as touching as the moaning of the sea breezes in the crowns of stone-pines and in the lentisk leaves that sliced the wind, as though they were so many little blades, to make it weep and sob in millions of little voices. Night would often overtake me, without being able to tear me away from the charm of the fictions with which my imagination delighted itself. Ah, what poems they would have made if I had been capable of singing them to others as I sang them within my own mind! But whatever has most of the divine in the heart of man is never manifested, for want of a language in which it can be articulated on earth. The soul is infinite, and languages comprise only a tiny number of signs fashioned by custom for the needs of communication among the commonalty of men. These are instruments provided with twenty-four strings in order to render the myriads of notes that passion, thought, reverie, love, prayer, nature and God arouse in the human soul. How can the infinite be contained in this humming of an insect beside its hive which the neighbouring hive does not even understand? I gave up singing, not for the want of inner melodies but for want of a voice and the notes in which to convey them.[18]

On the other hand it was one of the chief heirs of Symbolism, Paul Valéry, who said that the greatness of poets lay in their ability to seize masterfully with their words what they have only half glimpsed dimly in their minds.[19]

Interpretation presumes a world-view, a belief system; what Symbolism offered was a means of interpretation based on a world-view that was independent of religion and science but contradicted neither; it also through its world-view brought new reaches of what had been the tacit or inexpressible experience of humanity within an enlarged scope of expression. The achievement of the heirs of Baudelaire, particularly in France and Russia, in bringing into the scope of literature, new areas of human experience, such as Mallarmé's search for the perfect means of expression, one that was beyond the *hasard* or chance association, or Valéry's studies of his own creative processes and states of awareness, was one of the greatest civilizing forces of its time and one we need to absorb and study more fully for our own advancement.

Symbolism also provides an example of how a great cultural and social movement may be foreshadowed or accompanied by many different and unrelated recurrences from the past. This is to be seen in the movement for the emancipation of women which was gathering force at the same time that certain Symbolists were rediscovering the ancient expression of the ideal of the Eternal Feminine as wisdom.

The chief symbol of wisdom guiding discrimination and interpretation in our own and many other cultures is that of a woman. She is the Sapientia of the Books of Solomon who stands 'in the top of high places, by the way in the places of the paths' and she says of her origins:

The Lord possessed me in the beginning of his way, before his works of old.
I was set up from everlasting, from the beginning, or even the earth was.
When there were no depths, I was brought forth; when there were no fountains abounding with water.
Before the mountains were settled, before the hills was I brought forth:
While as yet he had not made the earth, nor the fields, nor the highest part of the dust of the world.
When he prepared the heavens, I was there: when he set a compass upon the face of the depth:
When he established the clouds above: when he strengthened the fountains of the deep;

When he gave to the sea his decree, that the waters should not pass his
commandment; when he appointed the foundations of the earth;
Then I was by him, as one brought up with him: and I was daily his
delight, rejoicing always before him;
Rejoicing in the habitable part of his earth; and my delights were with
the sons of men.[20]

This is the tradition that recurs constantly in Judaic and Christian
thought and in its parallel development in Sufism. The Goddess has many
forms: as the armed Athene who guides Odysseus and Herakles and as the
celestial Aphrodite through whom wisdom is manifested as love. She has
her light and dark sides – in Celtic mythology as Brigit, the goddess of
poets and learning, and as the hideous hag, the Morrigan, who becomes
beautiful when the hero consents to make love to her. In this she resembles
the aspects of the bride of Shiva as Parvati, who is his female emanation,
and as Kali with her necklace of skulls.

As in her many guises she represents universal wisdom, so she also
promises the possibility that we can share in that wisdom as we share
in the universal consciousness of which she is the knowledge. Like our
creative powers she is there to be unveiled, not to be striven for or made
out of our own endeavours. When an artist or a thinker most fulfils his
talents, it is through participating in her universal nature that he does so.
This is the recurrent effect on Dante, in her life and after her death, of
Beatrice. Even when he forgets her, she is the source of the visions and
inspirations that come to him. Only when he remembers her is he capable
of the truest and highest levels of interpretation and only then also is he
capable of the art of praise.

It was this tradition that was rediscovered particularly by the Russian
poet Vladimir Solovyov (1853–1900), who was to influence other poets
such as Alexander Blok. Like Dante, Solovyov had fallen in love when
he was nine with a girl whom he met in Moscow and whom he was to
identify with divine wisdom, or Sophia. He later had two other visions of
Sophia, one in the Reading Room of the British Museum in 1875 and the
last in the Egyptian desert the following year.[21] Out of these experiences
he wrote exquisite and powerful poems of celebration and adoration such
as 'Winter by Lake Saima':

You have dressed yourself in a powdery fur coat;
Quietly you lie in an untroubled dream.

Death does not breathe in the light-filled air,
In the transparence and whiteness of silence.

It is not in vain that I've sought you
In profound and motionless peace.
Your image is the same to the eye of the mind –
Enchantress of the pines and the rocks.

You are without spot as the snow on the mountains;
You are rich in thought as the winter night:
Resplendent you are as the Northern lights,
O radiant daughter of the darkness of chaos![22]

The visions made Solovyov see that, for God, the universe possesses from all eternity the image of perfect femininity.

He wills that this image should exist not for Him only, but that it should be realized and embodied for every individual being capable of uniting with it. The eternal feminine itself strives for such realization and embodiment, for it is not a mere passive image in the divine mind but a living spiritual being possessing the fullness of powers and activities. The whole cosmic and historical process is the process of its realization and incarnation in an endless multiplicity of forms and degrees.[23]

Quite independently of Solovyov, Teilhard de Chardin, serving as a stretcher bearer in the trenches in the First World War, drew on a similar experience to voice his cosmic vision in a long prose poem called 'L'Eternel Féminin', to which he affixed the dedication 'A Beatrix'. In this poem he saw the feminine as the principle of love, charm and attraction which binds all the matter of the universe together.[24]

Experience of love on the scale revealed to Dante, Solovyov and Teilhard de Chardin expands the possibilities of interpretation to a cosmic level because they were given a standard to which they could refer every other part of their experience. Such an experience of love changes and expands consciousness so that its universal nature is revealed. One of the most notable French poems of this century, 'La Jeune Parque' by Paul Valéry, has as its theme the awakening and expansion of consciousness in a young woman so that she recognizes her own nature and her delight in being born again in the waves of the sea and the gold of the sun. The themata of which we spoke earlier are the ingrained views of the universe that we, and especially scientists, are born with or acquire in early years: as views of the universe, they are aspects of natural laws; natural laws like archetypal ideas can be said to have an objective existence because they are our expression of the form of the universe. When the universe is seen as a single act of love, as a sublimely beautiful woman who is love and who is loving, then the forms of nature as well as the forms of art and thought are known as the forms and consequences of love.

Earlier we spoke of the missing feminine elements in the scientific images of man. I predict on the hypothesis of the Great Memory that out of the revivals and rediscoveries of feminine imagery and of matriarchal societies, a new statement of the Eternal Feminine will come into existence which will be crucial to the future ideals of our own humanity and will change science by changing our views of the universe. In the past the Eternal Feminine has awakened an art of praise: what we can look forward to is a return also of that science of praise that characterized the lives and work of so many great scientists in the past.

It is to the art of praise that interpretation aspires. Rilke, whose life-long struggle in his art was to rise above the personal and the limited sides of his nature, expressed his ideal of art in this poem:

O sage, Dichter, was du tust? – Ich rühme.
Aber das Tödliche und Ungetüme,
wie hältst du's aus, wie nimmst du's hin? – Ich rühme.
Aber das Namenlose, Anonyme,
wie rufst du's, Dichter, dennoch an? – Ich rühme.
Woher dein Recht, in jeglichem Kostüme,
in jeder Maske wahr zu sein? – Ich rühme.
Und daß das Stille und das Ungestüme,
wie Stern und Sturm dich kennen? – Weil ich rühme.

O tell me, Poet, what do you do? – I praise.
But how can you endure to meet the gaze
Of deathly and of monstrous things? – I praise.
But, Poet, how can you repeat the phrase
That names the nameless and unknown? – I praise.
What right have you to utter truth that stays
True in each disguise and mask? – I praise.
And star and storm, calm and noise, what conveys
To them you are their own? – That's why, I praise.[25]

11

The rosary bead: attention and execution

'In a nutshell' we say to express an idea or image in the most concise manner. The phrase came back to me recently as I passed by some cases in the Wallace Collection that had always fascinated me as a boy. These cases are filled with small precious objects – famous Renaissance medallions and curious reliquaries, portraits in coloured wax and enamelled jewels ripe with baroque pearls. What I chiefly remembered and found again was a rosary bead about the size of a large walnut carved from a piece of boxwood. It is ascribed to the workshop of Adam Dirksz in the early sixteenth century. The marvel of the bead is that it opens into two equal hemispheres. In one opened half you see St George raising his sword as his horse tramples the dragon. The princess stands chained ready for her doom in the middle distance. In the other half of the bead you see St Hubert on his knees as the stag steps from the forest with the crucifix between his antlers. To the right a mounted groom holds the bridle of St Hubert's horse while in the distance another huntsman rides through the overhanging trees. All the main figures are carved freestanding in both hemispheres and the details, extending to the towers and crenellations of the city behind St George and the figure of Christ on the crucifix between the deer's antlers, are represented with a Lilliputian exactitude to a scale for which millimetres would be too gross a measure. The vigour of St George signifies the active life whereas St Hubert is shown at the moment of conversion that will lead him from his hitherto selfish life obsessed with hunting into the contemplative life. The wholeness of life and the wholeness of the world come together in this tiny object which is charged with the emotive power of the stories portrayed in it, carved with the attention of the artist in order that it might be fingered with the attention of prayer.

As I gazed at it again, it aroused in me the same fascination I had felt in my boyhood and the experience stirred in me new thoughts about the concentration of meaning and emotion in art. It also reminded me of other, earlier medieval associations of the nut. Adam of St Victor, for example, saw a green hazelnut as an image of Christ, with the green sheath as his flesh, the wooden shell as the cross and the kernel as his loving kindness.[1] Dame Julian of Norwich says that when Christ showed her a little thing, the size of a hazelnut on the palm of her hand, he told her 'It is all that is made.' He also told her that it exists because God loves it.[2] It then came to me that all works of art, all condensations of thought and research, all great novels however fat, are in effect nutshells that are also worlds: they too are the result of special kinds of loving attention that last.

How does feeling enter worked matter except through attention and the skilled hand that is guided by inspiration in the atmosphere of attention? How is feeling so fixed in the notes set down by the composer that it may be resurrected and transmitted when played with attention by the performer? How does feeling enter words so that the reader knows – often instantly – that the language his eye re-creates for his brain is being charged with power that is both within him and from outside him? And how is it that such feelings can last through hundreds and thousands of years? These questions concern the crucial stage of communication between maker and enjoyer, researcher and understander, lover and beloved. The communication succeeds because of their love for the quality of attention that possesses them when they are fully engrossed and taken up with what they are doing. Stravinsky said: 'All creation presupposes at its origin a sort of appetite that is brought about by the foretaste of discovery', remarking also that his 'premonition of an obligation, this foretaste of a pleasure . . . shows clearly that it is the idea of discovery and hard work that attracts me'.[3] In other words, it was the state of making and the particular concentration of attention it required that excited him. It is the memory of that state and the hope that it will return that keeps most creative people going through troughs of blankness and despair.

The smallness of objects like the rosary bead that concentrate a vast tradition of devotion into a tiny space can often give us a feeling of what that attention must be like, more than larger or grander works. An Elizabethan miniature, the cloisons of enamel on a piece of jewellery or a reliquary, a haiku or brief lyric, a satisfying equation or a representation of a crystalline structure, in their different ways pierce the heart through the encapsulation of knowledge and skill. The concentration of meaning in all these forms of expression makes us intensify our attention and enlarge our sympathies so that we know something of what the painter, the goldsmith, the poet and the scientist felt when they made or expressed these different forms.

In the creative experience attention is both a gift and a skill. When an unexpected thought or inspiration comes, it attracts our attention to itself. Then the quality of attention we give to it is so enhanced it seems an extra gift of consciousness. When we set ourselves to execute or give form and body to that inspiration, we draw on the kind of attention built up throughout our education and our training which we have learned to give to our work. Every now and then, and sometimes as a continuous flow, we are given that extra state of attention with its accompanying feeling of the right coordination of all our faculties. It seems to come in this enhanced way when we have become wholly single-minded in our concentration on what we are doing – when, supposing we are the carver of the rosary bead, we are intent only on one link in the chains binding the princess or on one tine of the stag's horns in the apparition to St Hubert. 'Good is done in minute particulars,' says Blake.[4] Within the moment of time in which concentration is perfect, another mode of thinking and feeling expands from the narrowed centre of awareness – a feeling we get from the thousands of fine pencil strokes out of which Cecil Collins made his drawing *Resurrection* (frontispiece).

What happens then is as though ordinary awareness of time disappears. It is the reverse of the inspiration in which a new universe can be revealed between stepping from one flagstone to another. Hours can pass by and the creator is entirely unaware that they are flitting:

> He will watch from dawn to gloom
> The lake-reflected sun illume
> The yellow bees in the ivy-bloom,
> Nor heed nor see, what things they be;
> But from these create he can
> Forms more real than living man,
> Nurslings of immortality![5]

The narrowed field of attention in the moment connects with the wider field of consciousness by some alchemy or resonance.

Many people have inspirations and visions and many can interpret them: it is in the quality of attention that they bring to the manifestation of the inspiration that distinguishes their genius from the many with talent.

Yeats writes about that special quality of attention in his poem 'Long-legged Fly'. He brings before us Caesar in his tent with the maps of conquest spread around him, Helen of Troy dancing by herself 'a tinker shuffle picked up on a street' and then Michelangelo:

That girls at puberty may find
The first Adam in their thought,
Shut the door of the Pope's chapel,
Keep those children out.
There on that scaffolding reclines
Michael Angelo.
With no more sound than the mice make
His hand moves to and fro.
Like a long-legged fly upon the stream
His mind moves upon silence.[6]

The annals of Chinese painting over the centuries reveal many statements by artists about the condition they must reach when they paint. Wu Chen, known as the Taoist of Plum Blossoms, once said: 'When I begin to paint, I do not know that I am painting; I entirely forget that it is myself who holds the brush.'[7] Yet it was said of him that all the potentialities of the universe were present in the tip of his brush.

Artists painting their self-portraits often convey this special sense of attention. I think of Velázquez looking out from his canvas in *Las Meninas* or of the self-portrait of Tintoretto with his huge, staring, saucer-like eyes that seem to absorb the whole world with the intensity of his gaze. Especially I think of the series of Rembrandt's self-portraits from the curly-headed boy in the Rijksmuseum to the grandeur of the late work at Kenwood (figure 21), in which the bankrupt beggar is portrayed with the majesty of a monarch, or, at least, with a royal pride because in that work he is thought to have compared himself to Apelles, the painter of Alexander the Great.[8]

Sometimes an artist is fascinated by the recognition of that state in a fellow artist, as with the portrait of the young Delacroix attributed to Géricault, where the painter captures, as though it were the beam of a lighthouse out of darkness, the speed of comprehension and the revolutionary ardour in his eyes (figure 22). Other artists have responded to similar states in practitioners of other arts, as with Quentin Matsys's portrait of Erasmus. There is a similar feeling about the representatives of the liberal arts, carved above the south door of the Royal Portal at Chartres, especially the statue of Pythagoras who represents music, bending his head forward to attend to the zitherlike instrument on which he plays. My favourite example of this tribute by one artist to another is the portrait of Baudelaire by Courbet in the Musée Fabre at Montpellier (figure 23). Although Baudelaire is shown reading rather than writing, the quill pen standing erect in its inkpot, on the table against which he rests his book, denotes his readiness. Baudelaire is shown with his hair close-cropped, smoking a pipe as he reads, and much of his absorption is shown by the stillness of his wonderfully painted left hand resting on a cushion beside him. But even more is conveyed by the concentration of his eyes on his book and the two patches of light high on his forehead on either side of his widow's peak – as though, for all Courbet's realism, the symbolism of light and its association with consciousness and the attentive mind arises with the force of undeniable nature. One stands before this painting with a kind of joy that says: 'Yes, I have known that state; that state is a noble condition of humanity.'

In another context, Schiller in his *'Das Lied von der Glocke'*, the story of the casting of a great bell that will bring joy and peace to the city over which it will peal, makes his bell-caster say:

Da ist's ja, was den Menschen zieret,
Und dazu ward ihm der Verstand,
Daß er im innern Herzen spüret,
Was er erschafft mit seiner Hand.[9]

What crowns a human being with worth is this
And this is why he was given intelligence,
That he can feel in his inmost heart
What he fashions with his hands.

There is a special pleasure in doing something well with attention or in watching someone skilled in a sport or craft – like a fly-fisherman or a potter. In the case of objects such as fine furniture or old china one feels that the attention that went into their making is present in them long after their creators are dead. The quality of that attention that captured the spirit of the period when they were made catches our notice now. I take as an example a chair with which I have lived for many years: it is one of a pair I bought on a London pavement outside a junk shop. Their mahogany was coated in black varnish but they were still recognizable as sabre-legged chairs of about 1810. I slowly scraped the varnish off them to reveal their fine dark wood. I uncovered their seats to find the straw that had been harvested a few years after Trafalgar was fought and the hair from horses that had carried their last loads nearly two centuries ago and in reupholstering them I used as much of these materials as possible. Looking at this chair one day I thought of all the elements, forces, traditions and ideas that were necessary for it to have come into being, the earth, water, sunlight and air that had combined to form the mahogany tree in the Cuban or Honduran forest even longer ago, the felling of the tree and its seasoning and its transport across the Atlantic to the Pool of London and the arrival of its planks at the cabinet-maker's.

This was the point at which the wood was transformed into something beautiful, useful and lasting. The cabinet-maker had probably very little choice in how the chair was to look. He had to pay attention to the requirements of the customer, who also had very little choice, given that his or her tastes were formed by the fashion of the time, particularly by Thomas Sheraton and also by Thomas Hope. They were publishing designs heavily influenced by furniture portrayed on ancient Greek sculptures and vase paintings, in further refinements of the dominant Neo-Classical style which we have already discussed as an example of the Great Memory at work. The design comes from the ancient Greek *klismos* which had earlier been revived in the reign of Augustus and later in the reign of Hadrian, so it had already undergone at least two revivals.

The cabinet-maker is at the point of transformation: he did not make the wood; he did not devise the style even if he modified the design. If we think of two triangles overlapping, the lower one is the field of nature in which the mahogany tree grew while the upper, inverted one is the field of fashion, ideas and influences that goes back to ancient Greece and beyond to wherever the first chair was thought of and made. The field extends into the future, as well, for this is a style so comfortable and elegant that it has been copied again and again up to the present day. The cabinet-maker is centred in the fields of both triangles, in the lozenge made by their overlapping. What the cabinet-maker brings to his work is little but crucial: to manifesting a particular form out of seasoned matter he brings his craft skills, his physical strength, his aesthetic eye, his attention and his love of the wood and of his tools. The small will of his attention is united with the will of nature and the will behind the idea or form which he copies. He works within the field of his craft traditions and the field of fashion

I am introducing here an idea from physics: the field of influence, that mysterious concept that we take for granted. It can be seen at work in another form also crucial to our civilization: the violin, that summation of the Baroque period both in its curves and in the new voice of feeling it brought to instrumental music. Every one who makes a violin today follows a form largely decided by the great craftsmen of Cremona, Amati and his pupils, Stradivari and Guarnieri in the seventeenth and eighteenth centuries.

The impulse to evolve such an instrument from forms such as the *lira da braccio* was guided by the Neo-Platonic philosophy according to which, as we have seen in discussing Titian's *Le Concert champêtre*, stringed instruments were regarded as being more conducive to imitating heavenly harmonies than wind instruments. Just as opera evolved in the same period inspired by the wish to recreate the conditions of Greek dramatic art with its coordination of words, music and dance,[10] so the field of influence within which the violin developed was one driven by the desire to recreate the lost stringed instruments of Greece – the descriptions in recovered works of the ancients of the effect of the cithara, for example, on its hearers being such as to promote an acute sense of loss and a need to emulate and rediscover its expressive powers. Though it was known that the Greeks thought of music as their greatest art, no music and no instruments survived. It was a lost paradise of sound that the musicians of the High Renaissance were attempting to recover, something far more difficult to achieve than the comparable work of recovery in the arts and literature: it is as though the poets and dramatists of sixteenth-century Italy had only reports of the *effects* of the works of Homer, Aeschylus and Sophocles, not their actual verse, or the artists, sculptors and architects knew only reports of what ancient paintings, carvings and buildings looked like. The Great Memory was kinder to the poets and sculptors than to the musicians, but the musicians and their instrument-makers, once granted an ideal to which to strive, had a greater freedom of imagination, evolving the combination of instruments led always by the violins that became the modern classical orchestra.

The violinist who plays the instrument made by the fiddle-maker is similarly circumscribed in the conditions under which he performs. His interpretation will vary from that of other performers but he cannot change the form or content of what he plays. (I am speaking here of the western tradition of classical music – not of improvisatory modes for which the violin is admirably suited, as is shown by gypsies, players of Scottish reels, jazz violinists and musicians in traditions of Indian music.) His attention is cultivated often from early childhood by hours of practice and the aim of that hard work is to turn him into a virtuoso capable of mastering every difficulty to be met in the classical repertoire in order that he should be free to give all his attention to the interpretation of the work. The technical mastery will become part of his autonomic nervous system: what his attention is given to is the drawing-out of the emotional significance of the work. Now this is different from the spontaneous singing in the heart of the craftsman when his work is going well or indeed of the composer or the poet when the sounds and words flow effortlessly: it requires responsiveness to the moods of the work to be performed and the ability to draw out from himself the emotion which comes both from his own capacity for feeling and his understanding of the emotions of the composer. Carl Philipp Emanuel Bach wrote: 'since a musician cannot move unless he is moved, he must be able to project himself into all the emotions which he wants to arouse in the listeners: he makes them understand his passions and moves them thereby most fully to compassion.'[11]

The same ability to draw on experience and imagination is necessary for actors. In some traditions all the training is concentrated on being able to perform one part: it is said to take twenty years for an actor to be able to perform the part of Monkey in the Chinese opera of that name. In the western theatre, especially the commercial theatre, actors and actresses may be given no more than six weeks in which to create their parts. The processes an actor sometimes has to go through in order to enter completely into a role are movingly described by Arthur Miller in his memoirs, speaking of the rehearsals of *Death of a Salesman* when Lee J. Cobb, after weeks of walking through the part in the most wooden way, was suddenly possessed by the role.[12]

What he describes there is the achievement of a special kind of attention through which all the inner and outer aspects of the performance are coordinated. It is an attention which has to be worked for and hoped for and then suddenly seems to be given. For the period during which it is necessary for it to be present, once it has been achieved, the actor seems able to step into it at will. It probably comes about through the establishment of one central insight or image concerning the part analogous to the glue that holds together the eighty-four pieces of a violin. That insight is comparable to the revealing through constant reflection and practice, of the *Grundgestalt* or fundamental tonal image which the musician has to attain in order to be able to interpret and express a piece of music.

Goethe says in his late poem '*Vermächtnis*' that there is no greater vocation than to mark out new paths of feeling for noble souls. What is the nature of the attention that discovers those new paths of feeling? We have looked at the attention the craftsman pays to his hands and to the given form he has to reproduce and the attention the performer has to give to a role or piece of music that is also given. The attention of the creative artist, poet and original thinker or scientist has to be devoted to a much more difficult task: to fugitive visions, muffled images, evanescent sequences of thought and incompatible pieces of evidence. It can be thought of as a constant listening for a voice that is remembered for having spoken in the past and has never given promises that it will speak again.

One of the attractions of the creative state is that it is like being in love: the tortures are undeniable but the prize is too great for it to be forgone. This is how George Sand described Chopin at work:

Once he set himself to work, his surroundings fell into shade. He found it without looking for it or foreseeing it. It came to him at the piano, immediate, whole, sublime, or it sang itself in his head during a walk, so that he had to force himself to remember it until he reached the piano. Then began the most harrowing labour I have ever seen. It was a sequence of efforts, irresolutions, moments of impatience, devoted to recapturing certain details of the theme he had heard: what he had first conceived as a whole, he analysed too much in trying to write it down and his regret at not capturing it completely, he said, threw him into despair. He used to shut himself in his room for days, weeping, pacing about, breaking his pens, repeatedly changing one bar a hundred times, writing and rubbing it out as many times again, and beginning the next morning with attentive and desperate perseverance. He would spend six weeks on a page only to return to what he had written in his first draft.[13]

It is possible that torture of this degree is something which artists and poets are all the more likely to experience, first when, as in Chopin's case, they are inventing new forms or using forms that have only recently come into circulation; second, when they are creating out of an inner necessity, rather than in response to a commission. In painting the walls of the Brancacci Chapel of the Carmine Church in Florence, Masaccio and Masolino would have had only a few hours for each panel because they had to work while the plaster was still wet. They would have prepared for those few hours with drawings and with sketching the *sinopie* which they would have had to discuss with their patrons of the Carmine Church, but the achievement of a realism and a plasticity of form that was to revolutionize figural painting in the West was carried out in a maximum of six to eight hours for each section of plaster. There would have been no time for doubt or tantrums. The images had to be wholly and immediately present in their minds.

An artist who can work under such conditions resembles a performer in that there is only a short set period within which he can actually make the work of art. He must be prepared, in effect, to give a performance, drawing on all his powers of improvisation and spontaneity for what can only be done in that space of time.

The experience of time changes in states of creative attention. Whereas the initial inspiration that gives a vocation or directs the work of a lifetime may come in a millisecond, time that is spent in creative attention in making, writing or thinking may pass by with unobserved speed. When George Sand says of Chopin that he would spend six weeks on a page, it is likely that to Chopin those six weeks seemed like a day – an excruciating day perhaps but still only a day.

In that state time changes, space changes, the world changes. It is as though a window opens in time and only for the period that the window is open can this concentrated attention be maintained to receive and transform the gathered inspirations. It is like the gates into mountains in fairy stories that appear mysteriously and give the hero only a minute to decide whether to enter or not, or like the Logan stones, the rocking stones of the Cornish landscape that can only be climbed at midnight without disturbing their equilibrium. Sometimes it is as though an unseen protective barrier extending from his attention guards the poet or artist throughout the period that the window is open: no one telephones, no one starts a chainsaw a hundred yards away, no letter comes from a hurt bank manager; or else all these interruptors are powerless against the state of attention. The poet may know beforehand the ideas and some of the images that should go into these verses but only when he is in that state of attention and when he is actually making the continuous rhythmical sentences which he will be able to write down, does he know exactly what the moment will give. The time and the quality of his attention are crucial to how the ideas and images will manifest. He is listening to an intense singing in the mind, intense because the vibrations are so fast, they could only be reproduced by the voice as a continuous note: but in these vibrations there are the subtlest and finest changes of tone and mood that attract words and images out of unconsciousness to circle in the air of the singing and to give glimpses of themselves and of how they can be connected to the awareness of the poet.

'I am one who when Love breathes through me, takes note, and to the mode that he dictates within me, I set out the meaning.' So says Dante when asked by the poet Bonagiunta da Lucca what was the source of his *dolce stil nuovo*, his miraculous sweet style.[14]

Sometimes complete works are written in a period of time that is like a window of inspiration. In other cases only part of the work may have been written and the poet may have to wait for that state to come again. Sometimes it never comes again, as in the sad case of Ugo Foscolo and his poem known as the '*Frammenti delle Grazie*' – miraculously beautiful evocations of Greek and Italian landscapes and the goddesses of myth. Exiled in London, forced to support himself by such tasks as writing an essay on Italian poetry which Byron's friend John Cam Hobhouse paid for and then published in a book under his own name, he could never recapture fully enough the state he was in when he wrote the fragments, the state he himself described in writing about Dante:

Genius is born today as it always has been; more frequently and strongly where the climate is favourable to human development. I believe that in some individuals the organs of the intellect are not only tempered with the utmost strength and in equal proportion but are most rapid in their movement and of an inconceivable mobility while yet remaining in constant equilibrium. And so the various powers of the soul combine to unite simultaneously feelings, memories, reflections, images, sounds, forms and colours, and drawing together all these ideas in different and most original guises, make them seem new creations. It is certain that, at each thought and image that the poet conceives, at each phrase, word or syllable that he gathers, silent or muffled, he instantly uses all his faculties as a human being. And while he feels the passions that he expresses and reflects on the emotional impact of his art and meditates on the moral truth which derives from it, with his ear giving the greatest attention to any slight dissonance or consonance of the words, he joins the melody in the harmony of the sounds of the alphabet with the most exact proportions of modulation in the vowels and in the articulation of the consonants, and his eye sees, looks at and examines all the fantasms, and their shapes and attitudes and the scenes which he wishes to create and animate; and they seem new inspirations. The speed of production may come first; but the painstaking spending of time of perfecting is not a secondary gift, nor is it separate from genius. The incredible force and flood of thoughts demand it and both leave him perplexed as to disposition and choice. From this come the reworkings, endless corrections, improvements and dissatisfactions which sometimes make people think that the act of imagining is badly supported by skill in execution. But the height of the poetic imagination lies in seeing and aiming for a perfection which it is not given to others to understand or to envisage.[15]

Sometimes inspiration seems to wane and the creative force ebbs. Fortunately, it does come again, often inspired by the right kind of criticism or some inner shock or realization which is like a renewal of interpretation. It is as though the work itself keeps on saying to the poet: 'You haven't got me right: I am not as you have put me down; I am like this, not like that.' Then the poet must follow Ben Jonson's advice in his poem on the memory of William Shakespeare:

> For though the poet's matter nature be,
> His art doth give the fashion; and that he
> Who casts to write a living line must sweat –
> Such as thine are – and strike the second heat
> Upon the muses' anvil, turn the same
> And himself with it that he thinks to frame;
> Or for the laurel he may gain a scorn,
> For a good poet's made as well as born.
> And such wert thou . . .[16]

'The living line' – it is a phrase that sums up the mystery in what I am discussing. Following the great discoveries of science over the past two hundred years it is comparatively easy to discover the transformations of matter, the change of structure among molecules that produces a substance of quite different qualities from its constituent materials, to describe the action of chemicals in neuronal pathways and ganglia, or the flow of nutrients along a plant's capillary system and the changes in its cells as it reaches the stages of flowering and fruiting – easy when compared with our ignorance of what happens during the transformation of words and images into poems, or of notes into music, or of disconnected facts into a new scientific law. Each of the activities behind the poem, sonata and law are individual events or sequences of events, depending on the being and capacity for attention of a man or woman in historical time over a particular period. It is as though the poet and artist not only give their attention to the barely formed inspiration in their minds, but that they take in a particular energy through that window of opportunity of which I spoke above, an energy that is only available in that *kairos* or period of time.

Attention is applied consciousness, consciousness narrowed down for a particular object. Earlier we discussed inspiration and other aspects of the creative process as the effects of consciousness. Here again we come to the question of consciousness in relation to performance or execution. What seems to happen is this: attention is concentrated on each detail of the task in hand, the musical phrase being played in a particular moment, the working of two inches of a canvas, the rhythm and sound patterns of a single line of verse, while at the same time there is a general awareness of the form of the whole or, at least, of the direction the future work may take as a result of the discovery made in completing the present task. Discovering, or uncovering in the sense that Michelangelo spoke of in one of his sonnets when he said the form of the statue was already there in the block of marble waiting to be revealed,[17] is one of the great excitements of the creative process. One moment you do not know what you have to do next or what is going to happen; the next you are filled with a wonder and certainty of knowledge because you see and know the inner logic implicit in the development of a symbol, a rhythmic pattern or a line of thought.

It is through this concentration of consciousness in attention that the inspiration is made one's own. Ideas and images, stories and themata that may have a history of centuries behind them in other arts and philosophies are re-created in the given style and mood of the individual creator. In the state of creative attention there may sometimes occur a widening of the mental horizons within which the attention is subsumed. It is as though, to take the analogy of a field of force used earlier, the act of total attention brings about contact with a series of mental or psychic fields which extend far beyond the lifetime experience of the individual: fields of memory, of emotion and moods, of the tradition of the art or the science within which the individual works, and, most important of all, the field of universal consciousness. Handel wrote the whole of his *Messiah* in twenty-four days, in 1741, never leaving his house in Brook Street, ignoring the food brought to him. At the point when he had completed the second part of the oratorio with the Halleluja Chorus, his servant found him at his table with tears streaming from his eyes. Handel exclaimed to his servant: 'I did think that I did see all Heaven before me, and the Great God himself!'[18]

What all those overlapping fields can be thought to amount to, within the field of universal consciousness, is a host of potentialities, of choices to be made. The turning of attention towards them alters them, shows most of them to be not what is needed, while others announce themselves as the images or lines of thought to be developed. One of the characteristic features of this stage of the creative process is synchronicity: just as the world seems to provide and guard the time for making and expressing, so it also offers exactly when needed the right image or story perhaps from someone else's conversation, the right reference in a book that falls open at the relevant page, or the right surroundings in which to create, where every piece of furniture or every tree seems to offer a feeling or thought that can be incorporated into the current work.

So much is offered in this state, but what of the choice the creator has to make in all this wealth of impressions and memories? What is the difference between the numerous examples of automatic writing, for example, where the writer speaks of him- or herself entirely as the vehicle of spirit voices or disembodied masters, and the blind Milton shaping his verses in the night? Or between Adolf Hitler, who, some might think, would have been in a state approaching that of creative attention when he dictated much of *Mein Kampf* in a matter of months while in prison after the failure of the Munich putsch, and Einstein, with his phenomenal gift for concentrating on a problem whom Hitler was to drive into exile? Or between Stalin, who, by the extent of his collected works, must have possessed quite exceptional powers of concentration, and Osip Mandelstam, whom he deliberately and personally sent to his death in a prison camp and who was capable, like Milton, of composing all his verse in his head before he ever committed a word to paper?

These questions face us with another question: who or what is in control in the state of attention? Clearly, Milton, with his powerful memory, his inner visual sense and his superb mastery of language and verbal rhythms was in control of his work in a way that the medium in a trance could never be. What Hitler first dictated was in fact the product of the dispersal of attention rather than its concentration: it was the despair of the disreputable priest Father Bernhard Stempfle who undertook the task of editing the book and making it ready for publication. Hitler's attention was on projecting an image of himself as the saviour and the Führer of the German race, just as Stalin's attention was on creating a picture of himself as the infinitely wise teacher, friend and leader. Furthermore, Einstein and Mandelstam never wished to rule the world in the way Hitler and Stalin with their different motivations wished to. Einstein wished to discover truths about the universe and Mandelstam wished to express poetic truth. Exploration is different from conquest, at least in its beginnings. The wider implications of these thoughts will be considered in the next chapter: I raise them here to show they are not absent from my mind in considering a higher and more powerful form of the creative state, where creativity is an effect of the nature of the individual, rather than the whole object of the individual.

We can know that such forms of creativity are possible by the test 'By their fruits shall ye know them'. In Chinese art and poetry the highest achievements are tested by the standard of inner serenity. Thus Chang Chung-yuan says of the artist Ni Tsan (1301–74):

There was something in his paintings that none could describe or imitate since the secret of his achievement was hidden in his heart. From that illuminated chamber he reflected the heavenly light to his paintings and it was this transparency that enthralled the beholder. He painted simply to express his inner serenity; therefore whatever he painted – be it trees, branches of the bamboo, rocky banks – all became reflections of his inner exalted state.

Once Ni Tsan explained why he painted bamboo:

I-chung (the name of a friend) always likes my bamboo paintings. I am painting bamboo to release my inner serenity. How can I care for likeness and unlikeness; for abundant or scattered leaves; for slanting or straight branches? Perhaps . . . people may even take them for hemp or reeds. Why should I try to convince them that they are bamboos?[19]

Where other artists might try to free themselves by the expression of their emotions, Ni Tsan was already in a state of freedom where his creativity was untrammelled.

His early life overlapped with the later years of Meister Eckhart, whose purity of soul as expressed in his sermons and other writings has often been compared with the inner serenity of Taoist philosophers, poets and painters. When we read Meister Eckhart we are touched by a gentleness of spirit so immediately present it is as though he were in the room speaking his words to us. Frequently he speaks of the purity of soul as the Virgin in which the Christ may be born: also he speaks of a state which is neither conscious in the ordinary sense nor unconscious but one of dwelling in pure spirit, free of images.

There are people who seem to be born with this quality, which indeed has much that is childlike in it, and they carry the serenity of childhood into their later life as other people carry the fears or the imaginative gifts of childhood into their adulthood. Others acquire it through disciplines, sudden conversions, or as a series of transformations. I think of it as the state of freedom which it is the aim of art and other forms of civilized pursuit at least to recall or remember and at best to enter into as a permanent condition.

It is a state beyond destiny, beyond the Great Memory, and beyond the trammels of the past. It can be described by many of the images I have already touched on: the lost paradise, the Eden of the soul, the unitive condition of the spirit. Here creativity is one with the life and there is a permanent awareness of the great consciousness which is itself freedom. Here there is no division between the beloved and the lover: the lovely woman, the perfect friends, the saint whose simple presence inspires or heals are as creative in their beings as those who are inspired by them.

What I am attempting to describe is a state in which wisdom and justice are the guides of living and where the fullness of consciousness is the reservoir of creativity to be drawn on whenever needed. What I am also describing is an image of men and women such as I believe is needed today in order to transform our inheritance from the past and to create our new civilization.

Such must have been the states in which the great myths of past civilizations were devised – within the procreative moments when the eternal enters time, when the wisdom and knowledge present in universal consciousness were dictated by the gods or the muse or the angel to the listening scribe. Thus we are shown St John inspired by the Eagle to express the greatest voicing of the state of creative attention in western civilization when Christ says: 'the words that I speak unto you I speak not of myself: but the Father that dwelleth in me, he doeth the works.'[20]

Another way of seeing this universal consciousness is to regard it as an ever existing form of civilization, the civilization of Heaven, if you like – a theme I develop further in the next chapter when I speak of the redemptive spirit of civilization in history. As a civilization it is symbolized in many traditions as the ideal or heavenly city, the heavenly Jerusalem sparkling with jewels in Revelation, the blissful cities of Buddhist mandalas, and the Western Paradise of the Immortals. Blake saw it as the city of art, Golgonooza, and Dante as the court of Heaven within the white rose. It is the city of all possibilities where nothing great or true that has been manifested in time and has passed away in time is ever lost.[21]

There is an Indian symbol which combines the image of the city with the full state of creative attention. It is the Sri Yantra (figure 24). It is made up of a square frame with steps and doors on its four sides permitting entry to the sanctuary raised upon concentric circles with lotus petals and within those circles a pattern of nine triangles laid upon one another. The four triangles rising upwards are the male force, the lingam also known as 'the fire'. These indicate the male essence of the god whereas the downward-pointing triangles are female and correspond to the yoni or the Shakti, the female essence of the god's consort. At the centre is the heart of the devotee concentrated on his oneness with the deity of his choice. Interpreted as the state of creative attention it can be seen as a diagram of the coordination of all the faculties brought about by universal consciousness and each triangle overlapping is like the merging, without losing their distinctiveness, of all the fields of influence, memory, tradition, thought, feeling, discrimination, that must contribute to the work in hand.[22]

Figure 24. The Sri Yantra.

It does not come from our separated sense of ourselves, that higher state of creativity. 'Every good gift, and every perfect gift, is from above and cometh down from the Father of lights, with whom is no variableness, neither shadow of turning.'[23] If, however, we can learn to recover the sense of our oneness with the Father, with the true self that is in every human being, then all the possibilities of the heavenly city are open to us.

In Chapter 2 I spoke of the unprecedented scale of information about the past and the world that is characteristic of our present cultures, the undigested, uncoordinated farrago of images and ideas that the Great Memory has presented us with and of the need for ideals of humanity that will choose among and guide the offerings of the past. We are all creative, we each bring the world into existence at every moment we are aware of our perceptions. In addition to our gift for metaphorical thought, we all possess potentially one talent, and that is the talent for finding stillness in ourselves, the stillness that enhances discrimination, enriches consciousness and energizes our creative powers. Many of the ideals of the past are either of those who withdraw from the world or of those who ought to rule the world. The world now seems too great either to withdraw from or for one man to rule. It seems to me that the creativity of the future will grow out of a new spirit of cooperation where leadership is shared and by agreement, when new arts based on participation and spontaneity will arise from sharing in the one mind. It is something that scientists have already developed on an influential scale in their research teams with their binding-together of minds in a common pursuit and they have also revealed the inescapable vision of an Earth with its biosphere that is demanding a new ideal of humanity for the transformation of the past.

We must not forget that the city from which we derive our conception of civilization is an image of the feminine. Some of the earliest human settlements, such as the stone village of Skara Brae uncovered from the sand dunes of an Orkney beach, have been interpreted as following in the shapes of their chambers the symbolism of the Great Goddess, and so have the first known cities, such as Çatal Hüyük. The most powerful of all the ancient deities of Asia Minor was the Great Goddess, known as Cybele and as Diana of the Ephesians. Goddess of fecundity and inspirer of awe and terror, she encompassed the range of experience from savagery and terror to the most civilized of arts and pursuits: she was portrayed as riding in a chariot drawn by lions and wearing on her head a crown of city walls and towers.

One of the strangest episodes in Roman history is the story of how in 204 BC the Romans, perhaps realizing the lack of her great feminine powers from their largely male pantheon, formally invited the goddess to leave her ancient shrine of Pessos and to come to Rome, where she would receive even greater honour. They were advised in this by a prophecy in the Sybilline Books and by the oracle of Delphi. The goddess accepted and was escorted to Rome by five quinqueremes. From Rome, where later, under Claudius, she was incorporated into the state religion, her influence spread throughout the empire.

The symbolic and religious associations of the city with the feminine continued under Christianity: during a Saracen siege of Byzantium in the early tenth century St Andrew the Holy Fool saw the Virgin standing in the air above the city praying and spreading out her veil to protect the Christians, who were strengthened by this vision to save themselves and the city. This story has been brought alive in the West recently by John Tavener's composition *The Protecting Veil*, a work whose immense popularity indicates a longing and a need for the help of the Eternal Feminine. In other cases we can point to cities that have dedicated themselves to the Virgin, as did Siena before the battle of Montaperti in 1260. The building of the great Gothic cathedrals dedicated to the Virgin, such as Chartres and Florence, further maintained the association of the city with the feminine, nowhere more strongly than in the cathedral of Notre Dame de Paris which sums up the spirit of Paris. How will we heal the miseries and squalor of our inner cities except through the return of the compassion and wisdom of the Eternal Feminine and through the respect for the forms of creative attention offering mutual support on which civilized society depends and thrives?

12

Conscience and civilization

The Face of Glory pours out the divine creative energy at all times and for all ages. It is the energy of life, of consciousness and of delight. It is the Joy of Schiller's ode. The myth of the birth of the Face of Glory gives us a message: that the brute desires of life can be directed through the conscious inspiration of the god into a means of delight and enjoyment for others. In the measure that green becomes gold, civilization flourishes. In the measure that civilization flourishes, the Golden Age returns.

The instances of creativity I have been drawing on over the past chapters all point to states of awareness sometimes only fleetingly attained and sometimes known for longer periods in which the impossible becomes possible through the exceptional coordination of the faculties of the mind or soul. The picture of creativity that has been building up is that those moments of coordination arise, not only through the efforts of the artist or the thinker, but also through the entry and expansion of awareness into worlds that are pre-existent and already coordinated, worlds of ideal colour for the artist, of pure tone for the composer, of the vibrations of the universal language for the poet, of the laws underlying life and the universe for the scientist, and of the eternal ideas and archetypes for the philosopher.

Those worlds are another realm of Nature – in effect, her imagination. They are worlds of the mind and the emotions, full of living symbols that may appear to us as the subtle minerals of ideal mountains, the forms of the souls of plants and the spirits of animals and birds. They have their own intelligences and their own ecological systems. They are the realities in this sense. Though we are taught to look upon metaphor and symbol as signs towards reality that can be cast aside once we have reached an undisputable fact or truth, the opposite is the case. Metaphors and symbols are vehicles of truth in themselves and therefore gifts from above, not props we invent, in that they are of a higher order of organization and intelligence, tapping energy from different areas of the brain. The legends that say that once rivers, trees, flowers and animals had human sense and could speak are not false:[1] in these worlds they can still utter intelligible language. If we wish to look higher for the mind that unites these worlds of metaphors and symbols, for the all-containing universal mind, we will find it in ourselves in so far as we see ourselves, each one of us, as the metaphor of the universe. For there to be communication between that realm and the realm we think we inhabit we need the mediation of saints, poets, scientists and composers who are the miners of the mountains, the gardeners for the plants, the herdsmen for the animals and the falconers for the birds.

Many of the scientists whom I have quoted earlier believed that it was possible to create a greater and more efficient mind. Tesla said that he was going to make the brain of the Earth with radio; Bernal dreamed of the ecstasy of being part of the whole that would come about through the mechanization of the body and the development of multiple individuals. Others believe it possible to create giant intelligences through modelling the electrical circuits of the brain. Perhaps an embryo form of the concern with tapping into a greater mind may be seen in the current preoccupation with the Internet. It is interesting to note that materialist scientists should regard, as the ultimate goal of their science, the imperative to create a supreme intelligence into which they will be merged, in other words to make the transcendent deity with which they can experience the unity that they have been unable to find through their researches into microcosms and macrocosms. That they should have such a goal, however, places them much nearer to the position that I am setting out here than might on the surface be thought. The great difference lies in this: that they believe it necessary to create what already exists. From the viewpoint of the already existent conscious unity, creativity is an unveiling, a remembering of what is already latent and waiting to be given, a Platonic anamnesis. Thus the appreciation of the audience or the readership is fundamentally an appreciation at being reminded of the existence of those worlds in their own inner natures. For the creator and the audience to enter into those worlds or to be reminded of them is a recovery of freedom, a release from darkness or a return from exile.

Civilization depends on the constant rediscovery and re-enactment of the state of creative attention for its origins and its maintenance. It also decays when its members let themselves be cut off from the supreme experience of consciousness and devote their attention to imitating the past, to maintaining the outer forms of traditions, and to living on the cultural capital of their ancestors. Without realizing it they become the prey or the slaves of their imaginations instead of being at once the owners of their minds and the servants of the divine imagination. The energy to create still comes from the one source of consciousness but the inspiration comes from what is currently fashionable, from personal and private obsessions and themes. When it does draw on the deeper levels of dream life, it is the unredeemed and untransformed archetypes that are likely to dominate. Interpretation fails because the society surrounding the artist or the thinker has low expectations and uncultivated taste and because everyone neglects the thought that there is a vital connection between the transformation of the inner soul of the creator and the transformation of the matter, the ideas, the symbols, the myths or the tones with which he or she works. Much of Post-Modernist art and literature, playing with the detritus of the Great Memory, is typical of such shallow inspiration, and the violence and terror justified in the name of art and freedom of expression are fuelled by the dark archetypes of the unconscious mind. The creative power goes to the criminal, the unredeemed.

The constant factor in the origins of civilizations is the presence in societies of men and women who have achieved the inner transformation and who have through their example or through their own works brought about a significantly deeper transformation of art, thought and the inter- pretation of knowledge for their own and succeeding generations. They are the ones who are conscious, who have realized the full possibilities of their natures, and whose lives work a change in the climate of opinion through this subtle influence of their existence. They may be prominent in their time with great historical roles to play, such as St Francis and the present Dalai Lama, or they may live obscure and secluded lives, the greater influence of which is only apparent after their deaths, as in the case of Meister Eckhart, who was the channel for all that is best in the development of German art and culture. Through the integrity and consistency of their lives they set a standard for the service of others which many of greater name for their gifts to humanity have to follow.

> They are the lords and owners of their faces,
> Others but stewards of their excellence.[2]

To make a perfect life is the noblest form of creativity. Men and women who achieve such perfection live in the state of consciousness unveiled. By this I mean consciousness as the ground of life and being, the eternally existent, the source of life and of the physical world. This is the consciousness that is present or latent in all the states of human experience, from deep sleep to dreaming states to common and enhanced waking states. It is the hidden observer that has been found to remain inviolate even in subjects under hypnosis. It is the continuity that returns our seeming lost selves to ourselves when we wake after deep sleep. It is the giver of the moment of unattended joy and the detached helper in the time of danger and serious trouble. In Christian terms it is the Holy Ghost, 'the Lord and Giver of life', and in another phrase it is the Buddha nature. Time, like our bodies, is within that consciousness, and this is one explanation of why civilization recurs in history. It recurs because it holds history within itself.

It also explains the redemptive spirit that comes with each new civilization, the healing and consolation that art and true religion bring to the sufferings of the past, the power of regeneration that so often strikes the historian looking at the catalogue of natural disasters and those wrought by man when he sees the astonishing efforts to recover and preserve as happened in the Middle East and Europe at the time of the Black Death when perhaps as much as half the population perished in these regions and when in England, for example, a third of the agricultural land lay uncultivated for over a hundred years because the labourers who had worked the fields were wiped out with their entire villages. Yet that time of depopulation and worsening climate, which also saw the horrors of the Hundred Years' War and the origins of the Wars of the Roses, was also the period of the coming of age of English as a literary language, of great achievements in music, of new religious movements, and of the birth of the chief original contribution of the English to architecture, the Perpendicular style – and, behind and supporting all these achievements, the presence and influence of the English mystics, such as the author of *The Cloud of Unknowing*, Dame Julian of Norwich, Margery Kempe, Richard Rolle and Walter Hilton.

In order to demonstrate what I mean by the relationship between the inner transformation in the soul and the transformation of the matter or ideas in creative work, I give the following examples from various periods, including our own century. The examples also demonstrate how the expectations of the society in which a creative personality lives may limit or enhance the possibilities of those two linked transformations.

My first example is one of the most rebarbative characters ever recorded – the Viking poet Egil Skallagrimsson, who lived a long life in the tenth century (c. 910–90). *Egil's Saga*, incorporating many of his poems, is probably the work of Snorri Sturluson (1179–1241).[3] The period of the saga writers in Iceland can be seen as an example of a creative impulse that affects different parts of the world at the same time. Many of the greatest sagas tell the stories of notable individuals who took part in the founding of the settlements of Iceland from the ninth and tenth centuries onwards in the time up to the adoption of Christianity. The nature of the impulse is summed up in the word 'individual' because these sagas are roughly coeval with the first statement of the western conception of the individual in the sculptures of the Royal Portal and the transept porches of Chartres and the defence of the immortality of the individual soul by Aquinas against the Averroists. They precede Dante's innovation in introducing contemporary characters into *The Divine Comedy* who create the impression of their individuality out of their own words. The narrative mode of such sagas as *Burnt Njal*, the *Laxdaela Saga* or *Egil's Saga* has a modern realist and matter-of-fact tone that is unlike anything else in the literature of the period. On the other hand they are as much an appeal to a remote past as the contemporary retellings of the Arthurian legends and the Alexander stories and can be seen as much as them as examples of the Great Memory at work.

Egil was the child of settlers who had fled the tyranny of the kings of Norway to Iceland. From an early age he showed evidence of great physical strength, a proud and independent nature, and a gift for spontaneous and memorable poetry. At the age of six he killed another boy who had thrown him in a wrestling match. A fight took place between his family and the family of the dead boy in which seven men were killed. Rebuked by his father but encouraged by his mother, who saw in him the makings of a great Viking, he recited a poem predicting the slaughter he will wreak when he is given fighting ships. This early episode foreshadows a future career of bloodshed, enmities, fierce loyalties, acts of vengeance and unprovoked slaughter always followed or accompanied by verse. He is a true child of Odin, the god of battle and of poetry; he is a sorcerer, a healer, a lawyer, a drunk, a restless wanderer and a landowning farmer, a miser and a jealous guardian of his family honour; in short, a nest of inspired contradictions. His most famous poem is a grandiose lie. He had fallen into the hands of his worst enemy, King Eric Bloodaxe at York. Bloodaxe with much justification wished to execute him. Arinbjorn, one of Eric's chief followers who was a friend of Egil, told Egil to write a poem in praise of Eric Bloodaxe. Egil had only one night in which to compose this poem in order to save his life. He composed the poem, a twenty-stanza *drapa* rhymed and with refrains, and memorized it. The next day when he appeared before the king and recited the poem, it was revealed as so magnificent a tribute that Bloodaxe was forced to spare his life. Egil was allowed to depart in freedom. The poem became known as 'The Head Ransom'. Later in life when he had returned to Iceland, his world was shattered by the death by drowning of his favourite son. This followed the death of another son. He determined to starve to death. His daughter Thorgerd said she too would starve to death with him. Sharing his suffering, she gradually coaxed him to write a dirge in memory of his sons. At first he refused and then the poetic mood came upon him and he composed his lament:

> Purest of Possessions,
> Poetic craft, power
> That dwarf-devised
> Drew first breath;
> Now I feel it surge, swell
> Like a sea, old giant's blood,
> About the cragged cliff face
> Of the dwarf caves.[4]

His words are a palace, from his inner shrine the tree of words tells the story of its growth as he turns to lament his drowned son:

> Cruel crashed
> The curled sea
> Wave on the once well-formed
> Family shield-wall,
> Now broached and battered
> Like the beaten boat
> Of my son, smashed
> By the sea-storm.[5]

He can take no vengeance on the sea, he has no comfort in friends, and Odin whom he trusted has stolen his son. Odin who once favoured him now mocks him, but as he has taken away, so he has added another gift, which is unrelenting hatred.

> The end is all.
> Even now
> High on the headland
> Hel stands and waits,
> Life fades, I must fall
> And face my own end,

Not in misery and mourning
But with a man's heart.[6]

He was so cheered up by the poem he forgot about suicide. Odin, in giving him the poem, had not deserted him after all. He went on to live to an unregenerate old age. When he started to lose his sight and hearing, the women would laugh at him when he stumbled and fell. He wrote this poem about himself:

My bald pate bobs and blunders,
I bang it when I fall;
My cock's gone soft and clammy
And I can't hear when they call.[7]

Shortly before his death he announced his idea of what to do with all his treasure: he wanted to take it to the Althing, the assembly of Iceland, and scatter it among the crowd in the hope that everyone would fight over it. Foiled by his relations from doing this, he rode off with two slaves, taking his treasure with him, into the waste country. There he made them bury the treasure and then he killed them. Blind though he was, he made his way home, where he fell ill and died.

In terms of his own time he could be considered a universal man of the Viking Age, except for his miserliness. In terms of world literature he was a master poet whose images, even in translation, still bite into the mind like his sharp axe blade. In terms of our own age and conceptions of civilized behaviour, his was a world of artist-murderers to whose society we would deny the name of civilization. Just as their poetry, voicing their exultation in victory and their griefs in loss and defeat, was based on one of the most exacting crafts ever devised for complexity of imagery and metrical invention, so the weapons they took on their marauding expeditions and the ships they sailed in were all works of art, as were the gold rings and armbands that were the rewards granted by their leaders for slaughtering their enemies. Egil is so close to the old world of Scandinavian myth that even when he holds an honoured position in the army of King Athelstan, he is wholly untouched by the Christian civilization of the court of Wessex, then one of the most splendid in Europe. In his own world he has to live by its codes and its savagery, if he and his family and his landowning caste are to survive. From that world issued the race that was to define the boundaries of Christian Europe from Iceland to Russia and the Holy Land, that devised numerous technological innovations from ocean-going ships to the discovery of how to make hay for feeding cattle in winter, and that gave the world the concept of common law (the word law is of Old Norse origin) and the first practice of democracy in the modern age. These, as they were adapted and spread, provide further examples of the redemptive power of civilization. If we cannot compare his world with ours, even if we owe so much to what evolved from his world, what is the constant in his poetry that makes it so immediate and striking to us today? It is the flavour of a cruel but heroic age when poetry was an immediate response to life and its challenges. It is in Egil's case also his acknowledgment of the power of inspiration from a source beyond himself, the source he calls Odin. It is Odin who saves his life twice, first when he gives him the 'Head Ransom' poem for Eric Bloodaxe and, second, when he is turned aside from his suicidal mood in the lament for his sons. He is given the unitive experience but how he interprets it and what he makes of it is limited not only by his nature but by the society into which he is born.

Egil Skallagrimsson is married in my mind to the greatest artist of the twentieth century, Pablo Picasso. Picasso was the Viking of the world of art, burning the monasteries of academic painting and marauding along the estuaries of other arts from ceramics and sculpture to film and design for the theatre and ballet. He would speak of his art in terms of war.

Whatever the source of the emotion that drives me to create, I want to give it a form which has some connection with the visible world, even if it is only to wage war on that world . . . I want my paintings to be able to defend themselves, to resist the invader, just as though there were razor blades on all their surfaces so no one could touch them without cutting their hands.[8]

As he made war on the ossifying traditions of western art, so from the strangely intertwined strands of violent hatred and tenderest compassion in his nature he anticipated and recorded the cruelty and the dehumanization of society in western Europe. To me he is the greatest product of the Symbolist movement in art: where earlier Symbolists such as Gustave Moreau concentrated on the myths and moods of the past, Picasso made Symbolism modern. When he is distorting the human face and form to the most extreme and tortured shapes, he is depicting humanity in a Symbolist mode: he is showing the self-devouring pains and hatreds of the mind as creatures that can do nothing but grow out of true. He is equally a Symbolist in works in which he reveals the compassionate sides of his nature, such as the paintings of the circus people of his Blue Period, who are the toys and distractions of industrial society and, as such, types of the artist, and in the works of judgment such as his *Guernica*, in which the primordial symbols of his western Mediterranean world, the bull and the horse, the creatures of earth and the sea are the witnesses together with the lamenting woman under the light revealing the pile of corpses.

Picasso was fascinated by his own creative processes. He saw a contrary process at work in himself. 'Basically a picture doesn't change . . . The first vision remains, almost intact, in spite of appearances,' he said but he also remarked: 'A picture is not thought out and settled beforehand. While it is being done it changes as one's thoughts change.'[9] What he seems to have meant by these opposing statements is that, like the warning of the Boyg in *Peer Gynt* to 'go round about', he had to go through a process of greater and greater complexity until he reached a stage in which he returned to the first vision and by remembering it was able to reduce the painting to elements of greater simplicity. The process was necessary to preserve and include in the finished work all the numerous riches of meaning given in the first vision. Of the way in which he worked, his experience of creative attention, he said that he left his body outside the studio as Muslims take off their shoes before entering the mosque.[10] He was so much in love with that state and so terrified he would lose it that at times he would take four hours to get up in the morning, convinced that it had gone for ever.

His despair pursued him into old age. Despite his phenomenal energies and the temporary transformations of mood that success in painting brought him, he rarely achieved in his later works that calm and benignity which characterizes the mature and late styles of his friends Matisse and Braque. There was another reason for his despair. Someone remarked of him that he would have been a very great painter if he had lived in a true civilization. Giovanni Papini represented him as saying that in a world in which the majority of people no longer found consolation and uplift from art, he had become rich and famous in satisfying the appetite of the wealthy for whatever is strange, bizarre or scandalous.

When I am alone with myself, I am not bold enough to think of myself as an artist in the great and ancient sense of the word. Giotto, Titian, Rembrandt and Goya were true painters. I am merely an *amuseur public*, an entertainer who has understood his time and has milked as best he could the imbecility, the vanity, and the greed of his contemporaries.

It is a bitter confession, more painful than it may appear, but it has the merit of being sincere.[11]

This is similar to many tragic statements that he made. It is comparable to the feelings of William Morris who, in reviving the standards and taste of the Middle Ages in order to embellish the lives of everyone in society, discovered that only the rich could afford what he and his craftsmen produced, but with the added chagrin of being party to deception. Picasso's audience was not the one he desired and longed for: perhaps his admiration for Soviet society was based on the hope that it would prove to be that audience where the artist was one with the heart of the masses – even though that society in his lifetime was only allowed to see works of Socialist Realism and never anything fired with his revolutionary style and ardour.

He is the greatest artist of the twentieth century because he is the most representative and inclusive of all the themes and stresses in the mass psyche of western humanity. Whatever he condoned or fudged in his dabblings in politics, he never condoned in his art. The energy of the Green Man as the first gift of creative consciousness poured through him with phenomenal power. As he lacked the audience he needed, so he lacked the greater conscience that such an audience would have awakened in him.

All creative people, artists, scientists, thinkers, possess conscience in relation to their art or activity: conscience here is the intuitive voice that constantly reminds them of the standards they have made for themselves or are expected to achieve. It is the guiding taste of their being. There is, however, a greater conscience which is probably the most important civilizing force in guiding creative people and in expanding their inspirations so that they interpret them on a universal scale. This conscience is a life-transforming force. We have already spoken of the wholeness of a creative personality devoted in attention to making and discovery. Divisions, disunity and obsessions must all affect and weaken that wholeness. The Richard Wagner who wrote of Parsifal 'Through compassion the pure Fool finds wisdom'[12] is the Richard Wagner who wrote anti-Semitic pamphlets and whose mighty but incomplete reawakening of Teutonic myth, especially the archetype of Wotan, fed the violence and bitterness of National Socialism.

What conscience transforms is the world of the psyche, the images, the contemporary experiences, the gifts from the past, so that their violent and shocking emotions are directed to civilizing ends. In *La Vita Nuova* Dante describes how, heart-stricken by Beatrice's refusal to acknowledge him with a greeting, he had written poems lamenting her cruelty to him and blaming her. He could not even bear to be in her presence, so much did the loss of her greeting torment him. He met some ladies who asked him questions about the nature of his love, particularly about where he found happiness if he could not bear to be within sight of her. He answered that his blessedness lay 'in those words which praise my lady'. At this the ladies pointed out to him sharply the inconsistency between his actual practice in writing poems that blamed Beatrice and what he had just said. Dante was stung to his depths by the lie he had told and the slandering of Beatrice. He went away covered in shame.[13] The effect of his remorse came a little later when, in the episode related on page 131, walking beside a river his tongue spoke as though moved by itself the words *'Donne ch'avete l'intelletto d'amore'*, the beginning of the art of praise in his work and the raising of his imagination to a universal and cosmic level. This experience of Dante's may be compared to the metanoia, or 'change of mind', of the Gospels. Though we know in many ways less about Shakespeare in that we have no autobiographical writings from his hand, it is almost certain that he must have undergone a profound experience of conscience and of forgiveness such as caused him to write

Love is not love
Which alters when it alteration finds,
Or bends with the remover to remove.[14]

This is the experience that resounds throughout the later plays and without which he would never have achieved his universal position in the world.

The transforming effect of conscience is to be seen in the two examples I set against those of Egil Skallagrimsson and Picasso, the first a poet from a far more distant and legendary past than Egil and the second a contemporary scientist.

In ancient India there was a hunter called Valmiki who enjoyed killing and violence: to support his family he turned to banditry and murder. One day in the forest he came across seven holy men. These holy men had nothing he could steal and he found against his will that he was attracted to them. They told him that he was accruing a bitter future for himself through his misdeeds and they told him to ask his dependants if they would share in his guilt and his punishment. When he asked his dependants this question, they told him they wanted none of his responsibilities loaded on to them. Valmiki was so shocked by this rejection by his own kind that he returned to the holy men, who taught him to meditate. Through meditation and instruction he renounced his former life and began to discover his true vocation, which was that of a poet. One day he asked the sage Narada if he knew of a perfect man, one who was strong, responsible, absolutely truthful, consistent in word and deed, compassionate, learned, handsome, confident, free from anger but capable of inspiring terror when aroused. Narada said that such a paragon was extremely rare but that the prince of Ayodhya, Rama, possessed all these qualities. Valmiki, reflecting on what Narada had said, went to the river to bathe. There he saw a pair of herons mating. Even as he watched, a passing huntsman shot the cock heron. The female heron uttered a cry of distress which pierced Valmiki's heart so deeply that he rebuked the hunter, warning him of an early death for his cruelty. He was, in fact, repudiating his own earlier vicious cruelties. In his utterance, he spontaneously invented a new metre, the *sloka*, the great verse of Sanskrit epic poetry. On his return to his ashram, the god Brahma appeared to him and commanded him to write the story of Rama in this very verse form.[15] Valmiki set himself to compose and, inspired by the sage Narada, he found the episodes of the story rising as visions before his eyes. Thus he composed the epic of the *Ramayana*, the heroic and beautiful story of the births of Rama and his wife Sita, respectively incarnations of Vishnu and his bride Lakshmi, and of their sufferings when first he is wrongly disinherited of his father's kingdom and then when she is abducted by the demon Ravana. It tells of how Rama, with the aid of the monkey leader Hanuman and his followers, conquers Ravana's kingdom in Sri Lanka and rescues Sita, and how after further trials they both return to their true natures in heaven as Vishnu and Lakshmi. The 50,000 verses of the epic were preserved by generations of storytellers. It has been translated into the main languages of the subcontinent, most notably into Tamil by Kamban in the eleventh century and into Hindi by Tulsi Das (died 1616), a contemporary of Shakespeare. In these and other adaptations and translations it remains the most read and best loved of all the long poems in the world today, having been for centuries the chief cultural influence on the lives of millions in India and Southeast Asia.

Legendary though the story of the origins of the *Ramayana* may be, it is thought that Valmiki was a historical personage. In his telling of the story he became so much part of the scenes that his divine inspiration displayed before him that he himself appears in the epic and plays a role in it. The story of his conversion and of the conscience-stricken realization that turned him into a poet contains the same inner truth as the story of the Face of Glory. In that story Shiva makes the product of his anger devour himself so that the very source of the lion-headed man's hunger in his body and belly is consumed and all the power of rage is transformed into a protective and creative force designed to foster civilization among humanity. So too Valmiki, in portraying human perfection in Rama and Sita, drew on his experience of transformation to create a supreme masterpiece.

There have been many scientists guided by their love of nature and their own kind in the choice and direction of their work. Great numbers have suffered death, imprisonment and exile because of their faith or because their sense of truth conflicted with officially approved scientific doctrine – as in the case of the plant geneticists and other scientists in the Soviet Union who fell foul of T. F. Lysenko, who believed in the inheritance of acquired characteristics and who used his warm relationship with Stalin to crush his opponents. There have been others in more fortunate countries who, offered work that promised fame and security, have found it impossible in their consciences to accept. In giving the following example, I am not passing judgment on scientists who have not followed this hard path. We are individuals and conscience is individual.

My example is Glen Schaefer (1935–86). Brought up in rural Ontario, he showed early promise in atomic physics. He came to England to study for his higher degrees and he was picked out as one of the young scientists who would develop nuclear energy. The more he studied the subject, the profounder was his revulsion at the prospect of the work before him, especially the ungovernable nature of the effects of using nuclear energy. He refused all the offers made to him and found himself without a career.

At this point he turned back to one of the chief loves of his childhood, the natural world. He saw that there were many techniques in physics that had never been applied to the study of relationships in ecology and he introduced a new branch of science which he called ecological physics. He used these techniques in studying the effects of herbicides and pesticides and in studies of animal migration. By tracking swarms of locusts by radar across Africa he was able to demonstrate that nearly all the techniques hitherto used for destroying them were useless because of the speed with which they travelled and the power of their group intelligence. In studying the devastations of the pinebud moth in the forests of Canada he showed that the pest was most endemic in the areas where there had been most systematic and extensive spraying. The techniques he and his colleagues evolved became so refined that they could track the course taken by a single aphid across a huge wheat field. As a result of his work the concentrations of insecticides used were reduced to a tenth of their dosages in many instances so that only the target insect and not their natural predators would be destroyed.

Out of this work came what he called his third career, which was in metaphysics. To hear him speak of standing in a great forest and of feeling death in the silence where once there had been animal life and the sounds and sights of bird and insect life, all dead because of the indiscriminate use of chemicals, was a harrowing experience: the passion of his words transported one to that forest clearing where the dying trees stood round like judges pronouncing the same doom upon their unconscious destroyers.

He always remained close to his childhood and adolescence. As he had gone back to his feeling for nature when he made his fateful decision to abandon nuclear physics, so in the last six years of his life he returned to what he called the metaphysical influences of his grandmother and parents, which had been particularly strong in his earliest years. These influences included Christian Science and spiritual healing. At about the age of fifteen he knew he would have three careers: 'mathematical physics first, then biology, and finally metaphysics of man and nature'. The conclusion he came to is that nature is man in the sense that all is consciousness and is from one source of mind. One of the experiences that set him on his third career was looking at Blake's painting *The Ghost of a Flea*.

I was in the Tate Gallery wondering as usual how to do something better than to spray hell into the environment . . . [The painting] bolted off the wall into my mind, because the flea was in man form. It didn't have six legs, it had arms and two legs, but it was devilish. It had a bowl in one hand for blood – fleas are blood-sucking parasites at the present time – and it had a prick in the other hand to secure the blood . . . Blake told his friend Varley that, when he had this strong vision, the flea told him while he was drawing it, 'All fleas were inhabited by the souls of such men as were by nature blood-thirsty to excess.' Nature is the image of man's thought. Here we have an excess of a certain mentality exemplified in a blood-sucking thing 'out there.' Who knows what that thing would be like if we could redeem ourselves from that image? . . . all vision is known to be psychological in the last analysis. There's nothing 'outside' other than images of our collective mind . . .[16]

In this last stage of his career he suffered tortures over whether his metaphysical researches would damage his reputation as a scientist, not because of personal vanity but because the important messages he was pressing on governments and scientific institutions in many parts of the world would be weakened by the imputations of spiritual interests. This may seem surprising now when so many scientists are attempting wider descriptions of nature and the universe that try to account for the appearance of consciousness and intelligence. In his case, however, his conclusions were more revolutionary and prophetic, were based on personal experience and on his studies of the primitive Church, and required from him the most exacting standards. He saw the intelligence behind the material universe and the thoughts that are that universe, in his view, as being probably the collective unconscious of Jung. That intelligence, so he believed, was trivial in relation to the one intelligence of consciousness, which he called the Source. The collective unconscious 'delivers evil as well as good, it delivers error as well as truth because of its extreme limitation'. He believed that a microsecond of consciousness of the higher level, the Source, was infinite compared with any subdimension; 'a micro-second view of that will completely heal, redeem, allow walking on water . . .'[17]

The idea that nature can be changed and redeemed by the extent to which man has experience of God or universal consciousness has been expressed before. It underlies the stories of the miracles of Christ, of the Buddha, and of saints in many traditions. Alan of Lille, one of the great poets of the school of Chartres, described the transformation of nature, especially of all plant life, when God aids in the creation of the perfect man. Few scientists, however, especially not those concerned most with the environmental crisis, had ever linked the crisis to consciousness as the immanent good and none before or since, to my knowledge, has expressed it so succinctly.

Much of the riches of art and science is born at the level of the Great Memory or the collective unconscious, of the inner impulses of history, the level 'that delivers evil as well as good' – and this is the level on which Egil Skallagrimsson and Picasso interpreted and made use of their inspirations. Huge and capacious as it is, it is still a prison when related to the Universal Consciousness of which it is a manifestation, and when I say that the true purpose of creativity is to recover or gain freedom it is to the freedom of that fullness that I refer. One way to that freedom is through conscience, as in the examples I have given; other ways are through sacrifice, joy, mystical illumination and compassion – the ways that are under the guidance of the angel.

Civilization under the guidance of the angel shows as at Chartres what happens when religion, science, philosophy and art converge and are made to work together in a dynamic and long-lasting relationship. It also shows what can happen when the recovered images and ideas of the past, offered up by the Great Memory, are fully synthesized with the technology and the current needs of an epoch.

What happens, though, when human ingenuity and inventiveness flourish without the guiding spirit of wisdom, without the angel? I have drawn on examples of inspiration and inventiveness from the arts, technology and the sciences. Does what I have said about consciousness and inspiration apply to the discoverers of gunpowder, the makers of bombs, the devisers of Star Wars? Does it apply to the ingenious chemists who make pesticides and herbicides that destroy essential parts of food chains in ecological systems? Does it apply to the discoverers of drugs that are efficient at dealing with specific complaints and illnesses but have other effects, revealed only after severe damage has been done to patients or to their offspring?

First of all it must be said that many of the most deadly inventions of man have innocent beginnings: the first arrowheads are thought to have been ritual objects in rain-making ceremonies; the mixture that became gunpowder was first devised by Taoist alchemists as a recipe for physical immortality, not for projecting cannonballs;[18] the crenellations of castles and fortresses began as a snake pattern on Mesopotamian temples in honour of the Goddess; neither Louis Pasteur nor Robert Koch had any intention of germ warfare when they founded the sciences derived from bacteriology. Lord Rutherford, who first split the atom, believed it would always be a sink of energy, not a source of energy and therefore of no military interest.

On the other hand, how could Archimedes have refused his fellow citizens of Syracuse the benefit of his inventive skills when their city was attacked by the Romans? How could Giotto in the fourteenth century or Michelangelo in the sixteenth century, when Florence was in danger, not have worked on the fortifications of the city walls? Should Antoine Lavoisier have refused the comfortable quarters at the Arsenal in Paris where, among other studies, he improved the standards of gunpowder for use by the artillery of the French army? The chief consequence of that work was that a young military genius, the artillery officer Napoleon Bonaparte, was given a great technological advantage because his future victories over the rest of Europe depended in great part on his superior firepower.

There are recorded instances of inventors suppressing their inventions for fear of their consequences. John Napier (1550–1617), the deviser of logarithms, invented four devices he regarded so lethal that he begged his friends to keep them secret because whole armies could be destroyed by them: one was, in fact, a form of grapeshot which other, less scrupulous inventors also devised. The British cabinet at the time of the Crimean War rejected with horror a proposal from a member of the House of Lords for a lethal weapon that would have wreaked devastation on the Russians. Some German nuclear physicists deliberately held back their researches on an atomic bomb to prevent such a device falling into the hands of Hitler.

Many of the most notable contributions to global warming and pollution are owed to inventions that were introduced with benign intentions and were hailed as great benefits to humanity. Such were those of the American chemist Thomas Midgley, who solved two of the problems holding up the full development of modern technological society in the 1920s and 1930s. He solved the problem of knocking, or pinking, in motor engines by discovering that lead used as an additive to petrol helped the engines to run smoothly and efficiently. He solved the problem of finding a safe and efficient refrigerant for the refrigerator industry: ammonia, which was the refrigerant then in most general use, is both toxic and corrosive. He lighted on the class of chemicals known as chlorofluorocarbons, or CFCs. To demonstrate that chlorofluorocarbons were both harmless and not flammable, at a lecture to the American Chemical Society he inhaled CFC gas and then blew it at a candle, which was immediately extinguished. With the first of these discoveries he made more certain the increase in global warming from the exhausts of motorcars. With the second he unwittingly put into the hands of others the means of releasing to the upper atmosphere a chemical that is stable at Earth temperatures but is broken up by ultraviolet light in the stratosphere to release the free chlorine atoms that are destroying the ozone molecules which protect life on Earth from overexposure to ultraviolet radiation. His ingenuity never ceased to function. Late in life, when he contracted polio, he invented a special harness which hoisted his wasted and paralysed body out of bed. This worked excellently until one day in 1941, when he put it into action, it strangled him.[19]

How can we protect ourselves from our own imaginations that are too narrow to include in their vision not only how to make or do something now but also what the consequences of its introduction would be? And how can we protect ourselves from those dictators and rulers who have the kinds of imagination that see the possibilities for command, conquest and subjection in all technical advances? And is it possible to suppress or eradicate knowledge once gained? It would seem as though the only way in which humanity can lose knowledge is through the extinction of a culture, such as the destruction of classical writings in China under the Ch'in dynasty (221–207 BC) and the Christian and Muslim destructions of the Library of Alexandria, or by the wider cataclysm of a Dark Age such as overcame Greece between 1200 and 800 BC and most of Europe between 500 and 1000 AD. Dreams, however, survive and can be dreamed again. Dreams of space flight over centuries have led to our present awareness of the solar system and Earth's place in it. In Sanskrit literature not only are there legends of wars and battles in the skies but instructions on making the vehicles of flight. Lucian in the second century AD wrote of a journey to the moon. Among the stories about Alexander the Great is the legend of his space flight in which he was carried by griffons into the upper atmosphere. The legend of the Prophet Mohammed ascending to Heaven on his steed Buraq from the site of the Dome of the Rock probably fed the imagination of Dante when he came to describe his own journey up to Paradise. Other, later journeys include those of Cyrano de Bergerac and the suggestion by Bishop Wilkins, first secretary of the Royal Society, that the moon was inhabited, together with proposals of how to fly there. All these were to be replaced in scale and number as the growth in technology in the nineteenth and early twentieth centuries brought the likelihood of realizing the impossible nearer with the writings of Jules Verne, H. G. Wells and others. These authors stirred the imagination of scientists such as the Russian Konstantin Eduardovich Tsiolkovsky (1857–1935) to investigate the practical problems of the fuel mixes necessary to put a spacecraft into orbit. Many science-fiction writers, including H. G. Wells, had seen the military implications of space flight, but it required the imagination and power hunger of a dictator furnished with the right technological support for these implications to become reality.

Our picture of the Earth, a picture impossible for our forebears to conceive, our sense of the unity of the biosphere and of the interdependence of living things, our incipient new understanding of the depth and scope of consciousness and our hopes of international peace derive, paradoxically, from the resources Hitler put into making the first guided ballistic missile from 1936 onwards. On 3 October 1942 a prototype missile launched from Peenemünde reached an altitude of 50 miles and landed not far from its target over 100 miles away. The next year Hitler, dreaming of the day he would order 5,000 V-2 rockets to be fired simultaneously at London, gave the order for mass production to begin. Thousands of German scientists and technicians, led by Wernher von Braun, devoted their energies to the task. What has not been generally known until recently is that 32,000 prisoners from twenty-one nationalities were forced to work on making the rockets in tunnels burrowed into Mount Kohnstein in conditions so foul and subjected to a treatment so brutal that some 20,000 of them died. Hardly any of those responsible for the murders, the deprivation and the brutality were punished because the US Army repressed and sealed the investigations into what had happened so that Wernher von Braun and his colleagues, who were taken to the USA to become the pioneers of the NASA programmes, could work without embarrassing truths coming out.[20]

Hitler's hopes that this weapon would enable him to win the war were unfulfilled. Many of the rockets malfunctioned because of the heroic acts of sabotage carried out by the slave workers. What he had begun, however, continued during the Cold War in the Soviet Union and in the USA. Again it was war and the threat of war that brought about the deployment of resources and money on a scale that a purely scientific or exploratory venture would never have commanded.

We benefit from what we may not condone. The amazement of the astronauts who have been the eyes of humanity gazing down on the oceans of Earth has been bought at a price of ineffable and unnecessary suffering. Yet we cannot change and redeem that past: all we can do is to redeem the potential uses we will make of the knowledge we have gained now and in the future. This leads us once again to the question of choice and the part it plays in the redemptive role of civilization.

Among the gifts of the Face of Glory are the power to choose, the gift of free will, the gift of interpretation, the guidance of conscience and the will to praise. All these are granted us and we have the choice of making what use our training and our passions and our reason direct us to. The meaning or purpose that can be seen in history, beyond the patterns of economic cycles and social growth and decline and the chronicles of war and legislation, depends upon the exercise of choice by individuals. Perhaps the chief redemptive act for human beings is to recognize creation and the divine inspiration preceding it as an act of joy and to choose therefore to found their own creations from the urges to delight in their own souls. In this view of creation it will be seen that history itself is a work of art that is being constructed and constantly revised on a scale that seems to us of millennia but to the hidden artist is a matter of celestial days, that the initial inspiration to the hidden artist was the idea of humanity appearing as Adam does at Chartres over the shoulder of the Creator, that the essences of all lives that have ever been or will be are the notes, words or pigments of that synaesthetic work of art, that what we receive as impulses from the Great Memory are fugitive escapes from a memory that is as complete and whole as the idea of the work in the mind of the hidden artist, that all exercises of free will, whether towards the light of consciousness or away from it, are ultimately employed or redeemed in the overall form, and that the hidden artist, going through all the stages of incubation, renewed inspirations (which may be marked by the appearances of great civilizations on Earth), interpretation and execution, may still be astounded by the excitement of discovery in his act of creative attention. This is another way of expressing the idea of divine imagination at work in history, an idea that forces us to conceive in our own imaginations all creation as potentially to be redeemed by the Spirit which is also the human spirit. History is a work of art for which we are the inspiration and the materials and of which, when we are absorbed, through the state of creative and appreciative attention, into the will and mind of the creator, we are also the makers. The writing of the *Ramayana* illustrates my last point. Not only is Rama, the inspiration and the chief actor of the epic, an incarnation of God even though unconscious of his godly nature, but the ultimate narrator of the epic is also God as we trace back the source of the inspiration from Valmiki to Narada and from Narada to Brahma.

If God is the ultimate narrator, then who is the ultimate listener? Who is the hearer of the voice of conscience? The traditional image of conscience is of a woman as it is also that of the soul. It is the woman in us who listens to the still small voice, the woman that is lacking from the scientific image of man. It is the compassion and tenderness of woman expressed through conscience that transforms the green of life into the gold of civilization. The only occasion when the word translated as conscience appears in the Gospels is in the context of the story of the woman taken in adultery. The scribes and Pharisees who are about to stone her depart in shame because Christ's words 'Let he that is without sin among you, let him first cast a stone at her' convict them 'in their own conscience'.[21] In an interior and psychological sense we can see the woman taken in adultery as what our own lower intellectual natures, our scribes and Pharisees, hypocritically try to blame and suppress. In a modern context we can see the same woman as Nature stoned by the masculine attitudes of the scientific age and still to be redeemed and set free by the light of consciousness. It is immediately after this episode that Jesus says: 'I am the light of the world: he that followeth me shall not walk in darkness, but shall have the light of life.'[22]

Thus conscience, as a concept with a huge civilizing influence that stems from its one mention in this story, is also connected with the imagery of light which is associated, particularly in the Gospel of John, with Christ as the Logos, 'the True Light, which lighteth every man that cometh into the world'. The themes of the listener, of conscience as an inner voice and of light were brought together in this passage from the apocryphal Acts of John, written about AD 150. John has been called by an inner voice to leave the scene of the Crucifixion and to flee to the Mount of Olives. There in a cave Christ, standing in it and filling it with light, tells him that, though to the multitude below he is being crucified, he speaks to John 'that thou mightest hear those things which it behoveth a disciple to learn from his teacher and a man from his God'. He shows John a cross of light with multitudes around and in it and John sees the Lord above the cross, not having any shape but only a voice, 'one sweet and kind and truly of God, saying unto me: John, it is needful that one should hear these things from me, for I have need of one that will hear.'[23]

The cosmic Christ who is the divine imagination still has need of ones that will hear. We need to raise our own imaginations to that supreme level of creativity in order to heal the Earth and ourselves. We have been given back the great archetypes of wisdom and creativity in the Goddess and the Green Man in order to help us. To win that insight we need not the puritanism of current environmental thought nor the ecologically minded dictatorship that some movements wish to impose on us but something far more releasing to the imagination and to creativity – enjoyment, which means the capacity to become good listeners, enthusiastic encouragers of talent and the voicers ourselves of a spontaneous art of praise.

Part III

Clever reader, perfect enjoyer

13

The nature of enjoyment

I t is New Year's Eve on the edge of the desert of Thar in Rajasthan. We are sitting on chairs placed on the sand with a wood fire burning in front of us. The stars are brilliantly bright in the sky. The musicians, singers and dancers are squatting on rugs on the sand looking at us, the audience, as though we are the entertainment for them before their own performance begins. Two young men, both tall and exceptionally thin and wearing long pointed boots, are setting up their puppet theatre and hanging the puppets along the plain backdrop suspended from the frame of the theatre.

The musicians are from Muslim and Hindu families. 'Quite recently converted,' one of our Indian friends remarks of the Muslim musicians.

'How long ago?' I ask.

'In the time of the Emperor Aurangzeb,' comes the answer with no question but that an event of three hundred and fifty years ago is something recent. Our friend Prakash, as a member of a family of hereditary poets, has a special relationship with musicians wherever he comes across them. His family have been important in trying to preserve the musical traditions of Rajasthan which have depended for centuries on the feudal relationships of patron and performer. In a changing world these traditions need new sources of patronage for survival. One of the musicians to whom Prakash talks before the concert has travelled all round Europe as part of a troupe of musicians giving recitals. When the concert begins, Prakash sits closest to the musicians, urging them on, hushing some at times, indicating to others where they are to come in. What he is doing is also done to varying degrees by the rest of the audience who according to the rhythms and mood of the music beat time softly with their fingers and the palms of their hands or clap or at times get up and dance when invited by two glittering ladies who, as the mood takes them, stand up and dance and then retire to the back of the musicians. It is music that will never be heard again, in the sense that though it follows ancient formal guidelines it is all improvised for the mood of this one evening and this audience. The drums beat, the castanets clatter, as players of other instruments – the sarangi, the flute, the peacock's tail (or jew's harp) – follow one another in solos or perform in concert, the musicians raise their voices in song and the instrumental music starts again. One of the dancers, a pretty woman in silver and rose pink, starts singing another song and the audience erupts with displeasure. She is singing a popular song from an Indian film and the audience are outraged by this corruption of the evening. There is nothing for it but she has to stop short. Two of the other musicians, a husband and wife, are encouraged to sing a passage from the Rajasthan epic of the hero Babuji. The musicians rest while the languid young men in their long narrow boots leap to put on their puppet show.

They come from a caste of hereditary acrobats but they can only fulfil their true role as acrobats in performing for certain Rajput families. Puppeteering is how they occupy their time in the long periods when they are not performing for their patrons. All the feats of contortion, balance, daring and lift they are prevented by custom from performing for any audience except their patrons they transfer to the dolls dangling on their strings at the backdrop of their booth. Their most brilliant performance is that of a puppet that lifts his head off, tucks it under an arm, puts it back on his head and then tucks it under the other arm, all the time dancing wildly but in perfect time to the music.

The puppeteering is like the music in that the characters and what they represent are traditional and recognizable but the performance is improvised for that moment only. The quality of the performance depends to a great extent on the quality of the audience, their attention, their response, their awareness of the emotions and the skills that are being presented to them, and on what they want and expect from the evening. After the musicians have started to play again, at a certain moment they bring to Prakash, as the sternest but most appreciative member of the audience, his own instrument, the peacock's tail, and ask him to play. He takes the instrument as though to play it were a difficult but needful sacrifice and begins to play. A line of melody like a silver thread drawn out of the stars above us, beautiful with the beauty of inexplicable sadness, issues from the instrument. The drummers, their eyes fixed totally on him, wait for him to state the mood and then, having caught it, begin gently to strike their drums, responding to the slowing and the quickening of the melody. It is as though he is telling us a story or by taking us on a journey is making us part of a story that is a poem without words. We are given the pain and the rapture of the story and only the flavour of its narrative; we have also been given the point of the evening: the unexpected entry of the transcendent.

The moment passed as the consort of musicians began playing and singing more lively music. What had happened when Prakash played was that we had been granted the gift that we look for from all kinds of art: that we should be so taken out of ourselves that we feel utterly cleansed, delighted and changed.

When art or thought or understanding takes us out of ourselves in this manner, something very interesting may happen. Our state of consciousness changes, a singular feeling of purity unites our emotions with our awareness – and we become much cleverer. We become cleverer because we are taken up into a state akin to that of creative attention which I described in Chapter 11 in relation to artistic creation and scientific discovery.

The participatory audience, as in the instance I have just given, is probably the oldest kind of audience. It is evidence of a close-knit society to whose members their art and religion are means of bonding all classes together. Thus art, religion and sport bound Greek society together in ways that no treaties or leagues were able to bring about until the Macedonian Empire imposed order on the city-states. In ancient Ireland the poets were regarded so much as a national rather than a regional group that they could travel freely between warring tribes and it was as their audience that the Irish entered into a social bond that approached national unity.[1]

From the participatory audience formed by a whole society we turn to the way in which, in various unconnected cultures, there arose the need for writing down what formerly had been contained in everyone's memory. This process has led to the appearance of the audience of one – the individual reader. Why it happened is difficult to say. It is possible that there was in many cultures a strong resistance to the introduction of writing: the Druids, for example, rarely committed their sacred lore, myths or poetry to writing, depending on the excellence of their memories which they trained assiduously. It may have been that the sacred thoughts of the community were considered too holy to be written down. In other cultures it seems that the impulse to commit thought to writing as a general impulse is synchronous with that great change in human understanding that comes about the sixth and fifth centuries BC – the period of Lao Tzu and Confucius in China, of the Buddha in India, of the Zoroastrians in Persia, of the writing of Genesis and other earlier books of the Old Testament, and of the awakening of philosophy in Greece. It is the period of the discovery of the powers of the human mind and therefore of individual responsibility.

The ability to read was naturally restricted in all these societies to those who had the leisure and the opportunity to study. This meant that a writer had two audiences, the first those who could read and had access to the costly manuscripts, and the second those who could not read but attended public readings of his works. This, for example, is what happened in the case of Herodotus' history. Long as it is, it was recited in public to the people of Greek cities.

The ability to read and write both in Latin and Greek became much more widespread in late republican Rome and the period of the empire. To go by the graffiti left on the walls of Pompeii and Herculaneum, it was the medium of a lively popular culture as well as being essential for the administration of the empire and the international trade of the Mediterranean. Even the soldiers of the Roman army were literate enough to inscribe the lead missiles for their slings with rude messages to the enemy.

The way in which people read also changed. There is an anecdote of St Augustine that marks a great change in how people read to themselves at the end of the period of antiquity. He tells of how he came across St Ambrose who was reading by himself and he was amazed to see that St Ambrose was reading *without moving his lips*: 'his eyes scanned the page and his heart explored the meaning, but his voice was silent and his tongue was still'.[2] St Augustine had never come across this before. St Ambrose was demonstrating the possibility of a new process of interiorization in the assimilation of literature. To understand a thought or a narrative required the use of the eyes alone and not the participation of the facial muscles as well.

From that time has developed the kind of reading we do now when we are absorbed by great literature. I draw my examples in what follows chiefly from what happens to us when we give our attention to novels and then to poetry. If what I say seems at first too personal to me, I must state that I first set out the thoughts that follow in an article in the PEN magazine[3] and that I was astonished by the response I received from various readers, nearly all themselves authors, confirming that my experience was similar to their own. I received one negative response – from an eminent scientist who said he never liked or read novels in any way.

The central thought in what I said in that article was that when we read a novel with attention we take in easily and readily information we would find wholly unpalatable if given it in another way. A treatise on French law on bankruptcy under the reign of Louis-Philippe would be unreadable to most but that is what we absorb in passing when we read Balzac's *César Birotteau*. A related thought is that we become much cleverer when we read a novel that we enjoy. We may be as hopeless at history as Mrs Disraeli, who did not know whether the Greeks came before or after the Romans but was a splendid woman, yet while we read *War and Peace*, powers of historical synthesis, of empathy with people of a past age and an alien culture, of appreciation of strategic niceties and political nuances are among those we call into play, hardly noticing as we read that we are in possession of every ability and faculty that our teachers were convinced we lacked utterly. We will allow writers of detective novels to teach us chemistry and authors of science fiction to instruct us in astrophysics; we learn geography and geopolitics from writers of international spy thrillers and engineering from social-realist novelists. We may be incapable of remembering names and faces in daily life but give us the Barsetshire novels of Trollope and there is no Lumley, Arabin, Proudie, Harding or Grantly we are ever going to forget.

What happens to us when we read a novel with devoted attention to turn us into such clever readers? How did we learn to attend? First of all, we had to learn to listen, if learning is not too tame an expression for the feelings of delight with which a small child listens to a story. The first performers most children meet are their mothers and fathers and their grandparents, especially their grandmothers. Small children are by nature the participatory audience: they join in the emotions of the story, cover their ears if it gets too frightening, clap with pleasure when the princess is freed, and, if they are familiar with the story, are quick to point out if any episode or detail is left untold. They enter the cocoon of the magic narrative and their imaginations are coaxed into independence so that in an atmosphere of love they will learn to deal with a world that is often unloving.

It could be said that in western society we recapitulate in our own individual lives the process that has unfolded in history whereby the participatory audience has led to the audience of one. For individual children there may come a time when they discover reading for themselves and they are taken up into the special state or mood a book can arouse in us. For myself when young, books on a great range of subjects had that effect on me, not only the usual children's classics and myths and legends but, I remember, a history of ancient Egypt, a history of China, a children's version of The Faerie Queene and a child's book of science, all of which created in me a state of imaginative awakening and absorption.

Everyone reading this probably knows that state: it is when our awakened imagination seems to weave a tent of enjoyment about us. To myself I call it 'the state' for want of another expression. It is curious that, though in English we have phrases describing this state, such as 'I'm gripped', 'I'm hooked' or 'I am deep into . . .', we have no noun. I have been forced to a neologism and propose the term 'bibliophany': by analogy with theophany, which is a manifestation or revelation of the Deity, bibliophany describes the state when a book has captured us, mind and soul, and its contents seem to be revealed to us rather than merely read.

Thus there is a point in reading, say, a novel by Dickens or Henry James when we are gripped in this manner. It is essential to the full impact of the novel on us that we should be gripped in this way. Sometimes it can happen right at the beginning of a novel. I remember opening Solzhenitsyn's *The First Circle* and realizing during the reading of the first page that I was entering into a masterpiece that would lead me into experiences I had never had before while at the same time I was absorbed into the state of bibliophany, both welcome and familiar.

There are several strange things about bibliophany. Once the invisible convolvulus has come out of the novel, planted its roots in your soul and twined its tendrils about your mind, the state of bibliophany is nearly always present again when, after an interruption, you pick the novel up to continue reading it. You can have done all sorts of things in that interruption, gone to work, shopped, slept, quarrelled with someone, and, almost whatever you have done, bibliophany resumes its dominance over you as you go on reading. Yet once you have finished the book, however much you have enjoyed it, if you were to start reading it again immediately, bibliophany would have vanished – the convolvulus covert is dormant. The reading becomes an effort and the response becomes analytical, too ready to find faults or literary comparisons. You need to wait months or years before you can read the novel in the same way. Kipling spoke of a tap being turned off when a book seemed to complete itself.[4] Similarly with the completion of the reading of a novel it is as though an enchantment has been broken.

Another feature of bibliophany is that, even though your rate of reading increases sharply as you progress through the book, it may allow richer capacities of the mind to come into play. These include our capacities for making and entertaining vivid mental imagery, landscapes, human faces and bodies and the whole endless repertoire of our dream life called into play by bibliophany for the purpose of recreating someone else's story in our own souls. The effect may be accumulative over many books within a national or literary type. I have never been to Russia but the start of a story by a Russian writer that may begin something like this: 'On the outskirts of the village of — a few versts from the provincial capital of — a young man with a silken moustache and a discontented expression was tapping his boots with a whip, waiting for his groom to return with the local blacksmith to mend a broken wheel on his chaise . . .' will set me off through the huge Russia of my mind constructed by many experiences of bibliophany over years of reading Russian literature.

Our own visual response to literature does not depend on close, detailed visual description. In fact, too much of this deadens the exercise of the faculty, as in the case of Flaubert's *Salammbô*. Bibliophany builds up mental pictures out of tones of voice, conversations which convert from the closeness in spirit or distance of people talking to one another into feelings for the physical space in which they move or sit: out of a few words it can create a vast forest in the mind, as when the players of Bohemian horns make music in the woods outside Nancy and Madame de Chasteller invites Lucien Leuwen to take her arm as they walk together.

Once we have experienced bibliophany, we rarely stop hungering for it. When we cast our eyes over bookshelves, muttering, 'I need a novel to read,' what we are in fact saying is: 'I want to be in "the state" and I need exactly the right book that will induce the mood of "the state" as quickly as possible.' Another strange feature of such a state is that, though to the outside world we may seem abstracted and idle, we are often far more aware of ourselves and our surroundings than when we are engaged in seemingly more virtuous and approved tasks. Though I failed at many attempts to engage with *The Portrait of a Lady*, the moment when I realized that it had captured me is indissolubly linked with the physical impressions of the garden where I was reading it, the stone steps I was sitting on and the early roses of a hot May in the flowerbeds beside me. The opening pages of *À la recherche du temps perdu* evoke for me a teashop in Croydon to which I had fled from a barrack room of thirty companions when I was in the navy (and what was I doing in Croydon, so far from any navigable river, let alone the sea?) and the madeleine of Proust's description had its counterpart in the hot buttered toast I held in one hand while I turned the pages of his book with the other – transgressing one of the world's more sensible rules: that books and butter do not go together.

When we are caught up in this state we may be as fully aware, as fully conscious of the splendour of life and what it has to offer us while engaged in our reading, as from any sunset touch the world affords. What we gain from it, long after the book that aroused it has been put down, is the emotional flavour of the novel or story, something that may remain for years after specific details of the narrative may have seeped away. Through experience of bibliophany the book acquires a memorability for us it would never have had if it had been read as a newspaper article or a government paper: this is owed, of course, in the first place to the emotion put into the novel by the author[5] but also to the direction and right workings of our own emotional responses brought about by bibliophany when we are reading. Bibliophany awakens emotional memory, far more powerful than intellectual and literal memory in its range and efficacy: it draws on memory of former responses to literature, of our own experience of life and art, of factual, historical and social information we could never call to mind in an ordinary way; it also maintains the memory of what has already passed in the particular novel we are reading at the time, the past and interconnections of the characters, the landscapes they have lived among and even the changes in their income, enabling us to perform feats of synthesis and recall that would make us amazingly rich, clever and successful if ever we were able to transfer the use of these faculties to our working lives. Then it remains, after the book is read, to form part of our natures, our truly lived experience of life which is the fruit of the love of literature and art. Bibliophany is the condition in which we produce our own creative response to the creativity of others; without it there is no real understanding. It is the means by which the encapsulated experience of other lives and other times is transferred from generation to generation and from country to country – so that, as Solzhenitsyn has told us, nations may learn through literature and art what other nations had to learn through suffering.[6]

Poetry has been one of the chief means of the transmission of experience across the years and over national and linguistic boundaries. It awakens bibliophany by composing pictures in the mind through rhythmical sentences. A particular feature of what happens to us when we read poetry is the enhancing of the allusive qualities of the memory and mind. Poetry may seem today more than any other literary form designed for the audience of one but it constantly harks back to its origins, to the days when it was always recited or chanted. We read it at a speed much closer to that of speech – or even more slowly – than the rate at which we read prose. This is because it is a different language from prose, however much it may use the same words and sentence structures, and because it very often brings together, and requires the use of, more faculties in the soul.

To read poetry to ourselves we have to perform it to ourselves. We may not realize that this is what we are doing when we sound and savour the rhythms and contrasts of vowels in a Shakespeare sonnet or a stanza of Spenser's but we are being at once the reciter and the audience and in another sense we are also being the poet. We are re-creating the lifeless letters on a page or the unsounded characters in our memory and each one of us brings to the act of re-creation the unique contribution of our life experience up to the time of our reading the poem. Each reading of the same poem is comparable to an improvisation that can never be repeated wholly again, only with variations of mood and different patterns of emphasis and understanding.

This is another difference between the novel and poetry: that poetry takes and needs constant rereading in a way that the novel never can, except when it is studied by a teacher or student for purposes that are worthy but not part of this conversation. Though with each reading different meanings and significances may be revealed, the greater the poet, the more likely it is that we will be led into a mood that is wholly individual to that poet and what that mood is will be a general matter of agreement among most readers of all periods, so much so that the particular outstanding quality of these poets has been crystallized into a single word or phrase, as when we speak of the sublimity of Homer, the pathos of Virgil, the compassion of Dante, the magnanimity of Shakespeare and the humanity of Goethe.

Poetry, whatever the language it is expressed in, is an attempt to make that language aspire to the primal ineffable language. This is why in general we can say it is a different language from prose. Prose is content to be what it is: good English prose, good French prose, good Russian or good German prose. It may express eternal longings but it is not in its nature to quench those longings in a transcendent assumption to another plane of communication, which is the heartbreaking impulse within poetry.

The experience of reading poetry with all our hearts and souls bring us into a state comparable to the state of creative attention of which I spoke in Chapter 11, the state which is as essential to the act of creation as it is to the act of re-creation we perform in reading with attention. We undergo the same process as the creator of the work we study: we concentrate our minds on the words that are before us and a miracle of expansion of thought and feeling combined, sometimes momentarily and sometimes for extended periods, takes place in our minds. This brings me to another crux in my argument.

A transcendent aesthetic experience is the unveiling of consciousness within us. As the creative act arises out of consciousness, so the impulse when transmitted awakens the same state of consciousness in the reader, spectator or appreciator. A great act of appreciation is as creative in its impact and its consequences as a great inspiration.

In what follows as a discussion of the aesthetic experience gained through several of the arts and other pursuits such as philosophy and the sciences, I wish to give a true value to the worth of appreciation and therefore to the worth of the audience. I wish people to see the significance of the moments of transcendent awareness that great art can raise them to, not, of course, so that they can praise themselves for their fine feelings, but so that they trust and value them as points of entry into the wider continuum of understanding which is the eternal state of civilization of which we spoke earlier.

Such moments of transcendental awareness are the rewards and point of living in a civilized community — or at least in a community that does not actively ban the events or the publications or the exhibitions that provide the opportunities for experiencing these moments. As civilization depends for its maintenance and renewal on the one hand on the active creativity of artists, thinkers and scientists, so it also depends on what might appear to be the passive creativity of the audiences, enjoyers and supporters of what they produce. The antithesis is not as neat as I have put it: there is a great deal of passive reflection in creative work and a great deal of hard work goes into the education of a good audience on the part of the members of the audience themselves. In the preparation and study and learning that goes to make a good audience there has been in many ways as much creative effort as in the performance of the dramas and the music they have come to hear. The good audience joins in the re-creation of the original inspiration. Without audiences, listeners, admirers, enjoyers, the creative cycle is incomplete. They are extensions of the sounding boards of the instruments the musicians play, the looking-glasses of art, sculpture and architecture, and the greater hearts and minds to which poetry, literature and the insights of science and philosophy address themselves and where they find the solace of understanding.

Great poets need great readers; great composers need great hearers; great scientists need great thinkers and understanders. As much as the talents to create and discover have to be cultivated, so the talents of comprehension and appreciation must be developed in the cause of civilization. Martial in one of his epigrams says this:

Lector, opes nostrae; quem cum mihi Roma dedisset,
'Nil tibi quod demus maius habemus,' ait.[7]

Reader, you are my riches; when Rome gave you to me, she said
'We have nothing that is greater in worth we may give you.'

With the rise of Christianity, a new kind of audience developed in the congregations of the churches. There is an accumulated atmosphere of attention and devotion that attaches itself to the sacred writings, the liturgies, prayers, chants and hymns, and the buildings of the great religions. Every child taught a prayer or a hymn absorbs the atmosphere in which it is recited: there is a transmission of emotion over the centuries from the older to the younger generations. A special awe attends the liturgy of the Word in the Eucharist when the Gospel is displayed and censed and the lesson is chanted by the priest. As we stand to hear the Gospel, we take part in a way of hearing that, with various modifications, goes back over 1,500 years. The purpose of the ritual is to emphasize the special character of the words that are chanted or read to us and to induce in us a state of hearing in which we absorb what is told in the Gospel in a way that is intended to awaken our emotional understanding.

Curiously enough, for much of its history in the western Catholic tradition, the liturgy of the Word has been quite incomprehensible to most of its hearers because it was recited in Latin. It was up to the preacher to reveal in his homily or sermon what the Gospel was about. In this it exemplifies one of the many degrees of participation allowed the congregation at different times in the Church's history. It would appear that in the earliest days of the Church the *agape*, or supper from which the Mass evolved, was an event involving the full participation of all members of the Church present. They sat at a table, they sang, they got up to perform sacred dances and they shared the sacred elements of the bread and the wine. As Latin ceased to be the common language of the West, so it became the hieratic language reserved to the priesthood and with its sacred character ever more emphasized as the doctrine of transubstantiation was developed in the course of the twelfth century. In the same period everything was done with the help of art, architecture and music to exalt the sacred character of the Mass so that for the laity, who were now excluded from receiving the chalice, their only means of participating in the service was by watching a drama performed by the officiating priests and repeating their private prayers. There were, on the other hand, plenty of other ways in which they could participate, the pilgrimages with their popular hymns and devotions, the spread of the practice of the rosary, and membership of the various religious confraternities. There were also many more extraordinary rites, such as the annual parody of the Mass known as the Festival of the Fools when the clergy would appear in masks and women's clothes, censing the congregation from old shoes, and dance round the altar, after which they would travel round the town singing obscene ballads. Other traditions were observed in particular churches, as when the archbishop of Sens led his clerics and the mayor and corporation in a dance round the cloister and the cathedral or as at Laon where the story of Balaam and his ass was re-enacted in the course of a specially composed Mass and the congregation would bray in unison instead of singing alleluia. These jollities, alas, fell prey, for the most part, to the grim reformers, both those of the Roman Catholic Church and those who separated from it at the time of the Reformation.

What happened in those countries that adopted their own forms of Protestantism was that religion became participatory again. The Church leaders devised their own liturgies in their vernacular languages and invited the congregation to join in the responses and prayers as well as singing the psalms and the hymns. The Council of Trent, however, swung in the other direction, re-emphasizing the exalted and special nature of the priesthood in its sole right to confect the Mass and keeping the laity in the position of silent and attentive auditors. All that has now changed with the effect of the Second Vatican Council, the saying of the Mass in the vernacular and the active participation of congregations in the service.

Out of these changes in the degree of participation has developed another kind of audience – our modern concert audience. Polyphonic western music was first developed in the great cathedrals of northern France, most notably Notre Dame de Paris. There western man first learned to listen with delight and excitement to consorts of singers following different lines of music at the same time. The practice was extended to instrumental music and, following the developments already described in relation to the desire of the humanists to revive the glory of Greek music, both opera and the modern orchestra found their beginnings.

Audiences have their traditions as well as the arts. The audience that gathers together at a concert hall in one of the great cities of the world is in a tradition that stretches back to the congregations of the Middle Ages, the humanist courts of the Renaissance and the Baroque palaces of benevolent despots, and to the nobility and middle classes of Vienna and Prague who provided the first audiences for much of the current classical repertoire. The way we listen in the concert hall today, motionless and with silent attention, is something that has been developed over the centuries. There could be no music without us: I mean not only by this that the tickets sold and the taxes paid support the orchestra; I mean rather that without the attention and excitement of an audience to play to, our musical traditions would wither away because the cycle of communication would be broken.

The reason why the cycle of musical communication is so important in our culture today is that the experience of listening to great music together is one of the ways in which we come together in agreement. As Ariel Dorfmann's tragic play *Death and the Maiden* tells us, people divided by a political chasm widened by torture and repression can listen to the same music. Lenin in his last days found his only solace in hearing the *Appassionata* sonata played again and again to him, saying to Gorky: 'The *Appassionata*; I would love to listen to it every day. It is marvellous superhuman music. I always think with pride – perhaps it is naive of me – what marvellous things human beings can do,'[8] a thought that thousands of the victims of his revolution that he had sent to death or prison camps would have agreed with.

We listen to music in this way because we want to change ourselves. We know from past experience not only that we will receive general pleasure and refreshment from the music but that there is always a chance that the performance and our response to it will equally be of such a quality that the musical equivalent of bibliophany will happen to us, that, if only for fractions of a second, we will be lifted up into a state of unified joy. We will be freed once more to surrender ourselves to the joy in the present moment.[9]

To investigate further what happens to us when we listen to music I turn again to Beethoven's Ninth Symphony. We have already looked at, first, what was necessary to Schiller and Beethoven in their backgrounds and society for them to be able to create the works brought together in this symphony and then at what is known about their inspirations and the circumstances in which they composed. Let us imagine that we are at a concert at which it is to be performed: we hear first the Eighth Symphony, a much shorter work, radiant and full of the joy of the dance. We have already begun to listen more and more acutely. Then, after an interval, we watch the assembly of the huge forces of orchestra and choir and soloists. The conductor commands the horns and the strings and we are off on a journey through terror and tenderness.

The first movement not only announces cataclysmic change: it brings it about: earth forces and heavenly powers join in the work of stirring and rending the fixed and petrified strata of emotion in us: we are borne up on the crests of energy waves and crash down with them as they topple; we are delighted and awed at this dissolution of ourselves. The second movement with its titanic drum strokes and its shimmering restlessness is even more disturbing: it is as though the petrified crusts of ancient emotion and rigid thoughts broken up by the first movement are now put into a centrifuge for further and more intense processes of breaking down in order to make new and worthier forms. We are the toy things of Necessity and also the nurslings of immortality as we learn when the slow movement comes upon us like the waters of healing. We are already refreshed by the opening bars of the first theme when, never failing in its effect however often heard, that extraordinary melody of the second theme slips into our natures as though it had never been absent from us. Time is changed for us: we float upon the repeated and unfolding phrases of consolation as Beethoven plays with the variations upon his double themes; it could seem that we could stay in the heaven of the present moment for ever but the woodwind announces the coming of another mood and though the movement is allowed to end in peace it is followed instantly by the *Schreckensfanfare*, the fanfare of terror as Wagner called it, which causes an agony greater than any shock of the first two movements. The cellos and basses attempt again and again the famous theme of Joy while the other instruments are recapitulating themes from the previous movements: the cellos and basses are at last allowed to state the theme in full as though they are teaching the rest of the orchestra and the singers the song they will have to sing.

The terrifying fanfare is repeated but the baritone sings that we are not to follow that music but the sounds of Joy and he utters the first quatrain of the poem; 'Joy, beautiful spark of the Gods, daughter of Elysium, we enter drunk with fire, O heavenly one, into your hallowed place.' Thoughts with which the youthful Schiller was bursting but could only express crudely or too simply, in Beethoven's creative mind and with his passionate belief in the ideas and images of the quatrains, become endowed through song, through the richness of the solo and choral writing, through the orchestra's accompaniment of marches and choruses, and through repetition, a poem of a higher order of expression and communicability. Every part of this movement has at various times been criticized and condemned but it is like criticizing or condemning a mountain. No amount of criticism has ever lessened by a decibel the applause which has greeted fine performances of this work.

The overpowering effect on us that this movement can have is owed partly to the extremes, not of joy and misery, but of different kinds of joy: the exhilarating joy of human brotherhood on the one hand and the hushed joy of prostration before the Godhead on the other. It is also owed to the pentecostal revelation expressed in Schiller's words: '*Seid umschlungen, Millionen*', 'Be embraced, you millions' – not 'embrace one another'. The enfolding embrace is from the power of joy and it is that which enfolds us.

The whole work has had an immense influence. Sir Donald Tovey said: 'Of all single works of art, of all passages in a work of art, the first subject of the first movement of Beethoven's Ninth Symphony has had the deepest and the widest influence on later music.'[10] It is the last movement that has had the most obvious influence, being seized upon by people of all parties as an expression of their particular vision. It is indeed curious that a work that is devoted to universal brotherhood and universal joy should have so often been claimed as the voice of limited fraternities and as a delight reserved for selected groups: German nationalists, French socialists, the Nazis and the communists have all in turn called it their own. The European Union has made the theme of the last movement into its anthem and that too is a vulgarization as well as a limitation of its message.

One of the decisive interpretations of Beethoven's work as a whole was the book on him by the French socialist Romain Rolland, published in 1903. He took a sentence from a letter of Beethoven's to Countess Erdödy – 'the best of us obtain joy through suffering' – in which Beethoven was commiserating with her about an uncomfortable coach journey to Croatia, and he set up 'Joy through suffering' as the motto of Beethoven's soul and the message of the Ninth Symphony. Rolland's book in translation has had an influence far beyond Europe, notably in China and Japan, where its message has been interpreted in powerful but wholly different ways.[11] In China until recently there has been difficulty in extending universal brotherhood beyond the proletariat: however, through an equation of 'Joy through suffering' with the Marxist slogan 'Victory through struggle', it has been authoritatively stated that Beethoven was wholly behind the anti-feudal feelings of the people and in the whole work intended to voice the spirit of revolutionary struggle.

The first performance of the work in Japan was by German prisoners of war in 1918. Rolland's book was translated in the 1920s and the theme of 'Joy through suffering' came to have a deeper and deeper meaning particularly for students in the Second World War. In 1940 the custom was instituted of performing the Ninth Symphony on 31 December to mark the end of the year. Now there are many performances of the work, often on a huge scale, with choirs of from 3,000 to 5,000 not being uncommon, so that it has been absorbed into the social fabric of Japanese society, rather in the way that the Handel oratorios used to be heard in England with massed choirs and orchestras in performances having religious and social significances for performers and audiences far beyond the conventional reception of classical music.

Some have said with Adorno that the Ninth Sympony has been destroyed by social usage. To me the fact that it finds responses so different in cultures far removed from its origins shows that its richness of meaning and complexity of emotion continue to fascinate and to awake new interpretations. For westerners its themes of joy and brotherhood pose the supreme question of the history of this century: how could a society capable of thinking such thoughts and singing such songs tear itself apart and inflict such misery upon its members, and, in the process, so misinterpret its message that it became a justification of mass murder and racial discrimination?

I think of a story told me by a German Jewish couple who had taken refuge in London. They said that they had been protected by their wealth and position in Berlin during the rise of Hitler to power and believed that they only had to live quietly to wait for better times. They ventured out one day, however, to a performance of Beethoven's Ninth Symphony by the Berlin Philharmonic under Furtwängler. It became immediately clear to them that Furtwängler had turned the last movement into a Nazi hymn: it became under his interpretation full of violence and hate. That performance decided them: there was no hope left for them in Germany if such a work could be given such a message and they fled to England as soon as they could. To repeat this story is not to enter into the debate over Furtwängler's relations with the Nazis: so subtle were Furtwängler's interpretations and so varied with each performance, the warning they received may have been one he was intending to give. He did, on the other hand, allow himself to be trapped into conducting a performance of the work to celebrate Hitler's birthday in 1942, a performance that was widely used on film and radio for propaganda. Another story from the end of the war shows how deeply the Nazis had tried to claim the work: after the liberation of Belsen the camp commandants and warders were imprisoned in huts where their victims had been forced to live. A British officer passing these huts one evening was surprised to hear singing coming from them. He was even more surprised to recognize what they were singing to keep their spirits up: it was the 'Ode to Joy'.

Other, greater and more generous souls have been affected by it in other ways: Isadora Duncan wanted to make a ballet involving thousands of perfomers with the symphony so that its message should enter into people's hearts and minds through the dance. It was an answer to the paradox set by the conventions of the kind of audience for which Beethoven wrote, the static, motionless audience invited to participate but given no means of participation beyond listening – and this applies to all the great symphonic choral works that have followed in Beethoven's footsteps, such as those by Mahler and Rachmaninov. The paradox has partly been solved not in high art but in international popular music since the sixties in the vast gatherings at concerts where pop stars have used their influence to promote humanitarian and anti-tyrannical aims and to draw attention to the contrast between the affluence of the West and the starvation and the poverty of the Third World, and so spread a wider awareness of the world's social and environmental plight among the young who are expected to dance and to sing these thoughts into their own natures. We cannot say that Schiller and Beethoven set the model directly for this movement but we can say that they uttered first the statement in verse and music of the universal humanitarian ideal which has influenced it.

What actually happens to us when we listen in the concert hall to Beethoven's Ninth Symphony? The biological and sociological explanations would say, first, that we are enabled by our genes and education to like such music and, second, that we are enhancing the social bond by attending in the company of others the performance of a work that could be interpreted as glorifying the social bond. All can be explained in these terms, even the enjoyment and spiritual glory that we feel.

According to many psychoanalytic theories our joy and delight are responses to our masked desires: to return inside our mothers because the concert hall is a womb in which we are sustained by the amniotic fluid of the music; to go through the birth experience again without the inner shock and pain; to sublimate our sexual desires in a series of stupendous orgasms extending over an hour and a half; to bolster our lack of self-confidence by being absorbed in a demonstration of the will to power and to compensate for what is lacking in ourselves by feeling we belong to the right and the winning party; or to be absorbed into a manifestation of the archetypal powers that form our inherited birthright biologically transmitted through the collective unconscious. Whatever the theory, the result is the same: we are restoring our psychological homeostasis to a finer balance: that is the value of the concert and the test of its success.

There is another distinction to be made which cuts across all these theories and it depends upon this question: does listening or reading affect in any lasting or significant manner anyone beyond the individual who listens or reads? I do not mean this simply in the sense of enhancing the social bond or in the obvious cases where new ideas and images affect fashions and behaviour, but in the sense of asking whether, say, there is a wider influence caused by the changes in consciousness brought about in many tens of thousands of people in a great city, night after night, in the theatre and the concert hall, an influence that affects the dream and waking life of others, that brings to the surface dormant ideas and conceptions that would otherwise not have been brought to awareness. To put it another way, just as the creative moment, lasting perhaps a few microseconds, of fuller consciousness, may have outstanding consequences, so may the transcendent aesthetic experience, also lasting a fraction of the time it takes to read or hear the whole work, be a moment of expansion into an already existing state of consciousness. Thus, by an effect of resonance or the vibration of subtle energies, that expansion of consciousness may be more likely to be experienced by others.

My own answer to this question and to the question of what happens to us in the states I have described in relation to the novel, poetry and music and to the different kinds of audience is a symbolist answer. It is that we are seeking for truth and that when we are entranced by what we read or hear, we are in the lap of Nature, Nature revealed both with the force of life and in the light of consciousness – as we listened to our mothers and believed what we were told in our early childhood. The artist struggles to express the truth implicit in his inspiration, to tell the truth of what it is like to be himself during the conscious moments out of which his works arise: we too search for expressions of truth that will expand our imaginations to the imagination of Nature and will raise us to the state of receptivity and awareness signified by the Eternal Feminine. That state of receptivity brings about a change in our sense of ourselves: we become open, in flashes of consciousness, to the awareness of another permanent and immanent existence in which there is no division between the image and reality and no distinction between enjoyment and the experience of truth. The soldiers sleep, the stone falls away and we are reborn as creatures of light.

14

Matters of taste and the basis of civilization

Our remote ancestors in creating some of the earliest forms of
architecture were fascinated by the image of the womb or cave.
As at New Grange above the river Boyne where around 3100 BC they
raised 200,000 tons of stones into a mound, they liked to make a womb
of earth and stone to which they could return their dead. They also created
New Grange as a place of rebirth because they aligned the central passage
to its centre in such a way that at the time of the midwinter solstice the
rising sun sends its rays all the way through the passage so that they strike
upon the spiral carvings at the very heart of the mound (figure 26). In the
dark time of the year the Goddess, symbolized in her triple aspects of bride,
mother and hag or death by the mound, is impregnated by the sun.

To visit New Grange is to experience the architectural experience of
going into one's self. First there is the shock of seeing its restored exterior:
the mound is revetted with gleaming white quartzite set with sea-rounded
stones like cannonballs and set about with massive stones carved with spirals,
lozenges and chevrons. Then, skirting the portal stone, we enter the passage
lined with huge slabs that takes us into the centre of the mound where we
may experience that curious but happy feeling of becoming centred in
ourselves. It is an experience that may fall to us in other constructions
and buildings, such as the Breton island of the dead, Gavr'inis, and also
in much later buildings such as the crypts of great Romanesque churches
and the shrines of the Black Virgins.

Architecture can also send us on a journey of exploration in the other
direction. We go upwards and outwards to find ourselves in the cosmos.
It was one of the great achievements of the Gothic masters to develop
this effect.

Once when I was waiting inside the door of King's College Chapel,
Cambridge (figure 25) my attention was caught by what happened to each
visitor entering the chapel. Each one jerked his or her head back in surprise
at the sight of the vaulting. It was as though there was a lightning conductor

in reverse in the slim pillars that must have met their gaze first of all to sweep their attention so immediately right up to the fan-vaulting. What was also clearly visible in them was that the expression on their faces changed: from the wary expectation of boredom common to tired tourists, it altered to one of wonder and openness. It is something that we rarely do at the sight of the sky and only when some unwonted object passes over it. Architecture brings heaven nearer to our eyes and startles us with an intensified and condensed universe. As an example of the physical effect of architecture on human responses, it led me into seeing that the physical effort required for visiting great buildings – and indeed often for seeing paintings and sculpture – helps to bring about our aesthetic responses to these works of art.

There are obvious differences in the ways in which we encounter the visual arts from those in which we experience the literary and musical arts. With poetry, the novel and other narrative forms we experience them as sequences in time and the experience takes us inwards in order to awaken our visual imaginations. With the visual arts we seize their offerings as instantaneous wholes, as explorations of space. It is also that we 'go to see': we travel and walk in order to offer our visual perceptions for transformation.

One of the pleasures of looking at paintings in congenial company is that we can talk to one another as we look, about the work before us and about the feelings it arouses in us. We could, but we do not and we would not, say 'I liked that arpeggio' to our next-door neighbour at a concert. The nature of what we are looking at allows this ease of interchange which would be ridiculous in the context of most other arts. When we know a poem very well or a piece of music, we can hold the impression they have made on us in our minds and we can, from an interior point of view, see them as a whole or concentrate on them in detail. We cannot walk away from them in a physical sense as we can with a painting to view it as a whole and approach until our noses are almost touching the canvas to study a detail. We are given a degree of physical freedom, of alternations between movement and stillness, which is an essential part of the visual aesthetic experience.

What happens to us when we look at a great painting, a fine sculpture or a noble building? Again we enter a state comparable to that of bibliophany but of a very different emotional and physical quality. The painter sees on our behalf and shows us what he has seen either as a vision, a telling of a religious or traditional story or a landscape, portrait or still life. We are given his eyes and, more than his eyes, the thoughts, harmonies and emotions that were aroused in him as he looked and painted. To receive his eyes and to learn what happened and observed behind those eyes, we have, so to speak, to give up our own eyes. When we do not like or are revolted by a painting, it is as though we are rejecting the eyes its maker has imposed on us.

In the case of artists whose eyes we willingly accept, it is extraordinary how we can stand in front of scenes of torture, martyrdom and violence, wrapped in a dream of pleasure and yet at the same time pierced with pity and sorrow for what we see. I think, in particular, of a Pietà by an associate of Rogier van der Weyden in the National Gallery, London (there is also a version in the Musées Royaux des Beaux Arts in Brussels) where the gaunt Flemish Christ lies dead with his head in the arms of his mother, whose face is the face of one about to break into tears but whose force of grief is too great even for that physical solace (figure 27). The painting harrows the onlooker and at the same time transports him into a land of wonderful beauty where all artefacts and clothes, and all the limbs and faces of the figures, glow with a light of their own. We could step into that landscape with the certainty that it extends into a universe of its own and that wherever we went we would come across other people, other human beings, held similarly in moments of crisis and joy.

I think, too, of another painting I have been able to see twice in recent years. The painting is Titian's *The Flaying of Marsyas* (figure 28), long hidden in a Czech castle.[1] It is one of Titian's last works and the theme must have held the deepest meaning for him at a time when he was preparing for his own end. The satyr Marsyas has challenged Apollo to a musical contest in which he boasted his pipes would reign supreme over the lyre of Apollo. This is a theme, it will be remembered, that goes back to *Le Concert champêtre* (see pages 73–4) fifty years earlier in Titian's working life: it is the contest between stringed instruments as the voices of higher heavenly music and wind instruments as the sounders of animal passions. Marsyas fails in his challenge and his punishment is to be flayed alive. This flaying is what Titian chose to represent. Marsyas hangs upside down in the position of the Hanged Man in the Tarot card while Apollo and a helper begin the work of flaying him and the inhabitants of Arcady look on. Were such an action to be performed on a sheep or a goat before our eyes we would try to stop it or run screaming in horror from the scene. There was a grim contemporary reference in the punishment: the Turks had in 1571 flayed Bragadin, one of the Venetian commanders, alive. One of the features of the painting that make it so affecting is the wild fawn face of Marsyas with his huge eyes gleaming: his expression is ambiguous in its effect in that one moment one thinks that the eyes are full of animal fear and the next they seem bright with anticipation of enlightenment on the passage to a world of new experience. The ambiguity is reflected in the landscape of the painting, which shows a world full of forests alive with the anger of the gods and also contains the delightful swards and valleys of Arcady. The key to the painting is probably in Dante's lines at the outset of the *Paradiso*, when he calls on Apollo to draw his greater self out of his old baser self as once the god had drawn Marsyas out of his skin so that he, Dante, will be equal to the theme of Heaven on which he is now embarked.[2] We are taught to look on the scene by the old King Midas, another facet of the aged Titian, who sits and leans forward, hand on chin, pitying and watching what must happen in the self-sacrifice and surrender of the artist to his inspiration.

Sacrifice need not involve the suffering portrayed in Titian's Marsyas. In its original meaning sacrifice signifies making something holy – and 'holy' means 'made whole' or 'united'. Just as we go to a concert hall hoping that our natures will be changed, unified, so we go to the visual arts hoping for a similar cleansing and purification of our sense of ourselves. In both cases we can consider that we are performing an act of sacrifice: we are intending to sacrifice our wandering thoughts and our distracted emotions in a serious work of attention.

What helps us to accept and endure the painful and horrifying scenes portrayed by Rogier van der Weyden's friend and by Titian is the texture of the paintings, the way the paint has been applied to the board or canvas and the way it mediates to us the composition, colours, tonal values and lines of the paintings. Just as the beauty and sonority of the Alexandrine lines can palliate for us the intensity of emotion and the wickedness of human behaviour in a Racine tragedy, so the quality of the texture absorbs the physical shock of witnessing cruelty. Interestingly enough, this applies to the very different textures of the two works: the Rogier van der Weyden is worked to a smoothness that shows not the trace of a brushstroke; the *Marsyas* is painted with the rapid brushstrokes and thinned paints of Titian's last period. It is not the style that affects us so much as the humanity and depth of feeling that guide the artist's hand in creating the texture.

The capacity of texture to convey and soften emotion can be recognized in many other art forms, whether it is the fleshlike gleam of bronzes or the concentrated corrugations of wool and silk mingled in a tapestry. Our response to it can also be modified or intensified by the associated knowledge we bring to the understanding of a work of art. Every English and French schoolchild is familiar with the Bayeux Tapestry from reproductions. For centuries it used to be displayed in Bayeux Cathedral on great occasions as a memorial of the Norman victory over the English. No reproduction can convey, first, the surprise at how long it is and, second, the impact of the texture of the raised and knotted embroidery. There are further surprises. It is now regarded as the work of Anglo-Saxon embroiderers; in other words, it is the work of the conquered telling the story of their downfall. The central character is not William the Conqueror but Harold, whose story is told, like that of a Greek hero, as the tragedy that comes upon a man of noble character through neglecting his vows and through being forsworn. Each stitching by a needle of the cloth on which the story is embroidered could have been a piercing of the heart for the embroiderers at the conquest and despoliation of their land. The quality of the embroidery seizes one's attention like a great story being told to one because the stitching itself performs the narration.

How we see such works as the Bayeux Tapestry today must often be very different from how they were seen by their patrons and the contemporaries of the artists and embroiderers. First of all we are distanced by time from the traditions of the art we are looking at, but we are also in the strange position of loving art while living in a society that tolerates it without regarding it as necessary to our lives. I think in contrast of a tenth-century statue of Ganesha on the outskirts of a Rajasthan village, blackened by the offerings of vermilion applied to it over the years. I was shown a pile of recent letters lying before it, all invitations to the god represented by the statue from the villagers to weddings that they are arranging. I recall, also, my surprise years ago in St Peter's, Rome, when an old peasant woman, dressed in black from head to toe, came up to me, a young foreigner, to ask which was the statue of St Peter. When I showed her the famous ancient bronze statue with the toe worn away by the kisses of the pilgrims, she knew exactly what to do. She grasped the bronze foot and slavered over the toe with countless kisses.

More recently in Italy I was taken back into this older way of reacting to art in the church of Santa Maria Maggiore in Bergamo. There, several times a day, the sacristan puts on a performance. He unlocks the protective panelling that guards the series of intarsia pictures designed by Lorenzo Lotto and made by craftsmen in the early seventeenth century. They show various scenes from the Old Testament. The sacristan, wielding a lamp on a trailing flex and with an enjoyment of his task that repetition clearly increases because of the amazement of his audience, sweeps the light across the panels, making the woods with their different grains glow and flicker to a chorus of cries of 'Madonna!' and 'Bellissimo!' The performance reaches its climax when he demonstrates how the moon above Moses can be seen as full or crescent according to how he shines the light upon it. The cries grow to their loudest in appreciation and the appreciation is centred on the skill and the artifice of the works. There is a wonder in this audience at the glory of superb talent marvellously employed and I felt privileged to see these works in the company of such an audience, crying out in wonder as their ancestors in Bergamo must have done when by candlelight the panels were first displayed and Lotto and the craftsmen stood by, delighted at the effect of their work.

Today in art we face a challenge, that of coming to terms with the act of recollection of all the art and mythology of the past the Great Memory is forcing on us. In most of the bigger cities of the West it is possible to see in their museums examples of the art and artefacts from all the continents of the Earth, going back thousands of years in some cases and up to the present in others. We have already passed so far beyond the parish outlooks of our forebears that we actually expect to be able to appreciate items so different in their origins and purposes as early Chinese bronzes, Japanese screens of the Edo period, tribal art of the Congo, Mayan sculpture, Tibetan *tangkas*, and altarpieces of the quattrocento. We expect, naturally, to value different qualities in each of these and many more classifications and we can also expect to like the art of some cultures much more than others. Nevertheless there is an unspoken agreement in our societies, given that they have paid for the upkeep and display of these objects, that they are worth looking at because they provide instruction and delight and that there is a universal language or communication speaking through them across time and between cultures.

This leads me to another recompense for the divorce of art from our daily and religious lives. It is that, among all the paintings and objects that have the interest and charm of the period in which they were made, whether it is a seventeenth-century Dutch interior or still life or a mustachioed Gandhara Buddha, there are certain objects that have a different effect on us. They wake us up. They enlighten us with something of the degree of consciousness that was present at their making.

The comparative study of religions has shown that what the world religions have in common is evidence of people who have experienced mystical illumination and the special states of consciousness that are characteristic of illumination. The comparative study of mythology has shown that in societies completely separated by time and lack of communication the same archetypes and symbols and fundamentally similar stories have arisen, not only as explanations of causes and of the nature of the world but also as a means of conveying the incomprehensible and fundamental awe of consciousness. Thus, too, the comparative study of cultures and of art brings evidence of a constant that recurs and disappears and comes again in the course of history and this constant we recognize by its effect upon us. It is the sign of those who knew what they were doing.

As examples of works of art that possess this quality I think of the archaic Greek sculptures of *korai* and the Moscophoros, buried because they were damaged when the Persians fired the Acropolis and now unearthed and displayed in the Museum of the Acropolis, the Khmer heads of the Buddha in the Musée Guimet in Paris, numerous examples of Egyptian sculpture, many works by Chinese landscape painters, and the still-life paintings of Matisse in his middle period. The constant in them combines a sense of transcendent calm with a feeling of living intelligence as though the various kinds of matter of which they are made have been raised into consciousness. In many cases they consist only of fragments of the original work of art; nevertheless, what remains possesses the ability to move us and to awaken our own awareness into the state of creative attention.

Such works not only in their subject matter frequently portray an ideal of humanity, as in the case of the statues of the Buddha: they bring about an experience in the spectator such that the ideal is awakened in him or her through the special change in consciousness. That special state when we are completely aware of our surroundings, when our visual and spatial perceptions are enhanced to a superlative degree and when we are freed from other concerns, is an unveiling of latent consciousness. The unity of mind and heart, the coordination of our faculties and our bodies so that we even seem to move in a different and more composed way when we are in this state, may bring about other experiences, flashes of joy and even, for some, an intense auditory experience – except that it has nothing to do with the physical ear – a kind of inner singing that is paradoxically like a savouring of silence.

Our standards for art and civilization are set by such experiences, not by reading or writing or criticism. The experience is what determines what we study or think about. In such experiences we become the ideal to which we aspire. If we are to make an art of the future that synthesizes and surpasses everything we are being offered from all the quarters of the Earth by the Great Memory, the inspiration must come from a level of humanity that transcends all the differences separating races and period, from, in fact, the quality of consciousness that radiates across history and prehistory, from the cave paintings of the Dordogne to the sand paintings of Tibetan monks today.

That there is a deep longing in our society for the transcendent effects of art can be demonstrated by the numbers of those who every year visit our great cathedrals. A number of pilgrims and tourists, something equal to or surpassing the population of England at the time of the rebuilding of Canterbury Cathedral in the twelfth century, now visit that cathedral every year – 2.5 million people. The relics that once brought pilgrims in their hundreds and thousands have long disappeared: the power that was

263

in them has now, it seems, been transferred to the stone, wood and glass of the building itself. The buildings are, in some cases, being worn away by the unconscious devotion of the tourists who come to see them. That they come in such numbers must be owed in great measure to the particular effects that architecture brings about in the human soul.

Architecture, to take up a theme I mentioned earlier, is one of the arts that most demands participation, not only in the physical effort we have to expend in walking round and studying a building, but because when we take part in the use for which it was designed we often most fully appreciate a building's special qualities. To go round Westminster Abbey can still be a fine experience despite the ramps that have been put in place to spare the stones of the paving and the steps and despite the welter of tombs that hide so much of the medieval detail: but to be present, say, at the Christmas Eve service with 2,000 other people when the whole church is plunged in darkness before the acclamation of the birth of Christ is to have an experience of the building of a completely different order. Then the hugeness of the imaginations of Henry de Reyns who built the choir in the thirteenth century for King Henry III and of Henry Yeveley who built the nave for King Richard II in the late fourteenth century comes alive for us in an extraordinary way. The only light apart from a few candles comes from the square outside so that you see the flying buttresses in ghostly whiteness through the high windows and as your eyes grow accustomed to the darkness, so you can trace the form of the building from the dark ribs of the vaulting above down to the columns rising about you.

A great architect possesses generosity of soul. His works invite people inwards. Even the proudest monarchs need crowds to watch and admire and bow to them so that the vast spaces in the Forbidden City were necessary for the emperor to receive the kowtows of his subjects. Steps, gatehouses, avenues of approach, doorways and antechambers, even though they may be provided with defences against enemies, all have these positive aspects of invitation or at least of warning the visitor that he must be prepared in comportment and dress for what lies at the end of the succession of façades and entrances. Interesting studies have been made of the effects on subjects such as architectural students and control groups of surviving buildings of the Nazi regime.[3] These clearly are buildings that do not invite: built in a ponderous but simple adaptation of the Neo-Classical tradition, they were intended to give the impression of a Reich that would indeed last a thousand years. This impression, also intended to depress and cow the onlooker into an admiring acquiescence, outweighs all the other impressions one might expect to receive from a public building.

Architecture is also the most social and necessary of the arts. Rulers and patrons who would like to abolish all the other arts are forced to allow architecture into their states or their domains. One of the fundamental characteristics of European architecture up to the twentieth century was that, with the architecture of styles, there was an understanding that a new style, when set against older buildings in older styles, should harmonize in height and disposition with the constructions of earlier periods. One has only to walk past the buildings of the various science departments of Oxford University, mostly built from the 1920s onwards, to see a striking example of how that harmony disappeared. It is as though the architects and professors of each department were determined to be at odds with whatever buildings were next to them: not only did they build in determination to assert their identities in a variety of styles from Gothic revival to Brutalist modern; they also set their buildings at different angles to the frontage on the road so that each building should seem to be slighting its neighbours.[4] The farrago of buildings displays, as well as the decay of architectural neighbourliness, something else that had happened among their patrons: it is the division and fragmentation of science into separate fiefdoms.

What is conspicuously lacking in these buildings, given their connection with science, is that they are buildings without a cosmology or an objective system of proportion behind them. Not only does great architecture – in contrast to these – welcome the visitor but it nearly always shows him a picture of the universe he inhabits, a universe he is pleased to inhabit. This applies to several of the buildings I have discussed earlier, such as Chartres and St Paul's. The world's most famous sacred buildings all have these further characteristics – such as the complex of temples on the Acropolis, the Great Mosque at Damascus, Hagia Sofia in Istanbul and the Taj Mahal, to mention those where I have experienced it myself – that there is a magnetism about them, an excitement that makes the blood tingle with anticipation at the first sight of them and that as you approach and enter them you are filled with the mood entirely special to each building. I think particularly of the mood of the Taj Mahal that seizes everyone as they first see it framed in the gateway of the garden leading to the mausoleum a mood that seems to possess every tree leaning over the walls of the garden and every plant in the succession of beds. It is a mood of exquisite sorrow and delight mingled together, gathering in intensity as you approach the mausoleum and made almost unbearable by the subtleties, precision and grandeur of the building as you examine it more closely.

Great architecture changes one's sense of oneself. Through the avenue effect of walking down a nave of Gothic columns, through the effect of expansion as one looks up into a dome, through the intricacy effect of perforated screens or of the honeycombing of a mosque arch, through the recession effect of doorway opening after doorway, and through the surprise or ha-ha effect of coming upon an unexpected vista of a lake or a mountainface of trees, through these and many other effects, we are played with like toys that enjoy being played with. What is happening to us through the alerting and intensification of our perceptions is also opening doors and barred gateways into the hidden emotions and delights of our souls – and again, as with the ultimate impressions of painting, architecture that can have such an effect remains in us as a kind of music we have played to ourselves as much as it lasts in visual impressions.

What I have been describing in relation to the effect of the literary arts, music, art and architecture in this and the previous chapter is the change in kinds of awareness that each art is capable of bringing about in us, sometimes in solitude and sometimes through participation. The change is one in consciousness or rather in our consciousness of consciousness. What then is the self, the sense of I, that can be worked upon and varied by a line of verse, a song, a daub of paint or arrangements of cut stone or brick? And why is it important to know?

It is important because one of the most fundamental reasons for education is to bring people to the point where they experience bibliophany in reading or self-transcendence through listening to music or looking at works of art. It is important because a society in which such experiences are valued and are regarded as among the highest goods is likely to be more creative, more open to ideas and more free than societies in which they are feared and repressed. It is important because even in repressive societies where there is some access to the treasures of literature and art – or to the memories of them in prison – there the spirit can be free with its infinitely greater realms of freedom than those of the physical body. Above all, it is important whatever the merits of the surrounding society because the awakening of such experiences leads to the development and the self-knowledge of the individual soul.

In a world in which art, religion, philosophy and science accord, each of these modes of cognition would lead towards this knowledge of the self. It would be as natural for us to realize the expansion of consciousness as we contemplate a great idea or appreciate the workings of geological time as we look at a beautiful landscape as it is for this to happen when we are transported by music or respond to the spatial effects of a fine building. Not only would consciousness be enhanced but the same effect noted in regard to bibliophany would come about: we would be cleverer philosophers and cleverer scientists.

I write this at a time when there is renewed evidence of a turning away from science among the young and with the rueful thought in my mind that much of my working life has been devoted to helping children to become fired with a love of the natural world and of science. My work was with the Science and Mathematics Teaching Projects set up by the Nuffield Foundation in 1962 and it provided one of my chief experiences of working on a collaborative creative endeavour. The aims of the first leaders of the projects in biology, chemistry and physics included these: that children should learn by doing rather than by rote or having experiments demonstrated to them, and that through carrying out the experiments themselves and by discussing and analysing what they actually saw they would develop in each of them a spirit of enquiry which they would carry with them into adult life. To one chemist, Frank Halliwell, it was his hope and belief that when, for example, a child carried out a series of experiments on heating metals and weighing them, he or she would come to the same conclusions as Lavoisier in his original experiments on the nature of oxygen and the role of oxidation that helped to found modern chemistry. The child would experience for him- or herself the flash of inspiration. To a well-known physicist, Eric Rogers, the real aim of teaching physics, in addition to his conviction that there was an essential body of information from the time of Ptolemy onwards to the present day that should be handed on from one generation to the next, was that each child should experience at some time through physics 'wonder and delight'. They taught and based their materials on the historical method: the better they were as scientists, teachers and writers, the more likely it was that they would be profoundly aware of the traditions and history of their particular subjects.

There were strong political and economic reasons why this project and similar projects, particularly in the United States, should come into being. It was the shock produced in the West by the success of the Soviet Union in launching the first manned space flight. In trying to imitate what seemed the Soviet success in creating a scientific elite capable of such an achievement, the leaders of the new projects in the West ignored something that was crucial to Russian cultural traditions and education – even though increasingly a knowledge of those traditions was becoming available.[5] Russian education was a product of the Enlightenment rather than, as in the West, of the Middle Ages and the Renaissance, and its aims and traditions were set in the eighteenth century by the practice and ideal of such men as the poet-scientist Mikhail Lomonosov, who is regarded as the founder both of Russian literature and of Russian science. These traditions had to a great extent survived the Russian Revolution and they were helped by the success of the Soviets in establishing an equation between communism and science: they were both identified with progress. These different traditions avoided the fear and hatred of science endemic among western civil servants and educators reared in the classics and the arts.

Some of my colleagues and their contemporaries in the world of science felt the challenge of classical education so keenly that they tried to promote a new ideal, that of the scientifically literate person who would replace as the trained elite the classicists and historians of the past. Such scientifically literate persons would be the intelligent audience for science as well as providing the cadres of future scientists. They would shape the world in a rational way and they would hasten the scientific and technological utopia in its coming. Apart from this and what I say below, my scientist colleagues had little general ideal of what they wanted children to grow towards beyond the tradition of Christian humanitarianism in which they had been reared, and which they no more questioned than they did the mass of a known element. The division of science into separate fiefdoms was emphasized by the way in which some of my colleagues thought of their own subjects as cherished children to be protected from the false notions of the coarse and stupid children who were the other subjects: the physicists alone knew about energy, they deplored the ideas of energy common among chemists, and both physicists and chemists sneered at what the biologists considered to be energy. If these are criticisms, they are criticisms of the society and the general intellectual climate within which they had to work rather than of individuals; of a society living on the capital of its past, rather than creating and agreeing upon aims for the future that were beyond economic growth and material progress.

The great point about the projects was the recognition that the aim of science education was to arouse the unitive expression of intellectual satisfaction combined with wonder and delight. My colleagues were inspired by the desire to show that science is as beautiful as the nature scientists study[6] and to provide for their pupils the equivalent in scientific terms of bibliophany. Whether the Nuffield Projects and the similar projects in the USA will have had any lasting effect, it is at least ten years too early to tell. Great educational reforms generally take about forty years for their true effects to be seen: it took that long for the educational reforms introduced in England under Edward VI to appear in the generation of Shakespeare and his contemporaries and a similar period for the reforms of Lomonosov to appear in the generation of Pushkin – and in both these cases there was the dimension of an all-inclusive ideal of the kinds of human beings that education should lead to, which was only incipient in these projects.

I say incipient because the ideals were there but they were ideals of what the children should be as a result of their experience of science rather than that of the adults they should become. The chief and barely conscious ideal was that of the wonderfully responsive child, bright with intelligence, eager to explore, bursting with questions, and confident that his or her interaction with the world through knowledge or technology would be wholly benign. The ideals underlying these projects can now be seen in a historical perspective as one of the many impulses towards freedom and individuality that characterized the decade of the sixties. It would have seemed extraordinary at the time to relate a movement to awaken the spirit of enquiry in science to the impulses that provoked social and political rebellion, transformed fashion, saw the rise of international pop music and the drug culture and opened up to an extent barely known before a fascination with altered states of consciousness achieved either by traditional means or through drugs. A common theme, however, lay underneath the tweed jackets of my colleagues and the kaftans of the swinging generation: their underlying ideals were related to childhood and adolescence. Whereas in the art and popular culture of the years leading up to the Second World War the dominant male ideal was that of the young man on the brink of life, the hero at the point of setting out as an unconscious preparation for the trials of war to come,[7] now it was the time of the Flower Children, of children's rights, of education based on theories of how children felt and understood rather than of what they ought to learn, of student rebellion and sexual liberation. The release of these forces was partly political, with the lowering of the age for voting rights. It was also commercial: for the first time adolescents had money to spend and therefore were seen as a new and powerful market for businessmen. They became the new audience and the new patrons for whom the Beatles and the Rolling Stones were the voices of freedom and exploration. Their toys were the first fruits of the revolution in communications brought about by transistors and their music was driven by the Dionysiac rhythms of revolution.

Thirty years have gone by and the beat of those rhythms have helped to bring down the governments of old men in the citadels of East European communism and now threaten the old men of China. But still humanity needs an ideal of maturity rather than of adolescence. Such an ideal would be intimately linked to science and to the transformation of the scientific ideals of man of which we spoke earlier, to the necessity of redressing the balance of the feminine in those ideals and most of all the development of a science of consciousness, a science that gives a true account of our souls, minds and bodies and of the spirit that moves through all three modes of experience.

A major scientific discovery may, from one point of view, render unnecessary all the theories, conjectures and experiments that preceded it; from another point of view, its expression in a law or equation may be considered to be like a powerful metaphor in poetry in that it subsumes and includes within itself all the experience not only of the workers who make the discovery but of all their predecessors in the same field. I am thinking of discoveries of the order of Kepler's laws of planetary motion at which he arrived through the most arduous researches and changes of model, including his early proposal that the paths of the planets could be demonstrated to follow the circles that could be described around the Platonic solids when these were enclosed one with the other. That last theory seemed a perfect solution philosophically and aesthetically as well as scientifically except for the discrepancies that became clearer and clearer between the theory and his own observations of the path of Mars. He was driven to further researches and contemplations, which came right only when he changed his way of thinking. One important step came when, instead of making his calculations from Earth, he placed himself in his imagination on Mars and did his calculations as from that position.[8] This established that the motion of the Earth is not uniform but varies according to its distance from the sun. From this, through all kinds of blind alleys, he reached his triumphant discovery of the elliptical orbit of Mars, which led him to the statement of his laws of planetary motion. It was an extraordinary expansion of what Copernicus had begun when he set the sun at the centre of the planets. Now, however, the sun was not in the centre but in one of the foci of the ellipses: and what was in the other focus? Nothing? Or was it a return of the ancient idea of two suns, one the physical sun, known as Helios, and the other, the hidden or unmanifested sun which is Apollo and the light of the universal intellect?

A leap of the imagination of a comparable order will be necessary for science to develop a science of consciousness – a leap to the conception of studying it as a universal and unified noumenon rather than as the adventitious product of electrical discharges in separate human brains; a leap also to realizing the importance of symbolic thought and the part played by metaphor in developing scientific and medical investigations. I predicted earlier that the image of the angel will come to have ever greater importance in understanding the nature of consciousness. We have also seen other images much used in scientific writings, such as the imagery of conquest and violation: there is another image which, having risen from the past, may once again have a richer future and it is that of the hunter. Pasteur's genius in part subsisted in the clarity with which early in an investigation he formulated a problem and then pursued its answer through experimental methods. He saw his prey and then pursued it. He himself was delighted when, describing his discovery of tartaric acid and the experiments that led to the identification of laevorotatory properties in crystals of organic origin, a contemporary wrote: 'Never was treasure, never was adored beauty pursued over more paths or with greater ardour.'[9] As Crashaw said:

True Hope's a glorious huntress, and her chase
The God of Nature in the fields of grace.[10]

One consequence of the search for a science of consciousness will be a revival of certain human capacities that have become largely dormant in cultivated societies: those capacities I sum up in the imagery of the hunt. The powers of observation and coordination, the ability to identify with the nature of the creatures pursued, the seemingly clairvoyant anticipation of the behaviour of those creatures, the wordless communication of the team, the excitement and the delight of the chase, all these qualities and faculties so similar in many ways to the examples of creativity we have considered are already exercised by zoologists, biologists and the photographers and makers of films of animal and plant life, in the study of their subjects. These qualities and faculties, fascinating in themselves as subjects of investigation, are in fact necessary to the study of consciousness, to the development of powers of the mind fast enough to study the fugitive workings of the mind and concentrated enough to capture them in memory. In the study of consciousness we are both hunters and prey.

As a return from the past indicating the repossession of these faculties, I point to the extraordinary story over the past hundred years and more of the discovery of the art and the ritual underground sites of the earliest artists and scientists of Europe, the people who between the beginning and the end of the last Ice Age (33,000–10,000 BC) produced the first naturalistic art, as evidenced by the superb paintings and engravings of bison, deer, lion and other animals at sites such as Lascaux and Altamira, and also began to portray the human form, particularly the female form, in carvings such as the Venus of Willendorf and the Venus of Laussel.

The way in which we have lost that world and may yet recover it is told in a legend of much more recent date. I was led to it by looking at Poussin's late painting *Landscape with Orion* (figure 29)[11] and seeing in it fascinating connections with the Green Man, especially in regard to the fact that Osiris, the Egyptian form of the Green Man, is identified with the constellation of Orion. Orion, who is a giant and a hunter and also the most handsome of men, has three fathers, Poseidon, Zeus and Apollo: he is the child of earth by water, air and fire; he is also primeval humanity, of a size to accord with his heroic ancestry and with the intuitions and speed of reaction of our hunting fathers. He is also the universal man crucified in the cross of stars in the winter sky. Poussin in this painting shows him at a time of expiation: he had fallen in love with a princess, Merope, whose father promised her as his bride on condition he cleared his island of wild animals. Oenopion, the father, kept on putting off his promise because he was secretly in love with his daughter. Orion, in desperation, stole some of Oenopion's wine and in his drunkenness forced Merope to lie with him. Oenopion, in revenge, blinded Orion. His punishment, all the more terrible for a man who has lived by the quickness of his eye, would have seemed to Christian generations like an allegory of the wounds inflicted on humanity by original sin. The gods, however, have pity on him: an oracular voice tells him to travel towards the sun and the light of the sun will restore his sight. Orion found a boat and rowed eastwards. Guided by the clangour of the smithy of Hephaestus on the island of Lemnos, Orion plucked one of Hephaestus' assistants, Cedalion, from his work and set him on his shoulders to guide his steps.

This is the point in the story that Poussin depicts. Orion is walking out of a forest. Vapour, signifying his blindness, streams from the forest and hangs in front of his eyes, rising into clouds on which Artemis, goddess of the moon and ruler of the watery element, stands, watching the progress of the hunter as, with hand outstretched, he walks towards the dawn. On his huge shoulders stands Cedalion, directing him along the unseen path: this in itself is a reminiscence of the old story of the blind man carrying the cripple, emblems of the blind energies of humanity needing the guidance of higher wisdom. Hephaestus stands beside the path encouraging Orion. What fills the painting with the spirit of the Green Man is the landscape into which Orion walks. It is the time of first light, before the dawn, when the leaves of hundreds of trees start to stir into activity: the sea awaits the dawning sun in the distance and a craggy mountain overlooking the sea rises as though it is the summit destined for Orion to stand on like a colossus when he will turn the sockets of his eyes towards the sun and will find with his eyes restored the light of the sun come back to him once more. Orion is ourselves, our punished and redeemed selves, blind to the gods who help but still capable of hearing them and still alive to intuition and creative forces, stumbling into the healing light which will reveal to us the reason why we are created.

15

The creation of audiences

At the summer solstice of 1792 a group of Welshmen who lived in London gathered on Primrose Hill, close to the reputed tomb of the ancient British warrior queen Boadicea. Led by the poet Iolo Morganwg they set out a circle of stones with an altar on which a naked sword was placed. They constituted a *Gorsedd*, a gathering of the bards, and here the bardic traditions were recited. The rituals were based on the researches of Iolo Morganwg who not only made genuine discoveries but also liberally invented and wrote the sources himself that history failed to supply. From this ceremony Iolo and his friends were to lay the foundations of the future of the Eisteddfod, not as a local celebration as it had survived from the Middle Ages, but as the national centre of excellence for the revival and maintenance of the great Welsh arts of poetry and music. From this imaginative re-creation of the past arose a new and vital national consciousness in Wales, leading to the founding of institutions such as the University of Wales. What Iolo and his friends also created was a society with a fresh sense of the dignity and the grandeur of their ancient traditions: they made their fellow countrymen into a new kind of audience.

Thus, audiences have to be created, they have to be educated, and they have to learn to make themselves. There is a time when no Greek city possesses a theatre: the rites of Dionysos are performed in village and town squares but no one thinks of expanding or aggrandizing the rites or providing a special place for their performance. Then an impulse comes from the god that inspires the poets and playwrights and tells the citizens to gouge out scallop shapes from local hills into the semicircular ranks of seats that will accommodate the population of the city and where each section of society will find its own place – an impulse that is obeyed throughout the Hellenic world from Asia Minor to Sicily.

It may even be that the impulse from the god came through the audience that in the earliest days was also the chorus responding to the sufferings of Dionysos as portrayed by the first and single actor. To A. W. von Schlegel

273

as to Nietzsche the chorus was the quintessence of the audience and could be considered to be the ideal spectator, creating a bridge of authenticity between the myth portrayed and the minds and hearts of the rest of the audience.[1] We can think of the necessity for the Greek theatre and its sublimely simple shape as arising from the necessity for an orchestra, the space where the chorus with dance and song created tragedy as they brought myth and city together in a bond of re-creation and catharsis.

Audiences may be invisible and inhabit other worlds. Much of what we know of Egyptian art was created to be sealed up in tombs, where it represented to the soul of the dead pharaoh or noble the journey of judgment and redemption it would have to go on while providing simulacra of all the pleasures and necessities of life on Earth in the gardens, scenes of wildlife, boating parties on the Nile, representations of musicians, of cooks, servants, children and wives. It is as though at least half of all the students today who leave art school were to devote their lives to the sculpting and painting of objects that would, on completion, be buried underground. Similarly, much of Celtic art was made either directly for sacrifice to the gods or in the knowledge that one day it would be buried with a chieftain or noble lady or thrown into a river, bog or sacred pool. The most notable work of Celtic art to have survived is the Gundestrup Cauldron, a great silver cauldron superbly embossed with heads of gods and goddesses and mythological scenes, among them representations of Cernunnos, the Celtic form of the Green Man. When it was discovered just over a century ago in a Danish bog, it could be seen that it had been ritually dismantled into its constituent pieces, a clear indication that it had been placed in the bog as a sacrifice. Perhaps, as a symbol of plenty, the cauldron had been given to the gods in a time of dearth. Magnificent pieces of metalwork have been recovered from the Thames to which they had been consigned as offerings at Battersea, such as a famous bronze shield now in the British Museum. Again, it is as though whenever the City of London undergoes a particularly bad crisis, a painting by Turner should be taken from the Tate Gallery and thrown from the Embankment into the Thames, or whenever Wall Street is in a state of nervous jitters, a Rembrandt from the Metropolitan Museum should be hurled into the conjunction of waters at the feet of the Statue of Liberty. Furthermore, this would be done in the certain knowledge that works equal in depth of feeling and expression could be created to replace them.

The examples of Egyptian and Celtic practices are taken from societies that over centuries remained close to their founding myths and were directly in touch with archetypal expressions of the Great Memory. In such societies as we have suggested, myth is a stabilizing and conservative force. In the

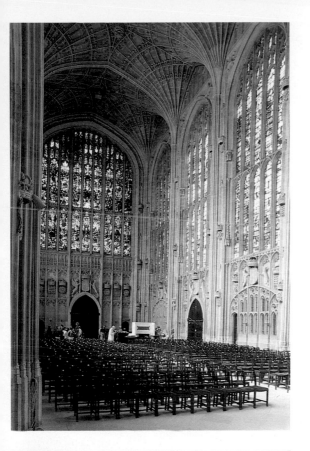

FIGURE 25. The interior of King's College Chapel, Cambridge, 1446-1515.

FIGURE 26. New Grange c. 3100 BC: the spirals on the great stone at this entrance with, above, the light box through which the sun's rays penetrate at the winter solstice.

FIGURE 27. *Lamentation over the Dead Christ*, mid-fifteenth century, by a follower of Rogier van der Weyden.

FIGURE 28. *The Flaying of Marsyas*, c. 1570, by Titian.

FIGURE 29.
Landscape with
Orion, 1658, by
Nicholas
Poussin.

FIGURE 30. Christ before Pilate: one of the thirteenth-century portrayals of the Passion story on the rood screen of the west choir of Naumburg Cathedral.

FIGURE 31. Judas and the thirty pieces of silver from the same sequence as in figure 30.

FIGURE 32. A view into the interior of the dome of the chapel at Anet, Normandy, built 1549-52 by Philibert Delorme for Diane de Poitiers.

FIGURE 33. Nijinsky as Petrushka, 1913.

FIGURE 34. *The Road to Mount Kailas* by Nicholas Roerich (1874-1947).

FIGURE 35. 'Night' from the triptych *L'Âge d'or*, 1900-01, by Baron Léon Frédéric.

dynamic society of the West the recurrences of ancient myths and ideas have been forces of radical change, and the speed with which they have been recognized and adopted is often remarkable. To take the imagery of air and the weather we earlier associated with metaphor and memory, these are changes in the climate of opinion which are changes in the minds and hearts of the populations of Paris, Florence, London, Vienna, Berlin or St Petersburg; in other words, in the audiences that have been essential to much of the development of western culture.

Sometimes artists and thinkers are far ahead of what audiences and readerships are willing to accept. In terms of the theory of the Great Memory it is as though they are drawing on aspects of the past and the emotional energies associated with them that are still too dormant in the unconscious mental levels of their contemporaries to meet with welcome or recognition. Beethoven said of his first Razumovsky Quartet that it was music for another age. Schubert expressed in his Ninth Symphony, the Great C Major, composed 1825–28 and never performed in his lifetime, an ideal world of a happy and blissful nature. Mendelssohn gave it its first performance in Leipzig in 1839 but when he tried to rehearse an orchestra in London in 1844 they burst out laughing, so incomprehensible to them was it and they refused to master its difficulties. The ideal poet-peasant (see page 62) whose vehicle Schubert became in writing his songs was only recognizable among his nearest acquaintance, who would perform his music in gatherings they called Schubertiads. Those were large gatherings compared to the audience Gerard Manley Hopkins won for his verse in his lifetime and for many years after his death. His particular appeal to the past was as a philologist and prosodist: he went to Old English and dialect forms to renew the vocabulary of poetry in English and to the accentual verse of Anglo-Saxon and Middle English verse for the examples on which he was to draw for the revitalized rhythms of his sprung verse. He also went to the past for a justification of his mystical insights or 'inscapes' in the neglected works of Duns Scotus. In his lifetime he had an audience of two, both poets, one his friend Robert Bridges, the other his former teacher Canon Dixon.

By his vocation in the Society of Jesus, Gerard Manley Hopkins was placing himself out of the way of the usual rewards of the successful artist. William Blake, on the other hand, lived in the middle of the artistic and literary life of London: he knew everyone who could have been of help to him. All too often, when he gained a patron it was for a short period and also, sometimes, to be deceived and let down. He had only one constant patron, Thomas Butts, of whom little is known except that the walls of his house could hardly be seen for Blake's paintings. It was he who received the following avowal from Blake:

I am not ashamed, afraid, or averse to tell you what Ought to be Told: That I am under the direction of Messengers from Heaven, Daily & Nightly; but the nature of such things is not, as some suppose, without trouble or care. Temptations are on the right hand & left; behind, the sea of time & space roars & follows swiftly; he who keeps not right onward is lost, & if our footsteps slide in clay, how can we do otherwise than fear & tremble? but I should not have troubled You with this account of my spiritual state, unless it had been necessary in explaining the actual cause of my uneasiness, into which you are so kind as to Enquire; for I never obtrude such things on others unless question'd, & then I never disguise the truth – But if we fear to do the dictates of our Angels, & tremble at the Tasks set before us; if we refuse to do Spiritual Acts because of Natural Fears or Natural Desires! Who can describe the dismal torments of such a state! – I too well remember the Threats I heard! – 'If you, who are organised by Divine Providence for spiritual communion, Refuse, & bury your Talent in the Earth, even tho' you should want Natural Bread, Sorrow & Desperation pursues you thro' life, & after death, shame & confusion of face to eternity. Every one in Eternity will leave you, aghast at the Man who was crown'd with glory & honour by his brethren, & betray'd their cause to their enemies. You will be call'd the base Judas who betray'd his Friend!'[2]

Blake is telling his patron that his prime audience consists of these messengers who not only instruct him in what he has to say but remain well aware of the extent to which he carried out their instructions. This appears from his conviction that, however difficult and miserable his circumstances might be through following their instructions, a far greater misery would fall on him if he were to disregard them. Again, it can be said that one of the many reasons why his contemporaries mocked or ignored him was because of the extent to which he was open to the offerings of the Great Memory and because he was so much in advance of his contemporaries. For example, 'Jerusalem', the poem for which he is best known and which now with the aid of television and radio resounds throughout the world on the last night of the Promenade concerts in London, draws on a legend connected with the story of Glastonbury that Christ as a boy was brought to the west country by Joseph of Arimathea.[3] To Blake, Christ as the divine imagination still walks upon the mountains green and in the mental fight to create Jerusalem in 'England's green and pleasant land' he calls on all his countrymen and women to make themselves the new great audience worthy of spiritual communion.

As a boy of thirteen apprenticed to an engraver, Blake was allowed to clamber about the royal tombs in Westminster Abbey drawing the effigies of dead kings and queens: from that time perhaps came his exceptional understanding of the Middle Ages. Gradually over the years since his death in 1827 Blake has been gaining the audience that the nature of his insights denied him in his lifetime. One of those insights, again so closely joined in meaning and practice to one of the most important means of audience participation in the Middle Ages, is his conception of the four Zoas and the fullness of the imagination when love, instinct, reason and inspiration work as one in the human soul for the realization of truth. The single vision of Isaac Newton, the level of thought and imagination of the Satanic mills by which he characterized much of science and the thought of the Enlightenment, was to Blake wholly defective when compared to the richness of experience symbolized for him by the city of art, Golgonooza, and the reunion of Albion and Jerusalem. One of the indications that the four Zoas are working together at their true efficiency would be, according to Blake, that visions and inspirations would appear in the soul, not as cloudy apparitions but exact and precise and full of detail.

At the end of his life Blake was given a commission by John Linnell to illustrate Dante's *Divine Comedy*. Never before or since has an artist illustrating a classic work done what Blake did: he made his illustrations at the same time an exposition of his own system of Christianity and the four Zoas and a work of active criticism of Dante and *The Divine Comedy*. At times the lover of Dante and the lover of Blake find themselves at war over the savagery of his criticisms and the caricatures of Dante's intentions: Beatrice, for example, is portrayed as the illusory goddess Vala, or Nature, and not as the illuminating truth and, if Dante expresses admiration of Caesar or any emperor, Blake regards such rulers as repressive tyrants like the heads of the Holy Alliance in his own day. There is a further irony in what Blake was doing: he was using his fourfold levels of meaning to interpret and criticize a work that, as described earlier (pages 184–5), was itself based upon and intended to exemplify the fourfold levels of meaning on which the Bible, according to medieval theologians, was constructed. Both Blake's idiosyncratic method and the medieval form of interpretation went back to Neo-Platonic origins. To dare another prediction, I believe that a fuller understanding of both the medieval fourfold method and of Blake's four Zoas is likely to come about, not as the mere restitution of antique modes of experience, but as supporting guides to the further development and recovery of the spiritual exactitude of the imagination and the inner eye.

The fourfold method of interpretation as practised in the Middle Ages provides an admirable example of how an audience or readership is brought into existence and maintained.[4] The method cultivated the visual memory in the context of religious study. The medieval view of the Bible was that its writings contained four levels of meaning, the literal truth of what it said, and three levels of allegory. These three levels consisted, first, of the level of allegory which interpreted the events of the Old Testament as types or foretellings of the birth and life of Christ and his followers so that, for example, the confusion of tongues at the Tower of Babel was related to its opposite in the Pentecostal gift of tongues to the apostles so that each man, listening to the apostles, heard them in his own language. The next level interpreted the Scriptures according to their moral or psychological meaning; the highest level, known as the anagogic or mystical, interpreted them as emblems of the relationship to God. It may seem, at first sight, a merely analytical process, a game of finding correspondences, but it is not so when, for example, we find that the procedure for using it, according to the instructions of Hugh of St Victor (c. 1097–1141), the great mystic and theologian, amounted to a technique of visualization. His instructions are that the reader concentrating on a story in the Bible, such as the Flood and the Ark, should create, as clearly as possible, with his inner eye pictures of the people involved in the story, the animals, the landscapes, the colours and the action. Only when this had been done and the images had been established in the mind should the reader then presume to dwell on the inner and allegorical meanings, letting them suggest themselves out of the images, rather than imposing them upon the passage. Hugh of St Victor saw it as a means of liberating the spirit and allowing the truth to flower within the soul.[5]

It was a technique practised long before Hugh of St Victor's time and this technique, together with the training in writing, book-binding, and illuminating which many monks would have undergone, helps to explain why so many of the clergy were such fine patrons. They had undergone a training in visualization which would have enabled them to appreciate the works of the architects, sculptors and workers in glass and in metals that they commissioned while at the same time making their patronage into a work of collaboration as they helped to design the patterns of the stained glass which, often, in their arrangements of stories draw out the typology of the Old and New Testaments. Though it was regarded almost as an esoteric technique to be reserved wholly to the clergy, except for sermons at the great festivals of the Church when sometimes the laity might be allowed to hear something of the allegorical and moral levels of interpretation, its wider effect through its influence over generations of priests and monks was enormous.

Hugh of St Victor was inculcating a method of reading that brought the soul to a state of peace. The nobility and educated members of the laity were to be brought closer to civilization by a similar idea. This was that the soul could be ennobled and purified through love and through the appreciation of poetry and music. This conception, coming from the Provençal troubadours and enriched by Sufi influences, was particularly fruitful in its effect on the poets associated with the court of the Emperor Frederick II in Sicily and southern Italy. We have already seen how this was further developed by Cavalcanti and Dante with the concept of the *intelletto d'amore*, the organ of understanding and wonder that could be awakened in the soul. Among the many strands woven into *The Divine Comedy* is that of an ascending openness to the mercies and benefits of art, symbolized by a progression through the nine Muses, beginning with Thalia, the Muse of Comedy, the Muse who explains why the title of the work is the *Commedia*, up to the Muse of the Heavens, Urania, and Apollo, the guide and master of the Muses.[6] The fires of Hell become the lights of Paradise, the howling of the damned turn first to the psalms of the repentant and then to the songs and carols of the blessed souls in Heaven, the naked sinners gripped in ice or writhing in torment become dancers exercising perfect control as they form the symbols of the Eagle and the Cross – all these may be seen and experienced as the transformation brought about in the soul of the reader of *The Divine Comedy*. Dante states very firmly that he has a practical object in writing the poem: it is to remove those living in this life from a state of misery to one of bliss[7] – in other words, bliss through experience of reading now as well as later through direct experience of the divine in Heaven.

This concept of ennoblement through appreciation was to flower again in Florence chiefly through the life work of the philosopher Marsilio Ficino (1433–99). Ficino and his friends, such as Cristoforo Landino, who wrote a notable commentary on *The Divine Comedy*, believed that philosophy was reborn in them for the first time since the classical period as poetry had been reborn in Dante. A half-length statue of Ficino by Andrea Ferrucci looks out from his memorial in the north aisle of the Duomo in Florence close to Domenico da Michelino's fresco of Dante standing before the three worlds of his poem. Ficino's warm and modest nature glows in his face as he is portrayed listening as though waiting for the creative moment when he would be given the inspiration for one of his spontaneous poems or when he was taken up to the highest contemplative state through his appreciation of music and poetry. We can look upon him as one of the most influential instruments the Great Memory has ever spoken through: not only did he translate the whole of Plato's works into Latin and oversee their printing (they were to be reprinted thirty times in the sixteenth century), he also translated numerous Neo-Platonic treatises and the body of mystical and cosmological texts attributed to Hermes Trismegistus, then thought to contain the theology of ancient Egypt. We can also look on him as one of the chief creators of our conceptions of what we may become at our highest as members of an audience or as the appreciators of art. Through his own writings, his vast correspondence and his standing and influence with Cosimo de' Medici and with Lorenzo de' Medici, he devised the philosophy for living which others such as Castiglione were further to develop and to spread with a wider currency. An essential part of that philosophy of living was the ennoblement brought about by contemplative experiences gained in the hearing of music and verse. These performances were like a form of benign ritual magic in their effect of drawing down influences from the stars, the gods and the angelic orders. Landino said that God is the supreme poet and the world is his poem.[8] Creation exists to be enjoyed and to be celebrated. Virtue was fed by such experiences: the ecstasy of being taken out of oneself through the effect of beauty was considered a renewal of the soul; and it was no disgrace to be so enraptured but rather the sign of nobility of spirit. There are later accounts of musicians who could bring about this state, such as Francesco da Milano, who could transport his listeners into 'so pleasurable a melancholy . . . they remained deprived of all senses save that of hearing, as if the spirit, having abandoned all the seats of the senses had retired to the ears in order to enjoy the more at its ease so ravishing a harmony . . .'[9]

The energies and ideas released by Ficino throughout Europe were to find some of their best expressions in English and Scottish society and culture under the reigns of Elizabeth I and James VI and I. There the tastes and expectations of the wider audiences of art and literature and of thought and science were set by the monarch whose life would be lived to a great extent in public as a living drama conducted with all the ceremonial and ritual that grew up in the Middle Ages around rulers regarded as the Lord's anointed. What we now enjoy in a concentrated form in the plays of Shakespeare and his contemporaries is the creation not only of the playwrights but of their patrons and audiences and of what went to form their tastes and direct their education.

The awed reports of foreign visitors to England speak of the almost liturgical nature of the behaviour of courtiers and royal servants not only when in the presence of Queen Elizabeth but whenever they were about their sovereign's business; for example, each person concerned with laying the table from which her meals were served would kneel three times before and after carrying out his or her particular task.[10] As for what happened when she was present, this is from an account of her going to chapel on a Sunday in 1598. Awaited by the Archbishop of Canterbury, the Bishop of

London, counsellors and gentlemen, she appeared preceded by noblemen and the Lord Chancellor accompanied by two gentlemen carrying the royal sceptre and the sword of state respectively; as she progressed she would speak to the ambassadors and others present in English, French or Italian (she could also speak Spanish and Dutch).

> Wherever she turned her face as she was going along, everybody fell down on their knees. The ladies of the court followed next to her, very handsome and well-shaped, and for the most part dressed in white. She was guarded on each side by the gentlemen pensioners, fifty in number, with gilt halberds . . . in the chapel was excellent music; as soon as it and the services were over, which scarcely exceeded half-an-hour, the Queen returned in the same state and order, and prepared to go to dinner.[11]

From such cameos we can see Elizabeth the Queen as being like the central crater of a gigantic volcano with her nobles and bishops as so many smaller craters placed upon her slopes. From her can pour the fires of justice and royal rage but also the fertilizing lavas that will nourish art and learning. To make occasions as splendid as these, each actor or actress on the stage of the court, each courtier, soldier and prelate was supported by hundreds of jewellers, goldsmiths and silversmiths, armourers, weavers and embroiderers, as well as choristers, musicians and composers of the Chapel Royal. To which, when we consider other occasions such as the tilting on Accession Day, we must add the masters of the horse, the armourers, the heralds, the squires and the poets who would devise the impresas, the emblems adorning the noble jousters, and the painters who would paint the impresas.

The skills of all these artists and craftsmen, whose work had to be of the highest standard in order to maintain the dignity of the monarch and her court, provided the base for training and emulation for the somewhat similar though smaller households of the noblemen and richer gentry. This love of conspicuous splendour added a further dimension to the impact Elizabethan drama would have had upon its audience: what they saw on the stage was what was also being enacted, generally quite close to them in London, at the court.

The communication of meaning and significance through symbolic gestures and ritual in the traditions of the court had its counterpart in Renaissance education. Here a skill inculcated from early years helped to create a knowledgeable and participatory audience. This came about because most schoolboys in the course of being taught rhetoric were also taught to be actors. The educational reforms under Elizabeth and her predecessors and the setting-up of over three hundred grammar schools in the country helped to make the teaching of rhetoric associated with the study of Latin and Latin literature something generally available. Not only were the schoolboys taught the many devices and forms of rhetoric then considered necessary for orators and clergymen, they were also taught a language of gesture which included postures and signs appropriate for every emotion and idea they had to express, indicated with the hands and fingers.[12] When Queen Elizabeth, educated also in the classics and rhetoric, visited schools, the two universities or the Inns of Court, she would be entertained by boys or undergraduates who would deliver orations or perform plays, again accompanying each trope or speech with the appropriate gestures. The patrons and educated people who formed much of the audience for the Elizabethan theatre were therefore prepared, through their own upbringing as a specially knowledgeable group, not only to appreciate all the classical allusions in the plays but also for understanding the language of gesture which the actors used. This language of gesture would have provided an extra dimension of communication, especially of mood and inner communication. They had no change of lighting to influence mood but they had their fingers and hands and arms to signal with in a language that would have been so natural to the audience, they would have received the meaning as instantly as they did the words. The great preachers of the day were also among the great performers of the day and the attitudes of their congregations to them were of men and women who desired instruction and wished to have it given to them with fire and drama, who, having at last been given the Bible in their own language, were determined to exercise their liberty to understand and interpret it. Here again was a new contribution to the background and the powers of concentration of the audiences: they were literate to an extent never known before.

The Elizabethans were similarly a good audience for music and for dancing because both these were important accomplishments at court and in social life. Every lady and gentleman was expected to be able to sing a part and the lyric impulse in their poetry was founded upon the love and practice of singing.

Music, like poetry, was considered to be capable of transforming and raising its hearers to higher states of consciousness and through the experience of those states to have a lasting moral effect in guiding them to virtue, courage and right action. Whoever was the chief recipient of Shakespeare's sonnets – Henry Wriothesley or William Herbert – it is certain, first, that he was a nobleman, and second, that he had to be urged to do his duty in marrying a young lady of suitable rank and fortune according to the wishes of his family. It has been suggested that the sonnets began as a commission to William Shakespeare from the Earl and Countess of Pembroke as part of an attempt to persuade their elder son Lord Herbert to marry. Lady Pembroke was the sister of Sir Philip Sidney and it had been for her that Sidney wrote his *Arcadia*. She had never ceased to mourn her brother's death and she devoted great efforts to keeping his memory alive and to furthering the influence of his works. She had had published not only the *Arcadia* but, among other works, his sonnet sequence *Astrophil and Stella* which had created a great fashion for the sonnet, a fashion Shakespeare took up in *Love's Labour's Lost*. Like her queen she was a polyglot and translated a French tragedy into English; she had a fascination with chemistry and with breeding livestock. She had also been the patroness of Edmund Spenser and Samuel Daniel and was to act similarly for John Donne and Ben Jonson. Here, following the ideas of John Padel, I am presenting her as one of the most likely candidates for originating the sonnets.[13] She typifies, in her intelligence, rank, wealth and ambitions, the wielder of patronage that most poets of the period would have liked to attract, not just because of her providing for creature comforts but because of her refined and exquisite taste. She was the audience who also inspired.

Out of that commission came the strange, passionate friendship between the young man, handsome, wilful, intelligent and perhaps sexually ambiguous, William Herbert, and his social inferior and moral and artistic superior, William Shakespeare, who was to become his tutor. Primarily Shakespeare was teaching Herbert how to be a patron and teaching him the mutual consideration which was its basis; 'this meant accepting his narcissism and by enlargement transforming his pride in his beauty (his "show") into a pride in his virtue (his "essence")'.[14] Other poets were to benefit from Herbert's training in patronage, not only the rival poet of the Sonnets, but also Ben Jonson, and Herbert and his brother were to be the dedicatees of the First Folio in 1623 after Shakespeare's death. Whether one reads the Sonnets in the order first published in 1609 or in a rearrangement such as John Padel's, there issues from the reading the impression of complexities of relationship, of love, betrayal, repentance, distancing and coming together again, together with the episode of the Dark Lady, all connected by certain themes such as time and what survives the passing of time. What constantly recurs among these complexities is Shakespeare's fascination with the self, with what he means in each context by his use of 'I', the self that is in disgrace with 'Fortune and men's eyes' or the self that stands in eternity, confident that in reputation and in worth it is free of the derelictions of time. Again there is the constant fascination with the nature of the self in the use of 'you' or 'thou': the beloved, the 'you', may be at one moment the cruel, the unkind or the untruthful and treacherous and, at other times, the repository of all the poet's earlier loves and friendships, the healer and bringer of balm to the world's hurts, or even the rose of the universe itself and the sun of transcendent understanding. With the growth of the relationship the creative urge has taken Shakespeare and his friend far beyond the original intention behind the commission to write the Marriage Sonnets, into something new in the connection between poet and patron, and writer and reader, into the private regions of the soul no one in European literature was to explore again with quite such penetration until perhaps Goethe or the French Symbolist poets. What we possess in the Sonnets is an autobiographical experimental novel which we read, not knowing for certain whether the pages are in the correct order.

The true novel was to come from the creation of another kind of audience. While a puzzled readership in London was trying to make out the story and meaning of the Sonnets, across the Channel a beautiful and gifted woman was creating a new kind of audience in Paris. She was Catherine de Vivonne, Marquise de Rambouillet.[15] Instead of an audience taking its standards and themes from the court, the audience she brought into being was formed in revulsion at the court. Henry IV, in winning the French crown and possessing himself of Paris by his conversion to Catholicism, brought the coarseness and licentiousness of the military camps where so much of his life had been lived to his court newly re-established in Paris. The atmosphere of the court was so disgusting that many of the wives of the courtiers withdrew to their own houses in Paris. This is what Madame de Rambouillet did in 1607 and in her *hôtel* in the rue Saint-Thomas du Louvre from 1617 to 1665 she brought together members of the nobility and literary persons in an atmosphere of easy interchange. Cardinal Richelieu, La Rochefoucauld and the Great Condé were frequently among the guests, as were such writers as Malherbe, Corneille and Voiture. Nobles and poets here met women on terms of equality and it was soon established that the women were recognized as the arbiters of taste. Many of Madame de Rambouillet's women friends, among them Mademoiselle de Scudéry, Madame de Sévigné and Madame de La Fayette, were to copy her in setting up their own salons so that the influence of what she created spread further and into fresh generations. One of the most influential consequences of her salon came from the discussions held there on the ideals of behaviour that should govern the lives and attitudes of her friends: out of these discussions, strongly influenced by the ideals of Ficino as expressed by Castiglione and by French imitators of *Il Cortegiano*, developed the concepts of the *honnête homme* and his female counterpart, the *précieuse*. These ideas, through published works and through their influence on the theatre, reached a wider audience.

The movement away from the court, despite Richelieu's attempts to control intellectual life through the academies and Louis XIV's later role as the fount of all patronage, is to be seen here and in other fields. The man who by his contemporaries was thought to be the finest living example of the *honnête homme* was not allowed to live in France after he had uttered some mild criticisms of the Treaty of the Pyrenees. This was the Sieur de St-Évremond (1616–1703) who spent forty years in exile, as an ornament successively of the courts of Charles II, James II and William and Mary, and who is buried in Westminster Abbey, in such regard was he held in London. Both Claude Gelée le Lorrain and Nicolas Poussin, the greatest of French painters to that date, preferred to live in Rome, and when Poussin was invited to return to Paris under the promise of notable commissions from Louis XIII, finding that he was to be directed in his choice of subjects rather than be allowed to follow his highly original studies of Stoic and other antique and Christian themes in which his genius excelled, he took the first opportunity offered him of returning to Rome and staying there. There his patrons were rich Italian and French collectors, of no great name, who trusted him to choose his subjects and thought themselves lucky to be able to purchase from him. In choosing his own subjects the artist was strong enough to take over some of the functions of the patron and among these could be considered the moral direction of the audience.

The novels and stories written by the circle of Madame de Rambouillet were considered successful if they sold five hundred copies and best sellers if they reached a thousand in sales, so small was the readership. The audience of the authors was made up of the same class who needed something to occupy their leisure. It was, for a short period, a system comparable to what had obtained in China for centuries, where the high arts of literature, painting and calligraphy were the preserve of the gentlemen scholars, who, clearly, were wholly professional in the time and effort they devoted to these arts but were enabled, by their freedom from the need for money, to declare themselves to be amateurs.

In the course of the seventeenth and eighteenth centuries the novel came to maturity in answer to a growing need among the reading public not just for stories and romances, but for narratives that posed moral, political and social questions and dealt with the relations between the sexes in ways with which the reader could identify and assimilate to his or her own experience. Should Madame de Clèves have told her husband that she loved Monsieur de Nemours even though she had no intention of giving in to that love? What would it be like to be cast ashore on a desert island or to be shipwrecked successively among a nation of miniature human beings, a nation of giants, a nation of scientists and a nation of horses? What would it be like to live by the Leibnizian doctrine that all is for the best in this best of all possible worlds? What would it be like to live either solely for the gratification of sexual desire or, on the other hand, entirely according to the feelings and the sensibilities of the heart? And what would it be like to be so overwhelmed by these sensibilities that the only escape from them is suicide?

This last question turned into a novel when the young Goethe happened to hear of the death by suicide of an acquaintance called Jerusalem. As he was to write later in his autobiography *Dichtung und Wahrheit*, 'at that instant the plan of *Werther* was found; the whole shot together from all directions, and became a solid mass, as the water in a vessel, which is just at the freezing point, is changed by the slightest shaking into ice.'[16] The publication of *Die Leiden des jungen Werthers* made his name across Europe.

Goethe was rich enough through inheritance to live anywhere he chose. Why he accepted when invited by the Grand Duke of Saxe-Weimar to live in the small town that was the grand-ducal capital is a choice only explicable in terms of what he made of it. Weimar gave Goethe the seclusion he needed for his studies and his writing, a theatre of which he became director in which to produce his plays, sufficient immediate social and intellectual contact with members of the court and the other great minds such as Johann Gottfried von Herder and, later, Schiller, and a base from which it was comparatively easy to travel for recreation and stimulation. What came from Goethe's life in Weimar was an astonishing productivity in verse of all kinds, plays, criticism, writings on botany, zoology, geology and his own theory of colours. Right at the end of his life Goethe wrote an address to the young poets of Germany. In it he described himself as their liberator and he was right to do so, because of the range of new thoughts, emotions and ideas he had introduced into poetry and literature. If he was able to continue to do so and to affect so powerfully a wider audience, it was because of the more intimate audience that welcomed and sheltered him at Weimar.

The chief of the younger poets he had liberated, Schiller also came to live at Weimar, finding, after an initial coolness with Goethe, the ideal surroundings for composing the works of his maturity. It was in Goethe's theatre that Schiller's theatrical masterpiece was first performed, the trilogy on Wallenstein, with its echoes of the rising power of the young Bonaparte contrasted with the great general of the Thirty Years' War. Schiller saw the theatre as the greatest potential means of uniting a nation. 'The stage alone can do this, because it commands all human knowledge, exhausts all positions, illumines all hearts, unites all classes, and makes its way to the heart and understanding by the most popular channels.' In a passage that repeats the themes of the 'Ode to Joy', Schiller speaks of the theatre as being where

> men of all ranks, zones, and conditions, emancipated from the chains of conventionality and fashion, fraternize here in a universal sympathy, forget the world, and come nearer to their heavenly destination. The individual shares in the general ecstasy, and his breast has now only space for one emotion: he is a man.[17]

The society that Goethe and Schiller helped to create was one of the most cultivated in recorded history. It is tragic to set against the words of Schiller the question of why that society, that cultivated audience, allowed itself to be torn apart by murderers and barbarians. Some years ago I had gone to see the cathedral at Naumburg and took advantage of the opportunity to see Weimar as well. It was at a time when the East German government, though wanting tourists, made everything as ludicrously difficult for them as possible. I was not allowed to stay in either Naumburg or Weimar: an extraordinary number of officials checked and counter-checked my documents; an extraordinary number of people who were not officials would express to me their detestation of the regime they lived under. In Naumburg I found I was not allowed to attend a service in the cathedral: to do that you had to be a recognized member of the Church with all the attendant disadvantages the profession of faith would bring upon you. I was, however, allowed in as part of a guided tour. A grey-haired bespectacled lady was our guide; the other members of the tour were all East Germans. The lady told us about the two choirs of the cathedral and gave us all the expected information: it was when she started to speak about the masterworks of the cathedral, the scenes of the Passion carved in the upper register of the rood screen of the west choir, that something happened to her and to us. For most of her audience there the story of the Crucifixion would have been something suppressed or unknown. She, the guide, was officially meant to describe the sculptures merely as art-historical objects but to perform her duty of instruction she had to tell the story the sculptures narrated. The sculptures are moving enough in themselves, deceptively simple, beautifully grouped like stills from a mystery play, always centred on the figure of Christ with the face of a peasant totally resigned to his fate (figures 30 and 31). As she told the story, her voice grew stronger and more vibrant and the attention of the visitors sharpened and their eyes became alive and fascinated. It was as though she was pouring into them a food of which they had been starved and making them aware that they would need it again. That lady needed locking up, she was so dangerous.

My visit to Weimar seemed at first to sum up the total tragedy that had been brought about by the destruction of German culture. Getting off the train at the station I was choked by the stench of broken and unmended drains. The smell followed me out into the street of dingy villas grey with peeling paint that was called Leninstrasse. I passed through Karl Marx Platz and another square, both lined by unfinished buildings of stained concrete with weeds growing among the slogans exhorting the working classes to greater effort. Then, without any preparation, I was in the Frauenplan, the centre of the old town of Weimar, all wonderfully kept, clean and painted, as though to do honour to Goethe was the one thing on which everyone in that society was agreed upon. There, at last, visiting Goethe's house with its sequence of rooms decorated according to his theory of colours or strolling in the park, gazing at the fleeces of wild geraniums rocking with the grasses of the meadows in which he had once taken such delight, I felt a form of freedom, as though his spirit was present, not just for me but for everyone in that ambience.

It was only there I felt that freedom. In other towns the miasma returned and I was brought face to face with a regime that was terrified of the interplay of ideas. I learned something of what happens when a government tries to control an audience and to manipulate it and when the audience is deprived on ideological grounds of its own traditions and its right to choose. 'Woe to that nation whose literature is interrupted by the interference of force,' says Solzhenitsyn. 'The nation does not remember itself':[18] the damage may not be only to the nation which is deprived of its past but to the whole human race because the whole of history ceases to be understood.

What had led to the division of Germany and the destruction of so much in the cultural traditions was paradoxically the desire for unity and the distortion of nationalism into racialism. Goethe in later life made himself unpopular by his opposition to German nationalism. He once said he felt a bitter sorrow at the thought of the German people 'which is so estimable in the individual and so wretched in the generality'[19] and he thought that the true destiny of Germans would be found not in national unity, which was a dangerous chimera, but through what Germans would take abroad. It is a prophecy that has been fulfilled in several ways: there can be no moments of any twenty-four hours when the music of the great German composers is not being played live in some part of the globe, quite apart from its reproduction on tapes and discs; the exiles from German nationalism going back to the time of Bismarck and later from Nazism have had a profound effect on education and culture wherever they have gone, especially on the development of science and scholarship in the United States; and it was from a small state bordering Weimar that Albert of Saxe-Coburg, a young prince raised in the spirit of Goethe's universal culture, set out in 1840 to marry the Queen of England and to become in consequence the last royal patron of Europe to exert a major and lasting effect upon international culture.

The Prince Consort invented and put in train the Great Exhibition of 1851, the first truly international exhibition. In a speech at the Mansion House in 1850 which was a manifesto for the coming exhibition, he said that nobody who had paid attention to the features of the era 'will doubt for a moment that we are living at a period of most wonderful transition, which tends rapidly to accomplish that great end, to which, indeed, all history points – *the realization of the unity of mankind*'. He thought that this unity was the result and product of national varieties and antagonistic qualities.

The distances which separated the different nations and parts of the globe are rapidly vanishing before the achievements of modern invention, and we can traverse them with incredible ease; the languages of all nations are known and their acquirement placed within the reach of everybody; thought is communicated with rapidity, and even by the power of lightning.[20]

What that gifted prince did was to provide for a new audience, the mass urban audience looking for advancement, education and instruction. He brought together all the achievements of the age, first in the Crystal Palace and then on a more permanent basis in the cluster of museums and colleges planned and instituted under his direction on the South Kensington sites. Though he was a product of the culture of Weimar, by widening the audience for the benefits of that culture, he was one of the leaders of change. It was also the effect of a series of inventions that changed that culture and its audience: steam-powered printing to be followed by electrically operated printing made possible the mass-circulation newspapers; the introduction of photography was followed by the moving picture and the art of the cinema.

The mass culture of early industrialized cities, the spectacles, circuses, melodramas, *cafés chantants* and music halls, with their participatory audiences, have all largely given way first to the cinema and then to television with their passive audiences. In the early cinema the discoveries of archaeology were rapidly taken up by commercial filmmakers so that a popular awareness of history, of a kind never known before, gave fresh opportunities for the influence of the Great Memory on current events. The high point of empires before the First World War sent filmmakers back to ancient Assyria and particularly ancient Rome for spectacles on a vast scale. The opportunities of spectacle in the cinema influenced the show parades of Fascists, Nazis and communists which were also recorded on film and shown to redound their political messages of power and invincibility to their followers and populations. Thus the cinema became a weapon of power politics, used by dictators for propaganda and also to establish them as ideals of humanity, as when actors resembling Hitler and Stalin appeared at the climax of films giving a general blessing to virtuous heroes and heroines. Again history was used constantly to establish a current political message, as in Eisenstein's *Alexander Nevsky* (1938) telling the story of the defeat of the Teutonic Knights, or in German films celebrating Frederick the Great.

In its commercial form the cinema brought about the rise of new kinds of heroes and heroines: the socially ambiguous actors and actresses of the past became the stars of the screen who were the objects of adulation and the setters of fashion on an international scale.

In its general effect the cinema has been superseded by television with its vast influence on power politics. Judged by the standards of the culture of Weimar, nearly everything television does that derives from the older culture, it weakens and trivializes: it loses the immediacy of the theatre and the concert hall, it makes opera ridiculous, and it is death to poetry because it imposes on the hearer's mind images less powerful than those he or she can evoke in his or her own imagination. It does best what no other form of communication has ever been able to do: it tells the weather of the world, not only in the physical sense but also metaphorically; politics, sport, social change, fashion, science and the state of the environment. It projects back to us the violence, the dreams, the vicarious ambitions and the involuntary thoughts of our own minds. It has become a new vehicle of the Great Memory not only because it is admirably suited to transmit the discoveries of archaeologists and of scientists investigating the past of the Earth but because in what is chosen for historical dramas or from the literature of the past there will always be significant clues to imminent changes in current society. Its power politically has been dramatically shown in the collapse of the communist states because none of those governments could hide from their citizens what was happening in their neighbouring states. Time and again, tyrannies have been powerless to ban the cameras, as in the case of the repression of the crowds in Tiananmen Square, Peking. As the witness of immediate history, television can have the effect that Schiller attributed to the theatre: it pierces us with a sense of our own humanity. It educates us about the animal and plant worlds and is arousing a fuller sense of the biosphere. On the other hand, television has increasingly fallen into the hands of the leaders of corporations and interests who are curiously anonymous and lack the sense of public and moral responsibility. They are interested chiefly in programmes that attract huge audiences and therefore advertising revenue. These people are the patrons who do not know how to be patrons and their ignorance creates a vacuum of taste that is dangerous for being open to sinister forces.

Earlier I said that science had not yet found its true purpose. It seems also that the means of mass communication which science has given us have not yet found their true purposes in any higher civilizing sense. We need to be ennobled in the spirit by what we watch and hear as our ancestors were ennobled by the art, literature and entertainment of their time. The desire to be ennobled must rise up within ourselves and perhaps, either in reaction against the passivity of the international audiences of television or even as a result of the concentration of millions of minds upon the same images and thoughts, a new sense of the world as a whole, and an understanding that humanity has eventually no path to follow but that of peace and toleration, will create a new audience that wants itself to create and to participate as once in Greece the chorus of the suffering god created the theatre or as in the rebuilding of Chartres the peasants and nobles yoked themselves to the carts bringing the stones and provisions for the southwest tower.

16

Patrons, impresarios and living inspirations

W hat we as part of the good audience or as cultivated spectators go
to hear or admire has been chosen for us by somebody else; that
somebody else is often not the composer or the artist but the patron or
the impresario who had an idea and commissioned it. Sometimes, as well,
the patron may be the living inspiration for the artist, as in the case of the
Emperor Akbar the Great (1556–1605) who in founding a new religion,
the Din-i-Ilahi, with strands drawn from all the great faiths known to him,
brought about the creation of new themes in art, architecture, poetry and
music celebrating the divine nature in himself. Such is the continuing power
of his personality that whether we stand in the courtyards of Fatehpur Sikri,
or gaze at a jade bowl carved for his use, or lift the tissues from a miniature
showing his portrait with a halo of light, we feel that he is the artist, not
the architect, the carver or the painter. Sometimes the patron may hope to
be that living inspiration, as in the case of Pope Julius II in his patronage
of Michelangelo and in his longing to found a dynasty for his family and a
lasting name for himself: but it is the statue of Moses on his tomb that is
remembered while he, the warrior pope, is recalled only as the incidental
cause of that masterpiece.

One of the most remarkable of all examples of the patrons who inspire
as well as commission is that of Diane de Poitiers, Duchess of Valentinois,
mistress to Henri II of France. The chance happening that she was christened
Diane permitted the numerous artists whom she patronized to play with all
the associations of the goddess Artemis/Diana after whom she was named:
goddess of the moon and of hunting, of the forests and of fountains, of
virgins and of chastity. So many contradictions were resolved in her that
she was like someone who in ordinary human terms ought never to have
been. A devoted wife who married her husband, Philip de Brézé, when she
was sixteen and he was fifty-five and who never ceased to mourn him after
his death; a passionate and irresistible mistress who was twenty years older
than her royal lover and who managed to guide him through his many other

affairs as well as making him look after his wife Catherine de' Medici; a devout and charitable Christian and the living symbol of the revival of the goddess religions of antiquity; a seemingly private housewife devoted to her embroidery and a subtle and powerful stateswoman consulted on all matters of policy great and small, whom no sensible ambassador ever neglected to cultivate, she was also possessed of the most exquisite taste and through her wealth and connections had the means of commissioning some of the greatest artists of her time, Benvenuto Cellini, Jean Goujon and Philibert Delorme among them, as well as being the patroness of Ronsard and other poets.

The power of her enigmatic personality to resolve opposites is still to be felt in her château of Anet in Normandy where the main entrance was surmounted by a famous bronze statue of Diana[1] and where the chimney stacks are carved as sarcophagi to commemorate her dead husband and where also the emblems of Henri II are constantly to be found. Her spirit especially fills the most beautiful remaining part of Anet, the chapel which Philibert Delorme designed for her between 1549 and 1552.[2] It is one of the finest examples I know of for producing the architectural effect of expansion of the mind to the universal. Formerly set within a wing of the château that is now destroyed, it seems a small construction from the outside with a dome fronted by two towers topped by tall pyramids; inside, however, the eye leaps up into the dome to see light pouring down from the lantern, round a swirling pattern of lozenge-shaped coffers, each containing emblems of fame or the winged heads of cherubs (figure 32). As the sun is thrown through the lantern on to one of these coffers, the gilded cherub's face seems irradiated with a heavenly smile and you see that the hair of the cherub is formed of leaves as though he were a celestial green boy of the garden of Heaven. As you look down you see that the swirling pattern of the dome is matched by the round marble inlay of the floor with the swirls marked clearly in black marble set between marble of other colours brought from the ruins of the villas of Roman emperors in Italy. The mirroring of the pattern between dome and floor enunciates the Hermetic doctrine that would have been familiar to patroness and artist: 'As above, so below.' Placed at the level of the drum from which the dome rises above the entrance is the gallery from which Diane de Poitiers would have heard Mass, in the sphere of the moon, at the lowest part of heaven.

A patroness of such a high order of taste and insight is a creative personality in her own right as much as or more than the artists who work for her and who come under her spell and are inspired by her. It is a special feature of French culture that there have been women such as Madame de Rambouillet, highly placed or in positions to have had a profound influence on civilizing movements that have passed far beyond the geographical bounds of France. One of the earliest is Agnes of Burgundy, wife of Guilhem III the Great, Count of Poitou and Duke of Aquitaine (993–1030). Under her influence a code of refined behaviour essential to the development of the art of the troubadours was made the rule of the court, which had excellent connections with the new humanism of the school of Chartres and which may also have acted as a filter for the transmission to Chartres of ideas from Muslim Spain. One of her descendants was Eleanor of Aquitaine, also famous for her court of troubadours.[3] We may also mention Blanche of Castile, who paid for the rose window of the genealogy of the Virgin in the north transept of Chartres; Madame de Maintenon with her patronage of Racine; and Madame de Pompadour and her encouragement of all the great painters of her time from Boucher to Chardin.

The patroness with the greatest influence is probably Agnes of Burgundy, but there is another whose influence on style and manners may be compared to her and to that of Diane de Poitiers and she is the Empress Joséphine. Her influence conquered lands even her husband could never subdue. As in the time of the introduction of Renaissance influences from Italy Diane de Poitiers was the vehicle for the Great Memory in recovering the lost treasures of antiquity, including the ideal of the nude, so Joséphine in her time was the vehicle for the recovery of Greek ideals of simplicity and purity of taste. She did not originate the new freedom in women's dress which resulted from the French Revolution but she gave her authority and her taste to the new style, as she did for every art and civilized craft, from painting to gardening, to which she gave her attention. Her gardeners and botanists introduced many plants and trees to France, among them eucalyptus, hibiscus, phlox, cacti, rhododendrons and dahlias; between 1804 and 1814 it is said that 184 new species flowered for the first time in Europe at Malmaison. She patronized the flower painter Pierre-Joseph Redouté and contributed generously to the publication of his *Liliaceae*. Like some gardeners, she came late to an appreciation of roses but nevertheless she acquired some two hundred varieties, on which Redouté was to draw for his most famous work. Though her remarkable collection of paintings was dispersed after her death, enough of the furnishings and decoration of Malmaison has been restored or returned to convey an idea of her taste. One of the most delightful surprises for the visitor coming there for the first time is to realize the subtlety and originality of her colour sense, shown in combinations of colours and textures that seem totally modern and original today.[4] She died in 1814 divorced from Napoleon and leaving debts that have scandalized later commentators, even though those debts were as nothing compared to what he spent on devastating Europe. Her actual legacy in terms of influence on modes, manners and taste is probably just as great as his and far more benign.

Hers too was the period when the French consolidated their supremacy in the arts of the kitchen. When Catherine de' Medici arrived in Paris to marry the future Henri II, she brought with her Florentine cooks who introduced to an amazed and gratified court new methods in the preparation of food and new standards of how the food should taste. The taste for such food spread to the nobility and the upper classes who could afford to keep chefs. At the Revolution large numbers of these highly trained chefs no longer had masters: in order to keep themselves they began to open restaurants where the middle classes flocked in order to enjoy these unexpected results of revolution and social turmoil. The spread of these tastes, allied to strong traditions of regional and peasant cooking, meant that the degradation in the standards and supply of food which had such a devastating effect upon the tastes of the English and upon many of their colonies brought about as an effect of the Industrial Revolution never substantially affected French tastes. As in Italy from which the great impulse came, in France there is a general agreement among all classes on what good food should be like. Recently my wife asked the lady at our hotel in Bourges if she could recommend a nearby restaurant. Certainly, said the lady, we would find it 'tout à fait correct', meaning that it would be up to the standards of any self-respecting French housewife. A restaurant that did not maintain such standards would soon be out of business. I give this as a parable that applies to civilization in general. It is the taste of the audience that decides the standards of art and, curiously enough, of science, as I hope to show.

Insight is essential to true patronage. The exercise of patronage is paralleled in creative experience by the stage of interpretation. Through the use of interpretation the artist knows what he should do with his inspiration: the patron similarly has an insight into how to make the best use of an artist's talent, or a scientist's discoveries. This kind of insight is of vital importance in furthering the creative impulse. In what follows I use the term 'patron' in a very wide sense, ranging from the disinterested help a friend may give in arranging a series of necessary introductions or suggesting themes or lines of investigation, to the religious and political aims of popes and monarchs. The term can therefore include many different motives but they often arise from need.

Think, for example, of the needs of a Norman-French bishop of Lincoln such as Remigius, who founded his see there in 1072 and whose cure of souls extended from the North Sea to the heart of England at Oxford. The majority of those souls spoke a variety of Old English or Norse dialects which he could not understand – and they would certainly not have understood him. They were also illiterate. Not only were they probably carrying on many pagan practices, but much of the Christianity they practised would, in his view, be vitiated by the corruption of the Anglo-Saxon Church he was expected to reform. To draw and attract these souls who could not read, he needed the help of architects and sculptors who would work to his bidding in order to make buildings so novel and awe-inspiring that ordinary men and women would be drawn into a new way of thinking and experiencing through enjoyment and wonder at what they saw. How far he succeeded in this would have depended on a particular combination of imagination and administrative and financial skills, together with the good fortune to possess wonder-working relics of saints of the Dark Ages. The possession of such relics was a great focus of local and regional pride and it was the desire to provide a worthy setting for such relics that brought in the funds for the buildings and the sculptures.

The bishop had notable models for patronage such as St Hugh, Abbot of Cluny, who reigned over the thousand dependencies of his abbey at its greatest period. The Cluniacs were using art and architecture to assert their authority over the pilgrim routes to Santiago de Compostela, to enforce a new code of peaceful conduct through their introduction of the Truce of God, and to spread the benefits of the Reform Movement in the Church. A little later we come across Abbot Suger of St-Denis, first patron of the Gothic style. Suger, who was not only abbot but twice regent of France and chief minister to two kings, had to combine at least two major motives in his patronage, one of them being the need to aggrandize the authority and prestige of the French royal house, then very circumscribed in its actual exercise of power, and the other being his desire to find expressions for his own highly developed aesthetic taste, inspired by the light symbolism of the writings of Dionysius the Areopagite. To him came a genius or geniuses with proposals of a new style and method of construction incorporating the pointed arch which would open out the area of the choir and the chancel of his abbey church to ever more light. (Curiously he never mentions the names of these artists in his account of the building of the church.) If he was lucky to find them, they were also lucky to find a patron so open-minded, so imaginative, and so well provided with the means of paying for their plans. It was his recognition of the possibilities in the new style that led in the hundred years following the completion of the choir of St-Denis in 1142 to its adoption far beyond the boundaries of the kingdom of France and to a transformation of architecture in western and central Europe.

Rivalry and emulation are also strong motivating forces in patronage as they are in the stimulation of creative endeavour. The Roman historian

Velleius Paterculus wondered why men of similar talents in the same field, such as the Greek tragedians or the Roman historians and orators, appear within a very short period, and then are followed by excellence in another field. He say: 'Genius is fostered by emulation, and it is now envy, now admiration, which enkindles imitation . . .'[5] He goes on to say that when we realize that we cannot surpass the achievements of others, we look for new fields in which to be eminent. He specially wonders at Athens; she surpassed all the other cities of Greece in masterpieces of eloquence: 'one would think that although the bodies of the Greek race were distributed among the other states, their intellects were confined within the walls of Athens alone.'[6] We may equally wonder at Florence as the city that produced Dante, Petrarch and Boccaccio, though in other ways she was comparatively late in competing with other cities in artistic and architectural terms. Here again we see the effects of rivalry. The cities of central and northern Italy, constantly at war with one another over trade, land and authority in the course of the high Middle Ages, were driven to outdo one another in the splendour and height of their public buildings, cathedrals, churches and hospitals, and the pleasure we now take in those cities is owed in great part to those bitter and ancient rivalries.

The many states and cities of Germany up to the unification under Bismarck practised a similar rivalry whether they were competing for kapellmeisters or founding universities to which they tried to entice the most distinguished scholars and teachers. Following the Humboldt reforms of 1806–13, the numbers of universities increased and with them the science laboratories, such as Justus von Liebig's at Giessen, which were to account for the pre-eminence of German scientists in the creation of modern chemistry and physics into the nineteenth and twentieth centuries.

Probably one of the strongest historical forces behind patronage is when the founder of a new dynasty needs to win over the loyalty of subjects and to establish an image of bounty and invincibility. The image nearly always depends upon the revival of traditions and ideas from the past; in other words, on the Great Memory, as we have already seen in relation to the Emperor Augustus in his establishment of the state religion of Rome and to Napoleon in his appeal to the Merovingian, Carolingian and Byzantine past. Here are two further examples from the thirteenth century, one from Byzantium and one from China.

After the sack of Byzantium in the Fourth Crusade of 1204, the city was ruled for over fifty years by leaders known to history as the Latin emperors. When the last Latin emperor was driven out and a Greek dynasty was established, the restored Greek emperors deliberately cultivated the ancient traditions of the sacred dances of the court which had been forgotten since the sack of the city during the Fourth Crusade, while at the same time stimulating the rebirth of the arts of Byzantium to the extent that they were soon influencing Italian artists such as Cimabue and Giotto.

At the other end of the world, Khubilai Khan (1214–94) had, by overcoming the Southern Sung Empire, finally subdued the Chinese, who were the most populous and educated nation on Earth, and he soon discovered that he had to take the place of the emperor he had conquered. The wandering Mongol had to appear to be the settled Son of Heaven. He responded by reviving ancient Confucian rites, long forgotten under the Sung, which involved public displays and ceremonials in front of vast crowds, which, in turn, required massive programmes of building, as in Peking, which he made his capital. The son of a Nestorian Christian mother, the cultivated Sorghaghtani Beki who has been compared to Eleanor of Aquitaine, he himself followed the shamanistic rituals of the Mongols while cultivating excellent relations with the Confucians, the Taoists and the Buddhists, among whom his wife was a devout follower. There came about under the Yuan dynasty, which he founded, an extraordinary new flowering of popular culture in the theatre and in literature, as well as introductions in art and ceramics and in the sciences and engineering, stimulated by the arrival of foreign influences from as far away as Venice and the Persian Gulf. The Chinese pre-eminence in making blue and white porcelain dates from this period because it was from the trading links with the Persian Gulf set up by Khubilai Khan that they learned the technique of using cobalt in their glazes. As the ruler of the largest empire on land ever known, he could not help bringing to his Chinese subjects, generally impervious to outside ideas because with much justification they were convinced of the superiority of their own civilization, a host of new thoughts and techniques, an interchange he actively supported.[7]

We see similar features in the courts of seventeenth-century Europe: Charles I emphasizing the doctrine of the divine right of kings by taking part in the climax of masques in the Banqueting Hall designed by Inigo Jones and with its ceiling painted by Rubens; or the young Louis XIV, apparelled as the sun god and dancing at the centre of the ballets performed at his court, to impress on the nobles who watched or took part with him that his rule was absolute and unquestioned. Charles I when Prince of Wales had spent a few weeks at the court of Spain, in a vain attempt to gain the hand of a Spanish princess: though he failed in his wooing, he saw the Spanish royal collection of paintings and fell in love with art; he also saw the newly built Plaza Mayor in Madrid. It only needed those few weeks of dazzling and novel impressions on his young eyes to enrapture him with art. When king, he was to form the greatest collection of works of art of his time and he laid out Covent Garden on the model of the Plaza Mayor.

The follies and caprices of extravagant monarchs and their queens and mistresses are often far better bequests to the future than the prudence of the wise. Shah Jehan aroused such resentment at the funds he was spending on the Taj Mahal, the mausoleum of his beloved wife Mumtaz Mahal, and that he was intending to spend on his own mausoleum, a black construction to contrast with the whiteness of the Taj Mahal facing it across the Yamuna River, that his son Aurangzeb deposed and imprisoned him. Shah Jehan's name is still blessed by every visitor to the Taj Mahal – and by all Indian tourist agencies – whereas Aurangzeb is remembered for the intolerance of his religious policies and the destruction of thousands of Hindu and Jain temples, in the course of which many masterpieces disappeared. He left a legacy of bitterness that has erupted in the recent destruction of the mosque at Ayodhya. What is produced by the artist for the private and selfish delectation of patrons becomes in later generations a common property of the cultural world. Titian produced the greatest series of secular paintings of his life when he was commissioned by Philip II of Spain to paint the works known together as the *Poesie*. They were intended to pander to the King's voyeuristic tastes and were considered so bold and voluptuous that they were kept hidden from the world in Philip's private apartments. They include such famous works as the *Diana and Actaeon* and *Diana and Callisto* in Edinburgh and *The Rape of Europa* in the Isabella Stewart Gardner Museum in Boston, readily on view to any member of the visiting public and known throughout the world in countless reproductions. Voluptuous they may seem today but in a wider sense than sexual titillation: the drama and psychological depth of these paintings, their colour, their original and brilliant compositions create a presence as works of art that erase the anecdote of how they came to be commissioned. When George IV died, *The Times*, though printed with a black border to mark the event, published an editorial which, without reserve, condemned the weakness, immorality and extravagance of the deceased monarch. Yet if London is still, for a great part, a beautiful city, that is owed to the taste as well as the extravagance of George IV.

There is another kind of patronage which does not need the resources of popes and emperors but consists of the imagination to see what talents exist in potential and what can be done to make them flower. Thus, according to Vasari, Cimabue came across the shepherd boy Giotto drawing on a stone and was so impressed by his talent that he took him into his studio.[8] Lorenzo de' Medici recognized the talent and character of the fifteen-year-old Michelangelo and treated him as one of his own sons until his death in 1492.[9] One of the most remarkable acts of patronage is that of the polymath Giangiorgio Trissino (1478–1550), dramatist, author of an epic on the Goths in Italy, a theorist of the Italian language who first saw the importance of Dante's forgotten work *De vulgare eloquentia*, and an architect. On 19 February 1534 he met a thirty-year-old stone mason named Andrea di Piero who impressed him with his ideas and designs; he turned him into the architect known as Palladio (after Pallas Athena) by educating him and taking him to Rome and by giving him his first commission. Without Trissino's insight we would never have had the series of public and private palaces and the Teatro Olimpico in Vicenza, the villas of the Veneto and two of the noblest churches in Venice, and what followed from those buildings over the centuries in other European countries and the New World, the spread of the Palladian style which even now is undergoing a new phase in its influence.

What Trissino possessed in his own strong creative urge and his originality of mind was, probably, the key to recognizing the potential gifts of the young Palladio; what he also probably recognized in him was a remarkable character. For what we love most in Palladio's work is not so much the extraordinary number of innovations he made in the uses to which he put the stylistic elements of inherited classical architecture and the new combinations of arch, column and pediment he invented as the sense of a warm and benevolent humanity that possesses us as we look at and enter one of his buildings. It was said of him that in giving the members of his workshop their tasks he was also able to pass on to them a sense of joy in their work. His buildings have a similar effect: Goethe wrote of his genius, his mastery, his richness, versatility and grace.[10] Palladio has the ability to make us feel glad to be human beings, glad to be at ease with our own natures whether we are looking at the barns and stables of one of his villas and slowly pacing the colonnades and great rooms of the main houses or contemplating the happy mysteries of the nave of San Giorgio and the crossing of Il Redentore. Like all great architects he constantly surprises us but unlike many others he surprises us with happiness: this was probably his intention, as we see when we read his inscription in the Teatro Olimpico where he says that the purpose of the building is to raise us to the bliss of Heaven. On being conducted through his rooms in the Palazzo Thieme in Vicenza I nearly shouted with surprise as the double doors were opened and there, opposite the doors, was carved the face of a Green Man with his wide yawning mouth forming the chimneypiece. Through his writings and engravings, Palladio managed to transmit his feeling of humanity to the best of his later followers, such as Lord Burlington, Colen Campbell and William Kent in Britain and Thomas Jefferson at Monticello in Virginia.

Without Trissino's discovery of Palladio, none of this great humanizing influence could have been given to the world.

A comparable story in science is that of the relationship between Sir Humphry Davy and Michael Faraday. Faraday's fate could well have been that of Thomas Hardy's Jude the Obscure. Born into a minor dissenting sect, apprenticed in adolescence to a bookbinder, poor and with little formal education and yet with a burning desire to pursue a life of discovery in science, at the age of nineteen he wrote for help to Sir Joseph Banks, the botanist and explorer who was then president of the Royal Society. Banks did not reply. A friend had given Faraday tickets to a series of lectures given by Humphry Davy at the Royal Institution. Faraday took notes of the lectures, bound his notes beautifully and sent them to Davy, who was so impressed by his understanding that he took him into the Royal Institution as his assistant and set him on the way to his great career, in which eventually he succeeded Davy as director of the Institution. Though Davy has been blamed for on occasion treating Faraday as a servant, he had the imagination to see what could be made of this young man, and, probably, a sympathy for someone of great intelligence in his circumstances, because he, Davy, had been born in Cornwall in a humble family with no chance of a university education and owed his own advancement to the successive patronage of a Cornish squire, Dr William Beddoes in Bristol, and then the internationally famous Count Benjamin Thomson, the founder of the Royal Institution, who himself had been rescued from destitution as a young American loyalist in exile by Lord George Germaine. The tradition continued at the Royal Institution where Faraday was succeeded as director by John Tyndall, who came from a poor peasant background in Ireland and had been helped in similar ways to realize his talents.[11]

Many of the patrons I have been discussing have fulfilled their role of patronage either because it was their hereditary duty or their political need to do so or because their own training and genius enabled them to recognize genius in others. In neither of these cases has patronage been the sole or chief employment of the patron: it has been incidental to their other occupations. There is a patron of another kind, whose whole being is devoted to vicarious creation through the talents of others: the great type of this patron for our century is Sergei Diaghilev.

My mother, who was a pupil of Enrico Cecchetti (1850–1928), the maître de ballet of the Imperial Ballet in St Petersburg, has described to me the impression Diaghilev would make when he came to watch Cecchetti's classes. 'We all knew,' she said, 'that he could do none of the things we could do but the force of his personality filled the room and affected everyone there. What you were aware of most of all in his presence was his taste.

He had such wonderful taste.' His taste was founded on an encyclopaedic knowledge of art, history and music; his personality, jealous, possessive, dominating, drew around him a host of talented people, any one of whom would probably have made their mark on their own in other circumstances but who, under his rule, together formed a revolutionary artistic force that took western Europe and the New World by storm. He was bitterly ashamed of the fact that his family fortune came from his grandfather's vodka distillery and he was driven to establish his place among the upper classes of Europe through his role as an impresario.[12] First through his journal *Mir Isskustva* (The world of art), he practised his skills in bringing artists, thinkers and poets together: then from the art exhibitions sponsored by his journal he moved into the productions of opera and ballet for which he became famous. His nose for talent led him to seek out the most gifted dancers, artists and composers whom he compelled, under the force of his personality and the brilliance of the ideas he suggested to them, to associate themselves with his productions. The artists he gathered around him, however cantankerous, vain and difficult they might have been as individuals, became for him the paints upon his palette. In promoting works such as *The Rite of Spring* he was releasing to a wider world the images and wild new emotions first conjured up by the Russian Symbolist poets and their contemporary musicians. In that work, with its portrayal of an ancient society which has to choose and sacrifice a virgin from their number in order to secure the fertility of their lands and the survival of the tribe, together with Stravinsky and Nicholas Roerich, the designer, he was being a vehicle of the Great Memory which channelled through to them by the strange pathways of scholarship and ethnography the forgotten but still vital energies of the past and made through them a spectacle so savage, vibrant and shocking that its first production in Paris in 1913 caused a riot between its admirers and its opponents in the Théâtre des Champs-Elysées so loud that at times the dancers could not hear the orchestra.

Dance has a special relationship with historical and racial memory. Not only does it present archetypal forces and symbols in ways that seem to awaken responses in the bloodstream and heartbeat of its audience but it also preserves the memory of how people lived and moved and made their gestures in the past – from the court dances of Thailand and Indonesia to the celebration of the sun in the Highland eightsome reel, from the pre-Buddhist religions of Tibet in the monastery dances to the clog-dancers of Lancashire expressing with their feet the resentments and passions the workers of the cotton mills were forbidden to utter in other ways. The photograph of Nijinsky in character as Petrushka, the puppet who comes to life and is murdered, gives a flavour of the accumulated agonies of the peasants of the Slav regions (figure 33). What Diaghilev brought about was, through the unlikely medium of classical ballet, founded as it is on traditions of the court, an explosion of violent and unbridled emotions, all the more glamorous because of the youth, beauty and breathtaking skill of his dancers, that has left a comet trail of influences upon the world of art. Before his time, ballet had become an appendage of opera or the theatre except in the two redoubts of St Petersburg and Copenhagen: after his time it became a matter of prestige that the major capitals of Europe and the great cities of the USA should possess their own ballet companies.

Diaghilev's career as an impresario setting free new sensations and emotions through physical movement has its counterpart in the extraordinary story of Baron Pierre de Coubertin, the *rénovateur* of the Olympic Games. It provides one of the clearest illustrations of the three parts of the hypothesis of the Great Memory, as will appear from what follows.

Pierre de Coubertin (1863–1937) came from a background of legitimist politics and traditions. His father was a painter of historical subjects, largely drawn from the history of the Church and the monarchy in France. De Coubertin rebelled against the repression of energy and the bitter nostalgia of the legitimists as he also rebelled against his Jesuit teachers who feared the development of individuality and physical maturity in their pupils and therefore allowed them only the most childish games. Going the opposite way from Diaghilev, he transferred his allegiance to France and to the young Third Republic. It is thought that he was still inspired by the ideals of his aristocratic background, especially those of *prouesse*, the performance of unique moral deeds of honour and of *patronage*, the provision of opportunities for *prouesse*, when he discovered his vocation as an inspirer and founder in the world of sport.[13] Though he loved sport, he was not built for success in most of the sports then practised: he was too small; the only things about him that were big were his eyes and his moustaches. Here again there is a resemblance between him and Diaghilev: what they could not do themselves, they devoted all their efforts to helping others to do.

His inspirations came to him in two visions. The first of these was at the tomb of Thomas Arnold in Rugby School chapel. Like many of his contemporaries in France, de Coubertin was drawn to the English ideal of the gentleman who, unlike the legitimists, would be actively involved in public affairs. This led naturally to an admiration for the English public-school system. De Coubertin visited many of the public schools but it was Rugby and the influence of Dr Arnold, already a presence in his life through his early reading of *Tom Brown's Schooldays*, that first crystallized his feelings and gave him his direction. Standing before the tomb in the chapel in 1886 – he was only twenty-three – he determined to bring to France *la pédagogie sportive*, or athletic education based on the ideals of muscular Christianity.[14] As a newly converted Republican, de Coubertin intended, through the institution of school sports, student self-government and athletic associations for all levels of society, to provide the means of France's full recovery from the defeats of 1871 and to set in train the creation of a democratic society. He was to travel widely, especially in the United States, studying the various forms of sport and gymnastics then practised and advocated. He had been impressed by various athletics meetings he had attended in England but it was probably the association of athletic games with the 1889 Paris Exhibition with its celebrations of the 1789 Revolution, its procession and rituals around the specially built Eiffel Tower, which prepared him for his second vision. Among the exhibits in the Palais des Beaux Arts was a reconstruction of the buildings of ancient Olympia based on the recent work of German archaeologists.

The Olympic Games had, of course, never been forgotten. There had been several festivals and meetings recalling them in name and spirit before Pierre de Coubertin, such as *les jeux olympiques* held on the Champs de Mars in Paris during the Directoire and the Olympic Games of Much Wenlock in Shropshire. None, apart from Much Wenlock, lasted for any time and none attracted international attention in the way that de Coubertin was to do in his work of re-establishing the games.

The Olympic Games were from their beginnings associated with peace, with the setting of standards, moral as well as physical, and with chronology. Their founding, according to tradition in 776 BC, set the chronology of the ancient world. They were held every four years under a sacred truce to coincide with the Festival of Zeus. At first only men and boys whose mother tongue was Greek were allowed to participate. Barbarians were allowed to watch but no married women and no slaves could be spectators. After the Roman conquest of Greece, Romans were permitted to take part. For a thousand years the Games were held until their suppression by Theodosius the Great in AD 393 in the decree that closed the oracles as well as the games of the ancient world.

Germany had uncovered what remained of Olympia: de Coubertin wondered why it should not be France that rebuilt its splendours. From that he said it was a short step 'to the less dazzling but more practical and fruitful project of reviving the Games, particularly since the hour had struck when international sport seemed destined once again to play its part in the world'.[15] He voiced an idea whose time had come and which was to lead to the restoration of the Olympic Games after an interval of 1,500 years, not at Olympia, but at Athens in 1896. De Coubertin visited the site of Olympia only after he had launched the idea of the restoration at a conference in Paris. In November 1892 he found himself in Olympia and there he had another vision; this time it was a vision comparable to the stage of interpretation of which we have written earlier because he saw the hugeness of the task he had landed himself with and the hazards that lay before him. This task he was to fulfil, despite all the attempts of politicians and persons eminent in sporting bodies to exclude him and to seize for themselves the glory, and despite the setbacks and tragedies of his personal life.

International travel, first steam-powered and then oil-fuelled, made international sport possible but it was the memory of the first series of Olympic Games, preserved by the odes of Pindar and the historical record of their importance in binding together the loose political system of the Hellenic world, that particularly provided the focus and decided the site of their revival. It is difficult for us now to conceive the immensity of the tasks that de Coubertin and his colleagues had to master: most of the events had no internationally agreed distances or standards. He himself invented the pentathlon and, with his friend Bréal, the marathon, a race unknown, of course, to the ancient Greeks and based on the distance he calculated between the site of the victory over the Persians at Marathon and Athens. Everything we now speak of as being to Olympic standards either in performance or in the provision of sporting facilities is the result of his drive and energy.

I said that his revival of the Olympic Games illustrated all three parts of the hypothesis of the Great Memory. The first illustration is obvious: something is revived from the past and that is the re-establishment of the Games. The next illustrates the ideals of humanity that guide the energies, physical and spiritual, that are expressed through the Games. In addition to reviving the practice of the Games, de Coubertin revived the ideals behind the Games, the ideals that had been celebrated directly or by implication by Pindar with the messages that by superlative effort and achievement an athlete would bring glory to his family and city and furthermore would enter the world of myth and the gods. From this ideal come the modern ideals of the perfect sportsman and the perfect sportswoman. This last was to be another effect of de Coubertin's responsiveness to the modern age: that women should be welcomed as competitors where in ancient times they had not even been allowed to watch. These ideas have set the standards for all other kinds of international sport and they are probably the closest humanity has reached in devising standards of behaviour and achievement that are acceptable in most societies around the world today.

The third illustration concerns the effects of a recovery from the past and the uses to which those effects are put. Like the International Red

Cross, the Olympic Games have kept their worldwide reputation, despite commercial and political pressures. No one government or dictator has succeeded in destroying or hijacking its aims. Hitler gained much useful propaganda from the 1936 Berlin Games: by the brilliance of the displays and the picture of a disciplined nation Germany was shown to have recovered entirely from the defeat of the First World War. On the other hand, Hitler's theory of Aryan racial superiority was shattered by the victories of one black American, Jesse Owens, who won three gold medals. It is unthinkable now that any nation or group should be excluded on racial grounds from the Olympic Games. Neither the Soviet Union, condemned for the invasion of Afghanistan, nor the United States, which led the boycotting of the 1980 Olympic Games, gained in prestige, either as host or absent guest. Every drug-taking athlete, once exposed, brings disgrace on his country as much as on himself: here we see interesting implications for the future development of the scientific ideal of man. This new ideal will be intimately linked to ideas of fairness, of conceptions of how far it is right to use the discoveries of science to improve on genetic endowments and acquired skills, and of how much it should be the pure mind and heart as well as the untampered-with body that enters the tunnel of the contestants and is tested before the gaze of thousands.

The reason for the comparative freedom of the Olympic Games from corruption and decline is owed in the first place to Pierre de Coubertin's character, to the purity and selflessness of his motives and to his ability to communicate his ideals with simplicity and memorable ritual. The ceremonies associated with the Games are also largely his creation, founded on the rituals at the opening of the 1889 Paris Exhibition. In his gift to the future he fulfilled, in ways that would have appalled his family, the urge for himself and others to perform deeds of *prouesse*: in re-establishing the Games he also fulfilled the duty of *patronage*, the provision of opportunities for others to participate by action or as spectators.

There is still something from the ancient Olympics that remains to be restored, an aim in which de Coubertin failed. This is in the competitions in music and poetry that were part of the original Olympic Games. These did take place in the earlier revivals but have since been dropped. I have elsewhere mentioned the importance of imagining what the lost music of Greece sounded like in the development of opera and other forms of western music. In 1893 the French school working in Delphi had discovered bronze tablets inscribed with the Delphic 'Hymn to Apollo' and with its musical notation. Gabriel Fauré wrote a choral accompaniment to the melody and it was performed at the congress held in Paris in 1894 which resolved to restore the Olympic Games. De Coubertin thought that this performance ensured the agreement of all concerned: 'The two thousand persons present listened in a religious silence to the divine melody risen from the dead to salute the Olympic renaissance across the darkness of the ages . . . Henceforth I knew, consciously or not, that no one would vote against the restoration of the Olympic Games.'[16]

The lack stems from a lack in our sense of wholeness of ourselves – one that may eventually be filled by the hugeness of the force of attention that is concentrated upon the Games. The crowds of Athens at the 1896 revival of the Games amounted to tens of thousands, as had their predecessors in ancient times. The audiences for the Olympic Games now amount to millions, thanks to television, and every four years the world is united in a vicarious life of effort and achievement and in admiration, which transcends national loyalties, of the beauty, grace, power and skill of men and women stretched to their utmost endeavours.

17

Love and the redemptions of space, time and matter

A wren hops in and out of the box trees on top of a low wall, stabbing at grubs or tiny insects on the bricks or in the soil of the bed the wall retains. It is unusual for wrens to allow themselves to be seen for so long, given the grumpy and suspicious nature of their kind. I seize the opportunity to watch for as long as possible. Apart from the sheer pleasure aroused by the neatness of his plumage and the brilliant life in his eyes, I am struck most of all by the quality of his attention. He is alternating his attention between two needs: one the need to provide himself with food, the other to preserve himself from attack and capture. It is my interpretation to divide the process into two when they are probably two aspects of one function. Next I think of what that attention is devoted to on a wider scale and I see that function as being the wren *making himself*. The attention of the wren makes himself and his progeny according to the ideal and the interpretation of his species. His keen eye for the waiting food and the hidden predator helps him to make the perfect life within the terms and code of his species. By making himself I mean the sustenance and the grooming that goes to make every feather perfect, every muscle trim and the nictitating membranes, flashing up and down over those brilliant eyes, efficient in their work of unceasing lubrication. I mean the urge for the cock wren to seek out a hen and to state through feathers, posture and song 'I am beautiful: love me' and for her to choose among the available males the one privileged to fertilize her eggs; I also mean the savouring of the pure emotion that probably signifies his wrenhood to the wren, his indomitable pride in being himself which is the ruling force behind his unwavering attention to his task of maintenance and survival.

This emotion is what earlier philosophers would have called the signature of the wren, the impress of the universal upon its individuality. In such instances we can glimpse the creative force of the Green Man as the imperative to make oneself. While formulating these thoughts I remembered the naturalist Charles S. Bayne, who, roused by the realization that many birds produce eggs that are beautifully coloured and decorated in ways and to an extent that can have no selective advantage, dared to suggest that the colouring of bird's eggs in its origins had nothing to do with utility. 'It is primarily a matter of temperament just as is the painting of pictures.'[1] All eggs when formed are white and the colours are washed on them in the oviduct. 'The bird paints her egg with her oviduct as the artist paints his canvas with his hands.' Where the cock bird in many species is permitted to make itself in a display of resplendent plumage, the hen often subdued in her own colouring can devote her artistic impulses to the eggshells of her progeny. A cuckoo lays her eggs in the nests of the species that reared her and there are many strains of cuckoo, each parasitic on a particular species. In time each of these strains tends to lay eggs that imitate more or less closely the colouring of its victim's eggs – but not all strains of cuckoo do this. The cuckoo that lays in a hedge-sparrow's nest makes no attempt to copy the hedge-sparrow egg whereas the eggs of the pied wagtail are always imitated. After stating that he thought individual birds and strains were more gifted than others, as in the case of human talents, Bayne summed up his thoughts thus:

The works of man are very wonderful, but the human hand which accomplishes them is only an organ. What can be accomplished with one organ can be done also with others. Man makes nets with his hands, the spider makes nets with her spinnerets which are not hands, and the caterpillar makes nets with its mouth. Similarly man produces beautiful colour schemes with his hand, using pigment derived from the earth; the bird produces equally perfect and elaborate colour schemes through the medium of the skin which is another organ, and also uses pigment derived from the earth and other more ingenious methods of colour production. The oviduct is another organ and with it the bird is able to enamel eggshells with beautiful pigments which are also derived from the earth. The essential difference between the artist's and the bird's painting is that the one is conscious and the other unconscious.[2]

Behind the conscious art of the artist and the unconscious art of the bird is the same creative energy directed by the imperative to make themselves. In the sense that I am using the phrase here, every creature that feeds, and that has its own physical boundaries and immune system, 'makes itself' and constantly 'makes itself' throughout its existence, whether the creature is the most primitive coral or one of a horde of the destitute picking over the huge rubbish dumps of Mexico City or a Cambridge mathematician coming from dinner in hall to look out over the Backs and seeing nothing but the symbols in his head. For most human beings their chief creative endeavour in making themselves and their children is the plain business of providing and surviving with the palliation of seasonal festivals and the satisfaction of carrying out crafts and tasks well. However difficult their circumstances, they are true to this first imperative of the creative urge: to make oneself so that one may be able to make the other.

Wordsworth said of the development of his infant soul that it was 'fostered alike by beauty and by fear'.[3] Schiller wrote that it is through beauty that we arrive at freedom.[4] Both fear and beauty intensify our awareness and our capacity for survival through attention. What most intensifies attention, beyond fear and beauty, is love. It is love that accounts for the similar origin of the creativity of human beings and of other creatures as it does for the drive or oestrus to 'make ourselves'. We attend to what we love as the wren attends to his own safety and his pride in his beauty for the overmastering love of his hen and their brood. Among our chief symbols of the relationship between creativity and love are the Green Man and Nature as the Goddess.

The Green Man gives out the works of Nature and the grass and plants of the Earth and swallows them up again in a ceaseless cycle of birth and death. Yet he, as he includes the cycle, is in his essence outside it, observing, creating and, above all, loving. The cycle of creativity, in each of its stages, creator, patron or performer, and spectator is equally one of reception and transmission, contrarieties that are part of the necessary whole. The Green Man as the lover of the Goddess signifies that the universe is the creation of love, that its laws are the forms of love, that the works of nature and the vicissitudes of history are the drama made by love, and that this love, immanent and perpetually existent in us as human beings, is the ground of our consciousness and the force driving us to make and remake ourselves. As creation in the universe results from an act of love to be regarded with wonder and affection, so creation by human beings should also be an act of love and should arouse the response of love. That experience of unconditional love in which knowledge is enlarged into a universal embrace is what completes the cycle of creativity, bringing about the state in which the glory of the creator's inspiration, the imaginative generosity of the patron, the interpretative gifts of the performer and the open-heartedness of the spectators or audience all meet. As an experience it brings about the redemption of space, the area through which we have the choice to radiate joy or misery, the continuum necessary for creative manifestation.

Love awakens attention and the quality of attention determines experience and the capacity for later recall in transmitting the essence of that experience in language, tones, colours, lines or symbols. Talent, training, skills inborn or acquired are all subsidiary to the capacity for experience, because that is what supplies the subject matter or the image which has to be expressed. There are, of course, many examples of talent being exercised without that experience and using invented experience but, in general, though they may dazzle and impress for a time, their essential emptiness is revealed to later and colder eyes free of the fashion in which they flourished.

As an example of what I mean by depth of experience I take the oil and watercolour paintings of Turner. His career was prepared for by a tradition arising from the influence of Claude, the two Poussins and Dutch landscape artists such as the Ruysdaels upon eighteenth-century English taste and on the artists patronized by the nobility and middle classes. Of all his great predecessors, none had ever seen landscape in the grip of weather or seas in motion as wholly and as fully as he did. Where they saw one mountain, he saw ranges of mountains, where they saw a sea, he saw oceans, where they saw the play of light, he saw the sun. What we experience when we allow ourselves to be absorbed into one of his great landscapes is not simply how a particular valley or mountain seemed on a day in the early 1800s, but the being of an individual we know as Joseph Mallord William Turner, his memories, accumulated thoughts and emotions, together with the wider feeling for nature that yawned open for humanity in the earthquake of Romanticism. In the deepest sense his was a Gothic soul: not only did he paint and record the masterpieces of Gothic architecture throughout Europe but there was reborn in him the hugeness of vision and the feeling for the accurate portrayal of natural forms that was one of the gifts of Gothic civilization. Another aspect of his art, which has been little commented upon, is how he could portray crowds of people as part of the elemental forces of nature, as in the crowds of Venice which seem like spirit vapours of the Adriatic or – the summation of this achievement – the sweeping clouds of souls in his last paintings. He brought a new experience of nature and of humanity to his contemporaries and future generations – an experience owed in part to his physique, his exceptional wide-angled vision and his capacity for enduring any discomfort or pain in the course of travelling, even, so it is said, to the point of having himself lashed to a mast so that he could observe the progress of a storm. He was the artistic counterpart to his contemporary Beethoven in his command of the Dionysiac forces of nature with the Apollonian calm and resignation of his dawn and evening landscapes and his pastoral evocations.

In the room devoted to Turner's paintings at Petworth House, Sussex, we can enjoy the results of a particularly fruitful example of friendship and patronage in the works painted for Lord Egremont, especially in the experience of looking out at the park and the lake and then at Turner's paintings of the same scene. As we turn from paintings to the view and back again, it is as though we are looking inwards into ourselves and then outwards into the world. In the later paintings of Petworth and other houses, especially the interiors, and in the late sequences of paintings of Venice, it is as though Turner had at times reached a stage of experience in which his soul was dissolved into the colours and impressions of what lay before him. The city, the lagoon, the prow of a gondola, the blazing reflections, the way a woman turns as she rises from a piano or the hanging of folds of velvet beyond an arch, all these as themes or subjects in the paintings bestow a special intensity of experience on the spectator: the paintings are of states of consciousness, of moments of absorption and unity, when the division of inner and outer is abolished, and the light of the world is one with the light of the mind. It is as though he is telling us: 'This is what my true nature is and in this dissolution of dream and waking, of inner and outer, is where you too will find the truth of your existence.' Just as we can hear certain late works of Beethoven, the last quartets and piano sonatas or the *Diabelli Variations* and we can say to ourselves: 'There is no music more *modern* than this', so Turner in his late works evokes a similar response. For all the theories and schools that have succeeded him, it is still Turner, through his depth of experience, who strikes me as, inexpugnably, the most modern.

It is strange, the force with which a long-dead artist can speak to us when the work of many of his contemporaries, for all their charm or talent, tell us only of the fashions of their time. We ascribe that force to originality, genius, exceptional gifts, but all those qualities derive from profundity of experience. It is also strange that often that profundity of experience is apparent in the earliest works of a creator – the experience and authority of the sixteen-year-old Rimbaud writing *Le Bâteau Ivre* or the delight and intensity of Juan Crisóstomo Arriaga in the three quartets written before his death at nineteen in 1826.

Whatever the length of life of the creator, there is a constant in his existence, the witness of his experience and the transmitter of what he has made of that experience: this is his individuality, his sense of I; the Turner who stood before the Reichenbach Falls and saw them as no one had ever seen them before and then painted their glory and their power; the Rimbaud whose eyes had never looked on the sea and whose only sources for the kaleidoscopic alternations of the imagery in the poem were the adventure stories of Jules Verne, Edgar Allan Poe and other writers, who could enter into the Tohu Bohu, the disintegration of the ego into a greater oceanic self, and was capable of expressing that experience in Alexandrine lines that hold and contain the willed chaos of his emotions; the Arriaga who had a talent for experiencing joy and who heard the quartet playing in his mind and could translate the experience into written notes.

When we speak of inspiration as the moment of knowing, as the moment when the scientist or the poet says: 'I know what I have to prove' or 'I know what I have to write', it is a special form of self-consciousness that they experience, a freeing of the mind so that they may continue to make themselves. The same freedom is what we as members of an audience require as a result of our appreciation and attention: that, for each one of us, our sense of ourselves should be exalted and expanded. We want, as part of the audience at an exceptional performance of an exceptional work, to be so changed by the experience that it is as though the creative wind of the Spirit is blowing through us.

One of the traditions that knows most about the importance of the good audience is that of the Sufis, who call the practice of attention *samai*. Al Ghazzali (1058–1111) says this of listeners whose hearts are consumed in the fire of God's love:

> If a form presents itself to their sight, their insight passes it to Him that formed it and if a melody strikes upon their ears, their secret thoughts pass hastily to the Beloved; and if there comes to them a voice disturbing or disquieting or moving or making to sorrow or making joyous or making to long or stirring up, that they are disturbed is only unto Him, and that they are moved is only by Him and that they are disquieted is only on account of Him; their sorrow is only in Him and their longing is only unto that which is within Him, and their being aroused is only for Him, and their coming and going is only around Him.[5]

The experience of conscious love is the highest to which an individual can aspire and for that to come to him he needs the company of others, physically or mentally present, and an object of that love. 'Open your arms if you desire an embrace,' says another Sufi, Jalalú'ddin Rúmí Mevlana, and again he says: 'Make yourself like to the community, that you may feel spiritual joy.'[6] I see one aspect of the last statement in the following way. When we join an audience giving attention to a lecture or a performance, we enter a different dimension of experience: we give to the speaker or the players through the quality of our attention just as we give to our fellow members of the audience and receive from them also by the same quality of attention. As attention sharpens and deepens, so the consciousness of the individuals changes and with that change the sense of time alters. It is as though we are no longer listening solely for our own enjoyment but we do so on behalf of everyone there to the extent that the supreme intellectual or aesthetic experience only comes about because of this selfless listening. There is a further dimension of experience, again only possible in the state of attention present in an audience wholly concentrated, and that is when the ideas being discussed are so immense in their cosmological and evolutionary implications or when the emotions expressed in the music are so universal, that the mutual activities of speaker and audience or players and audience seem subsumed into a state of prayer.

This last dimension of experience returns us to another idea, touched on in Chapter 15, which is that the true audience of our creative endeavours is not so much mortal human beings but rather God and His angels or the gods and goddesses honoured or portrayed in art. Rilke was reviving this idea when he wrote of the wonder that might be aroused in angels by showing them the simplest of human artefacts. He says that we should not boast of or praise abstract or unsayable things to the Angel but 'Praise *this* world to the Angel'.[7] We find such an attitude in the poems of Kabir (c. 1440–1518), a saint to both Muslims and Hindus, who identified himself with all beggars and outcasts but made all his verse a form of conversation with God, or the medieval writers of ballades who always addressed the poems in the envoi to the mysterious recipient of their meaning, the Prince. It is also there in the poems of the persecuted Dominican Tommaso Campanella, who wrote of how he seemed mad to the world but sane to the higher worlds, confident as he was that one day he would in a state of joy reach the place '*Ove io senza parlar sia sempre inteso*', 'where I without speech am always understood'.[8]

The supreme example of this attitude concerns the sculptor Phidias. When we visit Olympia we see today the ruins of the Temple of Zeus with the great shell limestone drums of the columns thrown about the site like draughts pieces as they collapsed in the sixth-century earthquake. On the podium is the empty space where there stood one of the most famous statues of antiquity, the huge chryselephantine statue of Zeus which Phidias made and the beauty of which was said by Quintilian to have given a new quality to conventional religion. Phidias was not concerned first of all with the responses of his patrons and contemporaries. Pausanias says: 'when the statue was completely finished, Phidias prayed to the god to make a sign if the work pleased him, and immediately a flash of lightning struck the pavement at the place where the bronze urn was still standing in my time.'[9]

That audience, the audience of first causes, of unconditional love, of the messengers between what Rilke called '*das Doppelbereich*',[10] is, in fact, the only audience for most of human creative endeavour, for the inventions and insights made and suggested before their time, or because no one would listen, for the unread poems of genius burned by uncomprehending relatives, for the solutions to mathematical problems that no one noticed. For every scientist such as Scheele, who discovered oxygen at about the same time as Priestley, or the Abbé Gregor Mendel, whose achievements were only recognized after death, there must be thousands whose works and thoughts, however original, are as lost as the writings of Aristotle that mildew destroyed before understanding eyes could copy them. For every Emily Dickinson or Gerard Manley Hopkins, there are even more thousands whose works of equal worth can never be read. Tom Stoppard's play *Arcadia* is centred on an adolescent girl who discovers the principles of fractal geometry in the early 1800s, long before the discovery of the computers necessary to carry out the development of the principles into formal conclusions.

Yet the makers of such lost works are still part of the general audiences of the climate of opinion that grants them the stimulus to create or to explore even if it denies them the recognition they might have deserved. Like Faust's, their redemption lies in the fact that they have striven and their very striving makes them into cultivated spectators and participatory readers. Another way of regarding the lives and fates of such people is that the essence of any higher human activity is that it should be a means of ennobling and transforming the individual who practises it: Mark Pattison said that learning is a compound of memory, imagination, scientific habit and accurate observation concentrated for a long period on the remains of literature. 'The result of this sustained mental endeavour is not a book, but a man.'[11] The quality of attention that we give to the arts and sciences we love redeems the time of our earthly existence.

Transformation, dedication, sacrifice, offerings, these are all the signs of a culture in which the God or Goddess is the chief audience. An epitaph for a monk and goldsmith in about 1300 runs thus: '*Ore canunt alii Christum; canit arte fabrili Hugo.*'[12] 'Let others sing praise to Christ with their tongues: Hugh sings Him with his work in gold.' Such attitudes are characteristic also of cultures that remain close to their origins and to the Great Memory. Art, poetry and religion are there to serve the divine and to bring down the blessing from the hidden listeners.

In contrast, many of our most notable modern artists, thinkers and scientists have maintained that there is no one there to listen and therefore all their work is within a wholly human dimension. Such attitudes have led to the solipsism of the artist and the irresponsibility of Expressionism. Or else they have allowed substitute invisible audiences to exert their influences: the ancestors whose cult is implicit in extreme nationalist philosophies, the watching face of Big Brother, the imaginary audience of the proletariat for whom Picasso longed to paint, the multiple individual composed of transfigured scientists of Bernal or of the master race for which Hitler's architects and artists worked to provide worthy surroundings.

We have already seen how Nazism and communism both drew on the Great Memory and on the scientific image of man and how with inadequate interpretations of the latter they debased the gifts of the Great Memory. Somewhat similar forces are to be seen at work today. The most powerful and sinister contemporary evidence for the unguided and uncivilized forces of the Great Memory is to be seen in an international scale in the rise of fundamentalism and of nationalism.

Fundamentalism is directed by a nostalgia for the past as much as it is by a fear of the present. Many American Christian fundamentalists, with their desire to revive the witch trials of Salem, their deliberate whipping-up of fears of Satanism, their reliance on the literal truth of the Bible in whatever translation they choose to read, and their detestation and fear of science and evolutionary thought are guided by a vision of the patriarchal religion and society of the early settlers of their country. Both Christian and Islamic fundamentalists in their statements on sexual morals are full of a nostalgia for the time before science, when ordinary people were ignorant of the physiology of their own bodies, when there was less requirement for divorce simply because so many women died in childbirth and less need for family planning because of the great incidence of infant mortality. The nostalgia for a once glorious past is prominent also in many of the current nationalist movements, such as the contenders in the former Yugoslavia. Nationalism such as that of the Croats and the Serbs is close to fundamentalism because of its exclusive and deterministic character.

Yet both fundamentalism and nationalism have positive and natural aspects. The positive side of fundamentalism is the desire for certainty and stability, the very bases of civilized society: the pity of it is that it represses the search for truth and incites to violence and war against all unbelievers. Where nationalism is concerned, our love of our own traditions, native landscapes and languages is one of the most powerful of all creative forces because it goes back so deeply into our childhood. Such a love is one of our guides in conserving our sense of identity – and the violence of the reaction to regimes which repressed national identities is in part the violence of resentment at the crushing of a natural emotion.

Arnold Toynbee in his *Study of History* saw among the signs of disintegrating cultures two complementary forces, one the 'archaizing' and the other 'futurizing'.[13] He gave many instances of 'archaizing' movements going back to the times of King Agis IV in Sparta and the reforms of the Gracchi in Rome and up to the nationalist movements of the 1930s. Stirred by his experiences in the First World War, he understandably detested nationalism. However, it led him to single out for special condemnation and mockery the efforts of the Jews in Palestine to revive Hebrew, of Kemal Atatürk to purify Turkish from its Persian and Arabic elements, of the Norwegians to recreate a language free of the centuries of Danish and Swedish domination, of the struggles of the modern Greeks to create a language capable of expressing the thoughts and concepts of sophisticated western society, and of the Irish to revive Gaelic.[14] To deal with only one of his examples, history, through the outstanding success of the Israelis in establishing their sense of national identity through their revived language and in making a society strong enough to resist repeated attacks from their neighbours, not to mention the appearance of a new and vital literature in that language, returns his jeers upon himself.

Rather than associate returns to the past, or archaizing movements, with disintegration or decadence, I hope to have shown through numerous examples how often such movements help to renew cultures or to introduce them. Though Toynbee rejected racial explanations for the breakdown of civilizations, nevertheless in his studies of disintegration and decadence, he shared in an obsession common to his intellectual predecessors and many of his contemporaries. There was thought to be a close link between memory and heredity and there arose the idea of organic memory, developed most clearly by the physiologist Ewald Hering in 1870,[15] who influenced persons as disparate as Sigmund Freud and the great physicist Ernst Mach. Theories of inherited degeneration spread rapidly through the medical profession and sociologists as they also influenced novelists such as Emile Zola and Thomas Hardy. The theory of organic memory rapidly became of great political significance with the growth of nationalist movements: the nationhood of a man or woman was to be decided by blood, not by language or upbringing in a particular society and adherence to the traditions of that society. To Hitler culture was blood and the mixing of bloods was responsible for the decay of civilizations as it also meant the degeneration of the memories that were transmitted with the blood. Although the defeat of Nazism has rendered such ideas almost unmentionable, the organic memory theory is tenacious and potentially more dangerous because it is not discussed. This is especially so in relation to the implications of DNA and the belief drawn from these implications that our identities are wholly dependent on our heredity. The results of the various genome projects, even though they are chiefly intended for the identification and future prevention of inherited diseases, will probably be marshalled for purposes of political control as they will also be devoted to the support of the unconscious fundamentalism of reductionism in science.

Where the Great Memory can be seen to be associated with decadence is when it is regarded not as a process but as an end in itself, where it is used to stop the flow of thought as in the case of reductionism or else when the resources of a society available for the arts and research are devoted to a preponderant extent to the preservation of the past. This last is to me a further example of unconscious fundamentalism: the barely questioned consensus that allows the support of thousands of professors and teachers devoted to the study and preservation of the art and literature of the past while denying virtually all help to the artists, writers and poets of today, that requires the endless acquisition of objects and works of art even though there are no facilities to conserve them, let alone display them, and that in the case of the new British Library, on which more money has been spent than on any other cultural object, certainly in the twentieth century and perhaps in all English history, the funds have been devoted to an object now agreed to be impossible of attainment, that is, the provision of space for every work of domestic origin, and, as much as possible, foreign works. Patronage lacks courage: it is safer to found a professorial chair than to support an artist, it is easier to present an old-master painting to an art gallery than to exercise choice over which contemporary talented individual or group should receive help, and it is a pleasanter mode of self-aggrandizement to rebuild a great library and to exercise the patronage of sitting on its board than to define the needs of the age, the artistic and scientific needs that are also the profoundest religious and social needs, and to set about satisfying them. One aspect of this unconscious fundamentalism is the fragmentation and specialization of subjects: another that follows from this is the irresponsibility of allowing an intellectual vacuum, which is also a vacuum of power, waiting to be filled by millennial and tyrannical forces.

These open and unconscious forms of fundamentalism are among the forces awaiting transformation if we are to escape wars on a scale undreamed of even in the imaginations of science-fiction writers. Yet because we know of all these movements and terrors with an immediacy never possible before, because we are part of a new kind of audience, the audience of instantaneous events, from all round the world, we, and even more those who rule on our behalf, know that we cannot hide from the world. A Saudi Arabian astronaut said of the experience of seeing Earth from space: 'The first day or so we all pointed to our countries. The third or fourth day we were pointing to our continents. By the fifth day we were aware of only one Earth.'[16] The rest of us do not have to go to space to have the same realization because it is being forced on us all the time by our daily experience of the media.

The symbol of the future for our age is the exploration of space, the expansion of awareness into realms and atmospheres where the human eye and other perceptions have never penetrated before. It is an image of the expansion of human consciousness into potentialities of transformation in a different order of existence, beyond and containing the physical world, and without the limits the physical world imposes. The symbol of the Great Memory for our age is the interior of the Earth, the crust, the mantle and the core. Just as earlier in the twentieth century the release of the once-living fossil fuels from the depths of Earth's crust provided the energy for the transport, power and communications of modern society, a phenomenon accompanied by an overwhelming mass of new information about the past of humanity and the Earth – information itself being a form of psychic energy – so now the further exploration of the depths of the oceans and of Earth's interior, much of it guided by the search for new energy sources, is revealing more and more extraordinary knowledge of the existence of huge colonies of anaerobic bacteria that from the beginnings of the Earth have been engaged on the creation of minerals. They are the chemists of the deep who liberate from their ores gold, silver, the constituents of brass, and iron, the symbols of the ages through which humanity constantly passes. They work away in the Hell to which Christ, according to the Apostles' Creed and the Gospel of Nicodemus, descended after his death on the cross to liberate Adam and Eve and other souls of the Old Testament. Where our ancestors placed the souls of the damned, modern scientists are finding bacteria. The descent of Christ to the underworld is an image of the transformation of the mineral world as part of the process of the greater art and science which is called the redemption of matter. It may be that this bringing of hitherto unknown life forms to conscious attention is another aspect of this redemption.

For millennia men knew nothing of the existence of bacteria, even though they were using cultures in the making of bread, cheese, wine and beer. The nature of the bloom on grapes and the forming of the noble decay on grapeskins reveal a new aspect of Dionysus: he has been all this time the god of bacteria. For the transformation of wheat and grape into bread and wine, enzyme-producing yeasts are necessary. Though certain Roman authors conjectured about the existence of invisible animalcules, there was no proof of their existence until Leeuwenhoek created his microscope, and their importance, both in human health and disease and on the greater scale of the biosphere, is a comparatively recent discovery. They were undetected stowaways in Noah's Ark. There were no bacteria in Dante's Terrestrial Paradise or Milton's Eden, yet without them there would have been no Dante and no Milton. Each discovery of a new form of life is a discovery of something that contributes to the understanding of the physical and psychic nature of man: bacteria provide the interface between all kinds of chemical and other operations in living things and in organic and inorganic matter; they are the agents of breakdown and decay, and of regeneration; they provide the enzymes of digestion and they turn the waste of the plant and animal kingdoms into the humus of new growth. The symbolic analogy provided to us now by our awareness of bacteria is that they represent the process of interchange between the waking and unconscious sides of our natures, as the enzymes digesting the food of experience and impressions and set into action by the creative moment. Their discovery deep in the crust of the Earth and in association with volcanic vents provides us with further analogies between our creative and social lives and the opening-up of the nature of the earth beneath our feet – which is also an opening-up of hidden memories.

Beneath the oceans of the Earth is another kind of ocean, an ocean of molten rocks, constantly in movement and carrying upon its waves the tectonic plates of the continents, thrusting against one another, pushing Africa against southern Europe, tilting Great Britain sideways from west to east, grinding the Indian subcontinent against the Himalayas, and threatening California through the San Andreas Fault. At the meeting points of these gigantic hidden carapaces, at the points where their stresses are most extreme, matter is constantly being sucked down below the Earth's crust and released by volcanoes as molten rock and gases into the atmosphere in a huge process of recycling. The discovery of tectonic plates is like an image of the massive unconscious forces that underlay the great wars of the twentieth century and the crumbling of empires and regimes that boasted of their longevity. The depths to which material from the crust of the Earth is taken down into the mantle and from which it is brought up again has been a matter of lively debate. What is not in question is the recycling process which again provides an analogy for the taking in of outside impressions into the dream and deep sleep levels of our natures. The greater and more extraordinary analogies await us the further we go into the depths of the Earth, the way, for example, the core acts as a dynamo creating the Earth's magnetic field, the intense heat and pressures of the core and, most extraordinary of all, the idea that the iron heart of the planet is either a single crystal the size of the moon or else a large group of crystals aligned with one another. As a crystal resonates and receives and transmits, so I see this as an analogy for the way our creative powers are stirred in their depths by the wakening of consciousness and for Mnemosyne as the mother of the Muses remembering what is necessary for creation. There is another image it recalls: the pythoness in the Delphic cave receiving and transmitting the divine messages from the sun god. It is an emblem of what we as individuals may become in developing our creative powers by making ourselves open to inspiration and the inner voice. It is also a prophetic image enabling us to look ahead to a time when the whole of humanity, without compulsion, responds to the one sound from the depths of the Earth, the sound that marries the conscious and the unconscious in the universal consciousness.

What the history of climates has been showing us is the encapsulated moods and ideas of Gaia over the short period, for her, of the last 150,000 years. It is an analogue of the climate of opinion within societies, the settled forms of behaving and thinking that in some cases may last as long as a few thousand years and in others may seem to have been everlasting but in fact are only a few hundred years old or a few decades old, and that may be changed in a matter of days by events such as the landing in Botany Bay or the first winter of the Pilgrim Fathers in New England or the month following La Grande Peur in the French Revolution when an extraordinary change came over people's attitudes and the unthinkable became the thinkable. The most recent example is, of course, the rapid collapse of communism in the states of Eastern Europe. The weather in the mind shifted to another quarter.

As a result of studies of the history of past climates, it appears that the climatic conditions on Earth at present are so unlike any known global conditions in the past, it is impossible to predict what the pattern of our future weather will be. This gives us another analogue: the unpredictable climate of the future is the unpredictable climate of future opinion. Our unassimilated and constantly growing knowledge of the world makes a set of conditions which has never been known before and which will require new arts, new sciences, new philosophies and new forms of religion for us to adjust and civilize the climate of future opinion. It is an analogy for the new step in human awareness, mentioned earlier as comparable to man's discovery of the powers of his own mind in so many separate civilizations in the period around 500 BC.

That discovery of the powers of reasoning led men away from the older participatory awareness of our remoter ancestors into a necessary stage of separation from Nature, the separation that has given us both our present environmental crisis and the unprecedented means of being aware of it on its global scale. In recovering the energy and insight of the hunter, the shaman and the wise woman, we would become the loving audience of Nature, realizing that our imaginations are as huge as hers and in fact include her imagination. It would also mean that we would begin to understand what we were given our individual selves and egos for: that we should become the transparent reflectors of the light of conscious love.

Standing above the Mer de Glâce recently, waiting for the sun to rise above the summits facing me, the thought came to me as I looked at this vast and beautiful river of ice surrounded by the stark and sky-piercing needles of the mountain: This is what the northern half of Europe, Asia and North America looked like 40,000 years ago. It was a cold thought for a cold and beautiful view and, though *then* no human society could have survived in the coating of ice over the continents, yet from the grinding of the rocks by the glaciers, blown by ferocious winds, came the rock flour, or loess, that was carried far off to the valleys and plains, providing the soil on which the bacteria were to work and from which, for example, the civilizations of China and of Europe were to grow.

From extremes of cold I have travelled to extremes of heat and then of cold again. Etna is a volcanic mountain that over a quarter of a million years has constantly made itself through its many orifices into a range of hills and summits surmounted by its ever active central crater. Ascending Etna you pass through towns and villages built out of lava and rise up from rich and fertile groves of orange and lemon trees to cooler climes of deciduous forest, followed by deposits of lava waving with yellow broom and pine woods. These in turn give place to slopes of increasing barrenness, cliffs and caldera of purple black varied only by washes of iron red and brave, huddled and clinging plants. As you go up even further in the cable car, you see the last stages of vegetative life disappear and your eye marks the twisted pylons destroyed in the outflows of the volcano that are all that remain of the systems of cable cars that preceded the one in which you now travel. When you disembark close to the smoking crater, you enter an atmosphere of seeming desolation and of a cold several degrees below zero and you stumble between the banks of snow that stripe towards the ragged protrusions of lava smoking and steaming on which you gratefully place your freezing hands for warmth.

It could seem that these upper regions of the volcano have nothing to do with humanity, except for some brave souls to record and to watch, but that for the rest of us we should flee and erase from our minds the eventual extinction of our species that can be predicted from the presence of such a mighty and inimical force. Yet, as we descend once more and pass through the regions of climate and vegetation we see what bacteria, plant life and weather and the activity of man have done in partnership to make the barren lava into one of the most fertile landscapes in Europe. Thus the raw forces of the Great Memory, which flow out upon human society like the magma from the hidden mantle of the past, can come to kill and to devastate but also to provide the minerals and the soil of new flowerings of civilization.

From whatever direction one looks at Etna it is an impressive sight, beautiful in its shape and its immensity, but there is no more remarkable view than that from the top of the cavea of the Greek theatre at Taormina with its sights of the blue Mediterranean and of the blue lower slopes of the volcano rising to the snowy summit with its plume of smoke rising into the blue of the sky. Goethe said of it: 'Never did any audience, in any theatre, have before it such a spectacle.'[17] The memory of that view reminded me also that Nietzsche said his fundamental reason for writing *The Birth of Tragedy* – his study of the impulses of ritual and music that led to the creation of theatres like Taormina – was to answer the question: 'How can we view scholarship from the vantage of the artist and art from the vantage of life?' which he then followed with the question: 'What is the meaning of the Dionysiac spirit?'[18] For every performance in that theatre the statue of Dionysos would have been placed on the stage as an acknowledgment both of the origins of the theatre and of the fact that the god was the prime audience for the performance. If one includes science and the conclusions of science in Nietzsche's category of scholarship and speaks of scholarship as the cooled and petrified surface of what burst through the crust of earth as the red-hot and flaming lava of the Dionysiac spirit, all these are the products of the Great Memory and, from the viewpoint of the theatre of Taormina, they are the raw materials of art and of civilization. Just as for the Greeks all their achievements and inheritance from the past in science, technology, myth and religion were brought together to make a civilization comprehensible and participatory to everyone present in that theatre, so for us we will only enjoy fully what we are given when we learn to regard all science, all scholarship, all social bonds as requiring the three redemptions of matter, time and space, and take part in their transformation into an art for which we are the makers and the audience.

These three redemptions will be brought about by love. In creating new objects and works we enter into matter with our hands, hearts and thoughts: we change the air about us by the quality of our speech; we redeem matter by the humanity we infuse into our creations and the love we express through them. We are in time, which we redeem both by accepting it and forgiving it and by the quality of attention we bestow on what we make and do. Time is necessary to unfolding, to growth, to the drama, and to the manifestation and maturing of love. Space is another word for memory: the place where something *was*, where the rose bloomed, where the face smiled, where the battle was fought, where the plough made a furrow and the prayer was uttered. Equally it is where all these manifestations or events will be in the future. In relation to creativity it is intimately related to causes, the beginnings of desires, thoughts and ideas, and the redemption of space means the purifying and refining of causes.

The strongest images of the creative power of love that the Great

Memory has been returning to us over the past decades have been those of the Eternal Feminine, whether as the Great Goddess of prehistory or as ideals, cults and symbols from later civilizations and societies or as a state of calm and unified experience. These images have appeared or been discovered synchronously with the surges in society that have brought about great changes in the political and social position of women. What is remarkable is that the images of the Feminine have arisen in many unconnected fields, some already mentioned and rehearsed here again. Thus archaeologists have revealed the matriarchal character of the earliest known religions from the time of the earliest European art onwards. Scholars have found the long-repressed evidence of the great role played by women and the feminine principle in early Christianity. All this has been quite independent on the one hand of the movement for the ordination of women and on the other of the promulgation of the Doctrine of the Assumption by the Roman Catholic Church, itself a return to and a reinterpretation of an event implicit in the past. Others have traced the transformations of the images of Isis and Horus and other female deities into the appearance of the Black Virgins of the early Middle Ages and even followed the fortunes of images of the Virgin taken by the Nestorian Christians to China, where these images helped to bring about the transformation of the male Boddhisattva Avalokitesvara into the goddess of mercy, Kwan Yin. In science, not only has the name of the goddess Gaia been revived to name the unified processes of the biosphere but what is often regarded as the most important discovery of the life sciences of the past fifty years, the way in which DNA transmits genetic information, is based on the helix, or spiral, one of the fundamental images of the Great Mother. In art similar images, including the recurrence of the biomorphic form, have given influential themes to western artists. More recently we have seen many attempts to reinterpret history as a sequence of oppressive patriarchal systems. Memory is personified as female: the scientific imagination has pursued and wooed, often brutally, the memory of the past. It is now time for a marriage in which that imagination with its knowledge will be transfigured by the love of the Eternal Feminine.

18

The perfect enjoyer

There is a triptych called *L'Âge d'or* in the Musée d'Orsay in Paris (figure 35). It is the work of Léon Frédéric in 1900–01 and its central panel is called 'Night', placed between 'Morning' and 'Evening'. The side panels are comparatively simple renderings of happy scenes but the depiction of night is far more effective in expressing what it must have been like to live in the Age of Gold.[1] It shows a group of people fast asleep in the open air in an Arcadian valley with forests beyond, and with flocks of sheep peacefully dozing. The people are sprawled on the ground against one another, their bodies naked or barely clothed, children, young men and women, people of mature and old age. Few images could have summed up more sharply the differences between that ideal world and the Paris of the *belle époque* where the only people to sleep out of doors were the drunken *clôchards*, the child prostitutes touting for custom in the Champs Elysées, and the outcasts of urban and industrialized society. A Belgian Symbolist painter, Léon Frédéric (1856–1940) had a strong social conscience and would have been well aware of such contrasts. By showing this group asleep in the open air, the artist tells us of a world of total trust and accord with the animal world and with other human beings: he tells us of an utterly benign climate; and he also tells us, from the way in which they sleep supporting one another, of a society that works together without compulsion and acts always in total agreement. We know that they will all wake up as one as they went to sleep as one and that they will agree easily and wholeheartedly on what pleasures they will enjoy in the day awaiting them. Their language and communication are poetry and song, their social governance is the dance, their heaviest industry is the gathering of fruits and plants, their science the profoundest knowledge of the inner nature of all creatures and vegetation: to them the stars are their intimate friends with whom they converse and their civilization is the enjoyment of the world that is given them. They are the perfect enjoyers.

There is another reason why they are shown asleep. Their slumber signifies the Golden Age which is asleep in most of us in our Age of Iron, and the effortless creativity which lies latent in us until a phrase perfectly spoken by an actress, a melody or an insight into a natural law, fills us with transient ecstasy.

There is painting of the same period by another Belgian artist Constant Montald (1862–1944), showing a forest glade with golden and silver trees shimmering against vertical bands of colour that suggest both a misty dawn and the purple-black of night. Through the forest young men and women come to drink from the basin of a fountain which is raised to the height of their lips. They perform an act of natural simplicity, coming to renew their loves, their sexual ardour and their creative powers in a composition of the utmost complexity. They too are perfect enjoyers, living in a world of eternal youth and knowing the source that renews their capacity for enjoyment, and, again, they speak to us of the hidden glade in the forests of our minds where for each of us there waits the fountain of renewal.

Neither of these works, even taking into account the swings of taste that allow us now to study and admire Symbolist and Art Nouveau paintings, can be considered great works of art. It is the desire to express themes beyond the consensus of their epoch that arouses my interest in them and I find the same interest in the work of another contemporary, the Russian artist Nicholas Roerich (1874–1947).[2]

Here it is not one work that we have to take into account but many hundreds. Roerich at an early age in the 1890s was fired by the belief that the true Russian culture was fundamentally Asiatic in its origins and that it was in danger of being overwhelmed by the borrowed influences of western civilization and the rapid effects of industrialization. He and his wife studied the folklore, dances and art of primitive Russia and he became, after a period with Nicolai Evreinov's Ancient Theatre, associated with Diaghilev, who suggested he should collaborate with Stravinsky. Roerich suggested two themes to Stravinsky, one of which was to become *The Rite of Spring*. Roerich gave him, in the course of conversations, the scenario based on the story of the sacrifice of the chosen virgin to the ancient Slav god Yarilo and he also designed the sets for the first production of the ballet in Paris in 1913. Driven into exile by the 1917 Revolution, Roerich continued his search for what he called the refined primitivism of the ancients, spending much of his time in the Kulu Valley in the Himalayas and painting more than six hundred paintings of the mountains and their shrines and saints (figure 34). Benois regretted that he painted so much, exclaiming that if only he had concentrated on fewer paintings, he could have made each one exhaustive of a particular theme. Individually his paintings are like stage sets, glowing with the marvellous Russian colour sense released by

Diaghilev's patronage and influence, for dramas we have to perform before them; seen in mass as a sequence of slides, they are like the preparation for an extraordinary animated film in which you would expect to see the Lord Shiva dancing on the peaks of the Himalayas or a mountain in its stillness revealing itself as the soul of a Boddhisattva. The cumulative effect of seeing his paintings in this way is to be taken to that lost land of saints and mystery which, for over a hundred years, since Alexandra David-Neel and other explorers of Tibet and Central Asia first set out in the hope of finding sources of enlightenment, has intrigued the European mind and nourished the belief that there, at least, are superhuman beings who have transcended all the limitations of mortal existence and who, by their contemplations and austerities, have achieved a perfection of inner freedom and ceaseless enjoyments, as an effect of which the rest of humanity, however unconscious of these benefits, has its lot lightened and made more endurable. This was the land of Shambhala, of Shangri-La, the subject of countless novels, including Kipling's *Kim*, and many films. The image occurs in James Elroy Flecker's 'The Golden Journey to Samarkand' where the pilgrims chant:

We are the pilgrims, master; we shall go
Always a little further: it may be
Beyond that last blue mountain barred with snow,
Across that angry or that glimmering sea,
White on a throne or guarded in a cave,
There lives a prophet who can understand
Why men were born: but surely we are brave
Who make the Golden Journey to Samarkand.[3]

I give these three examples, all based on the recreation of mythic pasts, the classical Golden Age, the Celtic fountain or cauldron of inspiration, and the primitive Slav Arcadia with its sources in a secret fastness of Central Asia, as prophecies of new ideas about creativity and appreciation.

The environmental crisis on Earth has been brought about by the alliance of scientists, technologists and industrialists since the beginning of the Industrial Revolution, often in connivance with politicians, generals and the press, all working on the same principle: 'We can change nature and matter and the means of heredity to whatever we like.' As the universe was conceived according to the fundamental metaphor of a machine, then the machine could be altered, tinkered with and fine-tuned to work or travel in the direction men told it to. The attitude has been one of telling the world what it is like and acting as the directors of the world. As the metaphors of nature are changing to ones of organic growth and development, of independent intelligence as extrapolated by some from the Gaia hypothesis, and, most revolutionary of all, of principles guided by universal consciousness, so, I predict, our attitudes will change from telling the world what it is like to listening to the world to discover the new myths and images that will guide the civilizations of the future. Instead of telling God that He is dead or that He does not exist, we will explore the nature of the consciousness on which all conceptions of the deity and all theories and experiences of nature, creativity and the life of society depend. It may then come about that we will save ourselves and redeem the balance with nature, by love and enjoyment of the glory of the world.

This change will depend on how we learn to understand what we were given our individualities, our sense of our own selves, for. Is it simply to fight in a world of competition for the satisfaction of our imagined goods, or to die in the causes of nation-states and ancient enmities? Or is it that our sense of 'I' was given us to be a vehicle of truth, consciousness and bliss, whatever our circumstances and whatever the talents we were given through heredity and nurture and that, following from this, the fundamental creative act is the service to which we put our individuality?

The first attitude is the way of barbarism; the second is the way to the renewal of civilization. It is not only scientists who are driven by the themata awakened in their early childhood; we are all born with and surrounded by the themata of our languages, nationhood, religion or social assumptions: these are the ingrained tendencies that, in the mass, accumulate to decide the particular drives both for destruction and for creativity within a particular race or nation. Like the themata, which we did not choose, the images of the Great Memory are given us as the matter of art, science and religion for us to recognize, and select among, and to transform. And if we do not recognize them and give them names, we will be more likely to repeat the faults than to emulate the excellences of our ancestors.

There are three levels of memory within the Great Memory with which we have to come to terms in our present age. Through their transformation we will be involved in bringing about the three kinds of redemption described in the last chapter. First, there is the recovery of the physical past of the Earth, the geology, the fossil record from the beginnings of life, the history of atmospheric changes and of the climate and the traces of the expansion and recession of the impact of human societies upon the surface of the Earth, with, in addition, the even huger views of the origins of the stars and the universe. This recovery has been the task of scientists largely over the past two hundred years, and though it is interpretable in its own terms of physical events brought about by physical causes, to the eye of the observer, it has uncovered more and more matters for wonder and further exploration of the diversity of life, its origins and its interconnections. It has also brought about a new conception of the unity of existence, of the envelopes of spaces, gravitational systems, suns, planets and biospheres. Through what we observe of the past, we draw on the energies of the past because information is itself a form of raw energy. The outrage of fundamentalists of all religions against the scientific picture of the past of the Earth and the universe is a reaction against the incipient power of these energies. The transformation of physical or organic memory is another aspect of the redemption of matter.

The second level of the Great Memory includes the recovery of the past of humanity, the legends and shibboleths of national identity, a revaluation of the different ways in which human societies have been and are bonded together, an amassing of the myths and folklore of these societies, the gathering together of the sacred texts of all religions, together with the emergence of a new kind of world history, increasingly freed of colonial assumptions. This is the level of human experience and therefore includes every kind of unreason and reason. Its recovery was begun by the historians, scholars and philosophers of the Enlightenment who shared and participated in the objectivity of contemporary scientists, applying to their studies techniques parallel to the taxonomic and investigative procedures of the scientists, such as the comparative method and textual analysis. It is the comparative method that has led to the beginnings of a new kind of world history, the realization of the advances made by China in culture and technology, enjoying the achievements of the Sung empire when Europe was undergoing the Dark Ages or the fact that in the eighteenth century, whatever was happening in England and France, China under the Manchu dynasty of the Qing was again the richest, most productive and populous nation on Earth, or that Mayan civilization had by the twelfth century evolved a calendar far more exact than the Gregorian calendar which appeared four centuries later, or, again, that, however important the courts of Europe were as centres of culture in the late sixteenth century, the court of Akbar the Great surpassed them all for its wealth, resources, cultivation of the arts and the exchange of ideas. It is this *new* view of world history which will render finally obsolete the earlier interpretations of the course of history such as the Marxist interpretation or the systems of Spengler and Toynbee. What may emerge from such a new understanding of world history is the complementarity of cultures and of the great religions in the sense that each has developed a special part of human potentiality and that the time is coming when, in the light of a fuller consciousness, the separate strands of past experience will be bound together in a new rope of salvation. The transformation of historical memory involves us in the redemption of time.

The third level of the Great Memory is the most profound and the most immediate because it is closest to the memory of the ever-present now. It is the realm of archetypal images and ideas, of the essences of colours, of the original intentions of language, and of what music is before it is turned into notes. It is the memory of acts of transformation and involves us in the redemption of space which we may also look upon as the redemption of causes.

In that memory is subsumed the experience of glory. Goethe in his late work *Die Trilogie der Leidenschaft*, inspired by his love for the young Ulrike von Levetzow, recalled in the first poem the pathetic shade of Werther coming back to look at what Goethe has himself made of his life and his entanglements with passion. With bitter irony he speaks of how movingly poets sing, evading the pain of the parting which is death.

> *Verstückt in solche Qualen, halbverschuldet,*
> *Geb ihm ein Gott zu sagen, was er duldet.*[4]

> Entangled in such pains and half to blame,
> O may a god grant them the power to tell
> What they endure!

In the second poem, known as the '*Marienbad Elegie*', he again begins with tremulous doubts and then the glory of the world bursts in on him:

> *Ist denn die Welt nicht übrig? Felsenwände,*
> *Sind sie nicht mehr gekrönt mit heiligen Schatten?*
> *Die Ernte, reift sie nicht? Ein grün Gelände,*
> *Zieht sichs nicht hin am Fluß durch Busch und Matten?*
> *Und wölbt sich nicht das überweltlich Große*
> *Gestaltenreiche, bald Gestaltenlose?*[5]

> Is then the world not real? Are rocky sides
> Of cliffs no longer crowned with holy shadows?
> Do not the harvests ripen? Green countrysides –
> Do they not border streams with shrubs and meadows?
> And does not the transcendent vault still reign,
> So rich in forms, so free of forms again?

In the final poem he asks who will soothe the agonized heart that has lost too much. Then music enters to offer the divinity of music and tears. His heart comes to life again and offers itself up in pure gratitude. It was then he felt:

> O daß es ewig bliebe! –
> Das Doppel-Glück der Töne wie der Liebe.[6]

O may it last for ever
The double joy of music and of love.

The point is of course that it cannot last for ever and that awareness drives us on always to renew the experience through other arts and plays and ideas. We long for the experience of glory, constantly offered us and constantly taken away from us.

Glory in Judaeo-Christian terms is first the splendour of the godhead and, second, the experience of transformation in which we, temporarily on Earth and for eternity in Heaven, are taken up into the sharing of that splendour. To be glorified is to become the perfect enjoyer. In Indian terms it is the participation in the *rasa*, the taste of the glory of atman mediated through the bliss of contemplation and the rapture of art. In modern terms, that is, in terms of consciousness, it is the experience of full consciousness, unveiled by the falling away of dualities and the coordination of the faculties into full absorption with the awakening experience. Glory is another aspect of the imagery of light associated with the expression of the nature of consciousness: it is another name for the halo or aureole of light and flames which are depicted in the portrayal of the saints, prophets and enlightened souls of many traditions from Christianity to Islam, from Buddhism to Taoism. It is the outward manifestation of the inner state of perfection of those who know that the ultimate witness of their being is present within them and is the source of their enjoyment. Dionysius the Areopagite says that the image of fire signifies the perfect conformity to God of the heavenly intelligences, the angels.

It is irresistible and invisible, having absolute rule over all things, bringing under its own power all things in which it subsists. It has transforming power, and imparts itself in some measure to everything near it. It revives all things by its revivifying heat, and illuminates them all with its resplendent brightness. It is inseparable and pure, possessing separative power, but itself changeless, uplifting, penetrative, high, not held back by any servile baseness, ever-moving, self-moved, moving other things. It comprehends, but is incomprehensible, unindigent, mysteriously increasing itself and showing forth its majesty according to the nature of the substance receiving it, powerful, mighty, invisibly present to all things.[7]

Wherever the traces of mystical experience are to be found in past history, they are associated with the imagery of light, from the Upanishads to Pascal's notes on his transforming vision of God, from the hymns of Akhenaton to the Sufi poets. The recovery of the mystical tradition has been one of the richest gifts of the Great Memory throughout the twentieth century: it has been brought about partly through the application of the comparative method which has shown how often in almost identical terms the mystics of the past have spoken of their unitive experiences; but there is a marked difference between the way in which it has been recovered and the way in which the scientists, archaeologists and scholars have recovered the lost knowledge and information about the past described in relation to the first two levels of the Great Memory. They have approached their discoveries and interpreted them according to the observer awareness of the scientific attitude, that of the detached, deliberately uninvolved commentator. The mystical tradition has only been recovered to its present fullness because the poets, philosophers and thinkers who have brought it back into currency have had the mystical experience themselves. This applies to earlier teachers and poets who have brought about this change drawing on their own and other traditions, such as Vivekananda, who brought the teaching of Ramakrishna to the West, Baron von Hügel and Evelyn Underhill who wrote on mysticism, W. B. Yeats, R. M. Rilke, T. S. Eliot, Martin Buber, D. T. Suzuki, and Ananda Coomaraswamy, the last two among the greatest scholars of this century. It applies equally to scientists such as Erwin Schrödinger and Wolfgang Pauli, and to more recent thinkers and writers such as Father Bede Griffiths, who did much to reveal the inner unity of the great religions. They recognized the truth within the experience of the past because they had, sometimes only in glimpses, sometimes in greater fullness, that experience of illimitable truth themselves. What they have done by communicating their experiences through their writings is to bring about a change in the climate of opinion, so that it is no longer necessary for people who have such experiences – such as, for example, Gerard Manley Hopkins or Emily Dickinson – to live in the terrible loneliness of having no one to whom they can confide. They have brought about an even greater change in the climate of opinion so that when from various sources, from India, Tibet, China and Japan, techniques of meditation were brought to the West, there were enough people prepared through desire and awareness to participate and to learn the practices of meditation. These techniques of meditation have had a profound inner effect upon many individuals and groups of people in the West. They have influenced the interior life of Christians and Jews making them look to meditative practices long disregarded in their own traditions, so that, for example, there is a widespread and influential Christian meditation movement, with its authority in the writings of St John Cassian, the teacher of St Benedict, and with links with meditators in other traditions, as well as spreading across the conventional limits of Christian sectarianism.

The recovery of the mystical tradition has its own strange coincidences, comparable to the discoveries of archaeology and their synchronous relevance to contemporary life and ideas. In 1896, contemporary with many of the movements such as theosophy reviving the mystical tradition, the scholar William Brooke bought for a trifling sum two manuscripts from a London bookstall. One manuscript contained thirty-seven poems and commonplace extracts. The other contained a remarkable prose work of devotions and effusions, now known as the *Centuries of Meditation*. There was no indication of authorship in these manuscripts. Investigations by Bertram Dobell showed that the author was an obscure parson called Thomas Traherne (1637–74) who had published only one work in his lifetime, a polemic against the Roman Catholic Church. Other manuscripts then came to light, another volume of poems in the British Museum, Traherne's notes on Ficino's commentaries on Plato, and, more recently, his *Select Meditations* in 1964. In 1967 the manuscript of his *Commentaries of Heaven* was snatched from a bonfire to which it had been consigned.

Traherne had been connected with a group surrounding Susanna Hopton, a learned and devout lady of the Welsh Marches, and it may well be that the poems and meditations were written for her circle.[8] It may also be that she and his brother Philip, who prepared the manuscript of poems subsequently found in the British Museum for a publication which never came about, were solely concerned with the possible value of his writings in the conversion or redemption of sinners and, judging them to be for the most part inadequate for that purpose, never devoted sufficient effort to their wider circulation. That they survived for the eyes of a later and more understanding generation is almost as great a matter of marvel as the longevity of the only volume of the verse of Catullus surviving from antiquity that appeared in Verona in the early fourteenth century.

To our century, increasingly ready to hear his message, Traherne has spoken of strange things: in the poems and the *Centuries* he tells of his state before birth when he was 'an inward sphere of light' and of his infancy when, though or because he could not speak, the 'fair face of Heaven and earth' spoke to him . . .

> And every stone, and every star a tongue,
> And every gale of wind a curious song.[9]

The poem 'Dumbness' from which that couplet comes describes his state of unity and enjoyment as a tiny child: in its companion poem 'Silence' he speaks of the joys of meditation in maturity, ignoring all the sacramental duties and works of mercy, for these were only made necessary by sin, in favour of the bliss which Adam knew before the fall and which Traherne also knew in his infancy. Here and in his other writings Traherne celebrates enjoyment which to him is a term that sums up the love of God together with the love of mankind and all created things.

> You never enjoy the world aright, till the sea itself floweth in your veins, till you are clothed with the heavens, and crowned with the stars; and perceive yourself to be the sole heir of the whole world: and more than so, because men are in it who are every one sole heirs, as well as you. Till you can sing and rejoice and delight in God, as misers do in gold, and kings in sceptres, you never enjoy the world.[10]

Enjoyment to him requires expansion of the mind and the soul: he had an exquisite and vast sense of infinite spaces where he found not emptiness but something else

> Dame Nature told me there was endless space
> Within my soul; I spied its very face:
>   Sure it not for nought appears.
>   What is there which a man may see
>   Beyond the spheres?
>   Felicity.[11]

This joy, this felicity, he links to his feelings for eternity. Turning Boethius on his head, who said that eternity is 'the complete, simultaneous and perfect possession of everlasting life' (see page 89), Traherne says: 'Eternity is a mysterious absence of times and ages . . .'[12]

Traherne is bolder than Blake or Wordsworth or Whitman and his work is still to be assimilated into our general culture because of the attachment to misery in putrefying conventional Christianity. How some of his thoughts have affected twentieth-century thinkers who have known this mystical experience may be seen by comparing his most famous words with the passage that follows:

All tears and quarrels were hidden from mine eyes. Everything was at rest, free, and immortal. I knew nothing of sickness or death or exaction; in the absence of these I was entertained like an angel with the works of God in their splendour and glory; I saw all in the peace of Eden; Heaven and earth did sing my Creator's praises, and could not make more melody to Adam, than to me. All time was eternity, and a perpetual Sabbath. Is it not strange that an infant should be heir of the world, and see those mysteries which the books of the learned never unfold?

The corn was orient and immortal wheat, which never should be reaped, nor was ever sown. I thought it had stood from everlasting to everlasting. The dust and stones of the street were as precious as gold. The gates were at first the end of the world, the green trees when I saw them first through one of the gates transported and ravished me; their sweetness and unusual beauty made my heart to leap, and almost mad with ecstasy, they were such strange and wonderful things. The men! O what venerable and reverend creatures did the aged seem! Immortal cherubims! And young men glittering and sparkling angels, and maids strange seraphic pieces of life and beauty! Boys and girls tumbling in the street, and playing, were moving jewels. I knew not that they were born or should die. But all things abided eternally as they were in their proper places.[13]

The passage that follows was published by the chemist and historian of science F. Sherwood Taylor in 1945. He was describing what had happened to him two years earlier when he had walked into the gardens of St John's College, Oxford:

the dahlias were still in bloom and the Michaelmas daisies were covered with great butterflies – tortoise-shells, fritillaries and red admirals. Suddenly I saw the whole scene take on a new figure. Every plant assumed a different and *intelligible* pattern, an individuality with a meaning that was the plant itself, which, by existing in that pattern, was turned towards God and praising Him. So with the butterflies; they were not merely lowly organisms, but intensely alive, clad in the livery of God, and in a fashion more personal than the plants ... The world was a prayer and I, fallen man, was the only being whose prayer was weak and broken. For there was nothing in my heart but love and tears and the avowal 'Lord, I am not worthy' ... At the same time everything revealed itself as interconnected. There was no visible link, yet round each centre of life there was an influence, as if each living thing were a centre in a spiritual medium. The vision faded after about half-an-hour, and though it has never fully returned, yet when my mind is recollected and my heart at rest, I can see the world of living things differently, and as partaking of that hidden life. Then I know that the scientific description of nature is as jejune as the chemical analysis of the painting of an old master. And, if the power of seeing nature thus is, as one may suppose, nothing to do with the power to write of it, how many millions must have lived and died in its consolation, unknown to the world? We have no right to dismiss this faculty as a rare one. It may be expressed by few, known by many, innate in all.[14]

Through the practice of meditation more and more people are having experience of states of awareness and unveilings of consciousness that are affecting their lives and the lives of those connected with them or influenced by them. One of the effects of this is that in religion they are beginning to trust experience rather than the magisterium or the traditional dogmas of their inherited faiths. They do not need authority in the way their fathers did. Another effect is upon the new subjects science is having to take into account, especially the nature of consciousness.

Implicit in the practice of meditation is an ideal of humanity, an ideal less glamorous perhaps than some of the ideals of former civilizations, such as the *uomo universale* of the Renaissance. In meditation the meditator is the audience of one in relation to the universal consciousness of God. The ideal is that he or she in meditating becomes the perfect and absorbed listener of the ultimate silence and the perfect enjoyer of the bliss of the present moment, taking the experience of calm and happiness into whatever are the activities of the daily life of that meditator. It is an ideal that goes beyond the limitations of our current religious and social boundaries and, if it seems to mean a withdrawal from what is called real life, it is a temporary withdrawal towards the source of life, the momentary experience of the ever-present trust of the Golden Age, the fountain of renewal in the forest glade of the mind, the peace of the mountaintop which is the place of propitiation, only in order that life should be engaged and lived more fully. I predict that in this ideal – which many people are now putting into practice – lie the solutions to what we will make of the mass of information, images and memories from the past with which we are overwhelmed today. Through realizing that ideal we may learn the necessary simplicity of what to keep and what to discard, how to interpret and how to manage our creative and imaginative powers. We may also become a new kind of audience with tastes refined into longing for new forms of participatory art and science.

Creativity is an outward impulse. In Christian terms it is the procession of the Word, resounding in space, manifesting in time and incarnate in matter. Thus a movement in the spirit is incarnated as music, uttered thought, a poem, a demonstration of the laws of nature, an artefact or painting and, in the cycle of creativity, it is returned to the spirit of the spectator and the audience. It is the outward embrace of love.

Also implicit in the practice of meditation is the premiss that the consciousness to which it aspires is universal consciousness. As a summary of how creativity may be understood under the same premiss, I recapitulate themes that have been expressed earlier and bring them together in what follows.

Within the universal consciousness desires arise. The desires create an unmanifested world, the divine imagination. The divine imagination contains all the possible ways in which the desires could be manifested. Within it is a principle of discrimination which decides which of the possible ways the manifestation will take. It could seem that the fulfilling of the desire will separate it from the full consciousness but we need not see it in that way.

With the help of the divine imagination of which our own imaginations are shadows, we can think of creation and non-separation in the following way:

Creation begins and continues as a single sound.

That sound includes all ideas, meanings and all expressions of meaning and all possible languages. It is universal consciousness letting itself be known as the Word.

That sound holds within itself all rhythms, melodies, chords and all the possibilities of music. It is universal consciousness letting itself be known as song.

That sound resonates in eternity and its resonances create voids and spaces and a diversity of experiences of time, the time experience of a galaxy, a tree, a man, a mayfly. It still holds within itself all lights and darknesses and all possible variety of colours. It also holds all natural laws and the principles of life and intelligent life. It creates beings capable of consciousness themselves who are the spectators and the audiences of its creation. It is universal consciousness letting itself be known as glory.

We, the human race, are the creation of that sound and as we are made conscious by its light and will, so we share in its creative possibilities. Where we think we invent, we discover: where we suppose we originate, we are supplied from the true origins. In our ultimate essence, our true individuality, we are that sound and through our existence we are ears to hear that sound and mouths to utter that sound.

We can also think of universal consciousness as the primal human being who sings that sound, creating worlds from its resonances, worlds which include that being's macrocosmic faculties of intelligence, the desires, memory and capacity for the reflection of consciousness, discrimination and the self-awareness of individuality. These faculties we also possess and, in varying degrees of combination, they are the means both of our creative acts and our acts of appreciation. We perform these acts to their fullest possible expression given our talents and environment to the degree that our faculties are expanded to the level and coordination of pure desire, complete memory and perfect reflection, just discrimination and the selfless experience of 'I AM' that characterize the effects of universal consciousness. If we do not experience these moments of expansion it is because of another gift of the one sound that accompanies discrimination and the expression of our individuality, and that is the gift of free will. It is in the will of universal consciousness that we should find our way back to the liberty of that consciousness only by the exercise of free will.

There are many traditional explanations of why we constantly fail to exercise our free will, from the doctrine of original sin acting as an inertial weight on our imaginations and our best impulses to the doctrine of karma carrying the burdens of past lives into the present. Northrop Frye, writing of Milton, says that liberty is the chief thing that the Gospel has to bring to man. 'But man for Milton does not and cannot "naturally" want freedom: he gets it only because God wants him to have it. What man naturally wants is to collapse into the master-slave duality, of which the creature-creator duality is perhaps a projection.'[15] One can define a duality without necessarily being taken in by it. The unity that transcends that duality is the unity of consciousness which is the common source of the creativity of nature and the creativity of humanity. The closer we come to unveiling that consciousness, the closer we come to seeing the true purpose of our creative powers and the more free we are made of the imagination of nature which we will come to discover as a vast network of living metaphors expressing the hugeness and variety within our own humanity.

Recently three of us, my wife, a friend from New York and myself set out on a fine autumn afternoon for a walk on our Sussex downs. The purpose of the walk was to find the late flowering orchid called autumn lady's tresses, so called because its white flowers are twisted in a spire and also are implicated with one another to look like a plaited tress of hair. It is one of the many flowers named in connection with the Virgin Mary and thought to be under her special care and to signify her attributes. It grows close to the ground with a beautiful humility and I have always found it a touching sight for this reason and also for the miracle of how it manages to reproduce itself. First it needs to be visited by bumblebees which, bringing the pollinia from other plants of lady's tresses, open up the flowers in searching for nectar and so fertilize the flower.[16] As in other wild orchids, its seeds are too tiny to include their own nourishment and they depend for germination and growth on being blown to sites where they come into contact with certain mycelia in the soil with which they form a symbiotic relationship and which provide them with the nourishment they need for their new generation. It is an emblem to me of how, despite the denial of creativity in fossilized institutions, tyrannies, and societies that cultivate mediocrity and depression, the wind of the spirit blows the seeds of creativity to far and unlikely patches of mycelia waiting to nourish them – the receptive souls of the artist and the thinker and their patrons and audiences.

There were none to be seen. We hunted the banks on either side of the chalk track, searching among the drying tufts of grass. As the track led upwards, so we followed it to where it gave out at a gate and stile beyond which was downland grass. As we passed through, our friend said: 'Do you ever feel the presence of the people who lived here in prehistoric times?' We were walking towards the banks of an Iron Age fort and though I responded by talking about the thousands of years of history around us I felt I was spoiling the mood of the moment her question had awoken. She had voiced into awareness the character of the place and as we passed along the defile formed by an opening between the banks, so the mood impressed silence on us as it also sharpened our perceptions. It was not only history that we walked upon but the memory of the crust of the Earth held in the deposits over millions of years of the sea creatures, the coccoliths, the lives and deaths of which had created the chalk downs about us. We came out at the head of one of the downland valleys known as bottoms. The hill we stood on curved steeply down to the valley whose floor we could not see: opposite our hill was another hill crowned with more earthworks. Both the hill we stood on and the opposite hill were bright green with grass still flourishing after heavy rains but the downland hill facing us at the end of the valley was completely black even to the curve of its summit as the sun stood high beyond it over the invisible sea. The simplicity of the forms that constituted this landscape, the cloudless blue sky, the way in which the steep curve of our hill intersected the facing hill so that they sheared curves into the blackness of the hill at the end of the valley, made us say almost as one that it was like entering an abstract painting – but it was the abstraction of the timeless, of the presence of the cause behind the transient, in effect, the living myth of the all-embracing Mother in her light and her darkness. We had set out to find a rare particular beauty and, denied that, were given the liberty of a general beauty.

In such moments we become the perfect enjoyers: through the richness of the human spirit, through the ability of art and science to break through the anxiety structures with which we cage our perceptions and stifle our spontaneity, we become again the possessors of the present moment, the only moment in which every word we utter is a leaf from the mouth of the Green Man and when the glory that we recognize is the reflection in ourselves of

THE FACE OF GLORY.

Acknowledgments

M y chief expressions of thanks are to my wife who has shared the journeys, the reading and the discussions that have gone to make this book. My second great debt is to my friend and former colleague in the Nuffield science projects, Dr Tony Mansell, chemist, historian and theologian, who has read my chapters and carried out researches for me, saving me often from error and, at times, docking my prolixities.

Carmen Blacker has helped me with passages relating to Japanese history and culture. Michael Loewe has helped me with passages concerned with Chinese history and art. Kirsten Williams has helped me with my understanding of Old Norse poetry. I am indebted to them for their assistance. I am grateful to the following friends and helpers who have commented on chapters or have provided encouragement and information: Emilios Bouratinos, Simon Brown, James Burge, Martin Caiger-Smith, Gerta Calmann, Mark Cohen, John Crawley, Prakash Detha, Dr Peter Fenwick, Victoria Glendinning, Robin Hamlyn, Dr Swana Hardy, Sir Terence Heiser, David Lorimer, Sir Neville and Lady Marriner, John Morley, Richard Morphet, Pamela Parsonson, Sally Payen, Barry Pluke, Isabel Raphael, Martin Redfern, Frances Taliaferro, Dr Rupert Sheldrake, Sir Laurens van der Post, Jaime Ward Jackson and Danah Zohar.

Clive Hicks, my friend and collaborator on eight books to date, has provided many of the photographs and commented on the text. Deborah Williams, my friend and former colleague, has searched for and found all the other illustrations. Leonora Clarke typed my manuscript with skill and kindness.

I acknowledge with thanks the following publishers and copyright owners for permission to quote from the works mentioned below: Routledge for the passage from Mary Midgley, *Science as Salvation* (1992) on page 95; Oxford University Press for the passage from Roger Penrose, *The Emperor's New Mind* (1990) on page 132; Sarah Codrington and the Nuffield-Chelsea Curriculum Trust for the passage from Sir Lawrence Bragg, *The Discovery of X-Ray Analysis* (1966) on pages 129–30; Maryanna Tavener for the passage from the works of her father, Glen Schaefer, on page 229; Penguin Books for the passages from *Egil's Saga* translated by Hermann Pálsson and Paul Edwards (1976) on pages 221–22. I also thank Elisabeth Collins for permission to quote from an interview given by Cecil Collins in *Temenos* 1 and also to reproduce as the frontispiece the detail of the drawing *Resurrection* by Cecil Collins belonging to the Britten–Pears Foundation. I thank Crown Publishers for the passages on pp. 81, 127, 148 and 210–1 from Chang Chung-yuan, *Creativity and Taoism*, originally published by the Julian Press in 1962 and Grove/Atlantic Inc. for the passage on page 149 from Shih-hsiang Chen's translation of Lu Chi's *Essay on Literature* from *Anthology of Chinese Literature, Vol. I*, ed. Cyril Birch © 1965 by Grove Press Inc.

I thank the editor of journals in whose pages some passages or thoughts in this book first appeared. These include passages in Chapter 3 from an article I published in *Parabola* in Summer 1989; in chapters 3 and 5 from an article on the Great Memory in the *Journal of the Institute of Noetic Sciences*, for which I thank Barbara MacNeill; in Chapter 4 from an article on Beatrice in *Beshara Magazine* for which I thank Jane Clark, and in Chapter 13 from an article on bibliophany in *The Pen*, for which I thank Peter Day. Other ideas were first aired in lectures and seminars at many institutions and bodies, including the National Science Foundation, Washington, DC; the Tate Gallery; the Highgate Literary and Scientific Institute; King's College, London; the Scientific and Medical Network; and the Arts Centre, Croydon.

Where support is concerned, no one has been a better friend to me than my bank manager, Martin Wheadon of Lloyds Bank. In this connection I am also grateful to King's College, London, for making me a senior research fellow of the School of Education and to the Harold Hyam Wingate Foundation for making me a Wingate Fellow for two years at the early stages of this book.

That this book ever reached completion is owed to the intuition, human insights, and inventive and technical skills of my friends in the medical profession, Dr Robert Lefever and my surgeons, Mr David Howard, Mr Meredydd Harries and Miss Penelope Lennox.

My warm thanks go to Liz Calder, my editor, and her colleagues in Bloomsbury Publishing for kindnesses and enthusiasm. I am deeply in debt to Ingrid von Essen who, in editing the book, saved me often from error and helped me to make obscure passages clearer. Juliet Nicolson, my agent, has been a great support in the later stages of the making of the book.

W. A.
London and Sussex
December 1995

Notes

The quotations from Dante are taken from the editions of the Società Dantesca Italiana, *La Vita Nuova*, ed. Michele Barbi, Florence (1932), *Il Convivio*, ed. G. Busnelli and G. Vandelli, *Florence (2nd edn, vol. I 1954, vol II 1964) and La Commedia secondo l'antico vulgata*, ed. Giorgio Petrocchi, 4 vols, Milan (1966–67).

The quotations from Shakespeare are from *The Complete Works*, ed. Stanley Wells and Gary Taylor, Oxford (1988).

Patrologia Latina refers to the Latin works in the *Patrologiae cursus completus*, ed. J.-P. Migne, Paris (1844–55).

Translations not given to other sources are by the author.

Introduction: The Face of Glory

1. This is my book *Green Man: the Archetype of Our Oneness with the Earth* with photographs by Clive Hicks, London and San Francisco (1990).
2. The story comes from the *Śiva Purāna*, tr. J. L. Shastri in *Ancient Indian Tradition and Mythology*, 4 vols, Delhi (1970), Vol. 2, pp. 881–90. See Heinrich Zimmer, ed. Joseph Campbell, *Myths and Symbols in Indian Art and Civilization* (1946), Bollingen Series VI, pp. 180–84 where he also tells the legend of the Face of Glory. Zimmer sums up his account of the Face of Glory thus:

   > This monster is a match for any evil. The principle symbolized in its eloquent deed, once grasped by the mind and assimilated by the faculties, will protect against both spiritual and physical disaster in the deepest darknesses of the jungle of the world. It represents the presence of the Lord in the moment of disaster: his readiness to take to himself and to comfort with his protection even those who have been his enemies; the paradox of life in death; and the wisdom of self-abandonment to the Lord. (*Ibid.*, p. 184.)

3. Sura 18, the Koran.
4. See Irene Nicholson, *Firefly in the Night: A Study of Ancient Mexican Poetry and Symbolism*, London (1959), p. 85.

5. See C. G. Jung, tr. Richard and Clara Winston, *Memories, Dreams, Reflections*, London (1963), p. 201.
6. Raniero Gnoli, *The Aesthetics of Abhinavagupta*, Banaras (1968), p. L. See also J. L. Masson and M. V. Patwardhan, *Śāntarasa and Abhinavagupta's Philosophy of Aesthetics*, Poona (1969).
7. See, for example, Jonathan Kingdon, *Self-made Man and His Undoing*, London (1993), for the effect of tools and technology on human evolution.
8. See '*Le Gouvernement de l'Imagination*' in *Salon de 1859*, Charles Baudelaire, *Oeuvres Complètes*, Paris (Pléiade edn, 1954), p. 779.
9. See the account in Arthur Koestler, *The Act of Creation*, London (1964), p. 118.
10. There is a contemporary link between modern Eleusis with its motorway and refineries and the scene of Persephone's abduction in Sicily. The chasm made by Hades became Lake Pergusa, near Enna, the only substantial inland lake in Sicily. This lake is now drying up under the effects of pollution; its banks are ringed by a motor-racing track.
11. This account is taken largely from the Homeric 'Hymn to Demeter'. See also Carl Kerényi, *Eleusis: Archetypal Image of Mother and Daughter*, New York (1967), and the account of Demeter and Eleusis in Anne Baring and Jules Cashford, *The Myth of the Goddess: Evolution of an Image*, London (1991), pp. 364–90.
12. It is to be found in the *Penguin Book of Greek Verse*, ed. Constantine Trypanis (1971), pp. 597–602. I have taken phrases from the prose translation by Constantine Trypanis in describing the poem. See the account of Sikelianos in Philip Sherrard, *The Wound of Greece: Studies in Neo-Hellenism*, London and Athens (1978), pp. 72–93.

Chapter 1: The creative imagination

1. See Lynn White Jr, *Dynamo and Virgin Reconsidered*, Cambridge, Mass. (1968), p. 84, and also Chapter 3 in my *Green Man* (1990), pp. 50–60.
2. Charles Darwin, *The Descent of Man*, London (2nd edn), 1882, p. 74.
3. In choosing these examples I thought at first my choice was made at random but even here I find there is a pattern: the composer, modulating through a series of keys to get back to where he started from, is constantly going round corners and it is the ability to go round corners that links his skill with the whippletree and the earwig.
4. Another version can be found in Matsuo Bashō, tr. Nobuyuki Yuasa, *The Narrow Road to the Deep North*, Harmondsworth (1966), p. 107.
5. Mary Warnock, *Memory*, London (1987), p. viii. See also her *Imagination*, London (1976).
6. S. T. Coleridge, *Biographia Literaria*, London (Everyman edn 1956), p. 167.
7. He actually said 'unity in multeity'. See Owen Barfield, *What Coleridge Thought*, London (1972), p. 79.

8. William Blake, *Milton*, Book the Second, 35, ed. Geoffrey Keynes, London (1961), p. 418.

Chapter 2: Myth and the Great Memory

1. Philip Wheelwright, *Heraclitus*, Princeton and London (1959), p. 20.
2. See the passage on Apollo and Cirrha in *Paradiso* I, ll. 13–36.
3. See the statement on myth by H. H. Shantanand Saraswati in *The Man who wanted to meet God: Myths and Stories that explain the Inexplicable*, New York (1996), pp. xi–xv.
4. See Bruce Chatwin, *The Songlines*, London (1987), and R. M. and C. H. Berndt, *The World of the First Australians*, London (1964).
5. I am building here on Joseph Campbell's discussion of the radical and innovative effect of myth on western society since the twelfth century. See Joseph Campbell, *The Masks of God: Creative Mythology*, London and New York (1974), pp. 6–7.
6. Erich Auerbach, *Literary Language and Its Public in Later Latin Antiquity and in the Middle Ages*, tr. R. Manheim, London (1965). He uses this phrase particularly of Eckhart, p. 332, but it may be applied equally well to Dante.
7. This was Cardinal Henry of Ostia in the eleventh century, quoted in John H. Mundy, *Europe in the High Middle Ages 1150–1309*, London (1973), p. 27.
8. The story is told in Kurt Weber, *Lucius Cary, Second Viscount Falkland*, New York (1940), pp. 127–29. Dryden was to borrow Denham's line in his 1697 translation of Virgil's *Aeneid*, the Second Book, 1. 763:

> On the bleak Shoar now lies th' abandoned King,
> A headless Carcass, and a nameless thing.

9. Sonnet 21.
10. *Aeneid* VI, ll. 183–211.

Chapter 3: The Great Memory in art, religion and politics

1. Edmund Spenser, *The Faerie Queene*, Book III, Canto III, stanzas 22 seq.
2. Quoted from G. E. Aylmer, ed., *The Levellers in the English Revolution*, London (1975), p. 109.
3. See the chapter on Sir Edward Coke as myth-maker in Christopher Hill, *Intellectual Origins of the English Revolution*, Oxford (1965), pp. 222–65.
4. The examples of the late Shah of Iran and of the revival of the Masada story are taken from Bernard Lewis, *History Remembered, Recovered, Invented*, Princeton (1975), pp. 3–41.
5. *Ibid.*, pp. 7–9.
6. The Italian priest is Ludovico Antonio Muratori (1672–1750), editor of *Rerum italicarum scriptores*; the English bishop is Bishop Percy (1729–1811), editor of

Reliques of Ancient English Poetry (1765); the Swiss critic is Johann Jakob Bodmer (1698–1783); the Russian scholar is Count Musin-Pushkin, who discovered the *Song of Igor's Campaign* in the late eighteenth century; and the Danish poet is Johannes Ewald (1743–81).

7. I take these works and editors from an even longer list in E. J. Hobsbawm, *The Age of Revolution: Europe 1789–1848*, London (paperback 1973), p. 321.

8. See the account by C. P. FitzGerald, *A Concise History of East Asia*, Harmondsworth (1966), pp. 207–39. See also H. D. Harootunian, 'Late Tokugawa culture and thought', pp. 168–258, and Kenneth B. Pyle, 'Meiji conservatism', pp. 676–720, in *The Cambridge History of Japan, Vol. 5 The Nineteenth Century*, ed. Marius B. Jansen, Cambridge (1989).

9. See Octavio Paz in his introduction to *Mexico: Splendors of Thirty Centuries*, Metropolitan Museum, New York (1991), pp. 6–7.

10. *Ibid.*, p. 20.

11. *Ibid.*, p. 21.

Chapter 4: Image of woman: images of man

1. Dionysius Longinus, *On the Sublime* IX, 2, ed. and tr. W. Hamilton Fyfe, London and Cambridge, Mass. (Loeb edn 1953), pp. 142–45.

2. See the description of the eleventh-century church of St Trond, near Liège, in Victor Mortet, *Recueil des textes relatifs à l'histoire de l'architecture et à la condition des architectes en France au moyen âge, XIe–XIIe*, Paris (1911), pp. 159–60.

3. See my *The Rise of the Gothic*, London (1985), p. 21, where I discuss in greater detail the tracing back of these images to the Neolithic period and the Bronze Age and the possibility that they were transmitted in crafts such as the making of corndollies.

4. *Vita Nuova* XXVI, 5–100.

5. *Purgatorio* VI, l. 45.

6. Guido da Pisa, *Commentary on Dante's Inferno*, ed. Vincenzo Cioffari, New York (1974), pp. 31–32.

7. See my *Dante the Maker*, London (1980), especially Chapter 18, 'The six guides and the four levels of meaning'.

8. For a full summary of the theories about *Le Concert champêtre*, see the essay by Alessandro Ballarin in the catalogue of the exhibition *Le Siècle de Titien*, Grand Palais, Paris (1993), pp. 392–400.

9. Sonnet 109.

10. Sir Philip Sidney, *The Countess of Pembroke's Arcadia*, ed. Maurice Evans, Harmondsworth (1977), pp. 463–4.

11. *Ibid.*, p. 464.

12. 'Last Verses' in *Poems of Michael Drayton*, ed. John Buxton, Vol. 1, London (1953), p. 286.

13. See *Meister Eckhart: A Modern Translation*, tr. R. P. Blakney, New York (1941), pp. 207–09.

14. John 14:10.

15. *The Dhammapada* I:2. tr. Juan Mascaró, Harmondsworth (1973), p. 35.
16. *The Geeta* VI, tr. Shri Purohit Swami, London (1965), p. 44.
17. *Ibid.* X, pp. 61–62.
18. Quoted from Chang Chung-yuan, *Creativity and Taoism*, London (1975), p. 124.
19. See the canzone '*Voi che 'ntendendo il terzo ciel movete*' (You who by contemplation move the third heaven) with which Dante opens Book II of *Il Convivio*.
20. See Chang Chung-yuan, *Creativity and Taoism*, London (1975), p. 57.
21. *Ibid.*
22. See *Mediterranean Fascism*, documents ed. Charles F. Delzell, London (1971), p. 43.
23. See Nirad C. Chauduri, *Scholar Extraordinary: The Life of Professor the Rt. Hon. Friedrich Max Müller, PC*, London (1974), pp. 313–14.
24. Adolf Hitler, *My Struggle* (*Mein Kampf*), London (1933), p. 258.
25. Karl Marx and Friedrich Engels, *The Communist Manifesto*, intr. A. J. P. Taylor, Harmondsworth (1985), p. 74.
26. *Ibid.*, p. 78.

Chapter 5: Time and the scientific images of man

1. St Augustine, *Civitas dei*, Part III, XI, 6, tr. Henry Bettenson, Harmondsworth (1972), p. 436. See also his reflections on time in his *Confessions* XI, tr. R. S. Pine-Coffin, Harmondsworth (1961), pp. 253–80.
2. The story is told in Heinrich Zimmer, *Myths and Symbols in Indian Art and Civilization*, Bollingen Series VI, New York (1947), pp. 3–11.
3. Boethius, *De Consolatione* V, vi, ed. Father Adrian Fortescue, London (1925).
4. Francis Bacon, Viscount St Albans, *Works*, ed. James Spedding, Robert Leslie Ellis and Douglas Denon Heath, London (1859), Vol. 3, p. 222.
5. Frederick S. Boas, *Christopher Marlowe*, Oxford (1940), p. 251.
6. See Stephen Jay Gould, *Time's Arrow, Time's Cycle: Myth and Metaphor in the Discovery of Geological Time*, Harmondsworth (paperback 1990), pp. 38–40.
7. *The Historical Works of Gervase of Canterbury*, Vol. 1, R.S. 73, ed. W Stubbs, London (1879), p. 27.
8. The whole Superman legend was given to Jerry Siegel in a vision during a sleepless night in 1934, according to his obituary, *The Times*, 1 February 1996. Superman as the scientist wholly in command of his physical nature and body could be regarded as an ideal that overcomes the dualism between head and loins of which we speak here, especially because of his emotional qualities and selfless actions.
9. Quoted from Mary Midgley, *Science as Salvation: A Modern Myth and Its Meaning* London (1992), p. 77.
10. *Ibid.*
11. The significance of Mary Shelley's *Frankenstein* in relation to the development of science is a recurring theme in Brian Easlea, *Fathering the Unthinkable: Masculinity, Scientists and the Nuclear Arms Race*, London (1983).
12. See J. D. Bernal, *The World, the Flesh and the Devil, an Enquiry into the Future*

of the Three Enemies of the Rational Soul, London (1929), p. 67, and also Mary Midgley, *Science as Salvation*, London (1992), p. 161, for her comments on Bernal.

13. J. D. Bernal, *Ibid.*, pp. 88–89.
14. *Ibid.*, p. 57.
15. *Ibid.*, pp. 94–95.
16. *Ibid.*, pp. 93–94.
17. See Nannette Aldred, 'A Canterbury Tale: Powell and Pressburger's Film Fantasies of Britain', *A Paradise Lost: The Neo-Romantic Imagination in Britain 1935–55*, ed. David Mellor, London (1987), catalogue of Barbican Art Gallery exhibition, p. 118, and see also Mass Observation Reports 836 (August 1941), 878 (September 1941) and 1485 (November 1942).
18. See David Mellor, ed. (1987) above.
19. J. W. von Goethe, chorus mysticus, *Faust Part II*, Act V, Berlin (1888), p. 499.
20. The production of both parts of Faust directed by David Freeman and with Simon Callow memorably performing the role of Faust was at the Lyric Theatre, Hammersmith. The translation is by Robert David MacDonald, *Faust: A Tragedy. Parts One and Two*, Birmingham (1988), p. 231.

Chapter 6: Freedom and creativity

1. Wren's son, also Christopher Wren, repeated the story in *Parentalia*, ed. E. J. Enthoven, London (1903), p. 292.
2. See Lord Teignmouth, *Memoirs of the Life, Writings, and Correspondence of Sir William Jones*, 2 vols, London (1806), and David Kopf, *British Orientalism and the Bengal Renaissance: The Dynamics of Indian Modernization 1773–1835*, Berkeley and Los Angeles (1969).
3. For an account of Rammohun Roy's influence see Kopf (1969) above and 'The Hindu Renaissance in Bengal' by Kusumith P. Pedersen, *World Faiths Insight*, New Series 21, February 1984, pp. 34–46.
4. Jacques Maritain, *Creative Intuition in Art and Poetry*, New York (1954), p. 3.
5. *Two Gentlemen of Verona*, Act III, Sc. II.
6. See n. 19, Chapter 4.
7. See John D. Barrow and Frank J. Tipler, *The Anthropic Cosmological Principle*, Oxford (1986), pp. 21–23.
8. Paul Davies, *The Mind of God: Science and the Search for Ultimate Meaning*, London (1992), p. 232.
9. *The Rig-Veda*, tr. Wendy Doniger O'Flaherty, Harmondsworth (1981), pp. 30–31.
10. Genesis 1:27. See chapters 6 and 7 on the cosmic person in the New Testament and in Hinduism, Buddhism and Islam in Bede Griffiths, *A New Vision of Reality*, London (1989), for further examples and discussions of these universal images of humanity.
11. P. D. Ouspensky, *Tertium Organum*, London (1981), revised tr. by E. Kadloubovsky and the author, pp. 193–94.

12. In his poem, *Resignation*, l. 85 in *Schillers Gedichte*, Berlin (1889), p. 56.

Chapter 7: The intellect of love: creativity as the moment of knowing

1. See Stella Kramrisch, *The Art of India*, London (3rd edn 1965), pp. 13–14.
2. Irene Nicholson, *Firefly in the Night: A Study of Ancient Mexican Poetry and Symbolism*, London (1959), p. 17.
3. *The Geeta* XI:2, tr. Shri Purohit Swami, London (1965), p. 64.
4. Claude Huart, *Les Saints des Derviches Tourneurs*, Paris (1918–22), Vol. 2, p. 172.
5. Rupert Sheldrake, *The Rebirth of Nature*, London (1990), p. xi.
6. *My Inventions: The Autobiography of Nikola Tesla*, ed. Ben Johnston, Williston, Vermont (1982), p. 47. See also John Briggs, *Fire in the Crucible: The Self-Creation of Creativity and Genius*, Los Angeles (paperback 1990), pp. 44–45.
7. Ecclesiastes 3:2.
8. *King Lear*, Act V, Sc. II.
9. Paul Valéry, 'Palme' in *Charmes*, *Oeuvres*, Vol. 1, ed. Jean Hytier, Paris (Pléiade edn, 1960), pp. 153–56.
10. See interview in H. P. H. Oliver, ed., *The Way of Discovery*, London and Harmondsworth (1969), p. 17.
11. Letter, February 1907, to Stefan Zweig in *Briefe aus den Jahren 1906–1907*, Insel Verlag (1932), p. 190.
12. For this pattern, see the essay on Pushkin by Dmitri Merezhkovsky in *Vechnye Sputniki*, Collected Works Vol. XIII, St Petersburg and Moscow (1911) pp. 304–18.
13. See William Blake, *Milton*, Book the First, 30, 31, ed. Geoffrey Keynes, London (1961), p. 413.
14. *Paradiso* XXXIII, ll. 94–96.
15. Quoted in Chang Chung-yuan, *Creativity and Taoism*, London (1975), p. 58.
16. Richard Wagner, *My Life*, London (1911), Vol. 2, p. 603.
17. Quoted in C. M. Bowra, *Inspiration and Poetry*, London (1955), p. 12.
18. Paul Valéry in his 1944 speech to a congress of surgeons in *Oeuvres*, Vol. 1, ed. Jean Hytier, Paris (Pléiade edn, 1960), p. 916.
19. See *Anthropologie in pragmatischer Hinsicht* in *Kants Werke* VII, Berlin (1907), p. 121.
20. Sir Lawrence Bragg, *The Discovery of X-Ray Analysis*, London and Harmondsworth (1966), pp. 4–5.
21. Charles Nicolle, *Biologie de l'invention*, Paris (1932), quoted in R. Taton, *Reason and Chance in Scientific Discovery*, London (1957), pp. 76–78.
22. Hildegard of Bingen, *Patrologia Latina*, 197, cols 17–18, tr. Charles Singer in *From Magic to Science: Essays on the Scientific Twilight*, London (1928), pp. 233–34.
23. *Vita Nuova* XIX, 1–3.
24. See Roger Penrose, *The Emperor's New Mind*, London (paperback 1990), p. 544.
25. *Ibid.*, pp. 545–46.

26. 'Die Sendung Moses' in Schillers Werke, Nationalausgabe, Weimar (1970), Vol. 17, p. 385.
27. Letter to Goethe, 18 March 1796, Schillers Briefe, Nationalausgabe, Weimar (1969), Vol. 28, pp. 201–02.
28. Quoted in Martin Cooper, Beethoven: The Last Decade 1817–1827, Oxford (1970), p. 416.
29. Ibid., p. 279.
30. See Nicholas Cook, Beethoven: Symphony No. 9, Cambridge (1993), pp. 19–25, for the details that follow of the first performance.
31. Ibid., p. 24.
32. Ibid., p. 93.
33. Ibid., p. 95.

Chapter 8: Manifestation and the individual

1. The suggestion by Lillian Schwarz is quoted in John Briggs, Fire in the Crucible, Los Angeles (1990), pp. 85–86.
2. Ibid., pp. 86–87, for this suggestion by Albert Lubin.
3. L. F. Haber, The Nitrogen Problem, London and Harmondsworth (1966), pp. 5–7.
4. See David Masson, The Life of John Milton, Vol. VI, 1660–1674, London (1880), pp. 464–66.
5. Quoted in Ruth Finnegan, Oral Poetry: Its Nature, Significance, and Social Context, Bloomington, Indiana (1992, reprint), from K. Rasmussen, The Netsilik Eskimos: Social Life and Spiritual Culture. Fifth Thule Expedition 1921–4, Vol. 8, Copenhagen (1931), p. 321.
6. Dante, Eclogue I, 58–63.
7. Sir David Brewster, Memoirs of the Life, Writings and Discoveries of Sir Isaac Newton, Edinburgh (1855), Vol. 2, p. 407.
8. Arthur Abell, Talks with the Great Composers, New York (1955) pp. 5–6. See also Malcolm MacDonald, Brahms, London (1990), p. 396, for warnings about the spiritualist interpretations Abell may have put on the interviews he obtained.
9. This is from a letter to his patroness Nadezhda von Meck, 17 February 1878, Florence, in The Life and Letters of Peter Ilich Tchaikovsky, ed. and tr. Rosa Newmarch, London (1906), p. 274.
10. William Blake, Milton, Book the Second, 34, ed. Geoffrey Keynes, London (1961), p. 417.
11. Purgatorio XXX, ll. 133–35.
12. This is the octet of 'Humanity: a sonnet', in Poems of the late Rev. Dr Richard Watson Dixon, a selection with portrait and a memoir by Robert Bridges, London (1909), p. 71.
13. From 'As kingfishers catch fire, dragon flies draw flame', ll. 5–8, in Poems and Prose of Gerard Manley Hopkins, ed. W. H. Gardner, Harmondsworth (1953), p. 51.

14. See Henry Corbin, *Creative Imagination in the Sufism of Ibn 'Arabi*, tr. R. Manheim, London (1970), p. 114.
15. Quoted in Max Hayward's introduction to Pasternak's *The Blind Beauty*, London (1969), p. 6.
16. Quoted in Chang Chung-yuan, *Creativity and Taoism*, London (1975), p. 233.
17. Lu Chi, 'Essay on Literature', tr. Shih-hsiang Chen, in Cyril Birch, ed. with Donald Keene, *Anthology of Chinese Literature*, Harmondsworth (1967), pp. 223–24. See also *The Art of Letters: Lu Chi's Wen Fu, AD 302*, translation and comparative study by E. R. Hughes, New York (1951).
18. Henry James, Preface to *The American*, Novels and Tales, Vol. 2, London (1909 edn), p. vii.
19. See the chapter 'Stages of control', Graham Wallas, *The Art of Thought*, London (1926), pp. 79 seq. See also the discussion of his ideas in Willis Harman and Howard Rheingold, *Higher Creativity*, Los Angeles (1984), pp. 21–22.
20. Isaiah 6:6.
21. *Abbot Suger on the Abbey Church of St-Denis and its art treasures*, ed. Erwin Panofsky, Princeton (2nd edn 1979), p. 121.
22. *Duineser Elegien* I, 1. 1.
23. *Briefe aus Muzot*, 337, tr. J. P. Leishmann in Rainer Maria Rilke, *Duino Elegies*, London (3rd edn 1948), p. 159.
24. From Rafael Alberti, *Selected Poems*, ed. and tr. Ben Belitt, California (1966), p. 233.
25. From 'The Theatre of the Soul', a conversation between Cecil Collins and Brian Keeble, *Temenos* 1 (1981), pp. 74–75. See also William Anderson, *Cecil Collins: The Quest for the Great Happiness*, London (1988), for further discussions of the theme in his work.
26. See, for example, Willis Harman, *Global Mind Change: The Promise of the Last Years of the Twentieth Century*, Indianapolis (1988).
27. See Bede Griffiths, *A New Vision of Reality: Western Science, Eastern Mysticism and Christian Faith*, London (1989), pp. 44–45.
28. This is taken from Gustav Theodor Fechner, *Ueber die Seelenfrage*, Leipzig (1861) p. 170. The translation is from *Religion of a Scientist: Selections from Gustav Th. Fechner*, ed. and tr. Walter Lowrie, New York and London (1946), p. 153.

Chapter 9: Metaphor, dream worlds and vision

1. *A Midsummer Night's Dream*, Act V, Sc. I.
2. 'Orchestra or a Poeme of Daancing', 43 in *The Poems of Sir John Davies*, ed. Robert Krueger, Oxford (1975), p. 101.
3. Boris Pasternak, 'Notes on the translation of Shakespeare's tragedies', *Soviet Literature* 7 (1956), p. 182.
4. *Poetics* XXII, 16–17, ed. and tr. W. Hamilton Fyfe, London and Cambridge, Mass. (Loeb edn 1953), pp. 90–91.
5. P. D. Ouspensky in his chapter on dreams in *A New Model of the Universe*, New York (2nd edn 1948), p. 254, writes of the artist in him who worked at making

his dreams out of material Ouspensky possessed but could never use in full measure while awake. He calls this artist 'a playwright, a producer, a scene-painter, and a remarkable *actor-impersonator*'.

6. From 'Autobiographical Notes' in *Albert Einstein: Philosopher-Scientist*, ed. Paul Arthur Schilpp, Evanston, Illinois (1944), pp. 8–9. See also John Briggs, *Fire in the Crucible*, Los Angeles (1990), p. 22.

7. See Willis Harman and Howard Rheingold, *Higher Creativity*, Los Angeles (1984), p. 31.

8. *Ibid.*, p. 39.

9. See Jacques Maritain, *The Dream of Descartes*, tr. Mabelle L. Audison, London (1946), pp. 9–11.

10. Roger Broughton, 'Biorhythmic variations in consciousness and psychological functions', *Canadian Psychological Review*, vol. 16, no. 4 (1975).

11. See Keats's letter to J. H. Reynolds, 25 March 1818, in *Letters of John Keats*, ed. Robert Gittings, Oxford (1970), pp. 79–82.

12. *Ibid.*

13. *Ibid.*

14. *The Upanishads: Breath of the Eternal*, tr. Swami Prabhavananda and Frederick Manchester, New York (1957), p. 121.

15. For these instances see John Livingstone Lowes, *The Road to Xanadu: A Study in the Ways of the Imagination*, Boston (reprint 1955), pp. 61–62.

16. 'Salamander' in William Anderson, *The Waking Dream*, London (1983), pp. 41–45.

17. René J. Dubos, *Louis Pasteur: Free Lance of Science*, London (1951), p. 101.

18. See *The Journals of Mary Shelley 1814–1844*, ed. Paula R. Feldman and Diana Scott-Kilvert, Oxford (1987), Vol. 1, pp. 114–20. See also the account of the journey in Richard Holmes, *Shelley: The Pursuit*, Harmondsworth (1987), pp. 339–43.

19. Quoted in the introduction by R. E. Dowse and D. J. Palmer to the Everyman edn of *Frankenstein*, London (1963), pp. xii–iii.

20. 'Mont Blanc', ll. 49–57, in Oxford edn (paperback 1976), p. 533.

21. *Ibid.*, ll. 139–41, p. 535.

22. Rudyard Kipling, *Something of Myself for My Friends Known and Unknown*, ed. Robert Hampson and intr. Richard Holmes, Harmondsworth (paperback 1992), p. 38.

23. Robert Louis Stevenson, 'A chapter on dreams' in *Across the Plains*, London (1920), p. 165.

24. *Ibid.*, pp. 166–67.

25. See Willis Harman and Howard Rheingold, *Higher Creativity*, Los Angeles (1984), p. 56.

26. *My Inventions: The Autobiography of Nikola Tesla*, ed. Ben Johnston, Williston, Vermont (1982), pp. 61 and 65.

27. This 'letter to a certain Baron' appears in E. Holmes, *The Life of Mozart*, London (Everyman edn 1932), p. 256. It is questioned because of its uncertain provenance.

28. See Claude Huart, *Les Saints des derviches tourneurs*, Paris (1918–23), Vol. 2, pp. 119–20.

29. See Proem to Book I, *The Mathnawi of Jalalú'ddin Rúmí*, tr. Reynold A. Nicholson, Cambridge (reprint 1982), Vol. 2, p. 5.

Chapter 10: Interpretation:
towards the art and science of praise

1. See Manoman Ghosh, *The Natyasastra: A Treatise on Hindu Dramaturgy and Histrionics Ascribed to Bharata-Muni*, Calcutta (1950), Vol. 1, pp. 100–17.
2. See Albert van der Schoot, 'The sound of emotion', in L. Ya. Dorfman *et al.*, *Emotions and Art*, Perm (1992), p. 285.
3. See the meeting with Charles Martel, *Paradiso* VIII, ll. 31–148.
4. See C. G. Jung, *Modern Man in Search of a Soul*, tr. W. S. Dell and Cary F. Baynes, London (1988).
5. *The Prelude* I, ll. 301 seq.
6. See Gerald Holton, *Thematic Origins of Scientific Thought: Kepler to Einstein*, Cambridge, Mass. (1973), and also John Briggs, *Fire in the Crucible*, Los Angeles (1990), pp. 25 seq.
7. See Briggs (1990), supra, p. 31.
8. *De Genesi ad litteram* II, 22, *Patrologia Latina* Vol. 34, cols 458–68.
9. *De musica* VI, XI, XII, *Patrologia Latina* Vol. 32, cols 1179–83.
10. See John Livingstone Lowes, *The Road to Xanadu: A Study in the Ways of the Imagination*, Boston (1955 reprint), pp. 155 and 204–05.
11. For a fuller discussion of Dante's use of fourfold interpretation, see my *Dante the Maker*, London (1980), especially Chapter 18, 'The six guides and the four levels of meaning'.
12. Quoted in Gary Schwartz, *Rembrandt, His Life, His Paintings*, Harmondsworth (1985), p. 228.
13. For a response to *Las Meninas* in the Impressionist period, see the many references to it in the book by R. L. S.'s cousin R. A. M. Stevenson, *Velazquez*, London (revised edn 1962).
14. Charles Baudelaire, *Mon coeur mis à nu* LIX, *Oeuvres Complètes*, Paris (Pléiade edn, 1954), p. 1224.
15. Nora Wydenbruck, *Rilke: Man and Poet*, London (1949), p. 95.
16. See Irving Sandler, *Abstract Expressionism: The Triumph of American Painting*, London (1970), p. 175.
17. See '*L'Art romantique*' in Baudelaire, *Oeuvres Complètes* Paris, (Pléiade edn, 1954), pp. 1027–28.
18. 'Première Préface des Méditations, 1849' in Alphonse Lamartine, *Méditations Poétiques*, ed. Lanson, Paris (1922), Vol. 2, pp. 361–62.
19. '*Choses tues*', *Tel Quel I*, in *Oeuvres*, Vol. 2, ed. Jean Hytier, Paris (Pléiade edn, 1960), p. 483.
20. Proverbs 8: 22–31.
21. He described these three visions in the poem '*Tri svidanya*' (Three meetings). See Vladimir Solovyov, *Nepodvizhno lish' solntse liubvi . . .: stikhotvoreniya, proza, pisma, vospominaniya sovremennikov*, Moscow (1990), pp. 118–24.

22. *Ibid.*, p. 96.
23. Vladimir Solovyov, 'The meaning of love' in *A Solovyov Anthology*, arr. S. L. Frank, tr. Natalie Duddington, London (1950), p. 174.
24. Pierre Teilhard de Chardin, *Écrits du temps de la guerre (1916–1919)*, Paris (1965), pp. 249–62.
25. Rainer Maria Rilke, *Späte Gedichte*, Leipzig (1934), p. 160.

Chapter 11: The rosary bead: attention and execution

1. Adam of St Victor, *Patrologia Latina*, Vol. 196, cols 1433–34.
2. Julian of Norwich, *Revelations of Divine Love 5*, tr. Clifton Wolters, Harmondsworth (1966), p. 68.
3. Igor Stravinsky, *Poetics of Music in the Form of Six Lessons*, tr. Arthur Knodel and Ingolf Dehl, Preface George Seferis, Cambridge, Mass. (1970), p. 67.
4. Blake also says that 'he who wishes to see a Vision, a perfect Whole, / Must see it in its Minute Particulars', *Jerusalem IV*, *Poetry and Prose of William Blake*, ed. Geoffrey Keynes, London (1961), p. 558.
5. Fourth Spirit's song, *Prometheus Unbound*, Act I, Oxford edn, pp. 224–25.
6. 'Long-legged Fly' in *Collected Poems*, London (1961), pp. 381–82.
7. Chang Chung-yuan, *Creativity and Taoism*, London (1975), p. 204.
8. See Gary Schwartz, *Rembrandt, His Life, His Paintings*, Harmondsworth (1985), pp. 350–53.
9. 'Das Lied von der Glocke', in *Schillers Gedichte*, Berlin (1889), p. 202.
10. Joscelyn Godwin, *Harmonies of Heaven and Earth: The Spiritual Dimension of Music from Antiquity to the Avant-Garde*, London (1987), pp. 104–05.
11. C. Ph. E. Bach, *Versuch über die wahre Art, das Clavier zu spielen*, Berlin (1753), p. 122 (facsimile reprint Leipzig, 1957).
12. Arthur Miller, *Timebends: A Life*, London (1987), pp. 186–88.
13. George Sand, *Histoire de ma vie, Oeuvres Complètes*, Vol. 4, Paris (1899), pp. 470–71.
14. *Purgatorio XXIV*, ll. 52–54.
15. Ugo Foscolo, *Discorso sul Testo e su le opinioni diverse prevalenti intorno alla storia e alla emendazione critica della Commedia di Dante*, London (1825), pp. 10–11.
16. Ben Jonson, 'To the memory of my beloved, the Author, Master William Shakespeare and what he hath left us', ll.57–65, in William Shakespeare, *The Complete Works*, ed. Stanley Wells and Gary Taylor, Oxford (1988), p. xlvi.
17. Michelangelo Buonarroti, 'Non ha l'ottimo artista . . .', no. LXXXIII in *Rime*, ed. G. R. Ceriello, Milan (1954), p. 77.
18. See Newman Flower, *George Frideric Handel: His Personality and His Times*, London (1959), p. 289.
19. Chang Chung-yuan, *Creativity and Taoism*, London (1975), pp. 223–24.
20. John 14:10.
21. For a discussion of civilization and the image of the city, see the title essay in Ananda Coomaraswamy, *What Is Civilization?*, Ipswich (1989), pp. 1–12.

22. See the description in Heinrich Zimmer, *Myths and Symbols in Indian Art and Civilization*, ed. Joseph Campbell, New York (1946), p. 143, pp. 146–48.
23. James 1:17.

Chapter 12: Conscience and civilization

1. See Novalis, *Hymnen an die Nacht V* in *Novalis Schriften*, ed. Ludwig Tieck and Fr. Schlegel, Paris (1837), p. 184, and also the opening of *Heinrich von Ofterdingen*, ibid., p. 5.
2. William Shakespeare, Sonnet 94.
3. See *Egil's Saga*, tr. Hermann Pálsson and Paul Edwards, Harmondsworth (1976).
4. *Ibid.*, p. 205.
5. *Ibid.*, pp. 205–06.
6. *Ibid.*, p. 209.
7. *Ibid.*, p. 235.
8. Françoise Gilot and Carlton Lake, *Life with Picasso*, London (1965), p. 253.
9. Rudolf Arnheim, *Picasso's* Guernica: *The Genesis of a Painting*, London (1964), p. 30.
10. Françoise Gilot and Carlton Lake (see n. 8 above), p. 110.
11. Giovanni Papini, *Il Libro nero: nuovo diario di Gog*, Florence (1953), p. 268.
12. *Parsifal*, Act 1, in Richard Wagner, *Gesammelte Schriften und Dichtungen*, Leipzig (2nd edn, 1888), Vol. 10, p. 342.
13. *Vita Nuova* XIX, 1–3.
14. Sonnet 116.
15. *The Ramayana of Valmiki: An Epic of Ancient India. Vol 1. Balakanda*, tr. Robert P. Goldman, Princeton (1984), pp. 127–29. See also R. K. Narayan, *Gods, Demons, and Others*, London (1965), pp. 125–42, for an account of how Valmiki came to give up his life as a bandit and to compose the *Ramayana*.
16. Glen Schaefer, 'The universe and the mind of man – which the reflector?', *The Bridge*, no. 5, London (1981), p. 23.
17. *Ibid.*, pp. 29–30.
18. Joseph Needham with Ho Ping Yü, Lu Gwei-Djen and Wang Ling, *Science and Civilization in China*, Vol. 5: *Chemistry and Chemical Technology*, Pt 7. *Military Technology; the Gunpowder Epic*, Cambridge (1986), p. 7.
19. See the entries on Thomas Midgley Jr in *The Dictionary of American Biography. Supplement Three 1941–45*, New York (1973), pp. 521–23 and Isaac Asimov, *Biographical Encyclopaedia of Science and Technology*, London (1966), p. 443.
20. The details of the V-2 rockets and the conditions in which they were made come from Paul Eddy's article 'Inside Hitler's death tunnels', *Telegraph Magazine*, 5 June 1994, pp. 18–32.
21. John 8:9. See the essay 'Conscience and conscious' in C. S. Lewis, *Studies in Words*, Cambridge (2nd edn 1967), pp. 181–213.
22. John 8:12.
23. Acts of John 98, in *The Apocryphal New Testament*, ed. M. R. James, Oxford (1924), p. 254.

Chapter 13: The nature of enjoyment

1. Ruth Finnegan, *Oral Poetry: Its Nature, Significance and Social Context*, Cambridge (1977; reprint 1992), p. 212.
2. St Augustine, *Confessions VI*, 3, tr. R. S. Pine-Coffin, Harmondsworth (1961), p. 114.
3. See William Anderson, 'Clever reader', *The Pen*, no. 23, autumn 1987, pp. 26–27.
4. Rudyard Kipling, *Something of Myself for My Friends Known and Unknown*, Harmondsworth (1992), p. 157, where he says of the *Jungle Books*, *Kim* and the *Puck* books that 'when those books were finished they said so themselves with, almost, the hammer-click of a tap turned off'.
5. I am aware that I am not in general applying what I say here to popular fiction. It is said, though, that popular fiction succeeds in so far as the author is convinced of the worth of the story he or she is writing and is sincere in the expression of the emotions of the story. In this connection see the essay by Rebecca West, 'The tosh horse', in *The Strange Necessity: Essays and Reviews*, London (1928), pp. 319–25.
6. See Alexander Solzhenitsyn's Nobel Prize Address *Lecture*, tr. Nicholas Bethell, London (1977), pp. 29–30.
7. Martial, *Epigrams* X 2, ll.5–6, ed. D. R. Shackleton Bailey, Vol. 2, London and Cambridge, Mass. (Loeb edn, 1993), p. 324.
8. Maxim Gorky, *Days with Lenin*, New York (1932), p. 52.
9. For a very interesting analysis of how different kinds of music affect us viscerally, emotionally or intellectually and how these categories decide different kinds of audience, see Joscelyn Godwin, *Harmonies of Heaven and Earth*, London (1987), pp. 87–95.
10. Donald Tovey, *Beethoven's Ninth Symphony*, London (1927), p. 7.
11. See Nicholas Cook, *Beethoven: Symphony No. 9*, Cambridge (1993), pp. 95–98 for what follows on the influence of Rolland's book in China and Japan.

Chapter 14: Matters of taste and the basis of civilization

1. See the entry on this painting by Francesco Valcanover in the Grand Palais exhibition catalogue *Le Siècle de Titien: l'âge d'or de la peinture à Venise*, Paris (1994), pp. 679–81.
2. *Paradiso* I, ll. 19–21.
3. See Martin Krampen, 'On some effects of totalitarian style architecture' in *Emotions and Art*, ed. L. Ya. Dorfman, D. A. Leontiev, V. M. Petrov and V. A. Sozinov, Perm (1992), pp. 203–15.
4. I find my comments are very tame compared to the criticisms of these buildings in Jennifer Sherwood and Nikolaus Pevsner, *The Buildings of England: Oxfordshire*, Harmondsworth (1974), pp. 276 seq.
5. Alexander Vucinich, *Science in Russian Culture: History to 1860*, Vol. 1, London (1965).

6. I owe this expression to my colleague in the Nuffield Projects, Dr Tony Mansell.

7. I have discussed this theme of the young hero in the 1930s in my book *Cecil Collins: The Quest for the Great Happiness*, London (1988), pp. 163–64.

8. See Arthur Koestler, *The Sleepwalkers*, Harmondsworth (1964), p. 329, for his account of Kepler and the motions of Mars.

9. René Vallery Radot, *La Vie de Pasteur*, Paris (1953), p. 87.

10. From 'Crashaw's Answer for Hope' from *The English Poems of Richard Crashaw*, ed. Edward Hutton, London (1901), p. 214.

11. The finest account of this painting is the essay of 1821 by Hazlitt. I draw here on the entry in the catalogue of the Royal Academy exhibition *Nicolas Poussin 1594–1665* by Richard Verdi (1955), pp. 309–10, and Robert Graves's account of Orion in *The Greek Myths*, Vol. 1, Harmondsworth (1955), pp. 151–54.

Chapter 15: The creation of audiences

1. *Die Geburt der Tragödie*, *Nietzsche Werke III*, i, ed. G. Colli and M. Montinari, Berlin and New York (1972), pp. 25–26.

2. Letter to Thomas Butts, 10 January 1802, in *Poetry and Prose of William Blake*, ed. Geoffrey Keynes, London (1961), p. 855.

3. There is an interesting possibility that the story of Christ coming as a child to Britain is a quite modern invention arising from Blake's 'Jerusalem'. Where Blake saw Christ's presence as the divine imagination in England, others have seen it as a literal journey made by Christ, making a new myth to add to the Glastonbury legends. See A. W. Smith, '"And did those feet . . .?"; the "legend" of Christ's visit to Britain', *Folklore* 100:1 (1989), pp. 63–83.

4. The chief account of the fourfold method is that of Henri de Lubac, *Exégèse mediévale: les quatre sens de l'Ecriture*, 4 vols, Paris (1959–64).

5. Hugh of St Victor, *De Arca Noe Morali*, Prol., *Patrologia Latina*, Vol. 176, cols 617–19. See also *The Didascalicon of Hugh of St Victor*, tr: Jerome Taylor, New York (1961), and *Hugh of St Victor: Selected Spiritual Writings*, tr. a Religious of CSMW, London (1962).

6. See my *Dante the Maker*, London (1980), pp. 325–28.

7. Epistle X, 15, *Dantis Alagherii Epistolae*, ed. and tr. Paget Toynbee, Oxford (2nd edn 1966), p. 178.

8. In his *Discorsi in Dante con l'espositioni di Christoforo Landino et d'Alessandro Vellutello; sopra la sua Comedia dell'Inferno, del Purgatorio e del Paradiso*, Venice (1564).

9. Quoted in Anthony Rooley, *Performance: Revealing the Orpheus Within*, Shaftesbury (1990), p. 8.

10. From Paul Hentzner's 'Travels in England, 1598', tr. W. B. Rye in *England as seen by Foreigners in the Days of Elizabeth and James I*, London (1865), p. 106.

11. *Ibid.* pp. 105–6.

12. See B. L. Joseph, *Elizabethan Acting*, Oxford (2nd edn 1964).

13. John Padel, *New Poems by Shakespeare: Order and Meaning Restored to the Sonnets*, London (1981).

14. *Ibid.*, p. 131.
15. See the account of Madame de Rambouillet and her influence in David Maland, *Culture and Society in Seventeenth-Century France*, London (1970), pp. 45–60.
16. *Dichtung und Wahrheit*, ed. Ernst Beutler, Zürich (1948), Vol. 10, p. 639.
17. *Die Schaubühne als eine moralische Anstalt betrachtet* in Friedrich Schiller, *Sämtliche Werke V, Philosophische Schriften*, Munich (1968), p. 101. There is a fine evocation of the theatre in London in the nineteenth century and what it meant to be a member of the audience by Robertson Davies in his 'The Devil's Burning Throne', in *One Half of Robertson Davies*, Harmondsworth (1978), pp. 179–200.
18. Alexander Solzhenitsyn, *Lecture*, tr. Nicholas Bethell, London (1973), p. 33.
19. Conversation with H. Luden, 13 December 1813, in Goethe's *Gespräche ohne die Gespräche Eckermann*, ed. Flodoard Freiherr von Biedermann, Leipzig (n.d.), p. 309.
20. Sir Theodore Martin, *The Life of His Royal Highness the Prince Consort*, Vol. 2, London (1876), p. 205.

Chapter 16: Patrons, impresarios and living inspirations

1. The statue now to be seen there is a replica of Cellini's *Nymph of Fontainebleau*, which is in the Louvre, Paris.
2. See Philippe Erlanger, *Diane de Poitiers*, Paris (1959).
3. See L. T. Topsfield, *The Troubadours and Love*, Cambridge (1975), p. 4.
4. See Ernest John Knapton, *Empress Josephine*, Cambridge, Mass., and Oxford (1964), pp. 267, for an account of Malmaison.
5. Velleius Paterculus, *Compendium of Roman History and Res gestae divi Augusti*, tr. Frederick W. Shipley, London and New York (1924), pp. 44–54.
6. *Ibid.*, pp. 46–47.
7. See Morris Rossabi, 'The reign of Khubilai Khan', *The Cambridge History of China*, Vol. 6, ed. Herbert Franke and Denis Twitchett, Cambridge (1994), pp. 414–89.
8. See the life of Giotto in Giorgio Vasari, *Lives of the Artists*, tr. George Bull, Harmondsworth (1965), pp. 57–58.
9. *Ibid.*, the life of Michelangelo Buonarroti, pp. 329–37.
10. Letter to Heinrich Meyer, 30 December 1795, *Goethes Briefe II*, Hamburg (1964), p. 213.
11. The extent to which scientists have come from peasant stock and from working-class and deprived backgrounds – in France, for example, following the route of the Ecole Normale Supérieure rather than that of the Ecole Polytechnique, which was that of the upper classes – has been the subject of interesting studies. See, for example, John Head, 'Personality and the pursuit of science', *Studies in science education* 6 (1979), pp. 23–44.
12. See Richard Buckle, *Diaghilev*, London (1979), who says: 'it seems to me likely that what first spurred him on was the knowledge that in St Petersburg and at Court he was nobody, a distiller's grandson', p. 4.

13. See John J. MacAloon, *This Great Symbol: Pierre de Coubertin and the Origins of the Modern Olympic Games*, Chicago and London (1981), pp. 6, 14–17 and elsewhere.
14. *Ibid.*, p. 59.
15. *Ibid.*, p. 138.
16. *Ibid.*, p. 171.

Chapter 17: Love and the redemptions of space, time and matter

1. Charles S. Bayne, *The Call of the Birds* with illustrations by C. F. Tunnicliffe, London and Glasgow (1945, revised edn), p. 137.
2. *Ibid.*, pp. 145–46.
3. *The Prelude*, Book I, 1. 302 (1850 version).
4. *Ueber die ästhetische Erziehung des Menschen, Zweiter Brief*, in Friedrich Schiller, *Sämtliche Werke: Philosophische Schriften*, Munich (1968), p. 314.
5. From Abu Hamid Al Ghazzali, 'On music', tr. Duncan B. MacDonald, *Journal of the Royal Asiatic Society* 66 (1901), pp. 198–99.
6. Jalalú'ddin Rúmí, *Selected poems from the Diwani Shamsi Tabrizi*, tr. Reynold A. Nicholson, Cambridge (1898), p. 167.
7. *Duineser Elegien*, the ninth elegy in *Duino Elegies*, tr. J. B. Leishman and Stephen Spender, London (3rd edn 1948), p. 86.
8. This is the last line of his sonnet 'Di sè stesso', *Opere di Giordano Bruni e di Tommaso Campanella*, ed. A. Guzzo and R. Amerio, Milan and Naples (1956), p. 854.
9. Pausanias, *Guide to Greece, Vol. 2. Southern Greece*, tr. Peter Levi, Harmondsworth (revised edn 1979), p. 229.
10. *Sonnette an Orpheus*, Part I, IX, 12.
11. See John Sparrow, *Mark Pattison and the Idea of a University*, Cambridge (1967), p. 2.
12. He was Hugues de Doignies from a monastery near Namur. The epitaph is quoted in Edgar de Bruyne, *Etudes d'ésthéthique mediévale*, 3 vols, Bruges (1946), Vol. 2, p. 411.
13. See Arnold J. Toynbee, *A Study of History*, Oxford (1939), pp. 49–97.
14. *Ibid.*, pp. 63–72.
15. See Laura Otis, *Organic Memory: History and the Body in the Late Nineteenth and Early Twentieth Centuries*, Lincoln, Nebraska (1994), pp. 10–13.
16. I am indebted for some of these images to Martin Redfern for his *Journey to the Centre of the Earth: The New Geology*, London (1991), and also Michael Alford Andrews, *The Birth of Europe: Colliding Continents and the Destiny of Nations*, London (1991).
17. *Die Italienische Reise* in *Gedenkausgabe*, ed. Ernst Beutler, Zürich (1950), Vol. 11, p. 324.
18. From 'Versuch eine Selbstkritik', *Die Geburt der Tragödie* in *Nietzsche Werke* III, i, ed. G. Colli and M. Montinari, Berlin and New York (1972), pp. 5–16.

Chapter 18: The perfect enjoyer

1. The whole triptych is reproduced in Robert Rosenblum, *Paintings in the Musée d'Orsay*, New York (1989), pp. 562–63.
2. See Jacqueline Decter, *Nicholas Roerich: The Life and Art of a Russian Master*, London (1989).
3. *The Collected Poems of James Elroy Flecker*, ed. J. C. Squire, London (1922) pp. 147–8.
4. *Trilogie der Leidenschaft: an Werther*, ll. 50–52.
5. *Trilogie der Leidenschaft: Elegie*, ll. 31–36.
6. *Trilogie der Leidenschaft: Aussöhnung*, ll. 17–18.
7. Dionysius the Areopagite, *The Celestial Hierarchies*, tr. editors of the Shrine of Wisdom, London (1920), pp. 62–63.
8. Thomas Traherne, *Selected Poems and Prose*, ed. Alan Bradford, Harmondsworth (1991), pp. x–xi.
9. 'Dumbness', ll. 61–62 in *ibid.*, p. 22.
10. *First Century*, 29 in *ibid.*, p. 197.
11. 'Felicity', ll. 4–9 in *ibid.*, p. 85.
12. *Fourth Century*, 7 in *ibid.*, p. 313.
13. *Third Century*, 2 and 3 in *ibid.*, p. 226.
14. F. Sherwood Taylor, *The Fourfold Vision: A Study of the Relations of Science and Religion*, London (1945), pp. 97–98.
15. Northrop Frye, *The Great Code: The Bible and Literature*, London (1982, paperback), p. 232.
16. See Charles Darwin, *The various contrivances by which orchids are fertilised by insects*, London (1888, 2nd edn), pp. 106–14.

Index

INDEX